CRAFTING INDIA'S SKILL ECOLOGY

This volume traces how the discourse of skill evolved in colonial and postcolonial India, from the mid-nineteenth century to the present neoliberal era. It introduces the concept of *skill ecology* to capture the broader political, economic, and social environment within which skills emerge, transform, and acquire meaning. Skill is examined here not merely as a technical attribute but as a historically contingent category, shaped by state policy, capitalist ideologies, and hierarchies of power.

Focusing on industrial training from the late colonial period – particularly the 1930s – through Nehruvian state-led industrialisation and into the era of neoliberal reform, the book explores how skilling became a terrain of collaboration and contestation between the state and the capital. It also reveals how social relations influence the legitimacy of skills, determining what forms of labour are seen as 'skilled' or 'unskilled' and for whom.

Combining perspectives from history, political science, and colonial and postcolonial studies, this interdisciplinary work offers fresh insights into the politics of labour and development in South Asia. It will be essential reading for scholars and researchers in modern history, political science, sociology, economics, social policy, and Asian studies.

Saikat Maitra is a faculty member in the Public Policy and Management Group in the Indian Institute of Management, Calcutta, India.

Sebastian Schwecke is the founding director of the Max Weber Forum for South Asian Studies (MWF) in Delhi, India.

Politics and Society in India and the Global South

Series Editors:

Tanweer Fazal, *University of Hyderabad, Hyderabad*

Shail Mayaram, *formerly at Centre for the Study of Developing Societies, Delhi*

Samita Sen, *University of Cambridge, Cambridge*

Awadhendra Sharan, *Centre for the Study of Developing Societies, Delhi*

Sanjay Srivastava, *University College London, London*

Ravi Vasudevan, *formerly at Centre for the Study of Developing Societies, Delhi*

Sebastian Vollmer, *University of Göttingen, Germany*

The Series is a collaboration of Routledge and the M.S. Merian – R. Tagore International Centre of Advanced Studies 'Metamorphoses of the Political' (ICAS:MP). It aims to publish books that explores core issues that are of concern in modern globalized societies.

Instead of the political system or politics in the narrow sense, this Series explores questions of what constitutes the 'political' in the contemporary environment. The volumes concentrate on multiple areas of politicisation: the role, forms and advances of civil society and social movements, the politicisation of law and rights, the drive for the democratisation of democracy, including modal changes of democratic procedures, and the diversification of forms of governance regarding state and non-state actors. Forms of social and political exclusion and questions of recognition and justice are covered.

The Series mainly feature edited volumes incorporating innovative social science research on the above themes. These volumes offer cross-disciplinary insights where collaboration of many top-ranking scholars on a single topic ensure state-of-the field studies. These are highly focussed with contributing chapters that link to the overarching theme of the respective volumes. A strong Introduction not only introduces the chapters and draw linkages between them, but bring new ideas and insights to the fore.

ICAS:MP is an Indo-German research collaboration of six Indian and German institutions. It combines the benefits of an open, interdisciplinary forum for intellectual exchange with the advantages of a cutting-edge research centre. Located in New Delhi, ICAS:MP critically intervenes in global debates in the social sciences and humanities.

Querying Childhood
Feminist Reframings
Edited by Mary E. John, Barbara Lotz and Elisabeth Schömbucher

For more information about this series, please visit: https://www.routledge.com/

CRAFTING INDIA'S SKILL ECOLOGY

Reproductions, Recalibrations, and Reimaginations

Edited by Saikat Maitra and Sebastian Schwecke

Routledge
Taylor & Francis Group
LONDON AND NEW YORK

Designed cover image: Getty Images

First published 2026
by Routledge
4 Park Square, Milton Park, Abingdon, Oxon OX14 4RN

and by Routledge
605 Third Avenue, New York, NY 10158

Routledge is an imprint of the Taylor & Francis Group, an informa business

British Library Cataloguing-in-Publication Data
A catalogue record for this book is available from the British Library

ISBN: 978-1-032-99616-5 (hbk)
ISBN: 978-1-032-99564-9 (pbk)
ISBN: 978-1-003-60484-6 (ebk)

DOI: 10.4324/9781003604846

Typeset in Sabon
by Apex CoVantage, LLC

SPONSORED BY THE
Federal Ministry
of Education
and Research

icas mp
Metamorphoses of the Political

Max Weber
Foundation
German Humanities
Institutes Abroad

In memory of Srabani Maitra

CONTENTS

FIGURES

AUTHOR BIOGRAPHIES

Usha Ajithkumar is Professor & Head, Department of Education at SASTRA University, India. Her research areas are education, pedagogy, ICT in education, innovation, TVET, and human rights.

Michaela Dimmers is an affiliated research fellow at the Max Weber Forum for South Asian Studies in Delhi and a doctoral candidate at the Department of Modern Indian History, Centre for Modern Indian Studies, University of Göttingen, Germany. Her research includes a social history of colonial prisons in British India, focusing on the penal experience within the colonial prison and coerced intermediation within penal systems, enslavement, and indentured labour in the Indian Ocean.

Pankhuree R. Dube is Associate Professor of Modern South Asian History at Middle Tennessee State University. Her most recent publications include articles in *Settler Colonial Studies*, *Arcadia: Explorations in Environmental History*, and *Social History*. Her first book project focuses on the life of the Pardhan Gond painter-intellectual Jangarh Singh Shyam (1962–2001)

Natalie Grote holds a master of education degree from the University of Cologne. She currently teaches English and business administration at the vocational school Handelslehranstalt Bruchsal, where she is dedicated to preparing her students for careers in business and beyond.

Barbara Harriss-White works on India's political economy, in particular informal capitalism, food, energy, waste, and many aspects of deprivation – all through field research. A former Director of Queen Elizabeth House, Oxford, and Founder-Director of Oxford University's Contemporary South Asian Studies Programme, she organised the world's first MSc in Contemporary India and co-founded Oxford's M.Phil. in Development Studies. She has written and (co)edited 40 books, published over 285 scholarly papers/chapters, and mentored 80 doctoral and post-doctoral scholars. Her book *Rural Commercial Capital* won the Edgar Graham prize. She is Emeritus Professor and Fellow of Wolfson College, Oxford, and Distinguished Research Fellow at the Max Weber Forum, New Delhi.

Douglas E. Haynes is Professor of South Asian History at Dartmouth College, the United States. He is the author of three major books, *Rhetoric and Ritual in Colonial India: The Shaping of a Public Culture in Surat City, 1852–1928* (1991), *Small-Town Capitalism in Western India: Artisans, Merchants and the Making of the Informal Economy, 1870–1960* (2012), and *The Emergence of Brand-Name Capitalism in Late Colonial India: Advertising and the Making of Modern Conjugality* (2023); he is a co-editor of several influential essay collections and special issues in journals. Focusing on his research on the history of late nineteenth- and early twentieth-century western India, he has covered such topic areas as cities and urban politics, artisans and merchants, capitalism, consumption and advertising, the Indian middle class, masculinity, conjugality, and sexual science. He is currently working on a history of management education and the making of managerial capitalism in India before 1991.

Ujjwal Kango is an assistant professor in the Public Policy and Sociology group at IIM Sirmaur. He completed his Ph.D. from IIM-Calcutta, with a dissertation focusing on platform work. His research examines the impact of digital platforms on the organisation of work, particularly the role of algorithmic management. In addition to platform work, his research interests encompass technology and policy, the future of work, and business and work history, from a political economy and sociological lens.

Saikat Maitra is currently a faculty member in the Public Policy and Management Group in the Indian Institute of Management-Calcutta. He received his Ph.D. in cultural anthropology at the University of Texas in Austin. His research focuses on how new labour subjectivities are emerging in Indian urban contexts due to the intersections between evolving work practices and the expansion of skill training under India's current 'Skill Mission'. In particular, he is interested in how skilling programs in India's formal vocational education institutions are creating a regulated labour force by stoking specific kinds of aspirations and desires in young adults as they seek to transition into an increasingly precarious labour market.

Soheb Niazi is currently a postdoctoral researcher at the Friedrich-Meinecke-Instiut, Freie Universität, Berlin, and an affiliated fellow with the Max Weber Forum for South Asian Studies, Delhi. His research is funded by the Gerda Henkel Stiftung. He has a PhD from the Department of History and Culture Studies at Freie Universität, Berlin, where he was a doctoral fellow at the Berlin Graduate School Muslim Cultures and Societies.

Samprati Pani is a social anthropologist working at the intersection of urban studies, the anthropology of markets, and the philosophy of process. She is currently an affiliated fellow at the Max Weber Forum for South Asian Studies, New Delhi. Her larger research traces the social, material, and affective life of weekly bazaars in Delhi, focusing on forms of doing and making around street trade. Her areas of interest span marketplace socialities, shop signage and design, urban spatial formations, and walking as a research technique. She is the editor of the blog *Chiragh Dilli*, which explores forms of writing about the city. Her writings on the blog explore everyday modes of walking, street life, and the ordinary city.

Matthias Pilz is Full Professor of Business Education and International Vocational Education and Training Research at the University of Cologne and Director of the German Research Center for Comparative Vocational Education and Training (G.R.E.A.T.). He is Editor-in-Chief of the *International Journal of Training and Development*. His research interests are in international comparative research in VET, transitions from education to employment, and teaching and learning.

Advaita Rajendra is a faculty member at the Indian Institute of Management, Sirmaur, in the Public Policy and Sociology Department. She completed her Ph.D. from the Indian Institute of Management, Ahmedabad. Her research explores how governing mechanisms (in)visibilise waste materials, waste infrastructure, and waste work. Her research interests lie in policy issues of labour, social hierarchies, and the environment.

Muthuveeran Ramasamy is a social impact professional currently serving as Chief Advisor at G.R.E.A.T. (German Research Centre for Comparative Vocational Education and Training) in India. He holds a Ph.D. from the University of Cologne and served as a senior researcher in the Chair of Business Education and International VET Research. Before his role at G.R.E.A.T. in India, he served as Project Director at VIT University in India and as a social scientist at the MS Swaminathan Research Foundation. Dr. Ramasamy specialises in skill development, sociology of education, workforce development, corporate social responsibility (CSR), and rural development.

Sreela Sarkar is Associate Professor of Communication at Santa Clara University. Her research critically examines technology and modernisation processes with an emphasis on urban India and the Silicon Valley. Sreela's ethnographic research focuses on labour and identities in the context of contested urban development and new policy initiatives targeted at marginalised groups. Her work has been published in communication studies, feminist studies, and STS journals and featured in popular publications and podcasts.

Sebastian Schneider, M.Sc., is a research associate at the Institute for SME Research in Bonn (Institut für Mittelstandsforschung Bonn); Sebastian received his doctoral degree from the Chair of Business Education and International VET Research at the University of Cologne, Germany. His research interests include international VET research, the attractiveness of VET, and research about small- and medium-sized businesses.

Sebastian Schwecke is the founding director of the Max Weber Forum (MWF) for South Asian Studies in Delhi, a German research institute under the umbrella of Max Weber Stiftung. He received his PhD in international political economy and political science from Leipzig University, Germany. His extensive historical and ethnographic research on extra-legal credit markets in northern India resulted in a post-doctoral habilitation in history at the Göttingen University, as well as the monograph *Debt, Trust, and Reputation: Extra-legal Finance in Northern India*, published in 2022. He was an associate professor at the Indian Institute of Management-Calcutta, from 2018 to 2020, where he co-edited the influential volume *Rethinking Markets in Modern India: Embedded Exchange and Contested Jurisdiction* (2020).

Sadaf Sethwala is a policy researcher. Her work examines educational policy making and practice, and explores how policies and institutional factors manipulate outcomes and aspirations for marginalised youth to help foster more equitable social and economic opportunities.

Christian Strümpell is a research associate at the Max Weber Forum for South Asian Studies, Delhi, and an anthropologist working on class, caste, gender, work, labour, and the state and social movements in South Asia and beyond. In addition to his research in Rourkela presented in this volume, he has undertaken further ethnographic research on export garment workers and metal workers in Bangladesh.

PREFACE

Skill and skilling are much-talked-about subjects in the contemporary Indian discourse. They are politically categorised as an important ingredient of India's future, and are equally present in many Indians' everyday lives: as aspirations, dreams, practices and routines, informal modes of learning, and credentials and also as certificates and bureaucratic forms, as something to acquire, maintain, and upgrade lifelong, or as something to show on a CV. Conversely, the attribute of being 'unskilled' serves as a marker of exclusion and low occupational and social status that stigmatises the respective person, and reduces entitlements in terms of contractual conditions, wages, and social benefits. The actualities of skill and skilling, however, frequently differ from their imagination by practitioners as well as political and administrative planners, and the histories of skill and skilling demonstrate a remarkable variation of understandings over time and space of what the terms 'skill' and 'skilling' encompass. In this volume we theorise skill and skilling in India as an ecology that emerges from non-linear, fluid, relational, and dynamic interactions between multifarious institutions, social identities, public policies, organizational forms, and labour practices. Such a complex system remains constantly attuned to transformations in its immediate surroundings at various scales, which might inhibit or accelerate the accretion of the meaning around skill and skilling. We draw on the notion of ecology with regard to skilling to also accentuate the notion of flows. The skill ecology critically depends on various levels of flows that encompass knowledge, funds, discourses, human resources, and technological innovations. However, the question of what regulatory influences direct such flows remains a critical point of exploration in this volume, where both the formal state and the informal forms of customary control exert at best partial and imperfect forms of regulation over this ecology. It is constantly navigated and contested between both formal and informal institutions and individuals. Such an ecology may be analytically captured in its fleeting expressions but remains sufficiently ephemeral to prevent static modes of projection and modelling.

The current formation of a skill ecology in India, driven by the market logics of reproducing and reshaping labour for the various industrial and services sectors through public-private partnerships, is therefore, part of a much longer historical evolution of occupation related training in India. While there is no scarcity of studies of higher education and associated institutions in colonial and postcolonial India, relatively less attention has been paid to the issue of occupational skill formation and skill utilisation vis-a-vis the philosophical underpinnings of skilling in India emerging out of hierarchies of social recognition, contestations of labour practices, formal and informal forms of knowledge transfers, and evolving perceptions of state-led institutional arrangements for promoting them. Moreover, there is a clear need to unpack the long-term historical contestations as well as the contemporary morphological transformations in the marketisation of skill training, the policy debates through which such marketisation is envisaged, and the social, economic, cultural, and political contestations about the valuation and conceptualisation of what constitutes skill in India.

Our emphasis on the complex and multi-scalar ecology paradigm of skill and skilling in India is to transcend these hardened binaries (such as between the formal and the informal), which tend to foreground certain perceptions about skill and skilling while remaining blind to others. We pay close attention to the points of collaboration, friction, conflict, and collusion between the putatively disparate domains of the concept of skilling imagined in a broad spatio-temporal context. Our hope is that more productive albeit fluid categories of skill and skilling might emerge as a consequence.

This edited volume brings together anthropologists and historians as well as scholars from related disciplines in order to present a nuanced picture of the skill ecology that has emerged in the course of the history of modern India. By building on existing scholarship, we critically reassess both the historical antecedents and the recent boom of the 'skill industry' through interdisciplinary social science perspectives. We seek to make critical contributions in South Asianist scholarship on the historical and anthropological understandings of skill/skilling in India and to the broader debates around 'education' and 'vocational education' with 'vocational education' seen as somehow occupying a lower status in the hierarchy of intellectual fields of inquiry. In doing so, this volume critically reflects on the periodic ebb and flow of social and political discourses, policy debates, and both the social consequences of and the social responses to the divergent attempts to institutionalise occupational training in India. Finally, we seek to move beyond binaries between education (knowledge) and training (practical) that reproduce class distinctions between administrative-managerial and 'labouring' classes by focusing on skill as the end product of learning processes, however way they are classified.

A vast segment of India's skill ecology remains tightly tied to historical antecedents of skilling predominant in earlier periods. However, even where segments of India's skill ecology appear to be untouched by more recent developments – such as in its rural economy, its artisanal industries, the commercial arenas defined as 'bazaars', subsistence industries and service sectors, or the broad category of India's 'informal economy' – they were and are hardly unaffected: ideas of and on skill have tended to percolate into even these segments, indirectly affecting them in manifold ways, even when ideas on skill and policies of skilling were strategically designed to exclude rather than include them. They have deflected and modified the forms of skill, in unanticipated ways, imposed on the workforce as much as the forms of skill sought to be acquired by individuals. They have devalued and partially introduced/re-introduced other skills and knowledge regarding work processes that had been in demand earlier.

The volume will include chapters attempting to re-think the histories of skill and skilling under conditions of rapid commercial re-orientations and industrial expansion in the late colonial period starting from colonial changes and interventions, through the state-led modernization in the Nehruvian decades, and up to the contemporary 'Skill Mission' emerging from both a groundswell of right-wing nationalism and intense pro-market ideologies of national growth. As is to be expected, the Indian state – both in its late colonial and in its post-colonial avatars – remains a constant refrain suturing together many of the narrative accounts through which skill and skilling in India must be traced. The attempt, however, is not to force a seamless narrative where the state remains a constant source of institutional support framing together the broader mandates of skilling; rather the chapters in this volume suggest how the periodic waning and subsequent resurgence of the importance of skill and skilling is often achieved through contestation and collaboration between multiple actors, of whom the state is often not the most important, even where it is the most visible. These contestations and collaborations lead to a process in which skill ecologies are shaped: as reproduction, as recalibrations, and as reimaginations.

In the context of labour, this volume will proceed from the double assumption that every labour process relies on certain levels of occupational skill, but that social relations of power always mediate the precise relationship between a labour process and occupational skill. These complex and unequal relations of power can for instance make certain categories of labour processes appear to be high-skill areas, while devaluating the high degree and sophistication of occupational skills involved in other work processes. This phenomenon is particularly true in India where the specific structural articulations of social power have led to the appropriation of major technological innovations, generated by the industrial revolutions since the eighteenth century under social conditions vastly divergent from those in many other parts of the world. Thus, the intersections between skill and the labour processes are context specific, dynamic, and localised rather than static, predictable, and universal. This crucial aspect of skill is critically manifested in India where complex laminations of socioeconomic and political power have fashioned distinct adaptations of technologies, different forms of organising the labour process when applying the same technology, diverging modes of combining skill with social status, specific combinations of processes of skilling and deskilling, as well as diverse patterns of skill-defined segmentation among the workforces. Consequently, the history and anthropology of skill and occupational training must simultaneously examine the formation of 'skill' as a category of the labour process as much as its development as a category of social status and hierarchy.

One central aspect in this reimagination of skill and skilling relates to the increasingly perceived need to create structures of certification for skills. In the process, the skill ecology shifted towards valuations of skill depending on information flows controlled by certifying agencies acting as intermediaries – whether or not these were part of the state – and skill as a category became increasingly detached from its meaning of an ability to *do* things. Instead, certifying agencies have emerged as the key actors *informing* the three main constituents of the skill ecology – capital, labour, and the state – of skills and skill levels available, and of those in demand or lacking, thus reimagining the supply and demand of skill (often also called skill utilisation) and shaping the responses of labour, capital, and the state towards the skill ecology.

The issue of certification has no doubt grown in importance in the period under review but its articulations are contradictory and need to be examined accordingly: while certification reflects, to some extent, a need for the standardisation of occupational skills and for a transferability of skilled workforces between companies, it can also be the expression of a business model of commercial or public providers of sometimes/often low-quality training that responds more to the trainees' aspirations for employment and upward mobility than to the needs of employers for any particular skill.

This collection of chapters will thus engage with the economic and sociopolitical processes that have provided the contexts for the transformation of India's landscapes of skill and the social hierarchies embedded in them from the middle of the nineteenth century to the contemporary period. They provide case studies of specific articulations of the 'skill question' in various socioeconomic settings and at different historical junctures. They analyse shifting ideological and policy imperatives and social conflicts framing the contents and the institutional infrastructures of 'skill development' at both the entrepreneurial and state levels. They take account of the unevenness of these processes across occupational sectors and India's historical geography of capitalism. Thus, the chapters provide critical insights for analysing a contested chronology and terrain of skill from colonial to contemporary India.

ACKNOWLEDGEMENTS

The idea for this volume emerged over the course of a conference organised at the Indian Institute of Management-Calcutta (IIM-C) in 2019 and sponsored by the M. S. Merian – R. Tagore International Centre for Advanced Studies 'Metamorphoses of the Political' (ICAS-MP) and the Public Policy and Management Group in IIM-C. Many of the ideas collected in this volume germinated and took, sometimes hazy forms, during this conference. A special note of thanks should go to Ravi Ahuja, Arun Kumar, Samita Sen, Bhaskar Chakrabarti, Rajesh Bhattacharya, Nimruji Jammulamadaka, and Manish Thakur. Many of their ideas, shared so generously, have decisively shaped some of the fundamental ideas of this volume. A very big thank you to Michaela Dimmers, not only for contributing an excellent chapter to this volume but also for suggesting ways to take this project forward. We would like to offer a sincere thank-you to Alyssa Miller for reading multiple drafts and providing nuanced comments, especially in the early stages of the book. The period of putting the book together was marked by two deeply tragic events. The first was the global pandemic, which saw the death of countless people globally and brought enormous suffering to many more. It would not be an exaggeration to suggest that so much of our received ideas on skill, labour migration, value chains, and the very understanding of capitalism has transformed due to the pandemic. The second tragedy, of a more personal kind, was the untimely passing away of our co-editor, Srabani Maitra, some of whose thoughts and ideas on skill still enliven this book in substantial ways. Any intellectual project is collaborative and this book also owes a huge degree of debt to multiple interlocutors, friends, and companions from around the around. Kamran Asdar Ali, Kaushik Ghose, and Kathleen Stewart from the University of Texas contributed immensely to many of the ideas spread across this volume. In India, Geetha Nambissan and Nandini Manjrekar have been critical in shaping our ideas on education, especially for those who are least privileged in society. We would also like to thank Debjani Mazumder for her patience and kindness in helping to compile the book.

1

CRAFTING SKILLS

Reproducing, recalibrating, and reimagining skill in modern India

Saikat Maitra and Sebastian Schwecke

Skill regimes in contemporary India

The separation of the 'Ministry of Skill Development & Entrepreneurship' (MSDE) from a severely truncated – at least in scope and ambit – 'Ministry of Labour' and the subsequent launching of the 'Skill Mission' in 2015 marks one of several critical moments in the wider historical narrative of skill development and skill formation in India. Occupational training officially now became regarded as a decisive element necessary to harness the much-celebrated and little-realized demographic dividend in India through greater degrees of market-oriented skilling of a young population. According to the Ministry of Skill Development and Entrepreneurship, this new regime of national skill training would not only be responsive to actual industry demands and requirements but also be delivered through a complex arrangement of both private and public institutions that maximized the reach and scope of the 'Mission'. The current Indian national government's emphasis on skill training to generate socioeconomic growth, employment and the production of a well-trained youth labour force is, while no doubt ambitious, not as unique or unprecedented as it is made out to be by the gushing contents of the MSDE's official website. While skill preservation is frequently linked to questions of attrition within internal labour markets, in India – at many levels of the economy – it is more often linked to preserving skills within regionally established economic clusters, partially offsetting the need to counter attrition at the level of the firm.

Similarly, ambitious – if at an entirely different level – are the various ways in which different segments of Indian society have imbibed and internalized discourses of skill. Whether it is prospective university and college graduates

DOI: 10.4324/9781003604846-1

undergoing the rigorous routines of coaching centres, the labour force of 'interactive service industries' subjecting and shaping their bodies according to the demands of employers, industrial and artisanal labourers applying for the recognition of their acquired skills, or young informal workers in the service sector visiting computer courses, the politically dominant perceptions of skill and skilling have become an everyday occurrence. However, the vast majority of the working-age population in India remains engaged in occupations that require skills that are fundamentally different from those offered by the skilling initiatives of the state and private capital. While skill and skilling are ubiquitous, it is the mismatch between the aspirations for skill(s) and the actual uses of skills along with the labour market outcomes associated with the returns on investment in skilling that drive their valuation.

Entering a very different segment of the Indian economy, the tone when discussing skill gets very different. People's responses in the commercially dominated economy of Narendra Modi's own electoral constituency Varanasi diverged significantly when asked to debate about the effect of skill policies for the last decade under the Modi government in India. 'There is no skill in the bazaar', was a common refrain, highlighting this seeming mismatch and pointing towards one of the many puzzles of the Indian economy – petty retail, in terms of its share in overall employment outside agriculture probably the single-most important economic segment, was not considered to involve any skill at all, and therefore could not possibly benefit from government policy, it was argued. Other respondents differed. If only the government recognized the right skills, petty retail in the bazaar would *be* skilled labour, and people would then benefit from the government's skilling policies through institutions of vocational education; yet a sense of pessimism-induced – or realism, possibly – caution persisted. How would people benefit? What would be taught at these institutions, and why would their graduates have improved their skills after passing a government examination (and likely paying for it, possibly through bribes but definitely in paying for tuitions)? How would their new skills allow them to be better entrepreneurs, thus helping in making ends meet? If people could become skilled in retail, how would this skill help attract new buyers when consumption – overall, but especially in this economic segment – was down?

Retail has often been overlooked in debates about skill, especially in India. Where skilling policies and programmes exist at all in this sector, they tend to focus on either accounting or comportment and appearance as in India's malls (Gooptu, 2009; Maitra and Maitra, 2018; Maitra and Schwecke, 2021). The fact that there supposedly were no skills involved in petty retail – within the bazaar or beyond it – is important in explaining its status as one of the dominant labour reservoirs in the country. Needing no formal entry requirements, many people can enter it – and make a very modest living without the hardships (and stigma) of hard physical labour. But are there really no skills involved in petty retail? Observing the functioning of petty extra-legal finance – a prerequisite for success for the vast majority of petty retail outlets in a city like Varanasi – the successful handling of these credit flows requires a vast repertoire of skills in communicating reputations, allowing debtors to re-negotiate the actual costs of credit through processes of defaulting, wilfully or otherwise, a lower-order version of the 'art of the deal' practiced among others by parts of India's corporate elite that accounts for major business success stories, even if it is not taught as a subject in India's prime management schools (Schwecke, 2022).

Saikat Maitra's work on employment skill training programmes in metropolitan malls (Maitra, 2016) raises a related set of questions in detailing the range of skills that were acquired by mall workers – and set them apart from the realm of petty retail: rote-learning of brand names, bodily comportment, physical grooming skills, and litanies of 'customer-friendly' phrases in half-mastered English. These newly skilled retail workers could hardly be expected to make a substantial difference to the information flows about products that could possibly increase the *productivity* (or value-generation) of the retail leg of the value-chain as opposed to merely producing entertainment effects for disinterested customers. If the workforce could not possibly be expected to acquire sufficient skill levels in areas relevant to the value-addition process their labour was employed for, why engage in skilling at all? Or, conversely, what was the workforce being skilled for? Was skilling the retail workforce in India's metropolitan malls in the end much more related to processes of imagination – the imagining of a transition process embodied in place-making that in turn required the employment of a certification process anchored in producing *difference* to the seemingly unskilled norm of retail as manifested in northern Indian bazaar towns or neighbourhood markets? Was the absence of a discourse on skill in the bazaar, then, a type of commercial counter-culture (Holt, 2002), or had it developed into one in the course of the emergence of mall-based orders of modernity? In other words, what are we looking at when we are trying to decipher what lies behind policies on skill and skilling in modern India, considering that it may, simultaneously, relate to one of the country's foremost requirements since colonial times as well as a range of very different objectives arising from the imaginaries of skill employed over various times?

Theorizing skill

Skill and skilling mean a myriad of things to many people, ranging from their associations with human capital development for national growth to transfer of knowledge systems along communal or familial ties. Their meanings reflect contextual circumstances and conjunctural patterns, individual perceptions, and structural developments. Skill is perceived and imagined, planned and strategized, valuated, recognized and certified, supplied and demanded. It is constantly reinterpreted at all of these stages. To make sense of skill – and in this way to make sense of skilling as well – we need to use both terms as embedded categories within broader socioeconomic processes and observe skill and the processes of skilling within the discourses and parameters that define them (Attewell, 1990). This raises the additional challenge that what might be recognized as 'skill' remains contingent on the intersections of several factors extending from formal technical proficiencies to social hierarchies nested in modes and hierarchies of production. Thus, in this volume, skilled workers are not assumed to be a uniform group sharing similar working conditions and privileges but as fragmented 'classes of labour' who are deeply stratified into formal and informal sectors of the Indian economy with enormous differences in wage structures, working conditions, and employment securities (Bernstein, 2006; Lerche, 2013).

Skill and skilling are much-talked-about subjects in the contemporary Indian discourse (Agrawal, 2013; King, 2012). They are politically categorized as an important ingredient of India's future, and are equally present in many Indians' everyday lives: as aspirations, dreams, practices and routines, informal modes of learning, credentials, and also as certificates and bureaucratic forms, as something to acquire, maintain and upgrade lifelong, or as something to show on a CV. Conversely, the attribute of being 'unskilled' serves as a marker of exclusion and low occupational and social status that stigmatizes the respective person, and reduces entitlements in terms of contractual conditions, wages, and social benefits. The actualities of skill and skilling, however, frequently differ from their imagination by practitioners as well as political and administrative planners, and the histories of skill and skilling demonstrate a remarkable variation of understandings over time and space of what the terms skill and skilling encompass.

In this volume we theorize skill and skilling in India as an ecology that emerges from non-linear, fluid, relational, and dynamic interactions between multifarious institutions, social identities, public policies, organizational forms, and labouring practices. Such a complex system remains constantly attuned to transformations in its immediate surroundings at various scales, which might inhibit or accelerate the accretion of meaning around skill and skilling. We draw on the notion of ecology with regard to skilling in order to also accentuate the notion of flows. The skill ecology critically depends on various flows that encompass knowledge, funds, discourses, human resources, bureaucratic conventions, public policy planning, and technological innovations. However, what regulatory influences direct such flows remain a critical point of exploration in this context where both the formal state and the informal forms of customary control exert at best partial and imperfect forms of regulation over this ecology. It is constantly navigated and contested between both formal and informal institutions, and individuals.

Such an ecology may be analytically captured in its fleeting expressions but remains sufficiently ephemeral to prevent projection and modelling. This volume draws on anthropologist Tim Ingold's conceptualization of *skill ecology* to argue that skilling processes need to be contextualized with regard to the ecology of the lives of the learners. Skill, according to Ingold, is often perceived from a Cartesian worldview, as of belonging more to the 'hand rather than the mind' (Ingold, 2018). Skill training in this logic implies imparting or transmitting knowledge 'by way of rules, schema or programmes into the mind of a recipient who then decodes them to be enacted by the body' (Woods et al., 2021). Traditionally skill training therefore has been focused more on the individual learner and his/her embodied expertise to acquire skills as 'a set of internalised rules or propositional commands that specify how movements are to be carried out and controlled by the body' (Woods et al., 2021, p. 2). Skill then becomes more of a 'top-down process of transmission' (Woods et al., 2021, p. 2) that practitioners attempt to impart or transmit to the learners.

Going beyond the mind-body duality, Ingold describes skills as a 'mode of thinking-doing that is indissolubly visceral and intellectual' at the same time (Ingold 2018, 160). According to him, skills should mean the capacities emerging out of an organic and inextricable linkage and feed-back loop between the mind and the body emplaced in a dynamic and textured environment affecting the mind-body connect. This is where the relational aspect of Ingold's conceptualization of skills becomes evident, as it entails that effective skills training should situate the learner in the context of an active engagement with the constituents of his or her surroundings affecting both the sensorial and corporeal capabilities. This is what may be described as the 'dwelling perspectives' of skilling (Ingold 2018). Skills are then neither 'innate nor acquired' but grown within an individual in relation to his/her environmental context (including the social relations structuring the work processes). Any skill training imparted without context ends up being simply a set of information rather than an 'enfoldment' that remains attuned to the embodied realities of the environment in which it is nestled (Ingold 2018). According to Ingold, life is generative – it is a 'creative unfolding' of many different forms within a field of relations and skill training needs to be engaged with and embedded within those different forms to be successful. Individuals and their environments are ever changing. Whatever interaction or knowledge is within an individual, they will only be meaningful when the learner can 'dwell' that training in a particular environmental context. Any context-free training is not skill but merely analytical abstractions (Ingold 2018). It would be as C. T. Woods explains, simply a 'filling up' (Woods et al., 2021, p. 3) of the learners' 'stored knowledge about the task and the environment to instil idealised ways of "being and doing" that fit established conventional templates' (Woods et al., 2021, p. 3). The ecological rationale is unique as it aims to 'restore balance between the organism and environment' (Woods et al., 2021, p. 3) when talking about skill training and acquisition. Woods further explains that *enskillment* as a type of 'local know-how or knack' that progressively emerges as an individual becomes intimately familiar with a task and surroundings" (Woods et al., 2021, p. 3). *Enskillment*, as developed by Ingold, talks about skill being perceptive, responsive, and deeply aligned with the changing ecology of the learners.

A. Brown argues that skill building depends on societal capacity underscoring the importance of understanding that 'social foundations' as critical to skilling, rather than simply thinking of skill formation in terms of national economy (Brown et al., 2005, p. 3). Additionally, Brown highlights the need to focus on the 'social purposes or goals' (Brown et al., 2005, p. 3), which skill development can address. The development of these goals is dependent on a deep, earnest societal commitment rather than simply assuming that a high skill society is an 'inevitable feature of knowledge driven economies' (Brown et al., 2005, p. 3). What the focus on human capital, linked to the acquiring of skills, has achieved is to take away the attention from various hindrances to employability such as class, gender, or race and to solely invest on 'talents, efforts, and achievements of individuals' (Brown et al., 2005, p. 7). Additionally, as Brown et al. (2005) argue, the reason that human capital theory has been invested on in both developed and developing nations is because '[i]t is indifferent to national history, culture, and identities because it conforms to the universal laws of economic development' (Brown et al., 2005, p. 7). For instance, the realities of technical and vocational education and training (TVET) in India is that the quality of training has more often than not failed to prepare young people to acquire skills that have a global appeal, nor has it been able to acquire necessary skills and credentials to compete in the local labour market. Furthermore, the supply-demand model is too market driven with decisions about TVET training being determined by employers with the role of a rapidly privatizing state simply being reduced to encouraging individuals to invest in their human capital. Too much focus on the supply side puts educational institutions and training organizations 'at the frontline in the battle for competitiveness' (Brown et al., 2005, p. 11). Human capital theory ignores that skills are socially constructed and not necessarily innate abilities of workers. Drawing on Ingold's work it can be argued that the individual's capacity to do work is not innate – it is socially created and needs to be socially sustained. Within that environment, sociocultural identities and relations of ethnicities, gender, class, race, or caste can and will impact motivation to learn or approaches to learning and skilling (Bryson 2017).

Students need to be committed and involved in what they are learning and it is only then that they can engage creatively in their work rather than simply prepare for a mechanical task under close supervision. Skill therefore, as Brown et al. (2005) argues, 'is not simply a question of acquired technical competencies through formal education and training, it also includes an ability to learn how to learn as a lifelong activity' (p. 15). Skill is not a disembodied, technical activity and has its cognitive, emotional, cultural and economic facets. David Finegold (1999), drawing on population ecologists in the management literature, compares skill ecosystems to biological systems in order to understand the conditions that are necessary for organizing skilling within the economy to thrive and grow. Finegold describes four elements that are necessary to sustain a high skill ecosystem. These are

> a catalyst – some event or external trigger that initiates the living reaction; fuel or nourishment – to sustain the growth of life on an ongoing basis, a supportive host environment – a set of environmental conditions that enables young creatures to grow to maturity; a high degree of interdependence – part of what makes this a system and not simply a group of separate organisms sharing the same physical space in that they are mutually interdependent, e.g. part of a single food chain.
>
> *(Finegold 1999, p. 66)*

The ecosystem needs a stable infrastructure and a work climate that is conducive to workers. This infrastructure includes, for example, local transportation that can give easy access to workers to get to their work efficiently. This steady communication system (internet, video conferencing, telecommunication) should be up-to-date for making virtual collaborations possible. Additionally, access to incubators and technology parks can help build networks and exchange of ideas and future collations. Finally, what is needed is a high degree of cooperation among the different actors such as educational institutions, employers, banks etc. so that together they can facilitate the learning processes and provide opportunities for growth. In sharp contrast, historically in India there have been very weak institutional linkages between firms, educational institutions, and training providers for adaptation to technology through skilling (especially life-long learning mechanisms) with quick short-term training seen as a solution to deeply entrenched problems of uneven skilling eco-systems.

The current formation of a skill ecology in India, driven by the market logics of reproducing and reshaping labour for the various industrial and services sectors through public-private partnerships, is part of a much longer historical evolution of occupation-related training in India. While there is no scarcity of studies of higher education and associated institutions in colonial and postcolonial India, relatively less attention has been paid to the issue of occupational skill formation and skill utilization vis-a-vis the philosophical underpinnings of skilling in India emerging out of hierarchies of social recognition, contestations of labour practices, formal and informal forms of knowledge transfers, and evolving perceptions of state-led institutional arrangements for promoting them. There is a clear need to unpack the long-term historical contestations as well as the contemporary morphological transformations in the marketization of skill training, the policy debates through which such marketization is envisaged as well as the social, economic, cultural, and political contestations about the valuation and conceptualization of what constitutes skill in India. Often the World Bank–driven prescriptive paradigms of skill and skill training for economic well-being of developing countries such as India exhibit a fundamental gap in the economic theory of human capital that it has not been able to comprehend the broader historical and social dimensions contributing to skill formation.

For too long, the ideas of skill and skilling in India have remained tightly inscribed around a binary opposition between the (formal) state-led economic matrices of human capital development and the romanticized informal *ustad/shargird* relationships prevalent in some artisanal traditions of production. A corollary of this (false) binary opposition is the exaggerated demarcations between ideas of formality/informality, industrial/artisanal production, pedagogy/practice, and ultimately modernity/tradition. Our emphasis on the complex and multi-scalar ecology paradigm of skill and skilling in India is to transcend these hardened binaries which tend to foreground certain perceptions about skill and skilling while remaining blind to others. The chapters collated in this volume instead pay close attention to the points of collaboration, friction, conflict, and collusion between the putatively separate domains of the two sides associated with the binaries mentioned here across various socio-temporal scales. Our hope is that a more nuanced and productive, albeit fluid, categories of skill and skilling might emerge as a consequence in theorizing labour, markets, pedagogic practices, and definitely skill in the scholarship on India.

Our edited volume brings together anthropologists and historians as well as scholars from related disciplines in order to present a complex picture of the skill ecology that has emerged in the course of the history of modern India. By building on existing scholarship, we critically reassess both the historical antecedents and the recent boom of the 'skill industry' through interdisciplinary social science perspectives. We seek to make critical contributions in South Asianist scholarship on the historical and anthropological understandings of skill/skilling in India and to the broader debates around 'education' and 'vocational education' that has steadfastly maintained a marked separation between the two spheres, with 'vocational education' seen as somehow occupying a lower status in the hierarchy of intellectual fields of inquiry. In doing so, this volume critically reflects on the periodic ebb and flow of social and political discourses, policy debates, and both the social consequences of and the social responses to the diverse attempts to institutionalize occupational training in India across time and space. Finally, we seek to move beyond binaries between education (knowledge) and training (practice) that reproduce class distinctions between administrative-managerial and 'labouring' classes by focusing on skill as the end product of learning processes which combine divergent intellectual and affective knowledge systems, irrespective of the stratified hierarchies of classification of knowledge. In this regard, Pankhuree R. Dube's contribution in this volume reminds us of the colonial devaluation of artisanal skills for being too embedded within the environment of the artisanal producer and therefore not consonant with 'modern' technological dimensions of skilling. Dube uses the theoretical formulation of 'haptic knowledge' to foreground alternate modes of knowing, doing, and ultimately 'dwelling' in the world and creating forms of knowledge systems.

Historically, we can distinguish three broad phases in the development of India's modern skill ecology, though it is important to emphasize the fact that these phases are not marked by clear ruptures, but rather by gradual and incremental transformations to the continuing evolution of skill and skilling in India. For instance, a vast segment of India's skill ecology still remains tightly tied to historical antecedents of skilling predominant in earlier periods. However, even where segments of India's skill ecology appear to be untouched by more recent developments – such as in its rural economy, its artisanal industries, the commercial arenas defined as 'bazaars', subsistence industries and service sectors, or the broad category of India's 'informal economy' – they were and are hardly unaffected: ideas of and on skill have tended to percolate into these segments, indirectly affecting them in manifold ways, even when ideas on skill and policies of skilling were strategically designed to exclude rather than include them. They have changed the forms of skill sought to be imposed on the workforce as much as the forms of skill sought to be acquired by individuals. They have devalued and partially replaced other skills and forms of skilling that had been in demand earlier. They have obscured the visibility of these other skills even where they have not replaced them fully.

Periodizing skilling in India

Based on this gradual evolution and aware of the continuities between them, we broadly distinguish three phases of the development of India's skill ecology that fall within the scope of this volume:

1870s–1930s – The Colonial Period: India's skill ecology was originally predominantly marked by experiential learning in a *laissez-faire* political environment that relegated concerns on skilling to the societal realm, marked by a kaleidoscope of practices in organizing labour by capital in terms of skill and skilling that – among other practices – prominently made use of kinship or community ties. Characterizing the dominant perceptions

> about skill training amongst capitalist entrepreneurs in colonial British India, labour historian Rajnarayan Chandavarkar suggested that 'Indian industry was built on legends' (Chandavarkar, 2008, p. 131). What Chandavarkar implied is that in the context of an established Indian industry like the cotton-textile industry of Bombay in colonial India, the reputation of managers, weaving masters, jobbers, and workers for efficiency and high levels of productivity depended not on any formalized training but on long years of experience, ingenuity, improvisation, and intuition learnt on the shop-floor (Chandavarkar, 2008, 1994). Industrial skill was learnt on the job and embodied in the personhood of individual workers who commanded enormous prestige and high reputation (Chandavarkar, 2008). The emphasis on experience as the sole determinant of skill training meant that there was a marked disdain for bookish knowledge along with a stringent belief in pragmatism where long years of trial and error in manipulating machines, raw materials, and social relations on the factory floor taught both management and labour the requisite skill levels for performing at an optimum level (Chandavarkar, 2008). This of course did not mean that there were no provisions for formal skill training for workers during the early years of Indian industrial growth from the mid- to late-nineteenth century. However, institutional skill training for workers in the form of Industrial Schools tended to be fragmentary, episodic, and not systematized (Kumar, 2019; Swaminathan, 2005).

By the late 1920s and especially from the 1930s, the industrial climate of colonial India was making the need for creating a modern, trained, and disciplined workforce more acute. This was primarily due to the increasingly hostile industrial relations developing between capital and labour where large industrial conglomerations, especially the jute and cotton-textile industries based in urban locations such as Kanpur, Calcutta, and Bombay, were witnessing a searing escalation of strikes, protests, and violent capital-labour confrontations (Chakrabarty, 1989; Chandavarkar, 1994; Joshi, 2003). For decades, the unwavering principle of profitability for these industries had hinged on the exploitation cheapness of an unskilled, migratory labour force along with low capital investments on relatively simple technologies of production and the dependence on the jobber system for maintaining internal labour discipline in the factories and mills (Bhattacharya 2007; Chandavarkar, 2008; Morris, 1965). Such principles of utilizing a cheap labour force and its disciplining, often in a violent, erratic, and 'rough-and-ready' manner by the jobbers in the cotton textile or jute mills, were essentially coming under serious questioning in the face of sustained and well-orchestrated labour strikes from the late 1920s under a nascent Trade Union Movement (Breman, 1999; Morris, 1965). But if industrial relations in the last decades of the colonial rule in India were putting the older systems of managing labour under scrutiny, new market threats were emerging in both the domestic and international markets for Indian industrial goods from the 1930s, a situation compounded by the recession of the Indian economy in the same decade (Morris, 1960; Sarkar, 1989).

Increasingly, the colonial Indian state was assuming an interventionist role through various labour committees, labour laws, and legislations to mitigate the fast-deteriorating industrial relations as well as to stabilize the market. The need for rationalization of Indian industries and the consequent demand for a skilled and responsible labour force was also emerging due to sudden and vast expansion of the Indian industrial landscape form the late 1930s and especially during the Second World War years (Morris, 1965). To meet the demands of war, Indian industry was expanding from its traditional bases of mining, textile production, and plantations to include heavy electrical engineering, automobile manufacturing, chemical production, rubber technologies, hydroelectricity, and production of machine tools (Chandavarkar, 2008). These industries, using sophisticated technologies for production, could hardly afford to restrict employment to a cheap but unskilled labour force that would be eventually trained through years of experience and by a 'trial-and-error' method of learning, as in the older cotton textiles or jute industries. The emerging advanced industries needed a large body of skilled and trained workforce who had adequate competence (in terms of both conception and execution of work orders) to run the capital-intensive machineries and new technologies of production. To go back to Harry Braverman's (1974) thesis of de-skilling and rationalization of industrial work, the modernization and rationalization of Indian industries was in fact creating a vast demand and institutional needs for skill training of workers and not their de-skilling. In any case, the history of industrial relations in the twentieth century suggests that the extreme forms of rationalization along with absolute control of work processes by the management invariably led to large-scale worker protests and dissents (Beynon, 2009). More specifically, industrial labour histories in India have accentuated the fierce quality of resistance marking workers' reaction to any absolute management control over work-processes that Braverman's theoretical framework of industrial de-skilling depends on (Chandavarkar, 1999; Joshi, 1999). Moreover, by amplifying autonomy and control as the primary yardsticks for measuring skill, Braverman's model reduces all (industrial) workers to the level of unskilled workers. This raises several theoretical problems. Firstly, it reifies the distinction between mental and manual labour by implicitly suggesting that the conceptual part of any task (the one controlled by management) falls on the side of skill while manual, mechanical functions are simpler and devoid of any connotations of skill. Authors such as Cavendish (1982) and Linhart (1985) amply demonstrate how assembly line jobs in factories demand incredible degrees of speed, dexterity, and resilience from workers, even in so-called 'unskilled' routinized jobs. Secondly, Braverman overstates the binaries between conception and execution where workers in manufacturing factories often have to adopt and improvise for achieving efficient production processes (Dunn 2004). Such improvisations are not necessarily foreseen by the management but are testimony to the workers own understanding of production learnt through experience, team-work, and skill training (Burawoy, 1979). In addition, the stark contrast between industrial workers and craftsmen is hardly tenable in the context of India and similar other post-colonial spaces, where factory spaces are often linked through chains of sub-contracting to informal craft workshops performing similar work complexities and with workers having similar credentials (Haynes, 2012; Parry, 1999; Roy, 2004).

Even before formal independence, the future Indian state authorities were committing themselves to furthering the processes of industrial expansion, rationalization, and creation of a modern, trained, and disciplined workforce. As early as 1940, the emerging Indian state's vision for modernization, expansion, and rationalization of the industrial sector as central to India's development was emphasized in the National Planning Committee chaired by the future Prime Minister Jawaharlal Nehru (Breman, 1999). As the eventual Independence of India in 1947 drew closer, the direct intervention of the Indian state in capital-labour relations for creating a cordial industrial climate and a responsible, modern labour force was becoming apparent (Myers, 1958). Thus, in this phase, the gradual unfolding of capitalism in India and the erratic entrance of the state brought about incipient changes in the skill ecology and the capital-labour relations underlying it, originally based on state-led discourses defining imperatives for political interventions into a skill ecology that predominantly remained beyond the state's reach. This erratic state intervention enabled processes of (a) defining skill and skilling according to the emerging ideals and needs of the state and (b) creating opportunities primarily for particular forms of capital to make use of and influence the direction of skill policies for the creation of market enclaves defined by the presence of labour skilled in these ways.

1940s–1970s – The Post-Colonial Developmentalist Phase: The paradigm of planned economic development with mildly socialist tendencies adopted by the Nehruvian Indian state after independence in 1947 assimilated industrialization as the primary growth sector from its second Five Year Plan extending from 1956 to 1961 (Parry, 1999; Roy, 2007). The Second Five Year Plan not only envisioned rapid industrialization of the country in heavy manufacturing sectors (such as iron and steel) through large-scale and intensive capital investments by the state but also took up the responsibility of training and skilling the workforce to meet the high-technology production scenarios of both state and private industrial enterprises (Kohli, 2006, 2012). Such training responsibilities had both

> utilitarian and ideological functions whereby the state's functions in labour reproduction (at the level of educating and training workers) were aimed to do the following: (1) fill in the demand for a large, skilled workforce in the resurgent industrial scene in India in the 1950s and (2) to push for a nationalist agenda for development that emphasized the transformation of young populations into a disciplined, modern, and responsible workforce through skill training and employment generating education. In keeping with the Second Five Year Plan's stress on industrialization, foreign collaborations and skill transfers for training workers were initiated for example with help from the Ford Foundation in the 1950s (Hilger and Unger, 2012).

As scholars such as Srirupa Roy have argued, the Second Five Year Plan was a policy document by the Indian state not only to boost industrialization and modernization of the economy through state led investments in sectors such as hydroelectric dams and the setting up of steel mills and other heavy industries by the state; it also envisioned a new Indian worker-subject who was free from pre-modern irrationalities and inculcated a scientific mind (Roy, 2007). Industrial training and technological education were seen as critical to developing the scientific bent of mind of the Indian population as a whole and of workers in the industrial sector more specifically – albeit without too much of an impact on the 'pre-modern' sensibilities of caste dynamics and hierarchies (Subramanian, 2015). Skill training was seen as fundamental for emancipating Indian industrial workers from their supposedly deep-rooted attachment to the rural, agricultural economy – a systemic process of social engineering for transforming the peasant character of industrial workers into an urban proletariat (Morris, 1960, 1965). This proletariat could then be employed and integrated seamlessly into the upcoming and modernized state-owned steel mills and company towns of Bhilai, Rourkela, or Durgapur.

This state/government perspective on the peasant, and therefore supposedly backward character of labour and the consequent need for skill-training, was furthermore validated by a powerful and influential body of social science literature emerging on India by a group of North American sociologists. The commitment of the Indian labour force to industrial wage labour was the fundamental problem raised by influential authors such as Kerr (1960), Moore (1951), Moore and Feldman (1960), Myers (1958) and Ornati (1955). For these authors, the Indian worker was essentially deficient and lacking in psychological commitment to modern factory regimes of work and the discipline, rigour, routinization, and the ability to follow commands that such regimes entailed. The key symptoms of this lack of commitment lay in the slovenly pace of work, slacking and pervasive absenteeism, the perceived inclination to go on wild-cat strikes at the slightest provocation, high rates of labour turn-over, and the tendency to migrate back into their rural homesteads for indefinite periods once they received their wages (Moore and Feldman, 1960; Myers, 1958). All the authors unanimously recommended to the Indian state the need to implant a new commitment to industrial wage labour among migrant peasant workers where commitment was understood as 'involv[ing] both performance and acceptance of the behaviors appropriate to an industrial way of life' (Moore and Feldman, 1960, p. 2). Extensive training in industrial skill was seen as a foundational means for developing a committed workforce out of the deficient labouring bodies with strong peasant roots (Myers, 1958). Even early critics of the commitment hypothesis such as Morris (1960, 1965) accepted that Indian industrial workers were sorely deficient in skill training because of a severe lack of investment in training of workers by the Indian industrial entrepreneurs and management (Breman, 2004).

This congruence and emphasis on training by both the Indian state and the critical social science literature of the 1950s led to the establishment of the first Industrial Training Institutes (ITIs) and the establishment of the state appointed National Council of Vocational Training for overseeing the curricular content. These institutions during the period of large-scale state led industrialization in India were measures for poverty alleviation and employability of youth populations by integrating them into the emerging national industrial landscape (Goel, 2011; Parmar et al., 2015; Sen, 1989).

During the same time-period, a vast majority of the workforce (in both nationalized enterprises and especially in private corporate ones) continued to be recruited as casual/informal workers with considerably less wages and benefits and were routinely demarcated as 'unskilled' or 'apprentice-trainees' – even while performing the same job complexities and holding similar credentials as the permanent labour force (Parry, 1999; Parry and Strümpell, 2008). Thus, Mark Holmström's (1984) evocative description of the Indian working class as a deeply stratified 'mountain' continues to be an apt metaphor in both colonial and post-colonial India. In this 'mountain' the ever dwindling 'labour aristocracy' of workers with formal job contracts and skill credentials occupies the summit with the increasingly vertiginous slopes being populated by vast numbers of precarious workers eking out a meagre, 'footloose', abject living (Engels, 1993; Hobsbawm, 1968). More often than not, members of underprivileged social groups such as Dalits, Adivasis, and women workers form this vulnerable labour force further compounding their economic and social marginalization (Sanchez, 2016).

This is thus a phase marked by the emergence of the state as a leading actor in defining the skill ecology, even while vast segments of the Indian economy remained untouched directly by the state's efforts to remake the skill ecology. Based on ideas of 'scientific management' and the 'rationalization of labour', the Indian state strategically (rather than erratically) selected economic segments in which it mediated capital-labour relations in skilling.

Initially, this intervention created heightened opportunities for capital to shape, control, and discipline labour within these segments with the aid of state-led skilling policies, though especially from the 1950s onward it also created opportunities for labour, in the process leading to a more balanced idea of state mediation between capital and labour. While economic segments not strategically selected by the state remained untouched directly, the expansion of the state's role in defining and shaping skill and skilling, especially in technologically complex labour processes in the expanding industrial landscapes, contributed to decreases in the valuation of experiential learning and modes of transmitting skills that relied on practices prevalent before this phase, thus also devaluing labour relying on these experiential skills. A clear impress of this strategic intervention by the Indian state is clearly evident in the institutional arrangements created for augmenting and harnessing the country's technical labour and managerial human resources – with the Indian Institute of Technology (IIT) and other degree-granting engineering colleges occupying the top tier positions along with the upcoming Indian Institute of Management (IIM), the diploma-granting polytechnic colleges in the middle section, and the foot-soldiers of the industrial workforce being provided by vocational institutions such as the Industrial Technical Institutes (ITIs). The intervention of the post-colonial state in developing the framework and institutional arrangements for vocational education as a key component of the tertiary education landscape in India should, however, not be overstated as the disproportionately large amounts of public funding and resources went into chiselling the resplendent edifices of higher educational institutions such as the IITs and the IIMs – as exclusive islands of social and educational privilege – that remained often cut off from the abject realities of obsolete course curriculum, chronic resource constraints, and low prestige of (public-funded) primary, secondary, and tertiary education in India generally (Jammulamadaka, 2017; Leslie and Kargon, 2006). This top-heavy approach to public education would continue to have critical and dilatory consequences in the broader objectives of skilling in the present times as well.

1980s to the Present – Skill in Post-Liberalization India: The present phase in the historical development of India's skill ecology is marked by processes in which the state did not so much withdraw from shaping it but instead shifted its role to that of a 'pro-business' facilitator of the demands of capital (Kohli, 2006, 2012), in the process blurring the boundaries between capital and the state concerning skill and skilling. In order to still avail itself of the benefits of the skill ecology, labour was forced into an atomization process of internalizing capital/state-dominated skill discourses, and to use a state/capital-dominated infrastructure for skilling. The scope for the strategic selection of economic sectors where the capital/state-dominated skill ecology prevails was massively expanded. Skilling became an area in which capital and the state were addressing perceived needs of labour without being redistributive, so that it increasingly supplanted other 'welfare' activities. The discursive formulation of creating employability through skilling initiatives of the state/capital dyad becomes especially critical after the post-liberalization period of the 1990s, which have seen a massive downsizing of formal government sector employment opportunities. The balance between state and capital changed with the entrance of consultancies into skilling as a central component that constitute new intermediaries informing the state's perception of the skill ecology and certifying the skills of labour, thereby informing labour of its 'recognized' skills. Skilling in this regard has become a necessary and powerful political rhetoric and ideological imperative that reinforces the aspirational attributes of 'muscular nationalism' in India today, where the state can still claim to be contributing robustly to the remaking of a self-reliant and prosperous citizenry despite expanding problems of unemployment and withdrawal of state protection of labour welfare. The celebratory claims of state/capital-led discourses and policy visions on skilling (usually employing references to vast numbers of youth populations receiving skill training) preclude the experiential modes of skilling that continue to prevail among the vast majority of the Indian workforce. Such experiential modes of learning are increasingly devalued unless 'recognized' through formal processes of certification and accreditation, and forced into a precarious niche of the labour market outside of the newly dominant skill ecology. The devaluation of non-recognized skills facilitates workers' initiatives to acquire 'recognized' skills from formal skilling institutions even where the infrastructure for skilling is not necessarily designed to produce (or in any way guarantees the imbibing of) relevant skills for their future 'unskilled' occupations, a process that can be described as 'skilling for unskilled employment'. The model of the skilled worker promoted by the contemporary regimes of skilling and influenced by neoliberal, economic rationalities is ideally a person who is able to take risks, is self-motivated, shows a constant inclination to adjust to shifting job requirements, and is enterprising enough to seek continuous self-growth (Cross, 2014; Bradley, 2000; Foucault, 2008). Instead of depending on state institutions for long-term social welfare, wage benefits or employment security, he/she supposedly is creative enough to seize whatever opportunities might arise, even under adverse socioeconomic conditions (Harvey, 2003). In low-end jobs, the preference for enterprising workers able to survive under contingent, flexible work practices has been heightened in India (following global trends) under the impact of economic restructuring (Levien, 2013). Employment in India is increasingly marked by a neoliberal agenda which includes removing perceived barriers to imaginations of a 'free market', along with the concomitant erosion of employment securities and workers' bargaining rights (Stanford, 1999; McQuaig, 1998). Within

> this neoliberal premise, self-reliance is paramount; as McElligott (2001) notes, this often translates into a market-driven approach to work-based skilling and training where workers must remake themselves into competitive, enterprising subjects. Ideologically skill training becomes imperative now within a social milieu where workers are made 'desperate enough' to have some credentials to break into the labour market – even for precarious, dead-end jobs with minimal or no labour rights protection (Carswell and Neve, 2013; McElligott, 2001, 16; Levien, 2013). Thus, discourses of work-related learning feed into a neoliberal agenda, whereby employees are conceptualized as possessing a 'bundle of skills' (Darrah, 1997), which they are responsible for upgrading on a regular basis. The workplace is conceptualized as a backdrop, and it is workers rather than workplaces that are deemed to be in need of constant improvement. This perspective is reproduced in skilling programs whereby skill development and training, conceptualized as depoliticized and individualized, is seen to be the necessary requirement for participation in the new economy.

There are reasons why skilling has for long been an area that was neglected in India, and arguably still is, even at a time when it has been foregrounded discursively as an aspirational category for self-development and self-sufficiency – extending all the way down from the nation trying to stake its claim in the global economy as well as for the individual desperately trying to find her sea-legs in the contemporary labour market. Partially, it reflects an economy externally and internally shaped towards the exploitation of low wages, corresponding to low average productivity. The recent uptick in discourses on skill may simply reflect spill-overs from still very isolated enclaves within the Indian economy that require increased skilling initiatives into wider segments of the economy, without these segments having developed the structural underpinnings needed to develop into economies supporting the nexus between increased skill-levels, higher wages, and higher productivity. At the same time, the Indian skill ecology may reflect class angles, particularly long-established elite preferences for accumulation and the manifest political fantasies of an 'Atmanirbhar Bharat' justifying its place as the technocratic 'Vishwaguru' or India's supposed position as the 'skill capital of the world'. The existence of a substantial reservoir of unskilled labour whether in agriculture, or in industrial or service professions, however, increases the real benefits accruing to elite segments of society from the relatively easy and internationally less competitive organization of productive forces centred on exploiting low wages. Intermittent spells of policy concern over labour productivity such as in the last decades of colonial rule and the immediate decades after independence were insufficient to fully overcome these patterns of India's political economy, while the present 'neoliberal' phase of skilling responds to contradictory pressures within the economy and – as of now – has not yet led to a consolidation of a marked shift away from this nexus for the vast mass of the Indian labour force.

It is imperative though to avoid falling into the traps of either romanticizing modes of skilling that appear to be the preserve of earlier prevalent historical phases and socioeconomic alignments or imbibing the narrative of 'formal' skilling as a milestone in a process of development – which itself romanticizes 'Nehruvian' and/or 'neoliberal' preferences or ideological predilections on skill and skilling. Ideas of skill and skilling in South Asian societies change with political discourses, in the process producing manifold effects on the practices of skill and skilling, the experience of which feeds back into prevalent ideas. The outcome of this complex process is the production of a kaleidoscope of often times contradictory structures and developments that define the prevalent skill ecologies. Rather, we argue, it is imperative to rethink the study of skill and skilling in ways that highlight the interconnected parts of the skill ecology, keeping in mind spatio-temporal variations.

There is, however, a **post-script** to this periodization provided by the harrowing experiences of labour, and especially migrant labour, in the country during the period of national 'lock-down' due to the Covid-induced pandemic. The uncertainty of sudden unemployment, the long-term loss of livelihood, or most spectacularly the ghastly sight of migrant labour trekking back to their place of origin did two things simultaneously. The televisual sight of a desperate and ragged workforce along with their families trudging across the nation's highways and by-lanes no doubt reaffirmed the critical importance of adequate skilling that could guarantee the continuity of livelihoods and a less precarious condition of employment. At the same time, the sight also lay bare the uneven trajectories of capital growth and distribution in the country leading to a deeply fragmented and precarious internal labour market along with the conditions of exploitation, and disposability such fragmentation ensures for a vast workforce, irrespective of their levels of skilling. Abandoned in the space between life and death, the precarious existence of the labour force in India is evocative of what Lauren Berlant terms as 'slow death' – the gradual attrition of not just a subject but an entire population once it is left to fend for itself in conditions of extreme deprivation without the minimal protection by the state (2007, p. 754). This postscript is important to add in any meaningful discussions of skill and skilling in India as it punctures the celebratory narrative of skill as a productivist category which opens the path for continuous socioeconomic mobility for the subject/population acquiring the right credentials for it. From this perspective, it may not be misleading to reimagine skill not in terms of economic rationalities but more as a political imperative of what Achille Mbembe articulates as *commandement*, as a political dictum ensuring obedience, discipline and submission by the sate-capital dyad in post-colonial and post-liberalization India today (2001). Skill and the prospect of some form of waged employment in this particular political rationale is not to 'reward a process of converting energy into wealth' through work and the manipulation of technologies by the worker but as a temporary privilege extended to her in return for the right tenors of obedience and submission (Mbembe, 2001, p. 45). Like all privileges, such recognition of skill along with the attributes of disciplining of the body-mind of the worker ensuring payment of wages (however nominal) might dissipate at any moment – either due to extreme conditions induced by a pandemic or due to the perceived recalcitrance of the workers – individual or *en masse*. A productivist path to the creation of social resources and an individual point of access to waged employment, skill exhibits in the post-colonial context of India also the modalities of control and disciplining where the rush to acquire legitimation of accredited skilling for the youth is a potential means of entering the good graces of the state and private capital. Such good graces may be extended in sporadic means, in ad hoc and mostly informal manners, but without this legitimation what is guaranteed is a perennial immersion in the lowest (and most brutalizing) confines of Mark Holmström's apt metaphor of the stratified 'mountain' for India's labour force (1984). Skill from this reckoning is also generative as it produces social docility and abjection to undergo training for any shot at gaining access to the limited munificence of the state or capital.

The reproduction, recalibration, and reimagination of the skill ecology

The volume includes chapters attempting to re-think the histories of skill and skilling under conditions of rapid commercial re-orientations and industrial expansion in the late-colonial period starting from colonial changes and interventions, through the state-led modernization in the Nehruvian decades, and up to the contemporary 'Skill Mission' emerging from both a groundswell of right-wing nationalism and intense pro-market ideologies of national growth. As is to be expected, the Indian state – in both its late-colonial and post-colonial avatars – remains a constant refrain suturing together many of the narrative accounts through which skill and skilling in India must be traced. The attempt, however, is not to force a seamless narrative where the state remains a constant source of institutional support framing together the broader mandates of skilling; rather the chapters in this volume suggest how the periodic waning and subsequent waxing of the importance of skill and skilling in various parts of the Indian economy is often achieved through contestation and collaboration between multiple actors, of whom the state is often not the most important even where it is the most visible.

Douglas E. Haynes, for instance, in his contribution depicts the role of state-led educational institutions and actors in disseminating managerial skills, yet also demonstrates how the state's role remained embedded within a demand structure shaped by private capital characterized by family-run businesses. Soheb Niazi, in turn, demonstrates the role of private entrepreneurship and agency in addressing questions of skill in meat markets in colonial north India, an economic segment largely untouched by the state at this time, and instead highlights the role of both individual actors and community structures in shaping skill and skilling. These contestations and collaborations between a multiplicity of actors lead to a process in which skill ecologies are shaped: as reproduction, as recalibrations, and as reimaginations.

This edited volume engages with a critical re-evaluation of the mechanisms of *reproducing* the skill ecology and inter alia the skill market through often-unanticipated alliances, frictions, initiatives, dissonances, and collaborations between unstable networks of both state and non-state actors. The state in this paradigm of skilling is hardly an unwavering entity but manifests itself through changing and even competing ideologies, visions of national development and socioeconomic needs, or perceptions about the sanctity of the market and relationships with private partners. In turn, private entities are also liable to constant processes of transformations, in their actual compositions – from localized informal private units with minimal capital investments to large financial institutions with enormous financial clout. Douglas E. Haynes in his contribution, for instance, depicts the cumbersome encounter between supposedly modern ideas of management imported from the United States, but adjusted to the Nehruvian state's preferences and, eventually, the managerial realities of Indian businesses, many of which remained far from convinced about the merits of graduates from the IIMs. Over time, the opportunity structures for skilling the managerial workforce that were created by the IIMs – together with broader developments concerning India's corporate worlds – facilitated shifts in the discourse on managerial skill that raised the acceptance of management graduates within Indian firms. In turn, Saikat Maitra and Sadaf Sethwala, studying Industrial Training Institutes (ITI), depict notions of unsuitability and low-status concerning ITI graduates among employers that clearly resemble the reserved responses of family-run firms to IIM graduates at an earlier epoch. In both cases, state-led skilling initiatives encountered entrenched structures of skilling and faced (partially ongoing) requirements of adjusting to these in which the state as the primary mover of institutionalization remained only one among many players. Muthuveeran Ramasamy's contribution, in turn, looks at the question of vocational training from a different perspective, highlighting how the process of institutionalizing skilling in line with the state's preferences produces pressures on young people in India to adjust accordingly, if merely to become employable under circumstances in which employers are looking for formalized and certified structures of training.

The mode of collaborations with the state through which private actors enter various niches within the broader skill ecology is also liable to change due to the imperatives of state regulations, profit motives through the marketization of skill training, the need to have a more highly trained workforce, or demands from a young labour force desperate to find a productive access to meaningful employment opportunities. However, skill is reproduced in manifold ways that are merely tangentially shaped by the Indian state. Most of India's informal sector today remains beyond the state's direct reach, and the intervention capacity of the late-colonial and early postcolonial state was much more restricted. Advaita Rajendra and Barbara Harriss-White study the formation of skill among informal waste workers – an economic segment in which the regulatory role of the Indian state could very well be expanded substantially, given the organizational patterns of waste economies, but where the Indian state remains almost entirely absent, thus facilitating room for the exercise of exploitation and discrimination through social structures. The chapter powerfully brings to light how social stratifications shape and mediate ideals of high versus low skill jobs with far-reaching consequences for entrenching structures of poverty and social marginalization. Shifting towards the colonial era, Michaela Dimmers studies skilling initiatives in an even more 'formalized' environment – colonial prisons in northern India – yet also finds manifold instances in which even overwhelming control by the state over an enclosed space did not generally lead to the significant expansion of the state's active stance towards skilling. Instead, even skilling programs for prison guards tended to be neglected, while skilling and education for inmates were introduced specifically as a disciplining tool and mechanism for control – despite occasional nods to ideals of 'reformation'. The themes of control and surveillance in the study of colonial prison labour resonate powerfully with Ujjwal Kango's chapter on a very contemporary labour process associated with the emerging platform economies in India. Through a nuanced ethnographic study, Kango posits the forms of super-exploitation and extreme control that are made possible through the digital interfaces of the platform economy. Skilling here is as much about the ability to adjust and push embodied capacities for work to their limits by the gig workers of the platform economy as to evade the hyper-surveillance to which they are subjected.

Even where the state is actively setting agendas for skilling, it rarely manages to fully encompass the entirety of the skilling process, and hence creates or reproduces peripheries of skill within the broader skill ecology. Sreela Sarkar's contribution in this volume is paradigmatic for these reproductions. Skilling the female workforce seeking informal employment in Seelampur, in her argument, is hampered by a lack of resources and attention even in a field that is discursively highlighted as central to the state's efforts such as computer literacy. 'Learning computers', she argues, emerges as drudgery through the low quality of skilling programs that are – in accordance with state planning – combined with the stagnant character of the relevant labour market segment. Not surprisingly, perhaps, such training produces a fruitless period in the young women's lives characterized not by the mobilization of their capabilities and social upliftment, but instead by waiting for the chance to move to jobs that largely fail to make use of whatever levels of skills have been acquired in the training programmes. Histories of skill and skilling in modern India need to address the centrality of the state for skilling, but also move beyond the state (and the state's perception) in order to address these issues of marginality of certain labouring bodies and the social dimensions shaping the politically charged processes of what gets or fails to make the cut for being recognized as 'skill', along with the impact of such recognitions on the quotidian lives of the vast majority of Indians today. Samprati Pani's contribution delineates the manner in which the state's apathy to street vendors – one of the largest labour reservoirs of the country – creates an image of vending as unskilled, despite the fairly high levels of skill simultaneously employed by many of the vendors throughout their precarious professional lives. Soheb Niazi's work on skilling in the colonial meat industry shows similar apathy in yet another (supposedly) low-skilled segment of the economy.

At the same time, many of the state's policies – failed or successful – need to be understood as responses to the ways skill and skilling were shaped by non-state actors, frequently even non-state actors that remained invisible to the state. Christian Strümpell explores the shaping of the 'workman's mind' – a hands-on approach to working with machines, and making them work – that is severely hampered by the social production of class and caste barriers. This divergence materializes in segmented relations on the shopfloor at the point of production in which highly educated engineers lack experience with machines while the workers handling them remain excluded from meaningful avenues for formal skilling that could facilitate their upward mobility in the respective niches of the skill ecology. Strümpell's work thus depicts on-going apathy in skilling initiatives – whether state-led or not – towards particular sets of skills, primarily sets of skills related to hard manual labour. In this, his work echoes the conclusions of Shahana Bhattacharya's study on skilling among leather workers and leather industry managers (Bhattacharya, 2018), which can be considered as one of the central texts in this field for colonial history – though Strümpell's study is located in the contemporary period, thus hinting at a persistent pattern.

In positing the episodic reproductions of the skill ecology through oftentimes non-linear and complex feedback loops between multiple social actors, the volume outlines how changing social matrices *recalibrate* the very meaning, scope, and understanding of skill. In order to unpack the processes of recalibration of the skill category, the chapters in this volume reconstruct the dynamic fields-of-forces where 'occupational skill' has been transformed repeatedly – fields-of-forces composed by the various historical actors who inhabited and changed the institutional forms and sites of occupational training as well as the social identities fostered by caste, gender, rural-urban migration, and class. Skill therefore often assumes elusive and ambiguous forms where the conjuncture of social, economic, and political forces gives shape to various transient forms of imagining it.

The emergence of the engineer as a figure epitomizing science and progress in the early and mid-twentieth century thus recalibrated industrial skills in manifold ways, producing its 'Other' in the downgrading of mere technical and thus 'non-scientific' and not-progressive skills in repairing and working machinery in industry (Strümpell in this volume). The notion of India as a rising information technology hub recalibrated the skill ecology in ways in which low-level computer literacy as studied by Sarkar in this volume gained sufficient acceptance – even respect – to be considered worthwhile in spite of its lack of applicability for workers in the informal sector professions available to them. Thus, acquiring these skills – however useless they would turn out to be in everyday work-lives – was considered meaningful by young women, and the growing realization of their inability to use the acquired skills, in turn, devalued the skilling exercise.

Skilling in the colonial meat industry, as shown by Niazi, did not generate similar responses, thus needing to fall back on the generation of community-specific responses since society at large failed to value the benefits of skilling in this industry. Bourgeois ideas of 'reform', in contrast, informed the colonial state's intent in setting up basic literacy education among prison inmates, as argued by Dimmers. Once released though, and thereby relieved of the pressure to discipline prison populations, the state lost its interest in the former inmates' fate to the extent that it did not even follow up on whether they were able to employ their newly acquired skills. Plausibly more literate on average than the typically rural communities they were to re-enter, multiple stigmas associated with caste, belonging, poverty, and imprisonment would likely have presented almost insurmountable obstacles to employment in accordance with their newly acquired education. At the same time, even in contemporary India the stigma associated with waste work is intrinsically preventing the successful acquisition of (recognized) skills among waste workers as argued by Rajendra and Harriss-White. Informal labour migration to the fast-growing enclaves of India's industrial economy in turn significantly undermines the long-term acquisition of skills even among formally skilled workers in that the migrant status is frequently accompanied by exploitation levels in everyday work that actively downgrade the acquired skill levels of these workers, as argued by Saikat Maitra and Sadaf Sethwala. Sebastian Schneider, Natalie Grote, Usha Ajithkumar, and Matthias Pilz (in this volume) demonstrate the relatively low prestige that is attributed even to teachers as the disseminators of skill when the target profession of the skilling exercise receives little recognition. Polytechnic colleges in contemporary India may constitute one of the better-working institutions of skilling, especially given their funding constraints, yet as with ITI at the lower end of this spectrum or the training received through learning-on-the-job (as discussed by Strümpell, and Rajendra and Harriss-White) the targeted groups in society for the respective skills tend to lower the esteem in which the upgrading of capabilities itself is held.

The actors, sites, and institutional forms of skilling have been diverse and a progressive reduction of this diversity in the course of 'development' cannot be assumed in relation to skill and skill training – contrary to many expectations in the development and modernization discourses. The *ustad-shargird* relationship between master-craftsman and apprentice, for instance, has been reproduced even in large-scale industrial settings; informal modes of 'learning on the job' have prevailed for long even with the simultaneous existence of skill-training institutions – their functioning and integration with labour processes constitute a major challenge for researchers. The proportions and relations between company training facilities, state institutions of occupational training, the skill programs of foreign, and international 'development' agencies as well as privately owned commercial training organizations thus need to be explored and emphasized for a meaningful exploration of India's skill ecologies. Haynes' work on managerial education and the employability of IIM graduates in the family firms dominating the Indian corporate sector is exemplary in showing the extent to which various forms of training coexisted simultaneously even at the very apex of the Indian economy. The interface between labour and skill, on the one hand, and between various prevalent social identities and occupational skilling, on the other, takes us to a central focus of this volume which is the relational and political nature of the skill category itself. Nowhere else is this relational attribute of skill training borne out more sharply than in the very labour processes providing grounds for bearing out the efficacy of skilling as well as the contested nature of its quotidian manifestations.

In the context of labour, this volume will proceed from the double assumption that every labour process relies on certain levels of occupational skill, but that social relations of power always mediate the precise relationship between a labour process and occupational skill. These complex and unequal relations of power can for instance make certain categories of labour processes appear to be high-skill areas, yet devalue the high degree and sophistication of occupational skills involved in other work processes. This phenomenon is particularly true in India where the specific structural articulations of social power have led to the appropriation of major technological innovations, generated by the industrial revolutions since the eighteenth century under social conditions vastly divergent from many other parts of the world. Thus, the intersections between skill and labour processes are context-specific, dynamic, and localized rather than static, predictable, and universal. This crucial aspect of skill is critically manifested in India where complex laminations of socioeconomic and political power have fashioned distinct adaptations of technologies, different forms of organizing the labour process when applying the same technology, diverging modes of combining skill with social status, specific combinations of processes of skilling and deskilling as well as diverse patterns of skill-defined segmentation among the workforces.

Consequently, the history and anthropology of skill and occupational training must simultaneously examine the formation of 'skill' as a category of the labour process as much as its development as a category of social status and hierarchy. It must engage with the manifold ways in which skill and skilling have been *reimagined* at various historical junctures. Through a combination of archival and ethnographic research we address these issues while bearing in mind two significant characteristics of Indian capitalism and the labour processes connected to it, namely the temporal and spatial unevenness in its growth, and the high degrees of informality structuring both production and the skill training driving such production. One central aspect in this reimagination of skill and skilling relates to the increasingly perceived need to create structures of certification for skills. In the process, the skill ecology shifted towards valuations of skill depending on information flows controlled by certifying agencies acting as intermediaries – whether or not these were part of the state – and skill as a category became increasingly detached from its meaning as an ability to *do* things. Instead, certifying agencies have emerged as the key actors *informing* the three main constituents of the skill ecology – capital, labour, and the state – of skills and skill levels available, and of those in demand or lacking, thus reimagining the supply and demand of skill and shaping the responses of labour, capital, and the state towards the skill ecology.

The study of polytechnics in this volume by Schneider, Grote, Ajithkumar, and Pilz hints at the importance of imagination. Being perceived as relatively less valuable for upward mobility in spite of their relative success in capability upgradation, polytechnic graduates tend to be perceived as lower skilled than graduates even from relatively dysfunctional colleges. Hence, the imagination of low skill supposedly inherent in specific professions undermines the effects of skilling policy, and skilling itself. Conversely, ITI graduates (as shown by Maitra and Sethwala) and graduates of other avenues for vocational training are valued for their certified skills even by employers who will not make use of the skills acquired, or in contexts of self-employment in which the disseminated skills have no bearing on work-related capabilities. Sarkar's contribution showcases how young women acquire basic computer skills not with the hope of employing them for their future lives, but as an enterprise in imagining skills in which certification of *a* skill is valued more highly by the targets of skilling than the capabilities actually imparted. The certification structure around 'learning computers' in this regard mirrors the depiction of 'reform' in the colonial prison system as depicted by Dimmers – as an ideological construct, professing a goal that cannot be achieved through the reality of skills disseminated or their use in future professional lives, but only in the reporting stage of its imagination.

The issue of certification has no doubt grown in importance in the period under review but its articulations are contradictory and need to be examined accordingly: while certification reflects, to some extent, a need for the standardization of occupational skills and for a transferability of skilled workforces between companies, it can also be the expression of a business model of commercial or public providers of sometimes low-quality training (along with low-quality education) that responds more to the trainees' aspirations for gaining *different* employment and becoming upwardly mobile than to the need of employers for any particular skill (Nambissan and Ball, 2010). By informing the constituents of the skill ecology, the reimagination of skill provides feedback loops into the reproduction and recalibration of this ecology. Policy discourses reflect changes in this reimagination process as much as the demands for skill by capital, as do the internalizations of (imagined, or imaginatively determined) needs among those individuals aspiring for skilling or the recognition of their skills or, for that matter, the perceptions of non-recognition of their skills by those classified as unskilled.

Where qualifications are not imagined as skills, their lack of certification thus informs the larger ecology of skill of their undesirability, and the undesirability of what the people inhabiting these particular niches of the skill ecology can bring to society. Waste management constitutes one of the foremost necessities of any complex social structures, yet its imagination as undesired, and therefore unskilled actively reinforces the problems associated with this economic segment, and thus also the undesirability of skills within it (Rajendra and Harriss-White). Similarly, the skills involved in coping with massive adversity inherent in contemporary street vending (Pani in this volume) or even the informal credit markets of north Indian bazaars (as mentioned above) have become devalued not so much because the skills currently valued are actually more difficult to learn and acquire, but because the absence of a certificatory structure renders them invisible. Somewhat ironically, the 'entrepreneurial' character of learning and applying these skills are valued highly in neoliberal skilling discourses in India, even though this valuation clearly does not extend to the economic segments in which they are acquired and employed. Wherever the lacuna in the imagination of skill renders capabilities invisible, in turn, the structure of certification (or non-certification) reinforces undesirability, thus pitching these sectors as labour reservoirs for those who failed to make it to 'desirable' professions.

This collection of chapters thus engages with the economic and socio-political processes that have provided the contexts for the transformation of India's landscapes of skill and the social hierarchies embedded in them from the middle of the nineteenth century to the contemporary period. We provide case studies of specific articulations of the 'skill question' in various socioeconomic settings and at different historical junctures. We analyse shifting ideological and policy imperatives and the social conflicts framing both the contents and the institutional infrastructures of 'skill development' at the entrepreneurial and the state level. We take account the unevenness of these processes across occupational sectors and India's historical geography of capitalism. Thus, the chapters in this edited volume provide critical insights for analysing a contested chronology and terrain of skill from colonial to contemporary India.

References

Agrawal, T. (2013). Skill development in India: An examination. *Journal of Education and Work*, 27(6), 629–650. https://doi.org/10.1080/13639080.2013.787485

Attewell, P. (1990). What is skill? *Work and Occupations*, 17(4), 422–448.

Berlant, L. (2007). Slow death. *Critical Inquiry*, 33(4), 754.

Bernstein, H. (2006). Is there an agrarian question in the 21st century? *Canadian Journal of Development Studies*, 27(4), 449–460.

Beynon, L. (2009). Controlling the line. In M. Mollona, G. D. Neve & J. Parry (Eds.), *Industrial Work and Life: An Anthropological Reader* (pp. 129–144). London: Bloomsbury Academic.

Bhattacharya, S. (2007). Introduction. In R. P. Behal & M. van der Linden (Eds.), *India's Labouring Poor: Historical Studies c. 1600-c. 2000* (pp. 7–20). New Delhi: Cambridge University Press.

Bhattacharya, S. (2018). Transforming skin, changing caste: Technical education in leather production in India, 1900–1950. *The Indian Economic and Social History Review*, 55(3), 307–343.

Bradley, H. (2000). *Myths at Work*. Cambridge and Malden, MA: Polity Press.

Braverman, H. (1974). *Labor and Monopoly Capital: The Degradation of Work in the Twentieth Century*. New York: Monthly Review Press.

Breman, J. (1999). The study of industrial labour in post-colonial India – the informal sector: A concluding review. In J. Parry, J. Breman & K. Kapadia (Eds.), *The Worlds of Indian Industrial Labour*. New Delhi: Thousand Oaks.

Breman, J. (2004). *The Making and Unmaking of an Industrial Working Class: Sliding down the Labour Hierarchy in Ahmedabad*. New York: Oxford University Press.

Brown, A., Tomassini, M., & Figueira, E. (2005). Participation in continuing vocational education, training and learning: Commentary on the implications for policy, practice and research. In *Learning While Working in Small Companies: Comparative Analysis of Experiences Drawn from England, Germany, Greece, Italy, Portugal and Spain* (p. 113). ESRC funded Centre on Skills, Knowledge and Organisational Performance. Oxford and Warwick Universities.

Bryson, J. (2017). Disciplinary perspectives on skill. In J. Buchanan, D. Finegold, K. Mayhew & C. Warhurst (Eds.), *The Oxford Handbook of Skills and Training* (pp. 1–22). Oxford: Oxford University Press.

Burawoy, M. (1979). *Manufacturing Consent: Changes in the Labor Process under Monopoly Capitalism*. Chicago: University of Chicago Press.

Carswell, G., & Neve, G. D. (2013). Labouring for global markets: Conceptualising labour agency in global production networks. *Geoforum*, 44, 62–70.

Cavendish, R. (1982). *Women on the Line*. New York: Routledge & Kegan Paul.

Chakrabarty, D. (1989). *Rethinking Working-Class History: Bengal, 1890–1940*. Princeton, NJ: Princeton University Press.

Chandavarkar, R. (1994). *The Origins of Industrial Capitalism in India: Business Strategies and the Working Classes in Bombay, 1900–40*. Cambridge: Cambridge University Press.
Chandavarkar, R. (1999). Questions of class: The general strikes in Bombay, 1928–29. *Contributions to Indian Sociology*, 33(1–2), 205–237.
Chandavarkar, R. (2008). The decline and fall of the jobber system in the Bombay cotton textile industry, 1870–1955. *Modern Asian Studies*, 42(01), 117–210.
Cross, J. (2014). *Dream Zones: Anticipating Capitalism and Development in India*. London: Pluto.
Darrah, C. (1997). Complicating the concept of skill requirements: Scenes from a workplace. In G. Hall (Ed.), *Changing Work, Changing Workers: Critical Perspectives on Language, Literacy, and Skills* (pp. 259–272). Albany, NY: State University of New York Press.
Dunn, E. C. (2004). *Privatizing Poland: Baby Food, Big Business, and the Remaking of Labor*. Ithaca, NY: Cornell University Press.
Engels, F. (1993). *The Condition of the Working Class in England*. London: Oxford University Press.
Finegold, D. (1999). Creating self-sustaining, high-skill ecosystems. *Oxford Review of Economic Policy*, 15(1), 60–81 https://econpapers.repec.org/article/oupoxford/v_3a15_3ay_3a1999_3ai_3a1_3ap_3a60-81.htm
Foucault, M. (2008). *The Birth of Biopolitics: Lectures at the College De France, 1978–79*. Ed. M. Senellart. Translated by G. Burchell. New York: Palgrave Macmillan.
Goel, V. P. (2011). Technical and Vocational Education and Training (TVET) System in India for Sustainable Development. Ministry of Human Resource Development Report, 1–2. http://adapt.it/adapt-indice-a-z/wp-content/uploads/2014/09/VT_Sustainable_Dev.pdf
Gooptu, N. (2009). Neoliberal subjectivity, enterprise culture and new workplaces: Organised retail and shopping malls in India. *Economic and Political Weekly*, 44(22), 45–54.
Harvey, D. (2003). *The New Imperialism*. Oxford: Oxford University Press.
Haynes, D. E. (2012). The organisation of production. In *Small Town Capitalism in Western India: Artisans, Merchants and the Informal Economy, 1870–1960 (Cambridge Studies in Indian History and Society)* (pp. 127–158). Cambridge: Cambridge University Press.
Hilger, A., & Unger, C. R. (Eds.). (2012). *India in the World since 1947: National and Transnational Perspectives*. Frankfurt: Peter Lang.
Hobsbawm, E. J. (1968). *Labouring Men: Studies in the History of Labour*. London: Weidenfeld and Nicolson.
Holmström, M. (1984). *Industry and Inequality: The Social Anthropology of Indian Labour*. Cambridge: Cambridge University Press.
Holt, D. B. (2002). Why do brands cause trouble? A dialectical theory of consumer culture and branding. *Journal of Consumer Research*, 29(1), 70–90. https://doi.org/10.1086/339922
Ingold, T. (2018). Five questions of skill. *Cultural Geographies*, 25(1), 159–163. https://doi.org/10.1177/1474474017702514
Jammulamadaka, N. (2017). A postcolonial critique of Indian's management education scene. In M. Thakur & R. R. Babu (Eds.), *Management Education in India* (pp. 23–42). Singapore: Springer.
Joshi, C. (1999). Hope and despair: Textile workers in Kanpur in 1937–38 and the 1990s. *Contributions to Indian Sociology*, 33(1–2), 171–203.
Joshi, C. (2003). *Lost Worlds: Indian Labour and Its Forgotten Histories*. Delhi: Permanent Black.

Kerr, C. L. (1960). Changing social structures. In W. E. Moore & A. S. Feldman (Eds.), *Labor Commitment and Social Change in Developing Areas* (pp. 348–359). New York: Social Science Research Council.
King, K. (2012). The geopolitics and meanings of India's massive skills development ambitions. *International Journal of Educational Development*, 32, 665–673.
Kohli, A. (2006). Politics of economic growth in India, 1980–2005: Part I: The 1980s. *Economic and Political Weekly*, 41(14), 1251–1259.
Kohli, A. (2012). Poverty Amid Plenty in the New India. New Delhi: Cambridge University Press.
Kumar, A. (2019). Skilling and it's histories: Labour market, technical knowledge and the making of skilled workers in Colonial India (1800–1910). Journal of South Asian Development, 13(3), 249–271.
Lerche, J. (2013). The agrarian question in neoliberal India: Agrarian transition by-passed?. *Journal of Agrarian Change*, 13(3), 382–404.
Leslie, S. W., & Kargon, R. (2006). Exporting MIT: Science, technology, and nation-building in India and Iran. *OSIRIS*, 21, 110–130.
Levien, M. (2013). Regimes of dispossession: From steel towns to special economic zones. *Development and Change*, 44(2), 381–407.
Linhart, R. (1985). *The Assembly Line*. Amherst: University of Massachusetts Press.
Maitra, S. (2016). The labor of self-making: Youth service workers and post socialist urban development in Kolkata. In A. Rao & A. Rajagopal (Eds.), *Media and Utopia: History, Imagination and Technology* (pp. 151–170). New York: Routledge.
Maitra, S., & Maitra, S. (2018). Producing the aesthetic self: An analysis of aesthetic skill and labour in the organized retail industries in India. *Journal of South Asian Development*, 13(3), 337–357. https://doi.org/10.1177/0973174118808129
Maitra, S., & Schwecke, S. (2021, November). Shopping elsewhere: Retail revolutions and the spectacle of retail in contemporary India. *International Journal of Asia Pacific Studies*, 17(2), Perspectives. https://ijaps.usm.my/?page_id=6497
Mbembe, A. (2001). *On the Postcolony*. Berkeley: University of California Press.
McElligott, G. (2001). *Beyond Service: State Workers, Public Policy, and the Prospects for Democratic Administration*. Toronto: University of Toronto Press.
McQuaig, L. (1998). *The Cult of Impotence: Selling the Myth of Powerlessness in the Global Economy*. Toronto: Viking.
Moore, W. E. (1951). *Industrial Relations and the Social Order*. New York: Macmillan.
Moore, W. E., & Feldman, A. S. (1960). *Labor Commitment and Social Change in Developing Areas*. New York: Social Science Research Council.
Morris, M. D. (1965). *The Emergence of an Industrial Labor Force in India: A Study of the Bombay Cotton Mills, 1854–1947*. Berkeley & London: University of California Press.
Morris, M. D. (1960). The recruitment of an industrial labor force in India, with British and American comparisons. *Comparative Studies in Society and History*, 2(03), 305–328.
Myers, C. M. (1958). Labor problems in the industrialization of India. *Thunderbird International Business Review*, 1(1), 7–8.
Nambissan, G. B., & Ball, S. J. (2010). Advocacy networks, choice and private schooling of the poor in India. *Global Networks*, 10(3), 324–343.
National Skill Development Mission: A Framework for Implementation (2019). Ministry of Skill Development and Entrepreneurship, Government of India.
Ornati, O. (1955). Wages in India. Economic Development and Cultural Change, 3(3), 241–259.
Parmar, D. K., Dave, S. K., & Jain, A. K. (2015). Empowerment of Dalits through vocational education and training. *International Journal of Scientific Research*, 4(9), 86–89.

Parry, J. P. (1999). Lords of labour: Working and shirking in Bhilai. *Contributions to Indian Sociology*, 33(1–2), 107–140.
Parry, J. P., & Strümpell, C. (2008). On the desecration of Nehru's 'Temples': Bhilai and Rourkela compared. *Economic and Political Weekly*, 43(19), 47–57.
Roy, S. (2007). *Beyond Belief: India and the Politics of Postcolonial Nationalism*. Durham: Duke University Press.
Roy, T. (2004). *Handloom weaving. In Traditional Industry in the Economy of Colonial India* (pp. 61–98). Cambridge: Cambridge University Press.
Sanchez, A. (2016). *Criminal Capital: Violence, Corruption and Class in Industrial India*. New York: Routledge.
Sarkar, S. (1989). *Modern India 1885–1947*. New York: Palgrave Macmillan.
Schwecke, S. (2022). *Debt, Trust, and Reputation: Extra-Legal Finance in Northern India*. Cambridge University Press.
Sen, B. (1989). Development of technical education in India and state policy-A historical perspective. *Indian Journal of History of Science*, 24(2), 224–248.
Stanford, J. (1999). *Paper Boom*. Ottawa: Canadian Centre for Policy Alternatives and James Lorimer and Co.
Subramanian, A. (2015). Making merit: The Indian Institutes of Technology and the social life of caste. *Comparative Studies in Society and History*, 57(02), 291–322.
Swaminathan, P. (2005). Making sense of vocational education policies: A comparative assessment. *Indian Journal of Labour Economics*, 48(3), 537–552.
Woods, C. T., Rudd, J., Gray, R., & Davids, K. (2021). Enskilment: An ecological-anthropological worldview of skill, learning and education in sport. *Sports Medicine–Open*, 7(1), 33. https://doi.org/10.1186/s40798-021-00326-6

PART I

Historical approaches to the study of the skill ecology

2

SKILLING AND MIS-SKILLING MANAGERS

The Indian Institute of Management, business education, and Indian capitalism, 1964–80[1]

Douglas E. Haynes

In recent decades, Indian capitalism has come to rely heavily on the role of a managerial elite staffed by graduates of business schools that offer training in 'professional' and 'scientific' methods of running large organizations. At the apex of this system of education are the Indian Institutes of Management (IIMs), now 20 in number. The initial two institutes in Kolkata and Ahmedabad were established in 1961 with funding from the Ford Foundation, and were associated with the Sloan School of Management at MIT and the Harvard Business School respectively. Today, the IIMs rank among the top business institutes in the world. Gaining a place in their MBA programmes is highly competitive, and graduates often find they can get their pick of job opportunities. The powerful position of alumni in Indian corporations seems to mark a transformation in the character of Indian business, which had long been dominated by family firms, managing agencies, and multinational companies. In much of corporate India today, an IIM education has been seen as a critical step in the acquisition of the skills needed to make business function more efficiently and innovatively.

This chapter suggests, however, that the skilling processes provided in IIM education fit quite unevenly into the world of Indian business in the period before India's 'liberalization'. It explores the training of managers at IIM Ahmedabad (IIM-A) and the subsequent role of its graduates in Indian firms from the 1960s into the 1980s. In examining skill formation among highly educated, 'professional' figures who came to occupy executive ranks of Indian firms, the chapter departs from other contributions to this volume and from most anthropological approaches, which have been concerned with training designed to facilitate employment and social mobility among actors nearer the bottom of India's social hierarchy. Management education,

DOI: 10.4324/9781003604846-3

in contrast, was part of a massive project to retool a segment of the Indian service elite, which had historically found employment in government and other educated professions, for participation in the structures of capitalism.[2] Like some of the other approaches to skill formation examined in this book, these methods involved not just transmitting new forms of knowledge and expertise needed to carry out specific jobs, but inculcating new standards of social comportment and new subjectivities believed to be necessary to inspire executives to carry out a larger transformation in the business world.

My work is informed by a critique of Alfred Chandler's (1977) classic works on professionally managed businesses in the United States, which have largely assumed that managerialism took hold because of its inherent superiority in coping with the complexities of modern capitalism. Such arguments have, in effect, been reproduced in an Indian context by business historians who suggest that features of Indian capitalism, particularly the supposedly outdated nature of the family firm structure, made the emergence of a managerial elite steeped in modern business methods necessary. Dwijendra Tripathi and Jyoti Jumani (2013), for instance, have argued that the formation of a professional class was largely a matter of Indian firms ultimately coming to recognize their rational interests. While Indian companies were originally apathetic about management education in the very first years of the IIMs, a crisis in Indian family business and the growing size of Indian firms made them recognize the value of employing highly trained executives after 1970:

> Splits in the old business families . . . further enhanced the value of management graduates for the private sector. In the older days, business families relied on family members to handle general management responsibilities. Post-splits there were not enough family members to occupy general management positions belonging to various factions. Under these conditions the services of professionals became almost indispensable for the young generation of leaders of the old business families.
>
> *(Tripathi and Jumani 2013: 212)*

In this chapter, by contrast, I see the development and deployment of managerial skills as a product of *political processes* at a variety of levels (Link 2017).[3] Management training emerged in India because it became part of a political vision for transforming India held by individuals primarily associated not with business but with the state, non-government organizations, and new educational institutions. In practice, however, the skills students acquired in the IIMs, and particularly the new norms of social conduct they absorbed during their education, were often unpalatable to Indian firms, which possessed very different kinds of internal politics. There the ideology of managerialism was usually irrelevant while the principles of deference, social reputation, and loyal service were often highly valued. Many graduates found themselves frustrated by their inability to deploy the expertise and the managerial practices that had been imparted in the IIMs. This chapter focuses on IIM-A, where the case method of business education was applied most rigorously.

Evidence regarding IIM-A graduates in Indian business structures before liberalization comes from three different sets of materials, each remarkable in its own way. First, I conducted interviews with many early graduates about their experiences.[4] A number of interviewees spoke with considerable candour on these occasions, sometimes defying my expectation that they might provide simple accounts of success that would fit neatly within linear narratives of the IIM's triumphalist rise.[5] Second, the published proceedings of a workshop at IIM in 1975 provides rich evidence on Indian business leaders' perceptions of graduates from the institute (Wadhwa and Garg 1975). At this workshop, representatives of industry (from both multinationals and family firms), alumni, and students offered their insights on the role of graduates within Indian business, often with considerable frankness. Indeed, when the three parties came together in an open forum at the Institute, the discussion fostered such an acrimonious atmosphere that the volume's editors chose to delete statements made on the occasion from the final report (Wadhwa and Garg 1975: 44). Nevertheless, the document clearly provides considerable evidence of business criticisms of the graduates within Indian firms. Third, significant information on the views held by IIM alumni about their job experiences comes from a social-psychological study of alumni conducted by Garg and Indira Parikh (1993), two professors at the Institute. Their research was conducted in confidence, and students clearly believed that they could express their perspectives without fear of losing anonymity. Overall, these sources come from two contrasting perspectives – that of former students on the one hand and that of businesses on the other. Together, however they provide a consistent picture of a dramatic clash between the social skills IIM MBAs had acquired in their education and the qualities Indian firms esteemed in their employees.

This chapter is organized in three sections. First, it explores the politics and the political visions that informed managerialism at a global level and in India. Second, it then discusses the features of an education at the IIM-A that emerged from these visions, suggesting that the pedagogical approaches followed in the institute, particularly the case method, shaped dispositions and social practices among its students that prepared them poorly for their actual experiences within Indian business, particularly in firms shaped on a family basis. Finally, it examines the tensions associated with the IIM alumni in their new positions, highlighting reactions to their roles from bosses and other managers as well as the dissatisfactions that developed among the alumni as a result.

Managerialism, the IIMs, and the ideology of development

Historically, training employees for participation in the managerial ranks of large businesses has taken many forms, as Rolv Petter Amdam has shown in his work. In Britain during the first half of the twentieth century, significant reliance was placed on recruiting managers through an old boys' network often based on Oxford and Cambridge connections, then readying them for work in a kind of apprenticeship system within the firm (often with a ceiling set by the presence of the owner's family in top positions). When this approach was introduced in British managing agencies and other businesses operating in India, it inevitably perpetuated the racial exclusion of Indians, who could not gain access to these recruitment channels and could not obtain training in home offices. Business education in the United Kingdom largely took off only after World War II. In Germany, engineering education rather than management school was often essential to employment in executive positions. When business schools did develop, they were part of a five-year programme which began with undergraduate studies and emphasized subjects, such as business economics and accounting, suited to employees occupying the lowest positions in a company's administrative hierarchy. The American system of business education, by contrast, was a postgraduate programme placing a premium on developing leadership skills. MBAs entered positions demarcated sharply from other white-collar employees, sometimes with the expectation of rising to the top of their organizations. Long-term apprenticeship was increasingly deemphasized; indeed, American MBAs often moved frequently between businesses, acquiring new skills in the process (Amdam 1996).[6] Even in the United States, however, modes of organization dependent on professional management techniques were far from universal in large corporations, particularly before World War II (Link 2018). In short, the mode of preparing executives for participation in complex capitalist organizations has depended on geographic, historical and political context.

In India, managerialism – the faith in the principle that relying on professionally trained managers would bring about a transformation of capitalism and the state and would consequently contribute to the reformation of the wider society – began to gain supporters during the 1950s. Managerialism was an ideology suggesting the value of skilled expertise that could be applied in every aspect of executive 'decision-making' and a method of forging 'leadership' at the highest levels of complex organizations (Wani 2023). By the late 1950s, managerialism came to assume a central place in the process of 'development', a key objective of American Cold War policymakers seeking to counter the spread of communism in the 'Third World', as well as a core ideological principle of the Indian state. American 'experts' and top Indian policymakers alike came to believe that management education was required in India because existing business and governmental structures were poorly prepared to guide the country's progress (van Haaften 2021). Douglas Ensminger (1972), at the time the leader of the Ford Foundation in India, which extensively funded the IIMs during their formative period, regarded the building of leadership as key to India's development; India needed 'change agents' ready to take up critical roles in the country's transformation (Wani 2023). Ensminger viewed India's five-year planning institutions, the Indian Administrative Service, and other structural features of Indian government as promoting unnecessarily bureaucratic decision-making processes. Indian businessmen, he reasoned, were overly cautious and conservative, and most firms relied heavily on family members and trusted employees hired through personal networks to supervise business functions, rather than professionals who were trained to formulate and apply innovative ideas (Ensminger 1972). Management education, which was intended to create managers who would be prepared to take actions on their own initiative rather than just follow orders from above, emerged as one of his central concerns. Americans who participated in the early IIMs echoed such views. For instance, Allen Cohen, a graduate student who came to Ahmedabad from Harvard in 1963 to create business cases for the IIM and to carry out his research on family business, told me in an interview that he had felt that India possessed a vast amount of untapped talent at the time, but that many businesses were then structured too personalistically or bureaucratically to meet the country's needs (2019). Managerialism, from this perspective, was the solution to overcoming such limitations.

A significant segment of India's top political leadership embraced the ethos of management. Rather than see this development as a straightforward outcome of American efforts, it would be more accurate to argue that both Indians and Americans were participants in a larger global context in which managerialism was acquiring a new status as a channel to modernity and 'nation-building' (van Haaften 2021). The thesis of 'mimicry' of American attitudes or neocolonialism (for instance, see Jammulamadaka 2017; Kumar 2019; Srinivas 2008) overlooks the fact that managerialism was lodged in a larger ideology with specifically Indian characteristics, one that deemphasized the Cold War context and allocated to the state an expansive role in development (van Haaften 2021 and Wani 2023). According to Prafull Anubhai (2019), who was a young manager in an Ahmedabad mill and a part-time faculty member at IIM-A during the 1960s and 1970s, 'management' had become 'a kind of a buzzword' that carried a magical power. The adoption of professional approaches to management was regarded as critical to forming the knowhow, the standards of efficiency, and the objective insights that the country required. Indian 'imaginaries' (van Haaften 2021) consistently stressed that scientific management would be critical to improving standards of government administration and social programmes as well those in businesses. Management associations were established in a wide number of Indian cities. State actors also took considerable interest. Humayun Kabir, a significant literary figure and a minister in different Indian governments during much of the late 1950s and early 1960s, became a particularly important champion of management education. In 1959, the Indian Planning Commission specifically encouraged a Ford Foundation–sponsored visit from George Robbins, Dean of the Business School at the University of California at Los Angeles, to make recommendations about the value and character of management education in India (Haynes 2020; van Haaften 2021). Vikram Sarabhai, member of an industrialist family in Ahmedabad, and a scientist who played an extensive part in India's nuclear and space programmes, was a particularly staunch supporter; he came to exercise a major role in convincing the government to relocate one of the IIMs to Ahmedabad when Bombay fell out of favour as a site (IIMA Institute Building Files 1961; Van Haaften 2021; Wani 2023). Perhaps informed by his own experience with the Sarabhai family of companies, which was diversifying from its original base in textiles at the time, he regarded the development of professional managers as key to breaking the traditional hold of the family in business. Sarabhai also regarded managerialism as essential to the success of organizations in the public sector and would later conduct a significant recruitment effort to woo IIM graduates to the Indian Space Research Organization (Karnik 2022; Wani 2023).

A concern with management studies within the Indian business world, by contrast, was comparatively limited at the time. Ahmedabad itself was something of an exception; there, a significant interest was emerging in local industrialist circles for somewhat different reasons. At the time, a kind of crisis existed in the city's textile industry, as the mills sought to introduce new technologies and 'rationalized' principles of work reorganization to reduce labour costs (Haensel Unpublished MS). These policies met significant resistance from workers on the shop floor. As a result of Gandhi's role in workers' protests after World War I, a labour environment had arisen that was based on the peaceful resolution of disputes between unions and mill owners; the industrialists in effect acknowledged that they could not force new policies down the workers' throats (Patel 1987). The important thing from the perspective of many mill owners was to devise work relations that would make changes acceptable. Haensel (Unpublished MS) and Wani (2023) have documented the role of management experts from the Tavistock Institute in London, particularly Andrew K. Rice, in proposing new organizational schemes in Ahmedabad that they believed would temper the societal disruptions generated by urban to rural migration and rapid social change, and thus permit continued industrial productivity. Their work in Ahmedabad was strongly associated with the local business elite, particularly the Sarabhai family (Wani 2023).

Ahmedabad business leaders gave voice to their commitment to managerialism in a series of conferences organized by the Ahmedabad Textile Industry

Research Association (ATIRA 1955, 1956, 1957, 1958, 1959, 1960) during the 1950s. Kamala Chowdhry, who possessed a U.S. PhD and was employed at ATIRA, was the key moving spirit in organizing these conferences, although she clearly gained support from local industrialists, including Kasturbhai Lalbhai, the city's leading textile magnate. The conferences possessed a global character; speakers before the conferences included Andrew K. Rice, Rolf Lynton, Andrew Towl of Harvard (a key proponent of the case method), Harriet Ronken (Center of the Advanced Study and Training, Columbo), Wynne Roberts, and other representatives of the International Labour Organization in Geneva. Business and government leaders from all over the country were invited to give presentations, but many of the Indian participants were from Ahmedabad. Subjects addressed on these occasions included the role of wages, workplace satisfaction, 'tradition and change', 'problems associated with technological change', 'resistance to change', and the value of consultants in addressing organizational problems. In effect issues related to labour management were linked to the logic of modernization. Elsewhere in India, enthusiasm for managerialism was uneven among industrial and commercial business people.

The role of management in transforming Indian capitalism, and the consequent impact businesses staffed with professional managers might then have on India's development, was set out strongly in the original IIM-A catalogue in 1963–64, perhaps an unusual place to find one of the ideology's most coherent articulations (HBS 1963–4). According to the catalogue, India was undergoing a period of significant and multidimensional social change, including shifts in the character of Indian businesses, a key participant in the country's progress:

> The corporation which was initially conceived simply as a convenient means of marshalling capital is rapidly becoming a vigorous entity among the social institutions of our time. If the past bears testimony to the subordination of business to other institutional organs such as the state, the religious groups, and the military, the present is witnessing the emergence of business institutions not simply as an integral part of our society but as the most significant moulder, in many substantial respects, of our total cultural pattern.
>
> *(HBS 1963–4: 1)*

The document placed the history of Indian businesses in an evolutionary scheme involving a shift from family-based firms to large corporations. In this view, management techniques had traditionally been learned through the job itself or were transmitted through face-to-face interactions within firms. However, business organizations were becoming larger and more complex; managers had to deal with 'new forces and changing motivations in people' (HBS 1963–4: 2), including unions and government regulations. In order to acquire the skills needed to advance their business firm and address its social responsibilities, managers needed access to new kinds of schooling. Managerial education would provide principles and 'repeatable controls and procedures' (HBS 1963–4: 5) that could equip future managers with the tools needed to cope with new situations. India's industrial development, from this perspective, depended upon the emergence of competent *managers*: 'The planned, rapid transformation of our society will be limited in a large measure to our ability to develop sufficient enterprise managers who have the knowledge, attitudes and skill required for efficient planning, organizing, staffing, supervising and control' (HBS 1963–4: 7). Trained professional managers were also needed to fill positions in government and in public sector firms.

Thus, by the mid-1960s, a significant segment of Indian political, educational, and (in Ahmedabad) business leadership had come to forge an ideological vision that regarded management education not just as essential to training people to carry out certain tasks within Indian firms, but also to stimulate them to become 'change agents' who would contribute to social transformation.[7] The modes of preparing young men to perform administrative jobs that had prevailed in mid-twentieth century Germany and England proved increasingly unattractive to exponents of India's modernization.

Skilling managers: the case method of business education

While the IIMs were created in part due to a drive to promote research on problems of business and public policy and to provide short-term training programmes for executives in Indian firms, their highest priority was the development of a two-year programme equivalent to an American MBA (the actual degree of MBA could not be awarded because the IIMs lay outside the formal university structure). The curriculum of the Institutes in Ahmedabad and Calcutta reflected a concern with building a cadre of professional managers who would have a broad understanding of issues facing Indian business and government, sophisticated technical tools to analyse business problems (including mathematical approaches), strong competence in English, and a national perspective. As the IIM-A catalogue put it, students would learn general principles for decision-making, that is, how 'these [business] sciences and methods of analysis can be used to communicate with each other, how their performance can be evaluated and predicated, how inter-related processes can be scheduled and controlled, etc'. Such a system 'equips a man to continue his education through experience once he has left the educational institution' (HBS 1963–4; unpaginated).

Education at the IIMs was, as the language in the quote indicates, a gendered project. While the initial proponents did not formally exclude females, they did not usually imagine women as occupying a central place in the Institute or in the larger agenda of promoting development through management training. The admission process at IIM highly favoured men; one successful female applicant in an early year recalled being asked outright in her admission interview whether it bothered her that she might take a man's place. Other faculty may have genuinely wished to expand the number of female students, but entrance tests requiring advanced quantitative skills and high levels of English seriously advantaged engineering students from the Indian Institutes of Technology and science graduates from elite educational institutions where women formed a miniscule portion of the student body (Tumbe 2020). In addition, upper-middle class families in India were generally reluctant to allow female offspring to travel from home to live in residential colleges. Some female students fought major social battles with their families in order to attend (many more probably lost such battles). At IIM-A, most of the earliest classes included a couple of women (out of a total of 50 to 100) and the percentage of women in any class rose to around 10% only at the very end of the 1970s.

Students in the IIMs received a general training that provided an overview of issues deemed to be relevant to management problems. At Ahmedabad, participants in the initial year of the programme had to take a set of courses that included Quantitative Aspects in Decision-Making; Managerial Economics; the Manager and the Indian Economy; Organizational Behaviour; Marketing; Production; and Written Analysis of Cases. All of these were taught by Indian professors (HBS 1963–4). Several years later, Finance and Managerial Accounting had replaced the Quantitative Aspects course, but mathematical methods were integrated widely into the curriculum (HBS 1969–70?: 2). Overall, students were to 'develop familiarity with concepts and techniques of management control and throughout must learn to understand and consider the relationships involved in administrative problems. They become acquainted with the general framework of business, delve into the fundamental factors . . . and consider the responsibilities of business to the Indian Society as a whole' (HBS 1969–70?: 2). Issues like business ethics and history that might have led to a questioning of capitalism's role in the Indian economy, by contrast, occupied only a limited role in the curriculum.

The programme's second year offered students an opportunity to do more advanced work, sometimes in the functional area where they hoped to land their first jobs, and to conduct research and take up projects. Interestingly, issues relating to 'industrial relations' – which would have prepared graduates for dealing with labour issues – were limited, sometimes appearing as an optional course in the second year. Understanding issues related to specific businesses was left to the on-the-job training that graduates would acquire in their new positions; education at IIM was never meant to be end of the process of skilling graduates.

While the acquisition of technical knowledge in different subject areas was a critical aspect of management education, IIM-A was also involved in inculcating new kinds of subjectivity and modes of social comportment that would contribute to the transformation of Indian businesses. According to the first catalogue, management required 'a modification of the sensibility', one that would result 'in a new and better control of the self and the outer world' and that sought 'understanding by development of a set of higher meanings' (HBS 1963–4: 5). Particularly central to the pedagogical mission of the institution was the larger project of preparing students for 'decision-making'. While a variety of methods were eventually employed in the classroom, the dominant and most distinctive technique, and the one most strongly championed by the institution, was the 'case method', an approach adopted and adapted from the Harvard Business School. In a nutshell, the case method involved the collection of information about a business firm and its problems, the composition of a written report, and discussion of the report in the classroom with an eye to considering courses of action that might help the firm to address some crucial shortcoming in meeting its objectives. In theory, case reports were written 'objectively', allowing for multiple approaches to the firm's problems (and sometimes even suggesting disparate identifications of what the crucial problems were). Classroom time was occupied not by lectures, but by often contentious discussions among the students, who were expected to be well prepared and to have read the cases beforehand. Students in effect became involved in role playing, that is, they were asked to imagine themselves in the position of the organization's leadership and to suggest decisions that would influence the firm's policies. The professor framed the discussion, asking questions, but, in theory at least, refraining from leading students to any predetermined conclusion.

Andrew Towl of Harvard, a leading proponent of the case method during the 1950s and early 1960s, argued that it stimulated the development of new social skills, those 'required to reach successful judgments and initiate successful action in problems involving other persons' (Bhavsar 2023: 15). The approach's rigour was emphasized by its advocates, who claimed that it trained the individual to be 'tough-minded', to make decisions when no single right answer existed but a course of action had to be taken. Its proponents argued that it provided a practically grounded approach to training students to handle business problems, one that would prepare them better to make executive decisions than mere exposure to theoretical ideas. The case method was rationalized in ideological terms as more inherently 'democratic' and anti-hierarchical because it permitted multiple viewpoints and encouraged contestations of the professor's authority. It was imagined as being applicable to decentralized organizations, where managers at various levels would be given considerable leeway in making decisions on issues under their purview. It also involved the creation of a new kind of relationship between academia and the corporate world, not simply because graduates later entered managerial posts in Indian business, but also because the collection of cases for the classroom involved gaining the collaboration of individual companies. It also placed an expectation on students to repeatedly assume the vantage point of top executive decision-makers within Indian firms and in the larger business world, and thus distance themselves from any questions they might have about capitalism in general or the ethics of particular organizations.

The case method achieved its ascendancy at IIM-A partly because of politics in the city and the institution. Admiration of the case method was likely in part responsible for Vikram Sarabhai's pursuit of a collaborative relationship with Harvard around 1960; earlier the Ford Foundation had been pushing for a link to UCLA, which did not stress the approach. Sarabhai would be the acting director of the institute when its two-year degree programme was established. Shrenik Lalbhai, son of Ahmedabad's leading business magnate and probably the city's only alumnus of the Harvard MBA program, pointed out the ideological rationale for the case method in the first management conference sponsored by ATIRA in 1955. There he critiqued lecture-based teaching methods: 'No amount of information, whether of theory or of fact, in itself improves insight and judgment or increases ability to act wisely under actual conditions of responsibility'. He went on: 'In business each situation is a new situation and there is no single right answer to any problem'. He specifically praised the value of the case method: 'The case method is "democratic" in distinction to the telling method. It reduces the importance of the instructor and directs the attention of the trainee toward his colleagues whose criticisms he must learn to face, and whose contributions he must try to understand and use'. After further stressing Harvard's contributions to management studies, he concluded his remarks by stating: 'I see no reason why Ahmedabad should not adopt such a down to earth realistic system and keep ourselves abreast of the progress in such a vital field in industrial management' (ATIRA 1955: 30–32).

The Harvard delegation that came to assist the establishment of the business school – including Warren Haynes, who headed the initial MBA programme – strongly favoured the case method, and three postgraduate students, Allen Cohen, Mel Copen, and Michael Halse, became involved in collecting cases. Neil Borden, a more senior faculty member, also came to India to gather case material. An even more crucial aspect of the exchange with Harvard were one-year visits by the new Indian faculty to the Harvard Business School; a group of five came to the Boston area in the year before the MBA programme began; another eight visited the next year (before there were any second-year students at IIM-A); and another group of six came the third year. The institute in Ahmedabad (in contrast to Calcutta) had specifically focused on hiring promising young scholars, some with U.S. PhDs, rather than reputed professors with experience in the Indian university system, who might have already developed commitments to existing teaching methods in India. At Harvard the IIM's new teachers largely became converts to the case method during their visits and most enthusiastically applied it in their subsequent courses. Many faculty were in effect true believers, who shared the vision of the institution and its dominant pedagogical approach as generators of the country's transformation.

The initial catalogue of IIM explained the logic of the case method to training executives:

> From the outset the students at the Institute discuss cases, i.e. real business decisions in which executive (*sic.*) take action and are responsible for the results. Each student is repeatedly placed in a position where, as an administrator, he must not only evaluate evidence but act with responsibility. He is compelled to meet, one after another, new situations in which he must grapple intellectually with fresh combinations of facts and half-facts, opinions, and ideas, there are no answers for him in any book.
>
> During his two years at the Institute, the MBA student is confronted with about seven to eight hundred cases. From this experience he acquires a background of facts and currently useful generalizations which afford guidance in changing sets of circumstances but which do not automatically furnish the solution to new problems; for new problems are seldom 'typical'.
>
> *(HBS 1963–4: unpaginated)*

Alumni of IIM-A repeatedly told me in interviews that they were expected to imagine themselves in class to be the CEOs of their companies. This was true in two senses. First, they were in effect to play the role of key decision-makers who would determine the direction the company would take. Second, they were to deal with the total range of issues someone at the top of the company would have to address, rather than to carry out a narrow set of functions delegated to them at the low end of an office hierarchy.

While the goal of the case method was ostensibly to provide a practical approach to business education, it was also designed to forge new psychological dispositions and new forms of social comportment among students. There was a high degree of pressure to pursue 'CP', that is, the professor's marks for classroom participation, which figured strongly in final grades. Students had to prepare the cases extensively, often studying well into the early morning with little sleep. Most of them had come to IIM-A from colleges and engineering schools that employed lecture and textbook approaches and were used to sitting quietly in class without engaging in heated discussions with their fellow students, disagreeing with their professors, or being criticized publicly. As Melvyn Copen would observe in 1965:

> Prior to joining the IIM, our students have never been exposed to anything like the case method. The philosophy behind this method is so different

from that to which they are accustomed in the classroom that I think an extremely difficult period of adjustment ensues, much more difficult than is the case with HBS.

(HBS 1965: 2)

Many students would later recount in interviews their fear of individual professors during class. In some instances, the classroom remained silent for long periods while the professors waited for participants to break the ice. Other professors cold-called students in class and pressed them again and again when answers seemed incomplete or uninformed. At least two professors were known to throw chalk in class when dissatisfied with student responses.[8]

A few students found the new classroom atmosphere, with its possibilities for expressing opinions openly, exhilarating from the outset. Others initially felt themselves almost terrorized. 'They broke down our confidence' said one former student, referring not just to the classroom experience but also to low grades many received, particularly in one required course – 'Written Analysis of Cases' (WAC) – where students learned to write concise summaries of business cases and provide recommendations on how firms might tackle key problems. Another referred to the classroom atmosphere as being like 'boot camp'. Stress levels were especially high because most students had been 'toppers' in their previous educational institutions and many now found themselves struggling to keep up. An IIM education was thus in effect involved in remaking its students psychologically as well as intellectually. Most alumni that I interviewed, however, told me that they got the hang of case discussion after a few months and that the second year of the programme was much easier. The toughness of the academic environment was seen by the Institute as essential for preparing students for the highly pressured positions of responsibility that they were expected to encounter in their jobs and for acting creatively, assertively, and self-confidently within these positions.

The case method disadvantaged students without some pre-existing skills. It put a premium on a command of spoken English, which some students (especially in early years) knew imperfectly before coming to the Institute. It favoured those whose knowledge of mathematics was strong since mathematical approaches were often stressed. Finally, it gave an edge to those with previous employment, who might be familiar with the kinds of problems real firms faced in the business world. Students without this background sometimes spoke up because of the class participation grade involved, but it was often clear their contributions did not represent the kind of experience possessed by their classmates who had worked before. Classroom success was strongly gendered, favouring male students who had previously accumulated the kinds of knowledge, experience in public self-expression, and self-confidence required at the IIM.

The actual cases provided to students during the first decade may have seemed quite disorienting. At first, few case investigations had been conducted by IIM-A, so most cases were imported from the Harvard Business School, involved American firms, and used American terminology. However, even 15 years later, when the Institute had compiled many hundreds of cases, professors often continued to rely significantly on Harvard case studies, which they often saw as superior to the cases written in India.[9] In subjects like Organizational Behaviour and Marketing, the cases often failed to consider key factors specific to Indian social values and business culture. One of the first female students, Dakshah Shah (2018), who came from a local industrial family and went back into the family firm upon graduation, mentioned that cases failed to consider the personal relationships critical to Ahmedabadi businesses. She also indicated that cases did not reflect the internal structure of such firms, which often did not divide executive positions along purely functional lines. She highlighted marketing cases as being particularly disconnected with Indian circumstances. The Harvard cases also assumed an environment of limited government regulation, conditions very different to those faced by businesses in India, where almost every student would have to deal with the complexities of the license permit raj. Students from the IIM's first decade regularly mentioned in interviews that most cases they encountered were about foreign businesses. Some of the 'Indian' cases were composed by American graduate students or by Indian researchers with little previous experience in the business world. At least one professor I interviewed would argue that reliance on American cases did not affect the learning experience, because the method's primary purpose was to impart a new mode of reasoning rather than to familiarize students with Indian commercial conditions.

While the case method in principle elevated a practical approach over theory, it was based upon a major pretence: that new graduates of the business school would be placed in positions where they would enjoy the authority to make key decisions about matters facing the firms that hired them. It envisioned an environment in which business structures would be transformed, where hierarchical organizations would be replaced by decentralized structures in which managers possessed significant autonomy, and where personal relationships like family and patron-client ties would give way to decisions made upon supposedly objective criteria and even mathematical calculation. These structural features were viewed to be the most rational, and the most optimally designed to promote change in individual firms and by extension to change India. In short, the discussion of cases involved a kind of role playing, but in roles that few graduates were likely to occupy in practice. Exercising these roles several hundred times during their period at the IIM-A no doubt conditioned their own outlooks and self-perceptions, as well as their expectations of the power they would enjoy in their jobs.

IIM graduates in the Indian business environment

Data on the careers of early IIM-A alumni indicates consistently that the training provided in the initial MBA programmes shaped a managerial ethos that was difficult to accommodate within the Indian business environment. At first, that is, beginning with the initial graduating class of 1966, the willingness of firms to send representatives to the campus to interview candidates was limited, and the Institute had to mount vigorous efforts to place its students (IIMA 1973: 23). The demand for graduates accelerated by the later 1960s, though placement remained a time-consuming concern for the Institute and its faculty. The average initial salary of a new MBA before 1972 remained below 1,000 rupees a month (IIMA 1973: 65), a bit more than the same individuals might have earned with two years' experience in a business (one professor referred to their salaries as 'paltry'). Finding placements during the summer between the first and second years – which was supposed to provide students with practical training – was difficult at first since Indian firms had little experience of hiring short-term employees and creating projects for them to complete.

With time, IIM graduates found much improved prospects, especially in a tiny range of especially large businesses.[10] To a great extent, multinational companies and other firms that had been created by foreign businessmen took the lead in hiring graduates. The internal politics of these firms promoted professionalization. Under pressure from the government and society to 'Indianize', such firms often actively sought to decolonize their structures by distancing themselves from a past in which executives had been hired through British old boy networks. In challenging racial exclusivity and the practice of hiring executives based on Oxbridge affiliations, they often came to stress standards in recruiting and promotion that could be perceived as objective and professionally based. There was perhaps no better way to demonstrate this than to hire students who ranked high in their graduating classes at IIMs. Hindustan Lever, which had been run largely by executives recruited through British social connections and trained through apprenticeship until World War II, took a prominent part in this process (Pant and Ramachandran 2017). Its chairman during the early 1960s, Prakash Tandon, regularly contrasted the company's reliance on professionals with the prevailing practice in Indian family firms. For the Bombay engineering company Larsen & Toubro, founded and led by two Danish entrepreneurs and historically run along the lines of British managing agency into the 1950s, the hiring of IIM-A-trained and educated managers may have helped counter the danger of nationalization that a firm undertaking large public projects such as nuclear plants must have faced.

Even within multinationals, integration of IIM graduates could initially be a rough process. In many cases, middle managers who had been recruited earlier through more personalistic methods, who had often lacked business degrees, and who served lengthy periods of apprenticeship, could make life hard for new graduates perceived as lacking experience and as possessing inappropriate ambitions to move rapidly upwards. New female hires in one major multinational company during the mid-1970s found themselves without clear responsibilities and were sometimes asked to serve coffee or to cut out newspaper clippings. Moreover, in many multinationals, managers underwent further lengthy training periods in which they familiarized themselves with different departments in the organization, participated in rural marketing campaigns, and came to appreciate the organizational culture of their companies. Some graduates later indicated that they gained much more from these on-the job programmes than they ever learned at the IIMs.

On the other end of the spectrum of Indian business, small- and medium-sized firms, which employed the vast majority of the country's industrial workforce, did not participate in the recruitment of graduates, nor did IIM alumni find them sufficiently prestigious to pursue employment there.[11] Firms in the informal sector could not afford the salaries of the graduates, even if they had any desire to employ them. Overall, one professor told me that businesses hiring MBAs were typically larger, 'progressive houses', while smaller firms tended to abstain from hiring graduates (Rao 2018). Although IIM-A's founding figures such as Vikram Sarabhai had hoped to recruit MBAs into government and state-controlled businesses, hiring in the public sector was also limited. Comparatively few graduates chose to join government or public sector firms, which offered lower salaries and generally possessed less modern reputations, and usually did limited recruiting on campus (multiple research interviews; Wadhwa and Garg 1975: 30–31).

The position was most fraught in large family firms. These firms were founded and headed by the leaders of major business families, and they were often staffed at the highest levels by brothers, cousins, and other relatives. Hiring within these firms had typically been carried out through personalized processes, usually without consideration of formal educational qualifications, and new employees were often expected to commit themselves on a lifelong basis. Many family firms were expanding during this period, but expansion rarely meant a transformation in internal structures and institutional cultures. Middle managers who had established positions of trust through their service to the company and years of building relationships with family members, often enjoyed positions of respect. Some of these businesses simply did not hire MBAs at all; few Marwari firms (Indian businesses founded by families from Rajasthan) made use of IIM graduates until the later 1980s. In some other cases, family firms hired graduates as 'showpieces' or 'ornaments', that is, as symbols that would identify the firm as 'progressive' and 'modern', without any clear delineation of what their roles would be. As one observer put it: 'Quite a few firms recruit management graduates only to be called progressive and professional. No plans are made to induct the graduate, nor are any attempts made to describe his job' (Wadhwa and Garg 1975: 20). Aspiration to the highest positions in these firms, which were usually held by family members, was impossible for non-family graduates in most cases. Integration could be tough even in firms that most aggressively sought to establish a modernizing reputation. Asian Paints, which insistently recruited IIM students from 1968 onwards, had serious difficulties retaining them (Parikh 2022). In Tata Administrative Services (TAS), which along with Unilever was the most prestigious of all employers, newly recruited managers often left after just a few years, choosing, for instance, positions in multinational banks, PhD programmes in the United States, and new roles as entrepreneurs (Wakhlu et al. 2022: 68–78). In many cases, TAS members felt their chances to advance by moving between firms in the Tata group were limited. Many, perhaps most, Indian firms simply would not hire female MBAs. Female graduates relied heavily on Indian banks for employment since so many other kinds of firms would not employ them. TAS adopted a formal policy of excluding female hires from the later 1960s until the early 1980s, actually reversing a policy of inclusion it had practised in its earliest years (Wakhlu et al. 2022: 79–91). Ahmedabad industrial firms, which had taken the lead in supporting the IIM's establishment in the 1960s, sometimes backed away from employing graduates during the 1970s, perhaps due to their experience with early hires. Speaking in 1972, Prakash Tandon, Chair of the Punjab National Bank and former Chair of Hindustan Lever, noted that he did not expect professional managers to reach leadership positions in Indian family firms until the next century (1974: 10).

Some of the difficulties were caused by the perceived irrelevance of the IIM curriculum to the roles graduates would play in their first positions. Business representatives in the 1975 IIM seminar suggested the 'educational content, concepts and situations' presented in management training were inapplicable to employees during their first five years of employment, observing that coursework was often poorly matched with the 'conditions, organizational culture, and the overall dynamics of Indian society' (Wadhwa and Garg 1975: 26). This comment might have been directed especially to the use of the case method in the classroom.

The subjectivities and modes of social comportment developed at the Institute caused even deeper concerns. Industry representatives indicated in the 1975 workshop that IIM graduates frequently experienced a kind of 'culture shock' as they entered the workplace (Wadhwa and Garg 1975: 19). They often came into their firms believing themselves qualified to participate in decision-making at the organizations' highest ranks. Instead they generally found themselves in entry-level positions where they performed routine functions like clerical work and ordinary sales (Wadhwa and Garg 1975: 22). Some graduates took a disdainful attitude towards on-the-job training. One observer in the IIM workshop suggested that new hires 'often do not apply themselves hard enough in their training periods. They also appear slack both in punctuality and discipline' (Wadhwa and Garg 1975: 22). Sometimes, businessmen observed, the graduates entered 'management training programs with a certain cynical attitude; it all seems irrelevant to them' (Wadhwa and Garg 1975: 22).

A related problem was the graduates' preference for staff jobs in office headquarters where planning was carried out and broader policies implemented, rather than 'line jobs' where executives interacted directly with workers and customers. According to industry representatives, shopfloor positions did not fit with 'the glorified picture of executive life that a management graduate has', and seemingly offered more limited possibilities for advancement (Wadhwa and Garg 1975: 29). A panellist at the IIM workshop observed:

> In the area of marketing, management graduates shy away from a salesman's role. In the production management area, they do not like to perform such functions as producing goods at a given rate and quality at the shop floor level. The only areas they like to get into in production management is production planning. They seem biased in favour of areas like project evaluation, product management, financial planning, materials management and budgetary control.
>
> *(Wadhwa and Garg 1975: 22)*

Another participant added that 'management education seems to displace everything the graduates learned during the five years of engineering [the education in engineering schools most students had received before they entered IIMs]' (Wadhwa and Garg 1975: 22). In practice, graduates seemingly were able to evade line jobs with significant success.

Even in companies that hired MBAs, graduates were often placed in areas that were viewed as secondary priorities in their firms. One example of this pattern was the extensive hiring in marketing, an area that was just opening up in many businesses. IIM-A was reputed for its marketing programme; students who had concentrated in other areas at the Institute were often recruited in marketing, a field where many firms could not hope to find qualified candidates through personal recruiting methods. Almost half of the IIM graduates during the first decade were employed in marketing (Tumbe 2020: 11). Godrej, one of the most prominent employers of IIM students, allocated its IIM hires almost exclusively to marketing (Godrej Archives Undated, 1976). With their involvement, the company redesigned its organization in the marketing area, creating a decentralized structure of product managers who exercised considerable authority over all matters related to specific products (Godrej Archives Undated). Graduates hired in marketing in many other companies, however, were little more than glorified salespeople. Those who had concentrated in some other subjects, such as finance, found limited openings in their fields.

Perhaps the most common sentiment among employers was that their IIM hires were arrogant and elitist. IIM students already possessed significant records of high academic performance before coming to the Institute, and an MBA education may have reinforced among them a condescending perspective of their own knowhow and capabilities. Some participants in the IIM placement seminar, including a few alumni themselves, attributed 'superior, elite, arrogant and other dysfunctional attitudes' directly to the 'content of the Institute's educational programme which orients them to identify with the top management' (Wadhwa and Garg 1975: 29). In a likely reference to the case method, one representative of the business world in the IIM seminar explicitly observed that 'the management graduate, as such, appears to communicate a kind of elitism, a kind of superiority over others. The result is a varying degree of adverse reaction and resentment from other groups in industry. This interaction results in an atmosphere of conflict' (Wadhwa and Garg 1975: 20). Graduates often emphasized their possession of special knowledge that others lacked; this attitude 'is interpreted by industry as arrogance and disdain for the experienced manager' (Wadhwa and Garg 1975: 30). Several graduates recalled that their bosses summarily dismissed decisions they made in their first year. A few reported learning quickly that the forceful demeanour that they had been trained to develop in IIM's classrooms was unwelcome, leading them sometimes to tone down the tenor of their comments and written report. Others, feeling that bluntness in criticizing company practices was justified, persisted in assertive stances until deciding to leave. Forty to 50 years later, many IIM alumni would acknowledge to me that their initial approaches to their jobs had often reflected arrogance.

In many firms, new hires were expected to act deferentially, a posture for which the case method, with its emphasis on assertiveness and on encouraging classroom participants to play roles as CEOs, had prepared them quite poorly. A business representative at the IIM seminar asserted bluntly: 'Does the management graduate recognize that the employer is the "boss"? [. . .] the organization is hiring him only as an executive and not as an adviser or consultant. Whether he likes or not, he is an employee' (Wadhwa and Garg 1975: 24). Refusal to show respect to middle managers was apparently common. A businessman in the 1975 seminar commented that 'the management graduate looks down on practicing managers who do not possess formal management education. He tends to see himself as a "cut" above other managers' (Wadhwa and Garg 1975: 20). One retired professor related to me an account of a student who incurred resentment by his failure to use the honorific 'ji' with his seniors; this professor blamed the business for its failure to professionalize, suggesting that the conflict was due to the inappropriate imposition of a social structure (family) on a work structure. Another student stressed the importance of referring to the boss in his company as 'saheb'. Adopting the language of Human Relations, industry representatives in the IIM workshop sometimes framed the issue as due to inadequate 'inter-personnel skills', perhaps not recognizing that the case method itself not only failed to emphasize the importance of imparting the social skills required in the Indian business environment but may have actively discouraged it.

To some extent, the apparent arrogance of graduates stemmed from the self-image of 'change agent' generated during their educations. Most firms employed the graduates simply to carry out routine functions rather than to effect organizational transformations. In other cases, IIM alumni had indeed been hired with the hope they might introduce innovative approaches, but company leaders could not allocate this role explicitly and exclusively to them without alienating middle managers (Wadhwa and Garg 1975: 30). The placement workshop report suggested that the management graduate 'wants his role of change agent legitimized by almost an act of proclamation' rather than through a substantial record of accomplishment on the job. New graduates aggressively put forward proposals for change in their organization, only to be told that that they should temper their criticisms and deemphasize the radical modifications that their proposals might involve. In short, the framing of the graduates' self-identity as transformational figures in a society-wide process of development created strong obstacles to their incorporation into meaningful roles in Indian business organizations.

Another problematic characteristic of the IIM students was their supposed lack of 'loyalty'. Young managers were socialized, both in their classrooms and in their highly competitive social interactions at the IIM, to think of themselves as possessing 'careers' that would involve steady advancement in status and financial remuneration but did not depend on devotion to a particular employer. They felt little compunction about leaving for jobs that offered better opportunities and more psychic rewards. Some transferred to new positions as many as seven times during their first three to ten years (Garg and Parikh 1993: 56). Family businesses, on the other hand, often expected lifetime commitment; the tendency of their IIM hires to move on to new positions could be very disconcerting and induce resentment. Firms intent on holding on to their IIM graduates sometimes found it advisable to establish programmes of career counselling, which would identify the new skills they needed to acquire for advancement.

Employers in all kinds of industry often found graduates difficult to work with: According to Garg and Parikh (1993: 13), industry's view of alumni were as follows:

> Overwhelmingly consistent. . . . According to them an MBA was technically sound and intellectually arrogant. He became easily disgruntled, changed jobs frequently, aimed too high too soon, and was unstable.

> Confident in his theoretical knowledge, he made light of the long experience of his superiors, criticized industrial processes and ignored ground realities. Industry did, however, concede that in some organizations the MBAs had not only stayed, but had also flourished contributing to the growth of the organizations.

At the core of all these problems was a tension between the social perceptions of IIM-trained graduates held by Indian business leaders and the identity of the graduates themselves. The former tended to regard the MBAs largely as employees, that is, as a form of labour, not as a class apart. The latter tended to feel that because of their unique form of training and their special position in the mission of development, they belonged to a privileged category of people called 'managers' who shared more in common with their bosses and owners than they did with ordinary workers.

Sources providing the perspective of MBAs confirm this strong sense of conflict between the values of the graduates and those of the business organizations they often entered. In my interviews, alumni often expressed the view that they had been placed in positions that gave them a limited sense of challenge or authority and that forced them to behave deferentially. One graduate described a climate in his firm where everything revolved around the personality of the family leader. Employees used to watch every morning for the arrival of the company head, and would scurry around saying 'the sheth has come, the sheth has come' when his car pulled in. A graduate who was hired in an Ahmedabad firm remembered feeling that his position was more that of an executive assistant than of a manager. He told me that the owner made all the key decisions and activity in the firm revolved around the sheth's persona. He felt he was used in the business as a kind of 'ornament' who could be introduced to outsiders as the company's MBA in order to impress them. He left this job after a year and found a position in another company where he was delegated real authority and the owner did not watch over him closely. Tellingly, the training of MBAs who found jobs *in Ahmedabad* provided them with little expertise to handle what had been the main priority of mill owners in initially supporting management education: the need to deal with labour as they sought to introduce new technologies. Hires who dealt with labour relations acquired the associated skills through years of on-the-job experience.

Garg and Parikh's analysis of young managers, though focused on the perspective of graduates and while steeped in the specialized language of social psychology, confirms the picture of cultural conflict in the workplace that emerges from interviews and the 1975 workshop. Only a few business firms, they suggest, had ready-made roles for graduates (1993: 52). Often the MBAs felt slotted into routine work that influenced company policy very little. 'Some of these [his reports]', remarked one graduate, 'were verbally appreciated and filed. Others were used for power politics to serve some senior people's needs' (Garg and Parikh 1993: 18). Some felt humiliated in the work environment. One commented: 'The injustices one experiences, after taking a job, regarding the probation period, confirmation of the job and the final placement make one feel frustrated. When hard work does not yield results one feels insecure and dejected. All these lead one to not stick around the place' (Garg and Parikh 1993: 19). Many felt they had limited opportunity to offer their opinions to those at higher levels:

> I am not sure of my approach to my superior . . . I have had a few confrontations. I believe I should be permitted to discuss matters . . . If my superior shuts me off, I feel suffocated. . . . I feel my superior and the whole organization are conspiring to keep me in my place.
>
> *(Garg and Parikh 1993: 21)*

While many MBAs thought of their roles as innovators, as 'executives who would introduce new techniques and correspondingly new skills' (Garg and Parikh 1993: 51), they often had little opportunity to implement change in practice.

Garg and Parikh argued that graduates adapted in three different ways to such circumstances. Some of them became transients and changed their jobs often; a few shifted positions several times in a short period looking for a more satisfactory experience. Others adapted, recognizing that 'finding a place which matched their potential, abilities, aspirations and dreams was only a myth'. A final group abided, waiting for opportunities that seemed to suit their needs before they took new career moves. With time, Garg and Parikh argue, 65% to 70% finally settled into positions where 'their behavior was acceptable and functional' (1993: 53–57). Seemingly, this tended to occur only after significant periods of struggle and after considerable adjustment to corporate culture. Garg and Parikh comment that in the end: 'the MBAs journey into the world of work, while materially rewarding, was psychologically dissatisfying and counterproductive to happiness. Their encounter with work only confirmed the omnipotence of the system' (1993: 62).

My interviews brought up yet another alternative to the three possibilities mentioned by Garg and Parikh: opting out of the management structure altogether. A few graduates found two main ways of doing so. One was to become entrepreneurs themselves. Several of the people I interviewed created their own companies during the 1970s, well before the major start-up era that began around 2000. This choice was a path that was not explicitly encouraged in management education at the time. Another possibility was to pursue PhDs outside India and then to take up academic careers in higher education, often in American business schools. In both cases, these choices were frequently adopted after briefly (and often frustrating) experiences in Indian industry.

Overall then, rather than entering decentralized structures that gave them considerable scope to exercise their expertise and their commitment to the values of professional management, graduates often encountered firms based upon the authority of founding families and the need to maintain the family's social reputation. In effect, many of them did not initially become 'managers' as the Institute defined the term. New forms of managerial capitalism were achieved only in fits and starts and as existing forms of business accommodated themselves to the slowly changing character of their executive workforce.

Conclusion

This chapter has suggested that the projects of skill formation on one hand, and of skill deployment on another, were lodged in clashing political contexts. The idea of management education in India was formulated by international agencies and reforming national leaderships who came to regard managerialism as a critical path to India's development. It acquired its specific shape in the IIMs, where it was seen as a method not only of imparting specific forms of technical knowledge believed to be essential to effective business administration, but also as a mode of generating 'leadership' with a special capacity for 'decision-making' and of forging 'change agents' who would guide the organizational transformation of both Indian capitalism and government and contribute to the country's progress. Consideration of the specific skills, subjectivities, and modes of social adaptation needed to thrive in Indian firms as they actually existed at the time was not a major part of the curriculum. Instead an IIM education in effect assumed that the organizational culture of Indian firms would have to be transformed into some ideal form in which the management skills imparted at the institution would become relevant.

A very different kind of politics was at work in a wide spectrum of Indian firms, especially family firms. These firms sometimes valued the specific forms of expertise graduates acquired in the IIMs, but they retained their priorities with the maintenance of the family reputation, the principle of deference to family members and other senior leaders, the stability of the business organization, sustained loyalty to the firm, and tactful social interactions rather than the brash assertion of 'leadership' as encouraged in IIM classrooms. Many graduates were hired primarily because their presence made it possible for the firm to project an aura of modernity, rather than for the skills and modes of social comportment graduates had developed at IIM-A. Indian capitalism showed little tendency to evolve towards structures in which the family would fade away into insignificance; instead the family's role adapted continuously to the increasingly complex tasks of business organizations in the country. The mismatch between the social skills transmitted in management schools and those valued in Indian businesses continuously produced tensions as the graduates entered their first jobs.

Yet by the 1990s, IIM alumni did acquire a degree of authority in Indian business. Despite the serious conflicts generated by the new MBAs, many firms continued to hire graduates, in some cases motivated by the prestige of appearing progressive. These graduates sometimes worked their way up the hierarchies of Indian businesses and gradually (though partially) contributed to reshaping organizational cultures through political assertions of their own. Rather than see management education as producing skills already required by existing firms, it is more correct to suggest that it created employees who eventually shaped expectations in their businesses as their numbers grew and as they rose to positions in middle, and occasionally senior, management. The process of 'liberalization' that emerged during the 1990s – a significantly transformed political context – would come to place a premium on expertise in finance, consulting, and marketing and on the ability to speak the language of global business that IIM graduates possessed. The status of IIM managers grew, and a kind of managerial capitalism did take form, though mainly in a tiny range of large firms at the top of the corporate world. Still, this did not happen without the continued generation of conflict created by the presence of IIM graduates within a larger field populated extensively by Indian family firms.

Notes

1 My thanks to Saikat Maitra, Jagrut Vyas, Kena Wani, and Stefan Link, who provided comments on earlier drafts of this chapter.

2 These arguments have been influenced in part by Subramanian (2019), though I have modified her perspective due to complexities I believe she has not examined, some of which pertain to omitting the importance of management education in her analysis of engineering graduates and some to her exclusive focus on Brahmins.

3 For the politics of business education in the United States, see Khurana (2007). For a previous argument consonant but not identical with my own, see van Haaften (2021).

4 I had completed roughly 100 interviews as of June 2023; only a sampling could be considered in this chapter though the other interviews would reinforce the analysis developed here.

5 A small number of interviewees preferred that I not reveal their names, at least for parts of the interview relevant to this chapter; here I have decided to withhold names of all interviewees and the firms where they worked when they were providing their own personal histories in business (specific references to interviews are provided in some other contexts).

6 I want to thank my student Jahnavi Bhavsar for highlighting to me the comparative history of management education and Amden's work specifically.

7 This was a term used widely by people involved, from Ensminger at the Ford Foundation to professors at the Institute.

8 This was mentioned repeatedly in interviews. At the same time, professors were known for their sociability outside the classroom, which included hobnobbing with students during evenings at the Louis Kahn Plaza.

9 Van Haaften (2021) stresses the eventual adaptation of the case method to Indian concerns during these years. No doubt, many cases were researched and written

at IIM and some of these became deployed in the classroom. Yet in interviews, former professors and students emphasized the continued role of American cases despite this development. One faculty member disparaged the quality of many Indian cases for classroom use. Since case writers eventually were well trained associates and sometimes faculty of IIM, I speculate that differences in classroom usefulness may have had more to do with the willingness of Indian firms to share crucial data about their internal workings and finances, especially during the early decades. More research, however, is necessary.

10 For an examination of placement from the Institute, see Patil (2021).

11 For one history of small industrial firms, see Haynes (2012).

References

Ahmedabad Textile Industrial Research Association (ATIRA). ATIRA Library, 1955. Proceedings of the First Management Conference, February 5th–7th.

Ahmedabad Textile Industrial Research Association (ATIRA). 1956. Proceedings of the Second Management Conference, January 20th–22nd.

Ahmedabad Textile Industrial Research Association (ATIRA). 1957. The Third Management Conference, February 2nd to 4th.

Ahmedabad Textile Industrial Research Association (ATIRA). 1958. Report of the Fourth Management Conference, February 7–9.

Ahmedabad Textile Industrial Research Association (ATIRA). 1959. Proceedings of the Fifth Management Conference, January 28th–30th.

Ahmedabad Textile Industrial Research Association (ATIRA). 1960. Proceedings: Sixth Management Conference, February 12th–14th.

Amdam, R. P. (ed.). 1996. *Management Education and Competitiveness: Europe, Japan and the United States*. Abingdon: Routledge.

Anubhai, P. 2019. *Research Interview with Prafull Anubhai.*

Bhavsar. 2023. 'The Case Method and Harvard Business School's Rise to Academic Hegemony'. Winter 2023. Undergraduate Student Research Paper, Dartmouth College.

Chandler, A. D. 1977. *The Visible Hand: The Managerial Revolution in American Business*. Cambridge: Harvard University Press.

Cohen, A. 2019. *Research Interview with Allen Cohen.*

Ensminger, D. 1972. 'The Ford Foundation and Management Education in India'. March 2, Ford Foundation Archives, Ensminger Oral History, Series, FA 744, Box 2.

Garg, P. and Parikh, I. 1993. *Young Managers at the Crossroads: The Trishanku Complex*. New Delhi: Sage Publications.

Godrej Archives. 1976. 'Analysis of MBAs'. MS 12-15-69-25, File 5863/3.

Godrej Archives. Undated. 'Reorganisation of Sales Force'. MS 12-15-69-25, File 3 C 1/34.

Haensel, Catharina. Undated. Unpublished MS. Wages and Shopfloor (Re-)Organisation: Rationalisation and Making of Scientific Wages. Draft of PhD Thesis.

Harvard Business School [HBS]. 1963–4. Official Catalogue of the Indian Institute of Management, Ahmedabad, 1963–64 (Typed manuscript). Ahmedabad: Indian Institute of Management. Baker Library Special Collections, Ahmedabad Records 1958–71, Box 12, Folder 1.

Harvard Business School [HBS]. 1965. Melvyn Copen to Vikram Sarabhai, Harry Hansen, Kamala Chowdhury and Warren Haynes. Ahmedabad: Indian Institute of Management. Baker Library Special Collections, Ahmedabad Records, 1958–71, Box 12, Folder 7.

Harvard Business School [HBS]. 1969–70?. Two Year Post Graduate Programme in Business Administration. Baker Library Special Collections, Ahmedabad Records, Box 14, Folder 23.
Haynes, D. E. 2012. *Small-Town Capitalism in Western India: Artisans, Merchants and the Making of the Informal Economy, 1870–1960*. Cambridge: Cambridge University Press. 2020.
Haynes. D. E. 2020. 'Harvard, the Case Method and the Indian Institute of Management, 1959–1970'. Paper Presented at the Meetings of the American Historical Association, New York, January.
IIMA Institute Building Files. 1961. Vol. 1. IIM Ahmedabad Archives. John Coleman, Ford Foundation, Delhi to Vikram Sarabhai, MIT, Cambridge Mass. April 29, 1961.
Indian Institute of Management Ahmedabad [IIMA]. 1973. *IIMA: The First Decade, 1962–72*. Ahmedabad: Indian Institute of Management.
Jammulamadaka, N. 2017. 'A Postcolonial Critique of Indian's Management Education Scheme'. In M. Thakur and R. R. Babu (eds.), *Management Education in India: Perspectives and Practices*, pp. 23–42. Singapore: Springer.
Karnik, K. 2022. *Research Interview with Kiran Karnik*. Delhi.
Khurana, R. 2007. *From Higher Aims to Hired Hands: The Social Transformation of American Business Schools and the Unfulfilled Promise of Management as a Profession*. Princeton: Princeton University Press.
Kumar, A. 2019. 'From Henley to Harvard at Hyderabad? (Post- and Neo-) Colonialism in Management Education in India'. *Enterprise and Society*, 20(2), 366–400.
Link, S. 2017. Unpublished MS. Business as Political Action: The Ford-GM Rivalry in the 1920s and the Limits of "Embeddedness".
Link, S. 2018. 'The Charismatic Corporation: Finance, Administration and Shop Floor Management under Henry Ford'. *Business History Review*, 92 (Spring): 85–115.
Pant, A. and Ramachandran, J. 2017. 'Navigating Identity Duality in Multinational Subsidiaries: A Paradox Lens on Identity Claims at Hindustan Unilever, 1959–2015'. *Journal of International Business Studies*, 48(6): 664–692.
Parikh, I. 2022. *Research Interview with Indira Parikh*.
Patel, S. 1987. *The Making of Industrial Relations: The Ahmedabad Textile Industry, 1918–39*. Delhi: Oxford University Press.
Patil, A. 2021. 'The Starting Recruiters of IIM Ahmedabad'. Paper Produced at IIM Ahmedabad) Research Paper. Ahmedabad: Indian Institute of Management.
Rao, T. V. 2018. *Research Interview with T.V. Rao*.
Shah, D. 2018. *Research Interview with Dakshah Shah*.
Srinivas, N. 2008. 'Mimicry and Revival: The Transfer and Transformation of Knowledge to India, 1959–1990'. *International Studies of Management and Education*, 38(4): 38–57.
Subramanian, A. 2019. *Caste of Merit: Engineering Education in India*. Cambridge: Harvard University Press.
Tandon, P. 1974. *Professional Management in India: Its Potential and Problems*. Ludhiana: Department of Business Education, Punjab Agricultural University.
Tripathi, D. and Jumani, J. 2013. *The Oxford History of Contemporary Indian Business*. Delhi: Oxford University Press.
Tumbe, C. 2020. 'The Rise of the Technological Manager in India in the 1960s: The Role of the Indian Institutes of Management'. *Management & Organizational History*, 15(2): 192–206.
Van Haaften, L. 2021. 'Management Science and Nation Building: The Sociotechnical Imaginary behind the Making of the Indian Institute of Management'. *Indian Economic and Social History Review*, 58(3): 333–359.

Wadhwa, C. and Garg, P. K. (eds.). 1975. *Placement of Management Graduates: Expectations and Experiences, Proceedings of the Placement Seminar, January 21 and 22nd, 1975*. Ahmedabad: Indian Institute of Management.
Wakhlu, B., Rajan, M. and Bhasin, S. 2022. *Tata's Leadership Experiment: The Story of the Tata Administrative Service*. Gurugram: Harper Business.
Wani, K. 2023. 'Pedagogies of Development, Conceptions of Efficiency: Modern Managerialism in Industrial Ahmedabad, 1950s–60s'. *Enterprise and Society*, 1–34.

3

HAVING TIME PASSED

Education, skill development, control, and labour in prisons of colonial India

Michaela Dimmers[1]

> It is the duty of the State to endeavour to reclaim and reform the prisoner in its hands by giving him the class of labour best calculated to interest and instruct him, to awaken his intelligence, to train him to habits of industry and application and so to fit him for free life.
>
> (Jails Committee 1921: 123)

Introduction

This chapter examines the how the colonial state of British India fulfilled its 'duty', proclaimed in the report of the Indian Jails Committee 1919–20, to 'instruct' and 'train' convicts incarcerated, or 'in its hands', by the colonial regime in order to 'fit him for free life'. By introducing literacy and skill development programmes, the colonial penal regime attempted to control every activity of the convict population. It did so not only by aiming to organize and regulate their movements and activities, but also by occupying them physically and mentally at all times during waking hours. By tracing such programmes and measures and their connections to labour, this chapter proposes a larger conversation about educational programmes and skill development measures in coercive contexts. It furthermore suggests that a contradictory situation was created, as people convicted of and punished for crimes received education they might not have received in the extramural world, while staff members employed from the extramural population, especially in the lower ranks of the prison administration, in charge of implementing penal coercion received such training much later.

DOI: 10.4324/9781003604846-4

Focusing on jails of the North-Western Provinces, later United Provinces, this inquiry provides a deeper understanding not only of penal policies and their developments, but also of colonial knowledge production. Defining education and training in the coercive environments of the colonial prisons in the mid-nineteenth and twentieth centuries largely as a mode of control and of improving the production of commodities, it puts into question the colonial argument of 'reforming' or 'rehabilitating' convicts through labour and education, thus, making him and her a 'useful members, to society' citizen, a term used in a report on the state of education of prisoners in Pentonville Prison, London, 1847. (Woodcock 1852: 161, App. G) Indeed, in many ways literacy training was not only part of skilling and skill development, but also, together with labour, one of the ways in the penal administration's official rhetoric this 'reclaiming' and 'reforming' of convicts was to be attained. Educational programmes and skill development were part of the coerced labour regime, intertwining skill development and labour into one inseparable entity. I argue that training and skilling, realized largely through prison labour, was mostly beneficial to the colonial prison administration and less so for convicts, who not only worked in jail industries, but assisted greatly in the running of colonial prisons, working, for example, as teachers, scribes, cooks, cleaners, servants, medical staff, in farming, and as masons. Furthermore, convicts, being employed as so-called convict officers for guarding duties, overseeing the labour of other convicts, as well as being on night watch, took over responsibilities of ensuring prison discipline (Arnold 2015: 216–218; Dimmers 2023).

Developing and maintaining modes of punishment through labour enabled the colonial regime to operate their prison cost effectively, all under the guise of punishment and reform. With literacy taught in increasingly structured programmes, held after a day of arduous labour, the colonial regime was able to control the convicts' time outside of working hours. Training and skill development measures, as other modes of labour, could enhance not only the quality of commodities produced, but also that of construction works inside and outside the prisons done by convicts. Through a combination of these elements, the penal regime endeavoured to control the inmates and their minds in their entirety. Hence, educational programmes, skill development, and training should be considered above all as techniques of control, as shown by Garland, agreeing with Foucault, defining it as a 'more effective exercise of social control', or in the words of Foucault 'not to punish less, but to punish better . . . to insert the power to punish more deeply into the social body' (Garland and Foucault, as cited in: Bailey 1997: 291–292; see also Foucault 1979: 82). The following sub-chapters will show how the colonial regime created a body of skilled workers supplying labour within the prison, but also how these programmes worked as mechanisms of control in order to 'punish better'.[2]

Controlling the body and mind: tracing literacy programmes and training measures for convicts

In July 1851, a literacy programme, taught by convicts known as 'monitors', was started for male and female prisoners in 'Mynpooree Jail'. William Woodcock, Inspector-General of Prisons for the North-Western Provinces, called this an 'experiment', which, to his knowledge, had been 'the only effort which, . . . has ever been made towards the reformation of criminals by the improvement of their moral condition'. He reported that during a visit to the jail the following year, he was met by 150 inmates wanting to show him the progress they had made in the programme and stated further that one third of prisoners had been taught to read and write *Devanagari*,[3] a few others Persian and Urdu. Six women classified as 'Aheerin', 'Chumarin', 'Koomharin', 'Pathan', and 'Thakoorain',[4] serving sentences of imprisonment between 5 and 14 years for *dacoity*, killing, or stealing children, or attempted murder had been part of this literacy programme. As reported, five of them had attained fluency in reading and writing Hindi, prompting the 'tehseeldar' to claim that these six would be the only women in the district 'who could read and write at all'[5] (Woodcock 1852: 9–10). Even though women's education comprised additional languages such as Urdu and English in some jails, they did not receive an education equivalent to that of male convicts, who were taught to read and write Hindi, in some jails, when the programme was expanded, also Urdu, Persian, and, in later years, English and in 'the higher classes', were also taught multiplication, 'arithmetic and mensuration' (Clark 1868: 73 Annual report Benares CJ; 1869: 22–23, 29; Annual report Bareilly CJ), 64, Annual report Agra CJ); 1871: 28D–29D, App. III, Annual report Bareilly CJ).

In 1852 a literacy programme was introduced in Agra Central Jail[6] and 'extended' to prisoners who were operating 'lithographic presses', 'from which cheap educational books and maps of very creditable execution are produced in considerable numbers' (Thornhill 1853: 10). Convicts detained in Agra CJ received special training in a monitor school to become, in effect, teachers. The report listed 29 male convicts who were placed in this school. They had to do manual labour for half a day, such as 'drawing water; occasionally carrying dry earth', and taught in the afternoon until evening for five and half hours, when their convict students had finished their day of arduous labour. Convicts selected as monitors were incarcerated for the most diverse crimes. They had been sentenced to terms of imprisonment between five years and life for crimes including murder, burglary, perjury, dacoity, including one case of dacoity with robbing a prosecutor, homicide, affray with homicide or with attempted murder, including children for ornaments, 'knowingly receiving stolen property', and forgery. Convicts who had previously openly defied prison discipline, by escaping or attempting to escape, including in a volatile manner, such as 'resisting capture, and severe wounding of captors', or '[e]scaping from confinement, with wounding of his guard', and '[b]eing accessory in the outbreak, and of having aided and abetted in the attack on the British detachment' were also among those trained and employed as monitors. None of them seemed to have shown a documented or explicit loyalty to the colonial administration, for example, by preventing escapes or other acts of disobedience. For most of these prisoners the main reasons for including them in this training programme were that they had been convicted to a life sentence and could teach other life prisoners, or that they were trained as a teacher to teach convicts in a penal settlement; ill health; and having taught before within the prison system. Some of these convicts thus selected had reportedly shown high interest in education and had progressed in their studies, some having learnt to read and write in jail (Thornhill 1855: 56–58, App. IV).

Literacy programmes for the general convict population were started in other jails in the province, such as Allyghur and Humeerpore, and were intended for introduction elsewhere in India (Thornhill 1853: 10). However, C.B. Thornhill, Inspector General of Prisons for the North-Western Provinces, questioned such programmes very early on, not expecting that they would have a 'marked reformatory influence', but viewing them as an instrument to enforce jail discipline and control the convicts' free time, which he deemed to be 'passed in . . . idleness', 'inactivity', and as a chance to recount past crimes, when prisoners were not engaged in 'manual occupation' (Thornhill 1854: 11). Lectures in religion and 'moral lectures', given mainly by representatives of Hindu and Muslim faiths, also took place and added to the controlled time for convicts. Such lectures can be understood as what Michael Ignatieff has defined as 'coercive moral education' (Ignatieff 1978: 117), in this context organized and regulated by the colonial state. All these measures echo the official penal discourse at the time of reforming convicts through coercive punishment, mainly hard labour, education, including 'coercive moral education', as well as literacy training and skill development, combined with general prison discipline. The perception, stressed throughout the sources, was that strict jail discipline would instil more general elements of discipline into the inmates' lives, since a lack of discipline was often perceived being the cause of criminality and subsequent incarceration. How life in prison was supposed to be organized and structured was outlined in the jail manuals of the time. The rules laid out therein demonstrate clearly that prison labour, which included skill development and training, was the main element around which the day was to be constructed (Clark 1863; Government of the United Provinces 1942; Government of the United Provinces of Agra and Oudh 1927; MacTaggart 1902; Walker 1882). When in place, education, on the other hand, was allocated outside the hours of labour, together with lectures, controlled the convicts' activities during the later parts of the day (see e.g. Clark 1871: 61D, annual report Fatehgarh CJ).

Even though the uprising of 1857–58 and its aftermath had put a hiatus on the literacy programmes, 'classes for instruction of boys and young men in the Central Prisons' had taken place and supposed to be expanded[7] (Clarke 1861: 7). Enumeration was extended at the same time, by including statistics on education in the yearly prison administration reports (Clarke 1861: 52). However, the categories in the statistics then used were documented in very broad strokes; without any gradation and irrespective of the proficiency of the inmates' literacy skills, every prisoner was included in these statistics.[8] The annual prison administration report for the year 1860 exemplified this, as it documented a large increase of 1,500 people who had learnt how to read for Agra CJ that year, in which no prisoner had learnt to read or write the previous year (Clark 1861: 25). But as the annual prison administration report for 1861 stated

> [o]f the large number in the Agra Central Prison who have learned since their conviction, a great portion know very little more than the letters; still the progress made is very creditable and deserves every encouragement.
> *(Clark 1862: 8)*

One year later, the purpose of the literacy programme targeting juvenile prisoners, who were at that time still housed with adult inmates, was spelt out: those with a prison sentence of more than one year were 'taught English, with the view of making them compositors and printers generally' (Clark 1862: 8). In 1862, eight juvenile convicts imprisoned for long terms in Agra CJ were taught English with the explicit goal to employ them at the prison's printing press (Walker 1863: 7c App. III Annual report Agra CJ), not only connecting education to labour, but also marking how educational training and skill development served the needs of the prisons. The progress in the literacy programme for juvenile prisoners was considered good, by contrast, progress for adults was judged to be 'nominal' (Clark 1865: 12). Juvenile convicts were taught by Indian teachers and Indian as well as European inmates[9] (Clark 1869: 64, App. III Annual report Agra CJ).

The documentation of the teaching methods gives insights to the educational programme's early formalization. A structured educational programme became evident in a circular of 1854, published in the jail manual for the year 1863, which included two lists with a 'Course of Study for Jail Schools' one each for classes one to four taught in either Hindi or Urdu, depending on the language predominantly used in the district in which the respective jails were situated. The list for the courses in Hindi was divided into three parts for (a) convicts, having been 'agricultural term-prisoners, who have been imprisoned of offences which are not ignominious', (b) for 'all other term prisoners', making exceptions for some convicts classified as 'agriculturalists', and (c) for convicts sentenced to life imprisonment. The courses in Urdu were also divided into three parts, but no specification for whom these courses were intended was given, presumably the same criteria were applied. The contents for the courses in Hindi and Urdu were listed separately. Except for the first class for groups (a) and (b) the contents of studying varied somewhat within the different groups of each class and included, amongst others, in class 1 multiplications, in class 2 arithmetic, stories with contents on moral and 'advice for Cultivators', in class 3 stories on health, and the study of maps of the convicts' 'own district', and for class 4 'explanation of village institution accounts', health advice, or 'natural theology'. The cost of the books and instructors was supposed to be covered by the revenue generated from prison labour (Clark 1863: XXXVII–XL, Circular No. 56 of 1854). According to the annual prison administration report for the year 1868 this course outline indeed was implemented[10] (Clark 1869: 23 App. III Annual Report Bareilly CJ). It is not established if, or to what extent, the convicts' own knowledge was taken into account as part of the course design or implementation. But the fact that agriculture, accounting, and geography were taught amplifies the intention that convicts should get skilled differently in agriculture or even the assumption that they would not be competent and experienced in these matters, which reflects the presumption of superior knowledge by the colonial regime vividly. The course work again demonstrates rather distinctively the connection between literacy, skill development, and the intent to create a labour force, trained to the colonial regime's vision of intramural but also extramural labour.

The teaching system at Agra CJ was detailed in the prison administration's report for the year 1860, in which '[a]fter dinner, the whole of the convicts are divided into classes of 15'. These classes were conducted by 20 convict monitors, aided by 225 convicts, literate before their incarceration, all supervised by 'hired teachers' (Clark 1861: 101 Annual Report Agra CJ). A teaching schedule was documented for Fatehgarh CJ for the year 1870, where classes for all convicts, except those of an advanced age or who were 'physically incapable', started at 4.30 pm. In order not to interfere with prison labour, classes were held for one hour in winter and two-and-a-half hours in summer, organized by barracks in groups of not more than 25 students, in front of the convict quarters. Most convicts were taught in Hindi, male convicts with longer sentences confined in this jail were taught Urdu, and students with 'good knowledge' of Urdu were taught Persian or English (Clark 1871: 61D). Exams were held and by 1863 between 6 and 30 good conduct marks were given for education in all the prisons running a literacy programme in the provinces (Clark 1863: CLVIc; Walker 1864: 35c App. III Annual report Meerut CJ). These good conduct marks had an immediate effect on various aspects of a convict's incarceration, as he or she could get certain privileges for a specified number of such marks; 50 good conduct marks entitled a convict to a visit from friends, 150 and 250 marks opened up access to different levels of posts as a convict officers, 'under special circumstances', and 500 marks could entitle a convict 'fit for recommendation to [the] Government for a reduction of a portion of his sentence, or release from Prison altogether'. What these 'special circumstances' were and who determined them was not specified. At the same time, good conduct marks could also be reduced as a punishment for infractions against prison rules[11] (Clark 1863: CLVIc). Exempted, officially at least for some time, from the literacy programme where it was in place, and hence also excluded from gaining good conduct marks for education, were those inmates classified in the more than demeaning category as 'too stupid to learn', a notion already used in 1862. This category was introduced into the official statistics in the annual prison administration report for 1872, which classified 19.8% of the convict population as part of this category. It remained in place until 1874 (Walker 1863: 7c App. III, Annual Report Agra CJ; Walker 1873: 14, 12A, 1874: 10, 12A, 1875: 12A). The use of such a category, even for a comparatively short period of time, not only demonstrates the attitudes on the part of the prison administration towards the inmate population in their care, but also demonstrates the hierarchical categorizations within penal enumeration, in this case the perceived and harshly categorized ability to learn.

As mentioned, the notion of the control of time as an additional layer of control was recognized by contemporary critics, who, very early on, had voiced their reservations of the literacy programme as a mechanism of reform (see e.g. Thornhill 1854: 11; Walker 1863: 9–10, 1864: 27). The criticism continued and with only quantifiable success measured, the calls to abolish the literacy programme grew louder. In 1891, the colonial administration agreed for it to be ended for adult convicts (Tyler 1892: 16). In 1925, however, a proposal was submitted, and endorsed by the United Provinces Jail Enquiry Committee of 1929, to introduce a mandatory literacy programme for any convict aged 25 or younger, based on the same reform argument as for the former literacy programme, but without any reference to it (Clements 1926: 5; Government of India 1929: 185). The proposal was granted in 1932 (Palmer 1933: 9, 3 of Resolution of Government). The age limit was changed in 1937, as '[n]ot only prisoners below 45 years but older prisoners with grey hair evinced keen interest' in education (Salamat Ullah 1938: 4, 1–2 Orders of Government No. 1847/VI – 1318–1933, Resolution, Government of the United Provinces). Some reports indicated that before being reintroduced officially, a number of jails had voluntary educational schemes, which were taught by staff members without compensation and after working hours by literate convicts. These voluntary programmes were on occasion noted in the annual jail administration reports (Clements 1927: 4; Government of India 1929: 185–186; Palmer 1931: 9, 1932: 9).

Education and training for juvenile convicts

The end, or rather the hiatus, of the official literacy programme in 1892 for adult convicts marked a change in attitude towards juvenile convicts. Having already been separated physically from adults in central jail reformatories, the educational programme continued for juveniles with a sentence of over one year. The difference in the approach to the educational programmes as well as skill development for adult and juvenile convicts was justified with the reasoning that, unlike for adult convicts, these measures had a reformative effect on juveniles convicts (Tyler 1892: 5,16, 1893: 4). The much more methodical approach to skill development taken with juveniles, again, not only interlinked education and training with labour, but suggests the intention to create a well-trained and literate juvenile labour force for intra- and extramural prison labour, as well as for the time after release. This was also reflected in the opening of a reformatory school in Bareilly on 1 April 1889, a compound originally intended as a prison for women. This reformatory school was opened for the specific purpose of housing male juvenile convicts, classified as non-habitual. It was turned into a juvenile jail in April 1909, (Clarke 1889: 4, 6 of Orders of Government; MacTaggart 1910: 3; Tyler 1894: 32), making the identification and classification of convicts not only as juveniles, but also as habitual or non-habitual, even more essential for convicts. Juvenile inmates classified as habitual continued to be incarcerated in the reformatories of the central prisons. Thus, this classification, together with the lengths of the sentence, decided the place of juvenile incarceration and the level and intensity of training as well as education they would receive, which in all the places juvenile male convicts were incarcerated in differed significantly. Additionally, it might have broken up the general 'convergence between models of adult and juvenile punishment' (Sen 2005: 11) to some extent, as in the Bareilly Juvenile Jail training and other measures considered reformative, and less productive, were put in the foreground.

Juvenile male convicts incarcerated in Bareilly were trained in professions deemed useful upon release. The Aman Sabha, an organization in Benares which worked for the aftercare of released convicts, facilitated employment for seven juvenile convicts released from Bareilly in 1923, working 'as a waterman on behalf of the Aman Sabha in the Criminal Courts of Benares', or 'employed as a domestic servant by a police officer', 'in private service by a Muhammadan zamindar', 'in the garden of a zamindar', 'as a groom of a rais', and 'as a weaver in a silk factory'. One ex-juvenile convict was working as 'as a bearer', but left 'after a few days'[12] (Clements 1924: 21). Of all these positions gained after release, officially only gardening and weaving were taught in the juvenile jail, the other people released, worked in positions for which no skill development or training was documented, which underscores the argument made in this volume that skilling, be it intra- or extramural, often did not necessarily produce related employment or reduced precarity. Instead, the majority of these former convicts worked in areas different to those they had been skilled in.

After the Aman Sabha was discontinued in 1924, the deputy collector of Benares took over the efforts to seek employment for ex-convicts. He documented finding employment for four released juvenile convicts, of which three started work in private households. All of them left within a short time span. The fourth person was employed 'in a gold and silver thread-making factory', and seemed to have stayed in employment (Clements 1925: 21–22). In 1939, an apprenticeship programme was started, in which juvenile convicts from Bareilly Juvenile Jail were trained extramurally 'in a factory, institution or under any employer of labour' without being guarded. Forty juveniles started such an apprenticeship in a timespan of seven months and were 'promised employment after release'; three of them were hired upon leaving the juvenile jail (Salamat Ullah 1940: 6). The low rates of employment after release, however, demonstrate that, as with adult convicts, the majority of released juveniles were left to their own devices, without any aftercare (Government of India 1926: 28). Therefore, also for juveniles any outcome of the training remained largely undocumented, and, by implication, the purported reformative effect of such measures could not be determined.

Especially for juvenile convicts, educational programmes and skill development continued to be developed and extended. An important change was implemented in 1938, when juvenile convicts classified as 'boys of the sweeper caste', were at last 'admitted to the school and they are now freely partaking with others in the various activities of the institution without any distinction whatsoever' (Salamat Ullah 1939: 5). Furthermore, in Bareilly Juvenile Jail, for example, first aid training, and competitive, predominantly physical games were added to the daily schedule (see, e.g. Salamat Ullah 1939: 5). Primary education was taught by house masters, as well as 'literate warders and the better educated juveniles who also work as monitors' (Palmer 1934: 8). As these monitors had multiple tasks and obligations within the jail, this teaching system was perceived as 'defective' and permission to employ two salaried teachers was sought from and granted by the colonial government. In 1935, two teachers were employed, who, in addition to their regular teaching, started instruction in hygiene and music and extended the syllabus to 'the upper primary standard' (Salamat Ullah 1935: 19, 1 Orders of Government 1936: 4, 1937: 3). Upon release, juvenile convict students received a school leaving or participation certificate (Salamat Ullah 1937: 3). By 1938, the Juvenile Jail School was 'recognized by the Department of Public Instruction up to the vernacular upper primary standard'. After inmates graduated from the 'primary classes' they were 'admitted into the English class' (Salamat Ullah 1939: 5, 1940: 6). Some juveniles received individual attention and some, exceptionally at this point of time, were allowed to sit general high school exams (see e.g. Clements 1930: 5). Training in 'poultry farming' was started and agricultural training was extended over the following years, covering contemporary methods in agriculture on 'a small model agriculture farm', taught in weekly classes by the Inspector of Agriculture for Bareilly.

Other industries continued and the sport programme was extended (Salamat Ullah 1937: 3, 1938: 3). Scouting for boys was another large scheme initially recommended by the Jail Conference of Inspectors-General of Prisons held in 1927 and approved in 1931 for a one-year trial period for the juvenile jail, against which dissent and criticism 'that it will only make them more efficient dacoits in the future' was voiced. By supporters, the programme was regarded as being 'a healthy influence in moulding the boy's character and in creating amongst themselves a true spirit of brotherhood, fellow feeling and self respect [*sic*]' . The convict boy scout group was 'affiliated to the Boy Scouts Association, United Provinces' (Government of Bengal 1928: 22; Palmer 1932: 8; Salamat Ullah 1940: 5–6). The colonial scouting programme was introduced in the reformatory schools of the other jails as well, and, in 1932, was made permanent in the Bareilly Juvenile Jail (Palmer 1933: 8; Salamat Ullah 1938: 3, 1939: 5).

These activities, being taught in different trades and industries, receiving school education, including English, music, and singing lessons, farm work, the availability of a terrain for team sports, training as boy scouts, and doing homework at night, added to the already established direct, indirect, and often oblique, levels of control over juvenile inmates, even if not all classes were attended by all inmates, here control, even though it might not have been the sole purpose of these different initiatives, had an, arguably intentional, added value for the prison administration.

Apart from this, juvenile male convicts, were, just as adult male convicts, recruited to join British forces in their Mesopotamia campaign, receiving a deferred sentence by serving British war efforts. A total of 1,343 convicts were sent to Basra from the United Provinces in 1916, including convicts in transit from other Indian provinces on their way to serve. The same year 70 juvenile convicts of unknown ages were sent from Bareilly Juvenile Jail to Basra as apparent volunteers.[13] The Inspector-General of Prisons for the United Provinces, Lt. Col. Henderson, seemed to have viewed these juveniles as representatives of the Bareilly Juvenile Jail, stating that he had 'little doubt they will do credit to the juvenile jail' (Henderson 1917: 2–5), taking uncritical pride in juveniles being sent into armed conflict.

The Bareilly Juvenile Jail deemed successful, the establishment of a reformatory school for female juvenile convicts in Fatehgarh was proposed. The proposal was dismissed by the Secretary of Government, not only because this would be 'inadmissible under the existing law', but also because the number of female juvenile convicts would have been too small to justify such a measure (Tyler 1896: 6, 5 of Orders of Government). Although no separate jail was established, in October 1899 a special ward for female juvenile convicts under 15 years, called "[a] depôt for the confinement of all girl prisoners convicted in the United Provinces", was opened in Lucknow CJ. Nine female juvenile convicts were admitted and four released by the end of the year. They were supervised by a 'European Matron of the Central Jail, and a specially selected Eurasian female warder', 'trained to the habits of industry', and 'given light work to do e.g. spinning, sewing and repairing old clothing'. They also received some literacy training in Hindi (MacTaggart 1900: 4–5). The reason for not starting a reformatory school for female juvenile convicts might not have been only legal or budgetary, but based on a gender bias. Hypothetically, the reasons for such a bias could also be found in the perceived limited employability of female juvenile convicts after release, echoing the reasons given for gendered training of adult female convicts. The jail conference of Inspector-Generals of Prisons of 1934 recommended 'inviting honorary assistance by suitable ladies in the training of female prisoners in recreation, Girl Guiding, First Aid and finer handicrafts' (Government of India 1934: 11). What 'suitable' meant and if these women were trained to instruct (female) inmates in any of these subjects remains unclear.[14]

Training and skill development programmes for adult convicts

The recommendation of the Committee on Prison-Discipline of 1838 to introduce 'teaching some trade to those who know none' with exceptions for some convicts due to their caste did not translate swiftly into any formal skill development (Committee on Prison-Discipline 1838: 105).[15] By 1927, 'vocational classes' for 'selected convicts, likely to benefit by the instruction given' were started in the central prisons, where 'instructors are employed to give teaching'. The prison industries taught in central prisons were '[d]yeing', '[w]eaving', '[c]arpentry', and '[s]mithy', with the exception of Benares CJ, where the weaving programme was started one year later. Not all of the prison industries were taught in each of these prisons; blacksmithing or 'smithy', for example, was only taught in Allahabad CJ. These vocational classes were listed separately in the annual prison administration reports until 1938, comprising the same industries in the same jails taught to the same target group as in 1927, one exception being weaving, which in 1928 had moved from Bareilly CJ to Benares CJ (Clements 1928: 14–15, 1929: 14, 1930: 14; Palmer 1931: 18, 1932: 17, 1933: 17, 1934: 16; Salamat Ullah 1935: 10, 1936: 12, 1937: 12, 1938: 12, 1939: 16). The majority of the convict population before and after the introduction of this vocational programme, however, remained in informal and unstructured training. For example, at Benares CJ, out of 656 prisoners released in 1871, 270 were trained in a trade. The trades and number of prisoners taught were '75 wool-spinning; 64 brick-making and burning; 30 mason's work; 25 sawing timber; 22 weaving; 17 blacksmiths; 15 twine-spinning; 10 carpenter's work; 7 gunny-making; and 5 potter's work' (Walker 1872: 1A, App. II Annual Report Benares CJ). Taking from the multitude of trades and industries which were practiced and in which convicts were being skilled, masonry, brick-making and burning in Benares CJ as an example, an average of

> 18.72 prisoners were engaged in building arches and dismantling them with a view to teaching prisoners masonry work, so that when masons were required in other jails they were available. The work is, of course, unprofitable, but absolutely necessary to keep up a supply of apprentice masons.
>
> *(Hall 1897: 18; see also MacTaggart 1900: 18)*

By training convicts in these industries, they could work in construction and repair work within the prisons, built a staff training school (Shaikh 1941: 18), and even be transferred to other prisons because of their – acquired – skills and not for reasons of, for example, jail discipline, hence the call for 'a supply of apprentice masons' (Hall 1897: 18). This programme was further formalized with the opening of a masonry training school for convicts in Lucknow CJ in 1940. In 1941, 47 convicts had been trained as masons in this school (Shaikh 1941: 19, 1942: 15).

The production of a trained workforce at minimal cost of either incarcerated or even – hypothetical – as released convicts was certainly beneficial for the colonial regime. A follow-up of the employment after release seemed to have been difficult. The prison administration report for 1871 indicated that the majority of police queries 'result in most cases in a report "not to be found."'. It was, therefore, believed to be a 'mere waste of time and labour (as far as helping prisoners to earn an honest livelihood after release goes) to teach trades which caste rules prevent prisoners from following when they leave jail' (Walker 1872: 1A–2A, App. II Annual Report Benares CJ). The annual prison report for the year 1861 stated that ten shops were opened in Benares by former prisoners of Benares CJ, out of which five closed again, the ex-convicts and former shop owners had 'taken service with merchants' (Clark 1862: 142, Annual Report Benares CJ), indicating that at least some ex-convicts did pursue a profession after release, even though, not the same they had been trained in, in the prison, as was the case with juvenile convicts.

For women, skill development was not only guided by views, the colonial administration had about incarcerated women, describing them as 'for the most part, of the lower and lowest orders of the native classes, extremely illiterate, narrow-minded, and with scarce [*sic*] any trace of female character such as would be expected of a European' (Clark 1869: 29, App. III report Bareilly CJ). Reproducing colonial gendered notions of labour within the intramural labour force, women were taught for example knitting, sewing, and weaving. For some convicts, these tasks might have resembled familiar tasks before incarceration, while for others it might have been unfamiliar work.

Such tasks seem to reflect not only distraught colonial ideals of women's occupations but also a very limited notion of what women were able to learn. Unlike for male convicts, the statistics in the annual prison administration reports listed the professions female convicts had prior to their incarceration as 'Married', 'Unmarried', 'Widows', and 'Prostitutes', thus defining occupations of convicted women through their relationships to men and, except for one, erasing any actual occupation the women might have had prior to their incarceration (see e.g. Jafarey 1947: 6A-7A; Tyler 1892: 12A; Walker 1875: 4A), which again reflects colonial ideas about womanhood rather sharply. As has been well established, women pursued occupations outside these ascribed roles and worked in various professions, including agriculture, diverse industries, and as domestic labourers.[16]

Education and training for extramural staff

For members of the extramural staff, literacy training was introduced only by 1940; from then on solely literate warders whose 'minimal educational qualification for the post is the Vernacular Middle Standard' were to be employed. '[I]lliterate warders' employed before this requirement were supposed to receive 'elementary instruction in reading and writing' (Shaikh 1941: 19). For 'the children of warders and the officials', a primary school was established ten years earlier at Bareilly Juvenile Jail, long after the juvenile inmates incarcerated in that jail received literacy training. In 1931, 22 male and 11 female children attended the school (Palmer 1931: 28, 1932: 27). In fact, educational and training measures for staff members were described in substantially less detail than those for convicts. Detailed accounts about training programmes for staff were documented to a much lesser extent than that of convicts in the official reports. The training measures for non-convict staff can be divided into two groups: (a) training for trainers and (b) training to ensure and improve jail discipline. Rules for the prison administration published in the jail manuals, reflecting the level of control that prison staff, especially lower ranking officials, operated under, served more as a reminder of their duties than as training (Clark 1863; Government of the United Provinces 1942; Government of the United Provinces of Agra and Oudh 1927; MacTaggart 1902; Walker 1882; all passim).

Extramural trainers were employed very early on to improve the training for the convicts. However, training for these trainers started much later. In 1938, for example, 'Dyeing Instructors' working at Agra CJ and Lucknow CJ attended a three months 'Refresher's Training' at the Government Central Textile Institute in Kanpur 'in calico printing, finishing and bleaching of cloth'. This specialized printing technique was then introduced in the central jails they were working in (Salamat Ullah 1939: 13). Cooperation with other governmental institutions was sought for training purposes, having trainers enter the prisons, for example, from the Government Agriculture College in Kanpur, which sent a staff member to Bareilly CJ to train staff and convicts in the techniques of sericulture for two-and-a-half months. New weaving designs were started in several central jails after weaving instructors received a 'refresher training at the Government Central Weaving Institute, Benares' (Salamat Ullah 1940: 14, 16). In addition to courses for trainers, booklets with information on various agricultural techniques were published or in print for the 'guidance of the jail staff' (Government of the United Provinces 1942: 247; Shaikh 1941: 10). All of these initiatives were ostensibly beneficial for the training of convicts, and keeping the prison industries up to date, in effect ultimately benefitting the output of commodities manufactured in the jail industries.[17]

Training to ensure jail discipline had already been proposed by the Jail Committee of 1889, which suggested military and arms training for 'all subordinates' and sought certain qualifications, like being literate, knowledge of English for certain grades of staff in the prison hierarchies, and proposed training for warders in central jails, as well as all staff, including the superintendent (Walker and Lethbridge 1889: 28, 31, 47, 158). In 1940, a staff training school, built by convicts, was opened in parts of the Lucknow Camp Jail, for which 'necessary additions and alterations' to the site were needed 'by jail labour'. Training started in two batches on 15 August 1940 and in January 1941. A total of '20 deputy jailers' and 76 warders were taught 'Criminology, Psychology, Social Psychiatry, Law, Agriculture, Accounting, Physical Drill, Musketry, Building, Factories, etc.' in courses lasting 'four and a half months' for warders and 'nine months' for deputy jailors (Shaikh 1941: 18, 21). However, the staff training school closed on several occasions, in 1945, for example, and '60 institutions, Camp Jail buildings' were temporarily transferred to the military authorities 'for accommodation and training of [a] Jail labour battalion'. The school reopened in August 1945 (Jafarey 1947: 1, 14; Shaikh 1945: 14). The school was still in place in 1947 (Oberai 1948: 14).[18]

In contrast to the more theoretical training delivered in the jail training school, military training for staff was introduced earlier. This military training included convicts working as warders, who received this training without arms; it was extended to convict overseers as well as convict warders and changed to 'elementary instruction in physical training exercises' (Government of the United Provinces 1942: 68; MacTaggart 1902: 277; Walker and Lethbridge 1889: 28, 52). Staff warders, employed from the extramural population, were supposed to 'drill for an hour daily, until he has become proficient', else 'eight drills in every month' had to be completed. In addition, they had to receive a monthly training with arms and firing practice, and were supposed to get an 'annual musketry course', as were other 'jail officers' (Government of the United Provinces 1942: 315, 318).

Calls to employ qualified staff, especially to the higher echelons of the jails, grew. The Jail Committee of 1889 articulated the need to employ 'trained subordinates' to higher posts, who were expected to have certain qualifications, such as a certain level of English and literacy, including in the local language, knowledge of administrative procedures and enumeration processes, as well as having character traits deemed essential for the position. The Jail Committee also wanted to make a promotion to a higher grade dependent on training (Walker and Lethbridge 1889: 31, 158). The suggested requirements to become an assistant jailer included being under 25 years, having passed 'a University examination', and having a 'sound physique'. The Jail Committee proposed a mechanism for promotion from assistant jailer, to deputy jailer, to jailer, which would have taken approximately 15 years. The committee assessed that 'it has been found impossible to obtain good, trustworthy Europeans or Eurasians on the small salaries offered by the service'. In case Europeans were incarcerated in central jails, the employment of 'a European jailor' was considered necessary. The Jail Committee recommended the employment of 'specially qualified non-commissioned officers of the British army, who have served for some time as warders over European prisoners' (Walker and Lethbridge 1889: 31–32). Furthermore, the committee's report proposed the introduction of training, as well as a probation period for warders and for superintendents of central jails (Walker and Lethbridge 1889: 47, 158). The Jail Committee of 1919–20 made similar proposals, and further suggested the employment of staff trained in the industries of the jails, rather than the practice, as reported by the committee, of having staff without any specific training, such as the superintendent and the jailer, in charge of the jail industries (Jails Committee 1921: 46–47, 53–54, 57, 66). By 1927, superintendents selected for employment without any experience working in prisons were supposed to be trained for a minimum of three months in a central jail to learn the 'duties of a superintendent' which included 'a study of the principles of penology, and of the Acts, rules, regulations and orders relating to jails' (Government of the United Provinces of Agra and Oudh 1927: 164). Clerical staff, intramural warders, and reserve guards received instruction and had to familiarize themselves with their duties, including, if necessary, additionally with the use of weapons. Clerical staff had to undergo a training in a prison and were neither paid nor 'posted for duty until the Inspector-General of Prisons is satisfied of his fitness for an appointment' (Government of the United Provinces of Agra and Oudh 1927: 166–67). A jail conference of the Inspectors-General of Prisons held in 1939 reached a consensus that superintendents should preferably be medical officers with military and sanitary training. This consensus was probably also due to the fact that psychology was deemed important for the position in order to treat prisoners. Other 'executive and clerical staff' were expected to have at least an 'Intermediate or an examination similar to the Senior Cambridge', but should preferably have been 'Graduates' (Government of India 1939: 18). Neither the jail manual for 1927 nor the one for 1941 mentioned any training or instruction requirements for female warders. The latter jail manual, however, prescribed that female warders should be able to do the tasks of a midwife (Government of the United Provinces 1942: 309–310; Government of the United Provinces of Agra and Oudh 1927: 203–204).

What becomes evident, considering the timeline of the training programmes for members of the extramural staff, in comparison to those for convicts, is the fact that the colonial prison administration invested much more resources, in the training of convicts, than in the training of extramural staff. Early staff training appears to have been mostly centred on physically controlling the inmate population to keep it in check and prevent outbreaks of violence and escapes. The later approach to staff training was more scientific or academic, certainly a reflection of the *Zeitgeist* of the time, which if viewed optimistically had the result of an improved inmate treatment, that is treating them not as a threat that needed to be controlled by any means necessary. This marked shift in professionalization needs to be considered further, preferably on a global level, in order to assess the trajectories of staff training and the extent such training changed the penal regime.

Conclusion

Terms or notions like education, literacy training, skill development, and training were fluid categories in colonial prisons, interlinked and embedded in the everyday schedule and life, not only for labouring convicts, but also for staff, who educated and trained convicts or oversaw and planned their education and training, while themselves receiving training seemingly to a much lesser extent. Even though vocational training was implemented, skill development for convicts appears to have mostly been unstructured training. For female convicts, colonial gendered norms were reproduced in training regimes. Notably, however, female convicts seemed to have had access to literacy and training measures. The purpose of such educational and training programmes for all convicts, whether structured or not, served multiple objectives for the colonial prison administration. For the macrocosm of the colonial regime, they could, under the guise of reform and rehabilitation, serve as a portrayal of colonial incarceration, as a 'punishment with a purpose', with the aim to turn colonial subjects convicted of a crime or multiple crimes into 'proper' and 'improved' or, as stated in the opening quote, 'reformed' and 'reclaimed' citizens. Teaching convicts trades and labour techniques to improve their skills, and offering an education of sorts, which most might not have received on the outside, could appear on the surface as benevolent and altruistic. However, combined with the aim of generating and improving intra- and extramural labour to serve the microcosm of colonial prisons, such programmes served also as mechanisms of convict control. The creation of a controlled labouring body with improved skilled labour techniques was used by the colonial regime for the upkeep and management of the jails as well as for improved jail industries. Under the guise of reform, an accessible labouring body was made useful to the colonial regime. By 'reforming' convicts, they could accordingly be appropriated for the purposes of the colonial state, in a way that was comparable to the transportation of convicts to penal settlements such as the Andamans or Australia. People deemed criminals and hence not being useful to the empire were thus made productive for it.[19]

In many ways, occupational training became part of the institution, in order not only to improve the quality of products and improving the way prisons were run and maintained, but also to show that the official dogma of punishment and reform was being fulfilled. At first sight, it might seem remarkable that convicts would receive literacy training to which many people outside of prisons had no access, including, for example, at least some of the extramural staff guarding them. However, viewing literacy training through the lens of prison discipline, as a mode of control, the colonial regime created mechanisms of controlling the inmates and their minds. Inmates had their time passed, only possible in Goffman's total institutions (Goffman 1961).

For the inmate population, however, literacy training might have been a means to pass time as well as a way to receive some privileges by earning good conduct marks, and – even though in many cases probably hypothetically – to get positions within internal prison hierarchies, such as a clerk or school monitor. The extent to which such knowledge had an effect on their lives after release cannot be quantified. It is impossible to discern what the impact of such programmes for the individual convict was. What is clear is that the colonial regime benefitted on a large scale from the system of enforced and coerced skilling and education, even if the latter was at times officially voluntary. Keeping in mind the circumstances, in which such programmes were conducted, it is not possible to assess the options of choice the inmates realistically had in this deeply coerced and coercive environment.

The fact that convicts were trained in agriculture, intermittently with special reference to the district they came from, demonstrates how the microcosm of the colonial prison operated under its own logics, which were at times running counter to those of the macrocosm outside the prison walls, in which farmers, especially from rural areas, presumably did not receive such training. The prison gave the colonial regime access to parts of the population to which it might not always had access to in non-penal contexts. Even though the official reasons for training convicts in various fields were rehabilitation, 'reform', and 'reclaiming' the convicts, training a workforce to produce a large variety of commodities for sale on the extramural market, to other governmental departments, or used for the functioning of the prisons, all at very low cost, seems another objective. Furthermore, the fact that the majority of the staff members were assisted by convicts in their tasks, who needed other qualifications, such as good conduct marks in order to be able to work in certain positions, is important here, as it blurred the line between the incarcerators and the incarcerated.

What this study also shows is that at least parts of the modes of control which prevailed in colonial prisons as well as the logics of a labour market were at times intertwined with colonial penal logics. The history of different modes of skilling and skill development in colonial prisons needs further inquiry. A more global and connected analysis of colonial prison labour through the prism of education, training, and skill development seems pertinent in order to better understand the inner workings of colonial prisons, as it underlines the importance of prison labour and the need for certain crafts and industries for colonial regimes and its prisons.

Notes

1 I am grateful to the editors and the anonymous reviewers for their comments. This research would not have been possible without the generous support of the German Research Council (Deutsche Forschungsgemeinschaft).

2 This was not unique to the mainland of British India; see for example: Chisholm (1991); see also: Sen (2000: 89–90).

3 *Devanagari* is a script mainly used in North India and Nepal in languages such as Hindi, Nepali, and Sanskrit.

4 According to Nesfield, John Collinson, United Provinces of Agra and Oudh [India]. Education Dept 1885, the Ahir caste (female variant Ahirin) was classified as shepherds and the Chamar (female variant Chamarin) caste as artisan "hide-skinner and tanner" (p. 20); some Chamarin worked as midwives (p. 43), the Kumhar (female variant Kumharin) as 'potters'; Pathans were classified as Muslims, and Thakurs (female form Thakurain), was defined as a honorific title for Chattri (p. 46).

5 Dacoity roughly translates as a form of banditry. A *tahasildar* was a collector of revenue. The report by Woodcock did not list the number of female convicts separately; therefore, no information as to how many women were incarcerated in the jail at the time is available. According to the 1853 census there were 367,836 female inhabitants living in Mainpuri district, that is 44.2% of the total population. However, this number 'was obtained by applying to the total number of houses, the averages deduced in the manner suggested in the instructions' (Christian 1854: 273). For another report on the literacy programme in Mainpuri jail, see: Reid 1852: 130–31.

6 In the following, central jail will be abbreviated CJ when in conjunction with a place name.

7 For prisons and the 1857–58 uprising, see: Anderson 2007.

8 A gradation of literacy skills was introduced in the yearly prison administration reports from 1870 to 1891. With the abolition of the literacy programme for convict adults, the literacy skills on admission, divided, as before 1870 into being illiterate, able to read, able to write, and able to read and write was incorporated in more general statistics on 'religion [,] age, and previous occupation': Clark 1871: 12B; Tyler 1892: 16, 1893: 12 A.

9 For reformatories for children, see: Sen 2005.

10 See pages 22–25 of the same report (Bareilly CJ) for details on skill development and literacy programmes in this central jail. For an outline of the development of a curriculum, see pages 22–25 of the same report for details on skill development and literacy programmes in this central jail. The disparaging and very discriminating language, especially expressed on page 24, is a poignant example for the interplay of the literacy programmes and 'reform'. For an outline of the development of a curriculum, see: Sen 2004: 90.
11 The rules for the reduction of good conduct marks are also listed in the annual prison administration report for the year 1863: Walker 1864: 22–23.
12 A *rais* was a person of high rank or social status, a *zamindar* was a landowner.
13 See Singha (2007) for the jail labour corps, including the recruitment of juvenile prisoners, also for serving the military outside Mesopotamia; see also: Singha (2020: esp. Chapter 3).
14 For female jails in the Panjab, see Sen (2002).
15 It should be noted that the members of this committee were against educational programmes, as they thought they would not only be too expensive, but also unfair to the non-incarcerated population: Committee on Prison-Discipline (1838: 117).
16 There is a vast corpus on women, labour, and education of women in colonial India; see for example: Sen (1999); Sinha et al. (2019); disparaging notions for poor women were used not only in the colony, but also in the metropole and globally; see for example: Zedner (1991a, 1991b).
17 For the prison industry see also: McGowan (2013); Rai Waits (2017); Swaminathan (1995); Yang (2023).
18 For an earlier discussion on the introduction of jail training schools, see also: Government of Bengal (1928: 10); Government of India (1926: 23–24, 1934: 11, 1939: 18); Government of the United Provinces (1930: 10).
19 See for example: De Vito et al. (2018).

References

Anderson, C. 2007. 'Sepoys, Servants and Settlers: Convict Transportation in the Indian Ocean, 1787–1945', in F. Dikötter and I. Brown (eds.), *Cultures of Confinement: A History of the Prison in Africa, Asia and Latin America*, pp. 186–220. London: Hurst and Company.

Arnold, D. 2015. 'Labouring for the Raj: Convict Work Regimes in Colonial India, 1836–1939', in C. G. De Vito and A. Lichtenstein (eds.), *Global Convict Labour*, pp. 199–221. Leiden [u.a.]: Brill.

Bailey, V. 1997. 'English Prisons, Penal Culture, and the Abatement of Imprisonment, 1895–1922', *Journal of British Studies*, 36(July): 285–324.

Chisholm, L. 1991. 'Education, Punishment and the Contradictions of Penal Reform: Alan Paton and Diepkloof Reformatory, 1934–1948', *Journal of Southern African Studies*, 17(1): 23–42.

Christian, G. J. 1854. *Report on the Census of the North West Provinces of the Bengal Presidency, Taken on the 1st of January 1853*, archive.org, online. Available online at: https://archive.org/details/in.ernet.dli.2015.195618/page/n7/mode/2up.

Clark, S. 1861. *Prison Returns of the North Western Provinces, for 1860*, British Library, London (IOR/V/24/2029).

Clark, S. 1862. *Annual Report, with Tabular Statements, for the Year Ending on 31st December, 1861 on the Condition & Management of the Jails in the North Western Provinces*, British Library, London (IOR/V/24/2030).

Clark, S. 1863. *A Manual of Jail Discipline and Economy, for the Use of Officers in Charge of Jails in the North-Western Provinces*, British Library, London

(IOR/V/27/171/89). Available online at: https://www.google.co.in/books/edition/A_Manual_of_Jail_Discipline_and_Economy/cJleAAAAcAAJ?hl=de&gbpv=0.
Clark, S. 1865. *Annual Report, with Tabular Statements, for the Year Ending on 31st December, 1864 on the Condition & Management of the Jails in the North Western Provinces*, British Library, London (IOR/V/24/2030).
Clark, S. 1868. *Annual Report, with Tabular Statements, for the Year Ending on 31st December, 1867 on the Condition & Management of the Jails in the North Western Provinces*, British Library, London (IOR/V/24/2031).
Clark, S. 1869. *Annual Report, with Tabular Statements, for the Year Ending on 31st December, 1868 on the Condition & Management of the Jails in the North Western Provinces*, British Library, London (IOR/V/24/2031).
Clark, S. 1871. *Annual Report, with Tabular Statements, for the Year Ending on 31st December, 1870, on the Condition & Management of the Jails in the North Western Provinces*, British Library, London (IOR/V/24/2033).
Clarke, S. 1861. *Prison Returns of the North Western Provinces, for 1860 [1859]*, British Library, London (IOR/V/24/2029).
Clarke, S. 1889. *Annual Report, with Tabular Statements, for the Year Ending on 31st December, 1888, on the Condition & Management of the Jails in the North Western Provinces and Oudh*, British Library, London (IOR/V/24/2036).
Clements, L.-CJ. 1924. *Annual Report on the Condition and Management of the Jails in the United Provinces, with Tabular Statements, for the Year Ended 31st December 1923*, British Library, London (IOR/V/24/2040).
Clements, L.-CJ. 1925. *Annual Report on the Condition and Management of the Jails in the United Provinces, with Tabular Statements, for the Year Ended 31st December 1924*, British Library, London (IOR/V/24/2040).
Clements, L.-CJ. 1926. *Annual Report on the Condition and Management of the Jails in the United Provinces, with Tabular Statements, for the Year Ended 31st December 1925*, British Library, London (IOR/V/24/2040).
Clements, L.-CJ. 1927. *Annual Report on the Condition and Management of the Jails in the United Provinces, with Tabular Statements, for the Year Ended 31st December 1926*, British Library, London (IOR/V/24/2040).
Clements, L.-CJ. 1928. *Annual Report on the Condition and Management of the Jails in the United Provinces, with Tabular Statements, for the Year Ended 31st December 1927*, British Library, London (IOR/V/24/2040).
Clements, L.-CJ. 1929. *Annual Report on the Condition and Management of the Jails in the United Provinces, with Tabular Statements, for the Year Ended 31st December 1928*, British Library, London (IOR/V/24/2041).
Clements, L.-CJ. 1930. *Annual Report on the Condition and Management of the Jails in the United Provinces, with Tabular Statements, for the Year Ended 31st December 1929*, British Library, London (IOR/V/24/2041).
Committee on Prison-Discipline. 1838. *Report of the Committee on Prison-Discipline to the Governor General of India, in Council Dated the Eighth of January, 1838*, British Library, London (IOR/F/4/1770/72749).
De Vito, C. G., Anderson, C. and Bosma, U. 2018. 'Transportation, Deportation and Exile: Perspectives from the Colonies in the Nineteenth and Twentieth Centuries', *International Review of Social History*, 63(S26): 1–24.
Dimmers, M. 2023. 'Caught in-Between: Coerced Intermediaries in the Jails of Colonial India', *International Review of Social History*, 68(S31): 237–251.
Foucault, M. 1979. *Discipline and Punish: The Birth of the Prison*. New York: Vintage Books.
Goffman, E. 1961. *Asylums: Essays on the Social Situation of Mental Patients and Other Inmates*. Harmondsworth, England: Penguin Books.
Government of Bengal. 1928. *Proceedings of the Third Conference of Inspector-General of Prisons Held at Calcutta*, British Library, London (IOR/L/PJ/6/1961, File 2014).

Government of India. 1926. *Proceedings of the Second Conference of Inspector-General of Prisons held in the Madras Presidency*, October 22 to November 7, 1925. British Library, London (IOR/L/PJ/6/1927, File 2433).
Government of India. 1929. *Report of the United Provinces Jails Inquiry Committee*, British Library, London (IOR/V/26/170/5).
Government of India. 1934. *Proceedings of Fifth All-India Conferences of Inspectors-General of Prisons, New Delhi*, British Library, London (IOR/L/PJ/8/487).
Government of India. 1939. *Proceedings of Sixth All-India Conferences of Inspectors-General of Prisons, New Delhi, 1939*, British Library, London (IOR/L/PJ/8/487).
Government of the United Provinces. 1930. *Proceedings of the Fourth All-India Conference of the Inspector-General of Prisons Held at Lucknow*, British Library, London (IOR/L/PJ/6/2009, File 3642).
Government of the United Provinces. 1942. *United Provinces Jail Manual. Containing the Rules, for the Superintendence and Management of Jails in the United Provinces, Revised Edition 1941*, British Library, London (IOR/V/27/171/95).
Government of the United Provinces of Agra and Oudh. 1927. *United Provinces Jail Manual, Revised Edition 1927*, British Library, London (IOR/V/27/171/93).
Hall, L.-CGC. 1897. *Annual Report on the Condition & Management of the Jails in the N.-W. Provinces and Oudh, with Tabular Statements, for the Year Ended 31st December 1896*, British Library, London (IOR/V/24/2037).
Henderson, L.-CS. 1917. *Annual Report on the Condition and Management of the Jails in the United Provinces, with Tabular Statements, for the Year Ended 31st December 1916*, British Library, London (IOR/V/24/2039).
Ignatieff, M. 1978. *A Just Measure of Pain: The Penitentiary in the Industrial Revolution 1750 1850*. London: Macmillan Press.
Jafarey, L.-CM. 1947. *Report on the Prison Administration of the United Provinces, for the Year 1945*, British Library, London (IOR/V/24/2042).
Jails Committee. 1921. *Report of the Indian Jails Committee 1919–20, Vol I Report and Appendices*, archive.org, online (ark:/13960/t6n01f41c). Available online at: https://archive.org/details/eastindiajailsco01indi/page/n3/mode/2up?view=theater.
MacTaggart, M. C. 1900. *Annual Report on the Condition & Management of the Jails in the N.-W. Provinces and Oudh, with Tabular Statements, for the Year Ended 31st December 1899*, British Library, London (IOR/V/24/2037).
MacTaggart, M. C. 1902. *Rules for the Management and Discipline of Prisoners in the N.-W. Provinces and Oudh*, British Library, London (IOR/V/27/171/91).
MacTaggart, M. C. 1910. *Annual Report on the Condition & Management of the Jails in the United Provinces, with Tabular Statements, for the Year Ended 31st December 1909*, British Library, London (IOR/V/24/2038).
McGowan, A. 2013. 'Convict Carpets: Jails and the Revival of Historic Carpet Design in Colonial India', *The Journal of Asian Studies*, 72(2): 391–416.
Nesfield, J. C. United Provinces of Agra and Oudh [India]. Education Dept. 1885. *Brief View of the Caste System of the North-Western Provinces and Oudh*, archive.org, online (ark:/13960/t7xk9jp8t). Available online at: https://archive.org/details/BriefViewOfTheCasteSystemOfTheNorth-westernProvincesAndOudh/page/n1/mode/2up.
Oberai, G. R. 1948. *Report on the Prison Administration of the United Provinces, for the Year 1946*, British Library, London (IOR/V/24/2042).
Palmer, L.-CC. 1931. *Annual Report on the Condition and Management of the Jails in the United Provinces, with Tabular Statements, for the Year Ended 31st December 1930*, British Library, London (IOR/V/24/2041).
Palmer, L.-CC. 1932. *Annual Report on the Condition and Management of the Jails in the United Provinces, with Tabular Statements, for the Year Ended 31st December 1931*, British Library, London (IOR/V/24/2041).

Palmer, L.-CC. 1933. *Annual Report on the Condition and Management of the Jails in the United Provinces, with Tabular Statements, for the Year Ended 31st December 1932*, British Library, London (IOR/V/24/2041).
Palmer, L.-CC. 1934. *Annual Report on the Condition and Management of the Jails in the United Provinces, with Tabular Statements, for the Year Ending December 31, 1933*, British Library, London (IOR/V/24/2041).
Rai Waits, M. 2017. 'Carceral Capital: The Prison Industrial Complex in Colonial India', in P. Haughey (ed.), *Across Space and Time: Architecture and the Politics of Modernity*, pp. 19–45. New Brunswick, NJ: Transaction Publishers.
Reid, H. S. 1852. *Report on Indigenous Education and Vernacular Schools in Agra, Aligarh, Bareli, Etawah, Farrukhabad, Mainpuri, Mathura, Shahjahanpur, for 1850–51*, archive.org.
Salamat Ullah, M. H. 1935. *Report on the Prison Administration of the United Provinces, for the Year 1934*, British Library, London (IOR/V/24/2042).
Salamat Ullah, M. H. 1936. *Report on the Prison Administration of the United Provinces, for the Year 1935*, British Library, London (IOR/V/24/2042).
Salamat Ullah, M. H. 1937. *Report on the Prison Administration of the United Provinces, for the Year 1936*, British Library, London (IOR/V/24/2042).
Salamat Ullah, M. H. 1938. *Report on the Prison Administration of the United Provinces, for the Year 1937*, British Library, London (IOR/V/24/2042).
Salamat Ullah, M. H. 1939. *Report on the Prison Administration of the United Provinces, for the Year 1938*, British Library, London (IOR/V/24/2042).
Salamat Ullah, M. H. 1940. *Report on the Prison Administration of the United Provinces, for the Year 1939*, British Library, London (IOR/V/24/2042).
Sen, S. 1999. *Women and Labour in Late Colonial India: The Bengal Jute Industry*. Cambridge: Cambridge University Press.
Sen, S. 2000. *Disciplining Punishment: Colonialism and Convict Society in the Andaman Islands*. New Delhi: Oxford University Press.
Sen, S. 2002. 'The Female Jails of Colonial India', *Indian Economic & Social History Review*, 39: 417–438.
Sen, S. 2004. 'A Separate Punishment: Juvenile Offenders in Colonial India', *The Journal of Asian Studies*, 63(1): 81–104.
Sen, S. 2005. *Colonial Childhoods: The Juvenile Periphery of India 1850–1945*. London: Anthem.
Shaikh, A. H. 1941. *Report on the Prison Administration of the United Provinces, for the Year 1940*, British Library, London (IOR/V/24/2042).
Shaikh, A. H. 1942. *Report on the Prison Administration of the United Provinces, for the Year 1941*, British Library, London (IOR/V/24/2042).
Shaikh, A. H. 1945. *Report on the Prison Administration of the United Provinces, for the Year 1944*, British Library, London (IOR/V/24/2042).
Singha, R. 2007. 'Finding Labor from India for the War in Iraq: The Jail Porter and Labor Corps, 1916–1920', *Comparative Studies in Society and History*, 49(2): 412–445.
Singha, R. 2020. *The Coolie's Great War: Indian Labour in a Global Conflict, 1914–1921*. London: Hurst & Company.
Sinha, N., Varma, N. and Jha, P. (eds.). 2019. *Servants' Pasts: Late-Eighteenth to Twentieth-Century South Asia*. Hyderabad: Orient Blackswan.
Swaminathan, P. 1995. 'Prison as Factory: A Study of Jail Manufactures in the Madras Presidency', *Studies in History*, 11: 77–100.
Thornhill, C. B. 1853. *Report of the Inspector General of Prisons, North-Western Provinces, for the Year 1852*, British Library, London (IOR/V/24/2029).
Thornhill, C. B. 1854. *Report of the Inspector General of Prisons, North Western Provinces, for the Year 1853*, British Library, London (IOR/V/24/2029).

Thornhill, C. B. 1855. *Report of the Inspector General of Prisons, North Western Provinces, for the Year 1854*, British Library, London (IOR/V/24/2029).
Tyler, J. W. 1892. *Annual Report on the Condition & Management of the Jails in the N.-W. Provinces and Oudh, with Tabular Statements, for the Year Ended 31st December 1891*, British Library, London (IOR/V/24/2037).
Tyler, J. W. 1893. *Annual Report on the Condition & Management of the Jails in the N.-W. Provinces and Oudh, with Tabular Statements, for the Year Ended 31st December 1892*, British Library, London (IOR/V/24/2037).
Tyler, J. W. 1894. *Annual Report on the Condition & Management of the Jails in the N.-W. Provinces and Oudh, with Tabular Statements, for the Year Ended 31st December 1893*, British Library, London (IOR/V/24/2037).
Tyler, J. W. 1896. *Annual Report on the Condition & Management of the Jails in the N.-W. Provinces and Oudh, with Tabular Statements, for the Year Ended 31st December 1895*, British Library, London (IOR/V/24/2037).
United Provinces of Agra and Oudh (India). Jail Department. 1915. *Jail Manual of the United Provinces of Agra and Oudh*, British Library, London (Asia, Pacific & Africa V 3420).
Walker, W. 1863. *Annual Report, with Tabular Statements, for the Year Ending on 31st December, 1862, on the Condition & Management of the Jails in the North Western Provinces*, British Library, London (IOR/V/24/2030).
Walker, W. 1864. *Annual Report, with Tabular Statements, for the Year Ending on 31st December, 1863, on the Condition & Management of the Jails in the North Western Provinces*, British Library, London (IOR/V/24/2030).
Walker, W. and Lethbridge, A. S. 1889. *Report of the Committee Appointed under the Orders of the Governor General in Council to Enquire into Certain Matters Connected, with Jail Administration in India, with Appendices*, British Library, London (IOR/V/26/170/2).
Walker, W. M. 1872. *Annual Report, with Tabular Statements, for the Year Ending on 31st December, 1871, on the Condition & Management of the Jails in the North Western Provinces*, British Library, London (IOR/V/24/2033).
Walker, W. M. 1873. *Annual Report, with Tabular Statements, for the Year Ending on 31st December, 1872, on the Condition & Management of the Jails in the North Western Provinces*, British Library, London (IOR/V/24/2033).
Walker, W. M. 1874. *Annual Report, with Tabular Statements, for the Year Ending on 31st December, 1873, on the Condition & Management of the Jails in the North Western Provinces*, British Library, London (IOR/V/24/2032).
Walker, W. M. 1875. *Annual Report, with Tabular Statements, for the Year Ending on 31st December, 1874, on the Condition & Management of the Jails in the North Western Provinces*, British Library, London (IOR/V/24/2032).
Walker, W. M. 1882. *Rules for the Management and Discipline in the North-Western Provinces and Oudh*, British Library, London (IOR/V/27/171/90).
Woodcock, W. H. 1852. *Report of the Inspector of Prisons on the Management of the Jails, from 1845 to 1851, and on the Present State of Prison Discipline in the North Western Provinces*, British Library, London (IOR/V/24/2029).
Yang, A. A. 2023. 'The Prison-Handicraft Complex: Convict Labour in Colonial India', *Modern Asian Studies*, 57: 808–834.
Zedner, L. 1991a. *Women, Crime, and Custody in Victorian England*. Oxford: Clarendon.
Zedner, L. 1991b. 'Women, Crime, and Penal Responses: A Historical Account', *Crime and Justice*, 14: 307–362.

4

PRACTICING SKILLS, PROCESSING SKINS

Urdu manuals on developing tanning as a rural trade (1940–46)

Soheb Niazi

Introduction

The crucial role of language as a pedagogical tool in the dissemination of technical education is undeniable, yet it has also represented a significant hurdle in the quest for knowledge in India. The ongoing emphasis on skill development in India prioritizes market-oriented training for the youth.[1] Although there is a drive to incorporate 'employability' skills, including proficiency in English, into technical education curricula, there is an implicit recognition that effectively acquiring and applying these skills remains challenging without a parallel effort to offer curricula in local and regional languages.[2]

This chapter revisits pedagogical efforts to impart technical knowledge in the vernacular[3] medium, focusing on Urdu manuals on tanning and leather production published in colonial India. It explores how discourses on new scientific technologies, particularly the introduction of chrome tanning for leather production, were received, translated, and re-conceptualized in Urdu.

Innovations in chemical tanning led by Western scientists created a divergence in tanning processes and methods between Europe and local rural tanners in India. The second half of the nineteenth century witnessed the growth and commercialization of the hides and skins industry, driven by an export market for Indian raw and semi-tanned hides (Bhattacharya, 2013; Roy, 1994). This commercialization, coupled with the adoption of chemical tanning, led to the emergence of new hierarchies within the leather industry. Butchers, hide suppliers, contractors, agents, tannery owners, and merchants formed a thriving network in the early decades of the twentieth century in India.

Following the boom in export trade, the establishment of chrome tanning-based tanneries and leather goods factories progressed gradually, mainly in

DOI: 10.4324/9781003604846-5

industrial cities such as Kanpur, Madras, and Calcutta. However, by the late 1930s and the 1940s, there was a growing recognition of the importance of developing rural industries for the progress of the 'nation in making'. It was this broad context that the Anjuman-e Taraqqi-e Urdu published manuals in Urdu to promote the adoption of chrome tanning methods in the rural countryside. Founded in 1903 in Aligarh and later relocated to Aurangabad in 1913 with the support of the princely state of Hyderabad, the Anjuman was a prominent Urdu publisher in the twentieth century. Abdul Haq, the organization's founder, led the effort to promote Urdu as a medium for scientific knowledge, aligning it with the progress of the nation (Haq, 1951).

Abdul Haq and his associates persuaded Imdad Ali, the manager of the Gwalior State's leather factory in Morar, to write articles on chrome tanning for the Anjuman's popular Urdu magazine, *Science*. These articles were developed into two Urdu manuals, *M'adnī Dabāġat* (mineral-based tanning) and *Nabātī Dabāġat* (vegetable-based tanning).[4] These manuals aimed to address a new readership from the *dihāt* (rural countryside) interested in practical work associated with the setting up of tanneries based on chrome tanning methods.

Based on a close reading of these Urdu manuals and insights from the debates on the history of science in colonial India, this chapter attempts to expand the discourse on technical education on tanning and leather production. It goes beyond the discourses of the technical institutes and schools founded by the colonial government to include perspectives that emerged from practitioners of the 'craft' such as Imdad Ali. Despite being written in Urdu, intended for a rural audience, these manuals are deeply rooted in the specific context of the twentieth-century development of chrome tanning methods. Consequently, understanding the tanning industry's specific context at the eve of the World War II is essential to grasp the publisher's objectives and Imdad Ali's proposals presented in these manuals. The chapter also underscores Imdad Ali's model of apprenticeship for the development of the rural industry, where the *māhir-e fann* or master craftsman leads the practicing and perfecting of skills associated with the *fann-e dabāġat* (craft of tanning).

This chapter is further divided into five sections. The first section offers a concise history of chrome tanning's development, providing context for Imdad Ali's manuals in the backdrop of the discussion on technical education in colonial India. The second section provides a brief overview of debates in the history of science and discusses Imdad Ali's specific use of Urdu terminologies in the context of various theoretical distinctions between craft and skill. The third section delves into the detailed publishing history and content of Imdad Ali's manuals. The fourth section focuses on analysing the 'skills' imparted by these manuals and their emphasis on the 'practice' of the craft, as well as the practical aspects of tanning processes. Finally, the last section explores Imdad Ali's proposed model for the organizational structure of rural industries and examines the usage and description of different skill hierarchies associated with specific labour processes that emerged with the introduction of chrome tanning in India.

Development of chrome tanning as a 'science' in colonial India

The escalation in the international demand for hides, skins, and semi-finished leather prompted a significant expansion and commercialization of the India's leather trade and industry. In the latter half of the nineteenth century, India witnessed a remarkable surge in export trade which escalated from Rs. 45 million in 1860 to Rs. 60 million in 1890 (Bhattacharya, 2018; Roy, 1994). This expansion in export trade did not diminish domestic rural-urban trade; instead, it brought about substantial changes in the processes of obtaining hides and skins involved with the flaying of carcasses and modifications in tanning methods. These changes were further accelerated by the introduction of new technological innovations, leading to the development of chrome tanning methods. These innovations gradually began to compete with traditional vegetable tanning methods without completely replacing them.

Scientists from Austria, Germany, and the USA pioneered advancements in tanning methods for raw hides and skins.[5] These innovations were driven by the growing demand to shorten the tanning process. The introduction of chemicals in pre-tanning and tanning processes reduced the time required, allowing for diverse leather production in terms of colour, texture, and elasticity, and established chrome tanning as a profitable scientific endeavour. The changes in the tanning process demanded the acquisition of new skills and knowledge, specifically an understanding of chemicals and the principles of chemistry. This shift necessitated a departure from the traditional skills associated with the craft of tanning that were handed down by 'communities of skills' over generations (Rai, 2022). The reduction of the time required for the tanning process highlighted chrome tanning's potential to amass higher profits, and its promotion in colonial India underscored the nexus of science and capital in the development of leather technology (Bhattacharya, 2018, 315).

At the eve of the introduction of chrome tanning methods during the first quarter of the twentieth century, the hides and skins industry could be classified into three main groups. Colonial reports, which documented various industries and detailed their work processes, typically classified it according to three criteria, first, in terms of trade – whether the processed hides and skins were meant for domestic supply or for export trade; second, according to the method deployed in the tanning process – the bag or pit methods; or third, according to the size of the tanneries, which led to a variations in the tanning process – large tanneries established in and around cities such as

Madras, Kanpur, Calcutta, medium sized with eight to ten workers or small household based tanneries that proliferated in rural areas (Chatterton, 1904; Walton, 1903; Chandra 1904; Martin, 1903).

Before the advent of chrome tanning methods, pre-tanning processes, including flaying, washing, liming, unhairing on the beam, bating, and scudding, followed similar principles across regions with slight variations. However, with the introduction of chrome tanning, while pre-tanning processes mostly remained unchanged, the tanning process underwent significant transformation.[6] In the traditional bag or pit methods, the use of vegetable materials, like the bark of *babul*, *myrabolam*, *tarwad*, or other plants prolonged the tanning process, as hides were immersed in successive pits with varying tanning solutions for several months. In the chrome tanning process, hides were pickled in a solution of sulphuric acid and salt or alum and salt. With the development of the 'single bath' process, the tanning time was reduced to just a few days. In India, currying or dressing of tanned hides was not common, as the majority of the export market consisted of 'semi-tanned' hides and skins. However, chrome-tanned leather gradually gained traction in the domestic market for finished leather goods. In this scenario, tanned hides underwent additional processes such as dressing or 'currying,' which included shaving, drying, machine staking, polishing, and dyeing to produce finished leather goods.

The introduction of chemicals into the tanning process and the subsequent development of advanced work processes resulted in the establishment of new hierarchy of skills. This was accompanied by a devaluation of certain skills associated with the 'traditional' craft of tanning. Shahana Bhattacharya's research shows how technical education in leather production, both in these institutes and more broadly, reinforced stigma and caste hierarchies associated with leatherwork and re-calibrated notions of skill to align them with the requirements of global capitalism (Bhattacharya, 2018). Her study compellingly argues that the process of 'deskilling' leather workers was enabled by a valorization of theoretical scientific knowledge of leather production and the simultaneous downgrading of practical knowledge and experience of workers at the shop floor. The invention of chrome tanning and the utilization of chemicals in the tanning process intensified an ongoing tension between two distinct perspectives on knowledge. One perspective elevated the leather chemist as the new industry expert, while the other emphasized the practical knowledge and experience acquired by working in tanneries as the domain of the master craftsman.

The process of 'deskilling' in the craft of tanning became notably evident when efforts were made to introduce chrome tanning methods in the rural areas; however, the adoption of these methods initially remained slow and gradual. The report on village tanning in the Bombay Presidency in 1930 noted, 'Though science has come to the aid of the Tanning industry in the West, most of the tanning work in this Presidency is still done by purely empirical and "the rule of thumb" methods' (Gaitonde, 1930, 13). The use of mechanical power was limited to only 3 out of 50 tanneries in the Presidency; the rest employed about 10 workmen who worked in one storied building that were in the form of a shed around a courtyard (Gaitonde, 1930, 13). Out of these three there was only one tannery that manufactured chrome leather only; the other two produced both vegetable and chrome leather; however, the latter were noted to lack 'scientific' guidance. Similarly, the 1930 report of the Hides Cess Enquiry Committee, noted that only about half a dozen tanneries were manufacturing finished leather goods and of these only two or three were large factories equipped with modern machinery.[7] The slow growth of tanneries that were mechanized or focused on finished leather goods was due to the huge proportion of raw and 'half tanned' hides that formed the largest share of the export trade.

At the eve of World War II, there was a marked decline in the share of hides and skins that were exported out of India. Out of the total exports of 10.344 million pieces in 1938–39, raw hides contributed to 5.5 million pieces, reduced from 11.4 million pieces in 1913–14.[8] During the same period, on account of the development of chrome tanning, the proportion of unwrought leather as export had increased from 35,000 pieces in 1913–14 to 8,40,000 pieces in 1938–39.[9] In terms of the share of hides and skins available for utilisation in India (17.5 million pieces in 1938–39), only 3.1 million pieces of hides were fully tanned for the manufacture of finished leather goods, out of which 2.1 million pieces (0.12%) were chrome tanned. The report of the marketing of hides in 1943 noted that, 'the tanneries adopting chrome tanning, although large individually, are not more than a dozen in India'.[10] In Calcutta, however, there emerged several Chinese tanneries that produced chrome leather at a cottage industry scale, and it was estimated that they utilised 0.3 million pieces of hides annually. In fact, in Calcutta (like in Kanpur), during the period of World War II, there was a boom in the number of leather goods factories that rose in number from 3,553 in 1939 to 9410 in 1944.[11] In these leather goods factories, the hierarchies of wage labour that were produced were markedly different from the rural and town based smaller tanneries. The factories included a long list of 'skilled' and 'unskilled' workers that were referred by various tasks and paid wages accordingly. Thus, the scourers, shavers, and fleshers were paid higher wages than the lesser skilled scudders or stakers or the unskilled coolies or handlers who were paid the lowest wages.[12]

The new hierarchies between skill and labour that the new chrome-based tanning methods produced posed significant challenges due to existing knowledge practices and the limited availability of chemicals and infrastructure for chrome tanning. These inadequacies, both material and structural, within the rural setup of tanning industries are evident in the discourse surrounding the definition of artisanal crafts and industries in general, and specifically in the context of tanning processes.

Imdad Ali's tanning manuals emerged in this background of the development of chrome tanning in India, which had a slow and gradual start in the larger cities. These manuals primarily focused on the *'amal* or 'practice' of the various tanning processes and their *'amlī* (practical) aspects. The model for the organizational structure of a rural industry based on chrome tanning methods that Imdad Ali proposes has the *māhir-e fann* or the 'master craftsman' taking a central role in practicing and perfecting the skills associated with the *fann-e dabāġat* (craft of tanning).

Before a detailed and close analysis of Imdad Ali's manuals, it is useful to contextualize their specific usage of Urdu terminology within the broader context of debates surrounding the history of science in the vernacular and the understanding of various distinctions between knowledge and skills associated with artisanal crafts.

Crafting skill: from art to science

As modern scientific methods and technologies were introduced and institutionalized in non-Western and colonial contexts, they also gave rise to local variations (Raina, 2011, 166). Historians of science, after the initial reluctance to analyse these local variations or categorizing them as pre-modern knowledge, have now embraced the examination of 'sciences as practices and bodies of knowledge, embedded in particular spatial contexts, and practiced by local actors with locally relevant political and cultural agendas' (Singh, 2021). Debates on the history of science in colonial India have witnessed a shift in frameworks of dissemination and dispersal of scientific knowledge and towards sustained attention to local agency, adaptations, and creative redeployment (Amstutz, 2023; Menon, 2021). Recent scholarship, drawing from regional language archives, has enhanced our understanding of how the interplay between colonial knowledge and indigenous knowledge unfolded in the pursuit of various scientific modernities (Lanzillo, 2021; Singh, 2022a; Singh, 2022b).

In colonial India, two aspects of local scientific knowledge are particularly relevant to this discussion: first, the translation of modern scientific methods and practices into regional and vernacular languages; second, the dissemination of scientific knowledge beyond the realm of experts or technical scientists to a broader audience through the medium of textbooks or through popular forms of writings such as magazines or journals published in various regional languages.

Imdad Ali's manuals on chrome tanning in Urdu were considered novel, as they were the first to address the 'science' of tanning in a vernacular language.[13] Nevertheless, they drew upon references from Western textbooks on the principles of chemistry.[14] However, his manuals were not mere 'translations' of these Western textbooks; instead, they emphasized the practical aspects of tanning. In this regard, they align more closely with the concept of translation as a crucial component of knowledge itself, that implies 'displacement, drift, invention, and mediation' (Raina, 2000, 57).

Imdad Ali's manuals constituted a vital component of a more extensive intellectual endeavour, which he shared with his publishers, the Anjuman-e Taraqqi-e Urdu. The Anjuman and its founder, Abdul Haq, actively promoted Urdu as a means of conveying comprehensive scientific knowledge and staking territorial claims for Urdu in the early twentieth century (Amstutz, 2017, 3; Datla, 2013). Much like other similar initiatives in various regional languages, the Anjuman aimed to disseminate scientific knowledge to a broader audience beyond experts, primarily through textbooks and popular magazines and journals.[15] It was within the pages of the Anjuman's foremost Urdu magazine, *Science*, that Imdad Ali's articles on chrome tanning methods were first published.

The prototype for science textbooks, particularly those designed for courses in Chemistry and Medicine, emerged in eighteenth-century Europe. Two distinct models of the textbooks appeared, first largely analytical in nature, while the second focused on demonstrating procedures (Raina, 200, 56). The former model pertained to pedagogical endeavours in 'pure' science, while the latter was associated with applied sciences. Imdad Ali's manuals on chrome tanning were structured in accordance with the second model, emphasizing the 'practice' and 'practical' aspects of the trade.

Translating and disseminating Western scientific knowledge into Urdu, as in the case of other regional languages, was a complex endeavour marked by tensions. Given Urdu's colonial history and its trans-local connections, the Anjuman and the intellectuals associated with it, found Urdu uniquely suitable for blending the contemporary British notion of 'science' with the traditional concept of *ulūm*. Consequently, they conceptualized Urdu *ulūm* as an integral part of the global scientific category, which was linked to, yet distinct from, provincial European 'science' (Amstutz, 2017, 16). The unresolved tensions within this project, which aimed to establish a global bridge between western science, local Indian knowledge, and older genres of Islamic learning through Urdu's connections with Persian, Arabic, and Turkish, were evident in the Anjuman's efforts to translate 'scientific' and technical terms (*Istilāḥāt*) into Urdu (Datla, 2013, 73–76; Haq, 1969).

Imdad Ali's writings are not devoid of these tensions; for him, *dabāġat* (tanning) could encompass both a 'craft' and a 'science', although his usage predominantly connotes the former.[16] In addition to the term *fann*, Imdad Ali refers to tanning as a *hirfa*, as seen in the subtitles of both the manuals – *chromī dabāġat bahaisiyat ek dehī hirfa* or chrome tanning as a rural craft.[17] Imdad Ali's description of *dabāġat* as a *fann* or craft, as opposed to a science, is also evident in his differentiation between the *māhir-e fann* and the *sciencedāṇ* (scientist) or the *kīmīyādāṇ* (chemist). The *māhir-e fann* is also distinguished from the *mālik-e kārḵẖānā* or the *kārḵẖānādār* (factory owner).

Regarding its etymology, the term *māhir* originating from the Persian word *mahārat* is employed to denote skill or expertise. Furthermore, *māhir-e fann* refers to someone who has mastered the *fann* with the highest level of skill.[18] Thus the *mahārat* or skill of the *māhir-e fann* or master craftsman is not only his knowledge of the technical aspects of tanning, but the *'amlī* (practical) aspects as well his experience of the *'amal* or 'practice' of the various processes associated with tanning. In this sense, Imdad Ali foregrounds the practical difficulties faced in setting up the chrome tanning industry in the towns and the rural countryside. In the tanneries proposed by Imdad Ali, the *māhir-e fann* or the master craftsman negotiates between scientific knowledge and artisanal craft to develop tanning as a profitable trade.

The notion of skill or *mahārat* that Imdad Ali deploys in his manuals is one that is developed through practice rather than solely rooted in scientific knowledge. In this sense, it falls under the category of tacit knowledge, regarded a crucial element of scientific knowledge as well as our broader understanding of 'making' and 'knowing' (Smith, 2014; Harris, 1992). The *māhir-e fann* or the master craftsman representing the pinnacle of skill plays a pivotal role in Imdad Ali's proposed apprenticeship model. This emphasis on apprenticeship diverges from some debates concerning the position of artisans and artisanal crafts in colonial technical education institutions and early Indian scientific discourse. These debates contrasted the apprenticeship system with the modern tutorial and evaluated hereditary skill against innovation and competitiveness (Raina and Habib, 1993, 104). However, Imdad Ali does not view the 'traditional' apprenticeship model as incompatible with modern chrome tanning methods. He believed that replicating multiple apprenticeship workshops based on the *shāgird ustād* relationship would be most beneficial for the growth of the tanning industry, thereby contributing to the nation's progress.

Imdad Ali's manuals aligned with the vision of the Anjuman and the intellectuals at Osmania. They constituted a part of a larger corpus of texts published with the aim of generating scientific and technical knowledge in Urdu, which could contribute to the advancement of local industries. These manuals were integral to a broader connection between science, capital, industry, and the concept of a nation in the making. Abdul Haq described them as appealing to individuals actively involved in the *sanatī taraqqī* (industrial progress) of the *mulk* (nation) (*M'adnī*, 1).

This association between science and capital was evident in Imdad Ali's proposed organizational structure, which acknowledged the hierarchy of skills brought about by the new chrome tanning technology. The pursuit of reducing tanning process duration, alongside the development of chrome tanning methods, led to an increased use of machinery, replacing manual labour. However, adopting chemicals in the tanning process and transitioning to machinery demanded more significant infrastructure and capital investment, which several small and medium-scale tanneries struggled to afford. The skill or *mahārat* of the *māhir-e fann* or the master craftsman was intended to serve the interests of capital and increase profitability for the progress of a native rural-based tanning industry. Notably, Imdad Ali preferred the apprenticeship model but disregarded any notion of 'community skills' or caste-based skills. While he briefly mentioned the traditional roles and skills of the *chamārs* or *qassābs* in a few instances, his understanding did not encompass skill reproduction through generational, social, and hierarchical passing of skilled labour within caste-based occupational communities (Rai, 2022).

Imdad Ali's Urdu manuals on chrome tanning

Sayyid Imdad Ali, who served as the manager of the Gwalior Estate Leather Factory in Morar, possessed several years of experience in various aspects of tanning and leather production. Known affectionately as '*Dabbāġh* Sahab' by his readers, Imdad Ali does not extensively divulge details about his own life in the texts and articles he authored.[19] The leather factory in Morar, founded in 1898, during World War I, was famed to have supplied tents, saddlery, footwear, and other leather goods to the colonial army, earning a reputation for their durability and high-quality finish (Garde, 1936, 93). As the factory manager, Imdad Ali likely maintained close ties with the government, which was the recipient of the factory's products, overseeing the production of quality leather goods.

Abdul Haq, the editor of the Urdu magazine *Science* and the president of the Anjuman Urdu Taraqqi Board, mentioned in the preface to the manual, *M'adnī Dabāġat* (1940), that Imdad Ali had been a regular contributor to their magazine for eight to ten years and had achieved expertise in both the *ilmī* (intellectual) and the *'amlī* (practical) aspects of the *fann-e dabāġat* (craft of tanning) (*M'adnī*, 1). It was Abdul Haq and his colleagues at the Anjuman-e Taraqqi-e Urdu who recruited Imdad Ali to write numerous articles for *Science* on tanning methods and processes, specifically related to chrome tanning. In the 1930s, Imdad Ali penned a series of articles for the magazine, which were subsequently compiled into two books, *M'adnī Dabāġat* (Ali, 1940) and *Nabātī Dabāġat* (1946).[20] These manuals aimed to address a new readership that included individuals interested in both 'science' and new technology, as well as those seeking practical guidance for establishing tanneries in the *dihāt* (rural countryside).[21]

The publisher of Imdad Ali's works, the Anjuman-e Taraqqi-e Urdu, shared a common vision with educators at Osmania University. This vision aimed to establish a standardized and uniform vernacular language 'that would perform a number of functions, quotidian, administrative, literary, scientific, philosophical and academic' (Datla, 2013, 58). With judicious funding from the princely state of Hyderabad, the Darul Tarjuma (Translation Bureau) was set up at the Osmania University in 1917. It attracted intellectuals from across the country and initiated an extensive programme to translate important works, curricula, and textbooks from various languages into Urdu (Datla, 2013, 63–68).[22] In the ensuing decades, Hyderabad evolved into a hub of Urdu literary production, hosting several organizations and literary presses founded by individuals associated with the Osmania University. Alongside the Anjuman, another organization, the Idara-e Adabiyat-e Urdu, founded in 1931, also played a role in Urdu literary production. However, it had a more localized focus compared to the Anjuman and consisted of founding members who had strong ties to the Osmania University (Datla, 2013, 124–129).

As previously mentioned, the Anjuman and the intellectuals associated with it viewed Urdu as a global bridge between Western science, local Indian knowledge, and traditional genres of Islamic learning in languages such as Persian, Arabic, and Turkish. With this vision in mind, the Anjuman and the Darul Tarjuma initiated the translation of 'scientific' and technical terms (*Istilāḥāt*) in Urdu (Datla, 2013, 73–76; Haq, 1969). As part of these initiatives, the Anjuman compiled several Urdu dictionaries of technical terms (*istilāḥāt*) across disciplines. These dictionaries included, the *Farhang Istilāḥāt-e I'lmīyāh* (Hasan, 1925), the Anjuman's inaugural dictionary of scientific terms; the *Farhang Istilāḥāt-e Kīmiyā* (Haq, 1939), a glossary of technical terms related to Chemistry; and the *Farhang Istilāḥāt-e Peshevarāṇ* (Dehalvi, 1933–1944), an eight-volume collection of technical terms and phrases associated with 'Hindustani' arts and industries.[23] In addition to these dictionaries, the Anjuman published a series of textbooks and manuals that encouraged home-based crafts or occupations that could provide a means of livelihood. Another publishing house, the Āzam Steam Press, published Urdu translations of English manuals that were part of training manuals in various industrial schools in America and Europe. These translations included *Hirfatī Kām* (Samiullah, 1919), a translation of Edward F. Worst's manual on craft work, and *Tālīmī Dastī Kām* (Beg, 1936), a translation of Alfred H. Jackson's manual covering various industrial crafts.[24]

Imdad Ali's manuals shared the vision of the Anjuman and the intellectuals at Osmania and his manuals were part of a larger corpus of texts published with a concern to produce scientific and technical knowledge in Urdu that could be utilised for progress of the local industry; however, as Abdul Haq, himself emphasized his book was unique as it emphasized on *'amal* (practice as well as the process) of the *fann-e dabāġhat*. Imdad Ali's manuals were part of a broader association between science, capital, industry, and the 'nation in the making'. Abdul Haq described the manuals as appealing to those who were active participants in the *sanatī taraqqī* (industrial progress) of the *mulk* (nation) (*M'adnī*, 1).

Abdul Haq and Imdad Ali often articulated the skewed relationship between Western science and technology and native industry and capital. They aimed to critique the system of scientific patents that restricted the use of science and technology to specific geographical regions in the West. Abdul Haq asserted that the times were changing (*zamāna badal rahā hai)* and that it was an economic necessity for the *mulk* (nation) to promote profitable occupations and industries. Chrome tanning was identified as one such profitable industry (*M'adnī*, 2). Similarly, Imdad Ali emphasized the importance of aligning the interests of scientists, *māhir-e fann* (master craftsmen), factory owners, and capital to promote chrome tanning. He pointed out that chrome tanning significantly reduced the time required to tan hides and skins, and such collaboration would ensure profitability (*M'adnī*, 4).

As the colonial state invested in technical knowledge and provided scholarships to Indian students for higher education in England, a select few students had the opportunity to study new and modern technologies (*M'adnī*, 9 and Bhattacharya, 2018). Nevertheless, this endeavour came at a considerable cost. Abdul Haq and Imdad Ali observed that students who pursued education abroad still lacked familiarity with the practical aspects of the craft, which could only be acquired through hands-on experience in a workshop or tannery. In the manuals, Imdad Ali frequently referred to financially disadvantaged *tālib 'ilm* (students) who couldn't afford expensive books, patented technologies, or the space needed for practical technical education. It was to these students that Imdad Ali offered both intellectual and practical guidance on the *fann-e dabāġat* (*M'adnī*, 35, 40 and 49).

To be more specific, the manuals were primarily intended for a rural audience, as Imdad Ali wrote with the aim of reaching his *dihāti bhāi* (rural brethren). This phrase was commonly used throughout the manuals when explaining various aspects related to the practice and processing of different types of skins. The composition of several chemical compounds was elucidated using terms that were local and familiar in the *dihāt*. Additionally, the processes involved were reiterated and summarized multiple times to facilitate comprehension for those who lacked technical knowledge about chemical tanning. Imdad Ali took care to ensure that both the *ajzā* (ingredients) of various chemical compounds and the *auzār* (tools) and machinery described in the manual were familiar and readily accessible to individuals in the *dihāt* (*M'adnī*, 154 and 164).

Towards the conclusion of *M'adnī*, Imdad Ali put forth a model for the organizational structure of the rural industry, aligning with his objective of 'the reform of rural industry and making use of the free time of the rural folk' (*M'adnī*, 188). Regarding the question of whether rural artisans, who typically tanned four to six skins a day, could compete with large factory owners, Imdad Ali believed that each would cater to different demands. While big factory owners primarily focused on exporting half tanned hides to Europe, the rural industry could meet the increasing local demand for finished leather goods (*M'adnī*, 189).

In this sense, both *M'adnī Dabāġat* and *Nabātī Dabāġat* were manuals that were written to promote chrome tanning as a rural industry. Based on articles published in the Urdu journal *Science,* these manuals detailed two distinct tanning methods: mineral and vegetable.[25] As mentioned earlier, the adoption of chrome tanning in India had a gradual start, with very few tanneries exclusively relying on chemical tanning; more commonly, they integrated processes involving both methods. Imdad Ali particularly emphasized this practice, especially for the benefit of his readers who were newly venturing into chrome tanning as a rural craft.

Addressing several practical difficulties that may arise during the process of tanning by using chrome salt solutions, Imdad Ali pointed out that if during the process one realised that the increased quantity of salts had led to some moisture on the skin, it was advisable to go for another round of tanning that would for instance include the bark of the babul tree. Though this would make the process of tanning longer than a purely chrome tanned skin, Imdad Ali insisted that this was still faster than a method that was purely based on vegetable-based raw materials and termed this method of tanning as 'mineral and vegetable mixed tanning' (*M'adnī*, 62–64). The emphasis on this mixed method as a practical alternative was in sharp contrast to the distinctions made by British experts to connote these two different methods as, 'traditional' and 'modern' used by the native' and European tanners respectively (Walton, Chatterton, 102 and Watts, 1908, 605).

Imdad Ali's manual took into consideration the initial apprehensions of Indian tanners, some of whom were hesitant to shift to the new methods. They expressed their concerns by pointing out that the *āb-o hawā* (climate) in India was not conducive to chrome tanning (*M'adnī*, 8; Bhattacharya, 2018, 314). The shift to chrome tanning required the use of expensive chemicals that were not readily available and required to be imported. Drawing from this practical experience in managing the Morar factory, Imdad Ali recognized the legitimacy of these concerns. He noted that several factories had failed in their attempts to shift to chrome tanning, resulting in their closure (*M'adnī*, 11 and 188). Thus, Imdad Ali insisted that his objective was not limited to proposing these ideas on paper; he believed that without experiencing the practical challenges associated with adopting the new tanning methods, such proposals would be of no benefit to the country (*M'adnī*, 188).

Another concern contributing to the hesitancy of tanners who relied on vegetable-based tanning was the fear that the introduction of chemical tanning would threaten the survival of their industry and hinder their ability to compete with this new technology (*Nabātī,* 20). However, as previously emphasized, this fear was unfounded. Chrome tanning did not completely supplant the traditional tanning processes. Instead, as Imdad Ali meticulously elaborated in his detailed and vivid descriptions of the tanning processes, both methods were employed in their respective ways to expedite the tanning process.

The two manuals share several similarities. Although they emphasize different tanning methods, as previously mentioned, the various processes associated with these methods often exhibit more similarities than differences. Both manuals commence with a brief history of the *fann-e dabāġat* (*M'adnī*, 3–12 and *Nabātī,* 7–28). Imdad Ali noted that in the Western tradition, before delving into the specifics of any *fann*, one must begin by tracing its history (*Nabātī,* 9). He explained the reasons behind using the term *dabāġat* to describe the tanning process.[26] In colloquial Hindustani, the phrase, *chamrā pakānā* (literally, cooking leather) was commonly employed to refer to the English term 'tanning' (*Nabātī,* 9). *Dabāġhat,* on the other hand, specifically denoted the practice of cleaning and decorating animal skin. According to Imdad Ali, it was a more appropriate choice than the colloquial phrase, which he regarded as highly misleading.

This discussion of the etymological roots of the different terms in Urdu and English sets the stage for the unresolved tensions between various tanning methods and the hierarchies of skills that emerge from the associated work and labour practices. For Imdad Ali, the history of tanning dates back to pre-historic times when humans began to use animal skin for clothing. He proceeds to narrate the history of tanning and the utilization of leather in the Rig Veda, the practices of mummification in Egypt, the export of Moroccan leather to Spain in the eighth and ninth centuries, and scientific advancements in modern Europe and America to arrive at the *jadīd tarīqā-e dabāġat* (modern method of tanning).

M'adnī Dabāġat is organized into ten chapters, each dedicated to the flaying, tanning, and curing of skins and hides of various animals including small birds, squirrels, deer, goats, sheep, bulls, buffaloes, and cows. The manual provides detailed explanations of the technical aspects involved in the labour-intensive processes of tanning, complemented by an extensive use of diagrams, sketches, and photographs. Additionally, as an appendix, the book offers valuable information for rural practitioners who wish to establish their own workshops or expand their businesses. This section includes a list of merchants across the country who supply various chemicals and a tariff rate list for the chemicals used in the tanning process (*M'adnī*, 157–163). The book concludes with a proposed model for the organizational structure of a rural industry that can be adopted and replicated in different regions of the country (*M'adnī*, 184–190).

Nabātī Dabāġat was published in 1946, six years after the publication of the first manual. To establish his legacy, Imdad Ali stated that since the publication of the first book, he had received numerous letters of appreciation, and several individuals had expressed their desire to become his *shāgird* (apprentice) (*Nabātī,* 5). He declared that it was for their benefit that he decided to write a full-length book on methods based on vegetable raw materials. Some chapters of this manual had previously appeared as articles in various issues of the magazine, *Science*. This manual was twice the length of the first one, consisting of 24 chapters. One of these chapters elaborated on various vegetable-based tanning materials, primarily different trees whose barks could be utilized for tanning purposes (*Nabātī,* 125–150). The primary focus of this manual was also on the practical aspects of the trade. It provided detailed information on topics such as the construction of the building and structure of the *kārkhāna* (workshop or factory) (*Nabātī,* 29–73). Several chapters in the manual addressed specific stages in the tanning process and the corresponding spaces required within the tanning unit. These spaces included a large *hauz* (tank) for water, a storage space for raw materials, a warehouse for skin washing, lime storage, and old and fat-related processes. Other chapters delved into the specific processes involved in tanning methods based on vegetable raw materials, including the careful flaying of skins and their preservation, the preparation of bark-based solutions, the crafting of army boots, and the dyeing of various kinds of leather.

As previously mentioned, Abdul Haq stated in the preface to the first manual, that it was one of the first manuals on tanning in Urdu. However, it is important to note that there was a thriving tradition of writings on artisan industries in the nineteenth century, predating the establishment of the Anjuman-e Taraqqi-e Urdu Board (Lanzillo, 2021). Lanzillo points out that these early Urdu-language manuals typically engaged with narratives of material and technological change, perceiving them as integral parts of regional or religious histories related to their respective trades.

In contrast, Imdad Ali's manuals, published several decades later, did not perceive themselves as part of any 'religious heritage', despite the well acknowledged participation of Muslims in the broad network of the meat, hides, tanning and leather industries. Instead, Imdad Ali's manuals closely resembled government monographs published on tanning and leather work in various provinces of colonial India (Chatterton, 1904; Walton, 1903; Chandra 1904; Martin, 1903). However, Imdad Ali's Urdu manuals fundamentally differed from these monographs. They were designed to 'teach' practical skills to their readers and, as a result, were far more comprehensive and detailed, with a focus on the 'practice' and 'process' of tanning. In this regard, Imdad Ali's Urdu manuals were akin to English manuals published in London and prescribed in leading tanning schools in Europe. Nonetheless, the English manuals were considerably more expensive and difficult to procure in India.[27]

The following section of this chapter will focus on Imdad Ali's descriptions of the different processes connected to the two tanning methods and the practical considerations related to them. According to Imdad Ali, it was the *'amal* (practice) of the skills utilized in these processes that was not typically taught in technical education institutions but ultimately determined the fate and success of a newly established rural tannery.

Practising skills, processing skins

With the advent of chemical-based tanning, it became an assumption that an understanding of chemical compounds and the fundamental principles of chemistry was essential for any practitioner of the trade. As noted in the previous section, colonial technical institutes began to regard tanning more as a 'science' than as a 'craft'. Consequently, the pursuit of knowledge related to leather production became more exclusive, confined to those who had received technical education rooted in scientific methods and the principles of chemistry. However, for practitioners of the trade like Imdad Ali, who possessed a deep familiarity with the local industry in India and a nuanced understanding of the unique needs and requirements of rural artisans, the broader adoption of chrome-based tanning could only be successful if it harmonized with tanning methods familiar to rural tanners.

Imdad Ali acknowledged in his manuals that his *dihātī* brothers lacked knowledge of *kīmiyāvī usūl* (principles of chemistry). Moreover, not all the raw materials and chemical ingredients readily available in big cities like Kanpur, Calcutta, or Madras could be easily obtained in the rural countryside. Thus, he incorporated several practical adjustments that could be applied in the tanning processes accordingly. In his writings, he provided extensive explanations of the *'amal* (process) of tanning and its *'amlī* (practical) aspects, which could be understood by a novice or a student.

When describing a process that required some technical finesse on the part of the *kārīgar* (craftsman), Imdad Ali went on to provide detailed insights into the labour-intensive process. For instance, he described the process of softening the skin, a necessary step in case the skin had become hardened due to excessive exposure to the sun – a regular complaint of the merchants who procured hides and skins.

> Spread out the skin on clean floor or a mat with the flesh side of the skin facing upwards. On top of the skin, spread a clean scrap newspaper. The one who has to work must sit on it and start work so that the hide does not become dirty. Place the right foot slightly behind and the left foot ahead, with the (khurpī) hand shovel in the right hand, hold the skin with the left and move the hand shovel in the direction of right hand. In the beginning, the left hand (in which the skin is placed), must be lifted from the floor or wooden plank as little as possible. Gradually when the skin softens, then begin to lift the left hand more, so that when it becomes quite soft, then bring the left hand till the right hand that holds the hand shovel.
>
> *(M'adnī, 52–53)*[28]

Imdad Ali offered detailed explanations to address various practical difficulties encountered by rural practitioners throughout different stages of the pre-tanning processes, such as the removal of excess moisture, lime or hair from the skin. In such a situation, Imdad Ali frequently presented straightforward solutions and accessible solutions for the *dihatī* practitioner. For instance, to determine whether the skin had eliminated all traces of lime, Imdad Ali proposed a simple method involving *haldī* (turmeric), a readily available substance in the countryside (M'adnī, 86). The method entailed dipping a cloth in *haldī*, cutting a portion of the skin, and then wiping it with the *haldī* soaked cloth. If the cloth turned red, it indicated that the skin still contained some lime, and the lime removal process should be continued for a while longer.

Imdad Ali's manuals are abundant with examples and practical explanations of principles of chemistry from a *gharelū* (domestic) perspective. Despite the complexity of chemistry in textbooks, Imdad Ali managed to describe intricate chemical processes in the simplest manner possible. He recognized that the detailed chemical compositions could be overwhelming for rural practitioners, and he accordingly offered guidance on chemical tanning through straightforward examples (*asān misāl se dabāğat ki kīmīyāgīrī*) (*M'adnī*, 70). Given that many of his readers would be attempting these processes for the first time, Imdad Ali frequently summarized their descriptions, making them easily understandable and implementable (*M'adnī*, 164).

In various sections of the manuals, Imdad Ali provided formulas for creating specific chemical solutions, detailing each ingredient and its required quantity. One such *nuskha* (formula) that he shared for the convenience of his *dihatī* brothers was Dr. Proctor's chemical solution for chrome tanning, developed in 1898 (*M'adnī*, 67).[29] Similarly, he explained the process of producing chromic oxide, which served as an acid in the chrome tanning solution. In this context, he advised that as soon as one added sugar to the solution, they should immediately distance their hands from it, as it would bubble up and overflow from the container. To help readers grasp this unfamiliar concept, Imdad Ali likened the bubbling process to a familiar one – when *gurh* (jaggery) was produced from sugarcane (*M'adnī*, 173). In another example, Imdad Ali elucidated the technique of flaying the skin from the head of animals without horns, a process involving intricate knife skills. He drew a parallel between these knife skills and the finesse required when removing the rotten part of a fruit by encircling the tip of the knife around it (*M'adnī*, 30).

Imdad Ali employed another method to simplify complex chemistry, which involved describing and emphasizing critical colours used in the chemical processes by their colloquial names, easily comprehensible in the countryside. Consequently, when removing excess moisture from the skins, the use of *ghīr* bark would cause the flesh side of the skin to turn *katthaī* (brown), while the use of babul bark would result in a *badāmī* (almond brown) hue and employing *dhow* leaves would yield a *halkā zard* (light yellow) colour (*M'adnī*, 63). Other tools deployed by Imdad Ali's manuals are various diagrams, sketches, and photographs that aid the readers in visualizing the labour-intensive processes during various stages of tanning. Several diagrams are presented that describe how to stretch or treat the skins during the process of flaying, softening, polishing, or drying (*M'adnī*, 26, 32–33, 112, 114, 132 and *Nabātī*, 229, 238, 293, 295, 303, 329, 416–7). Additionally, the texts contain architectural drawings and designs of various building and structural components of a proposed factory or workshop (*Nabātī*, 30, 32, 49, 52, 54, 57 and 69). Both manuals include images of various *auzār* (tools) and machines used in different processes, especially for practitioners looking to expand their trade at a later stage.

Complex labour processes are accompanied by visual cues in the form of images, and these pictures provide detailed instructions for close examination (*M'adnī*, 182). For example, the rather challenging task within the currying process, involving the removal of hair from lime-soaked skin on a beam using a specific knife held and utilized in a particular manner, is accompanied by photographic aids (see Figures 4.1 and 4.2). Imdad Ali emphasized that this process is intricate, requiring not only experience and expertise but also intelligence, and thus fetched a higher income within the trade compared to other skills. Imdad Ali described the skill involved in the *chilāyī* (scraping) of the skin with the following instructions:

> The craftsman holds the right handle of the knife in his right hand and holds the tilted handle strongly with the left hand forcefully scraping the thick skin to peel it layer by layer to even out the thickness in the process.
> *(M'adnī, 178)*

Hierarchies of skills, divisions of labour

Imdad Ali's proposal for an organizational structure in a rural industry based on chrome tanning methods offers insights into the hierarchies of skills and the division of labour associated with the tanning industry. Each tannery necessitated a diverse set of skills to be deployed at various stages of the tanning process. These skills varied in difficulty, challenge, and expertise, resulting in a dispersion of labour. These divisions, in turn, gave rise to hierarchies based on roles and functions determined by the tannery's structure.

Imdad Ali identified four essential requirements: *māli imdād* (financial aid), a *sadr zakhīrā* (central storage) for raw materials, a truthful and selfless *kārpardāz* (manager of supplies), and an experienced *māhir-e fann* (*M'adnī*, 184–88). As the manager of the leather factory patronized by the Gwalior State, Imdad Ali recognized the importance of financial assistance in establishing and running a successful trade based on chrome tanning methods. Capital was indeed a primary requirement, particularly in the initial stages of setting up trade. According to Imdad Ali, such assistance could come from wealthy patrons, princely states, or the government (*M'adnī*, 185).

FIGURE 4.1 The skin on the beam on which it is scraped

Various terms were used to describe individuals considered as sources of capital, with *sarmāyādār* denoting the capitalist, distinct from the *mālik-e kār<u>kh</u>ānā* or the *kār<u>kh</u>ānādār*, which referred to the factory or workshop owner. While the capitalist or factory owner provided the capital, the *māhir-e fann* or the master craftsman, played the most crucial role in the organizational structure of the industry. In Imdad Ali's scheme, the *māhir-e fann* was the expert possessing knowledge in the technical aspects and chemistry of tanning, as well as practical experience in tanning processes. The *māhir-e*

FIGURE 4.2 Images of the various stages in the process of sharpening the knife for scraping the skin

Source: M'adnī, 174.

fann might have received formal training at technical schools in India or abroad, but Imdad Ali, himself, did not study abroad; he mastered the craft of tanning through years of *tajurbā* (experience) at the leather factory of the Gwalior Estate.

However, the *māhir-e fann* was distinctly different from the *sciencedāṇ* (scientist) or the *kīmīyādāṇ* (chemist), such as Shultz or Eitner, who 'discovered' various chrome tanning methods. While the scientist or the chemist possessed knowledge of *jadīd* (modern) scientific research, the *māhir-e fann*, in addition to this knowledge, had the practical experience required in a tannery. Imdad Ali highlighted this difference on several occasions when he prescribed processes that deviated from modern principles of chrome tanning as practised by Western scientists. For example, concerning the use of *siyāh phitkarī* and *zard phitkarī*, Imdad Ali emphasized that the latter was too hazardous for a novice to use and recommended a reversal in the order of alum solutions. Here, Imdad Ali pointed out that the *tajurbakār* (experienced), *māhir-e fann* would understand that, in the *dihāt* a judicious variation of scientific principles would be more effective for the novice *dihātī dabbāġhkār* (rural tanner) (*M'adnī*, 70–73). These distinctions between the *māhir-e fann* and the scientist/chemist suggest that, for Imdad Ali, the *fann-e dabāġat* or tanning was more of an artisanal craft, despite chrome tanning's heavy reliance on the knowledge of the chemical principles.

Another facet of Imdad Ali's proposed organizational structure involved the *māhir-e fann* assuming the role of a *ustād* (master) responsible for training a specific number of *shāgird* (trainees) under his mentorship and guidance. This *ustād/shāgird* relationship followed an apprenticeship model characteristic of artisanal production traditions (Rai, 2022). By retaining this role for the *māhir-e fann*, Imdad Ali indicated his preference for this model, at least for establishing tanneries in rural areas, as opposed to the technical education being promoted in industrial and art schools in the urban centres of colonial India. The *shāgird*, having received training under the *māhir-e fann's* guidance, would then venture to rural locations to put their learned craft into practice. Imdad Ali emphasized that they should personally engage in each of the processes involved in *dabāġat* and teach various skills to *dihātī* inhabitants in their presence. Each *māhir-e fann* would oversee three to four rural locations, with each location being supervised by a specific *shāgird*.

In addition to the skills related to the tanning processes, the managerial responsibilities were to be handled by the *kārpardāz*. As the manager of the supplies, the *kārpardāz* would oversee the central storage facility, a place designed to store various raw materials and make them readily accessible. This storage would also serve as a platform for selling tanned skins and hides at competitive prices. For Imdad Ali, the role of the *kārpardāz* was pivotal for the success of a rural trade. The *kārpardāz* was expected to possess a working knowledge of basic mathematics and accounting and an ability to manage financial matters, including expenses and savings. Additionally, the *kārpardāz* needed to be familiar with the *tafsīlāt-e fann* (details of the craft) of tanning to effectively supervise the quality of hides and skins.

Selecting an ideal location for the workshop or tannery should be based on the local *āb-o hawā* (climate) conditions, and the availability of raw materials should not pose significant challenges. At such a location, one *ustād* could train four *shāgird* over a span of four to five years, and each *shāgird* could then establish similar workshops or tanneries in nearby areas (*M'adnī*, 186). In each of these locations, *dihātī* (rural) inhabitants should receive training in the methods and processes of tanning. Once individuals have acquired the necessary skills and techniques, they should be provided with assistance to initiate their independent ventures. Over time, the initial location would evolve into a central storage facility where raw materials could be stockpiled and distributed to local areas. This central storage should be connected to *mandīs* (marketplaces), where hides and skins could be purchased and sold at fair prices. In Imdad Ali's model, the *dihātī* practitioners should have access to raw materials at affordable wholesale prices. From the net profit, 1 anna per rupee should be set aside as a fund for emergency purposes.

While it was emphasized that the *dihātī* practitioners of the trade, along with the *māhir-e fann* and his various *shāgird*, should have the knowledge of the practical aspects of various tanning processes, they did not constitute the workforce or labourers possessing specific skills required for different stages of the processes. These labourers were generally referred to as *mazdūr*, and when engaged in more specialized tasks, they were called *kārigar* or craftsmen. The responsibilities of the *kārigar* encompassed tasks such as flaying, skin scraping, and hair and lime removing, as well as softening or polishing the skin.[30] As noted before, specific tasks were elaborated upon with precise instructions tailored for the labourer performing them. These instructions were often accompanied by diagrams and photographs to serve as visual aid. With the introduction of chrome tanning, several processes required expensive machinery, which began to impact the labour process, like in many other industrial settings. Some tasks that previously required a specific number of *kārigars* could now be accomplished with fewer workers who simply had to operate these machines. However, this scenario was more applicable to large-scale tanneries or leather goods factories. Imdad Ali recognized that the costly machines required for various chrome tanning processes, especially those assisting in the 'currying' of leather, might not be accessible to local *kārigars* in rural areas (*M'adnī*, 155). For instance, chrome tanned leather demanded a more refined polishing process compared to leather tanned from tree bark. In this context, Imdad Ali ingeniously described a method for constructing a wooden machine based on locally available materials in the countryside (see Figures 4.3 and 4.4) (*M'adnī*, 180–181).

Operating these machines required specific skills that the *kārīgars* needed to acquire through training, a responsibility that fell upon the *māhir-e fann*. Such training did not necessitate separate formal technical education in an industrial school. The utilization of these machines not only made the labourer's task significantly more manageable but also reduced the overall labour force required. This was evident in processes like 'sleeking' or drying wet

شکل نمبر ۵۰

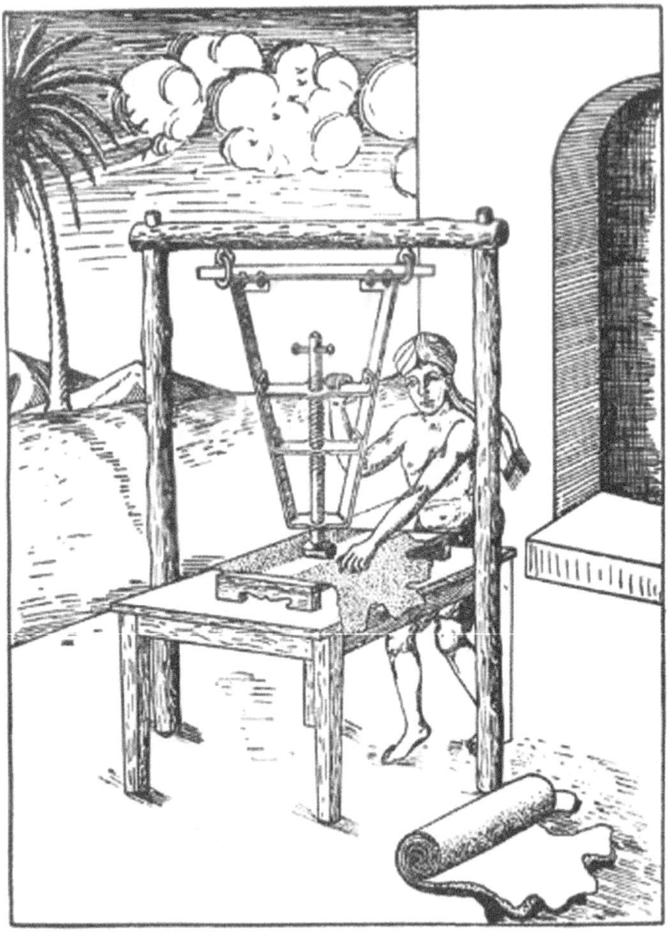

بالش کی مشین لوہے کی

یہ نالی‌دار لوہے (angle iron) سے تیار کی گئی ہے

FIGURE 4.3 The machine for polishing skins with angle iron

hides after scraping them on a beam (as described in the previous section). In the past, sleeking was entirely a manual process, but with time, machines took over this task. Imdad Ali proposed a simplified version of the 'sleeker' constructed from wine drums with attached stone slabs (see Figure 4.5). This setup considerably accelerated the sleeking process, as now only one *mazdūr*

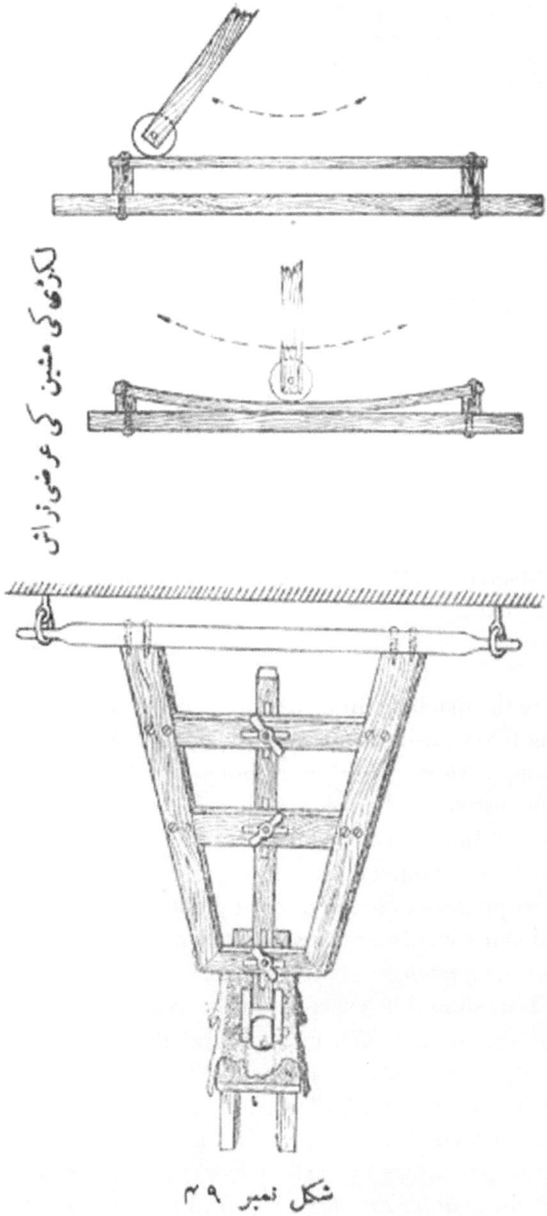

FIGURE 4.4 The various parts of the machine for polishing skins

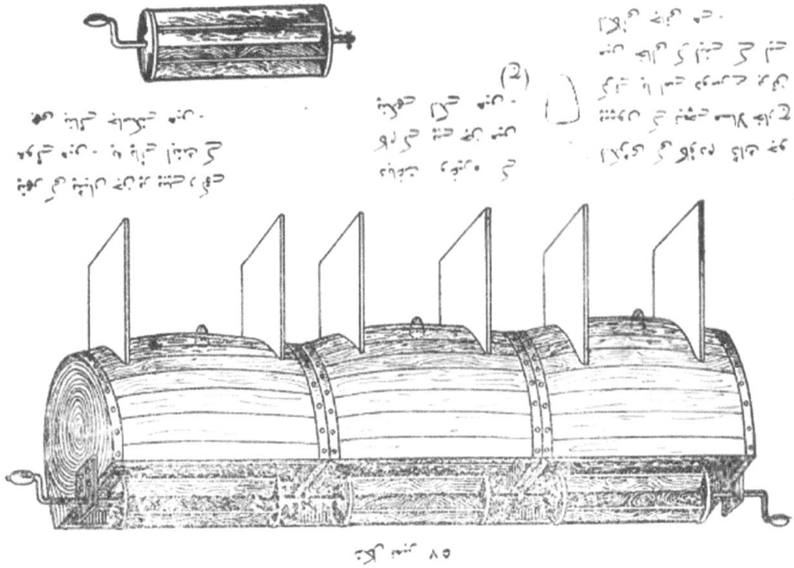

FIGURE 4.5 Machine made out of wine drums with stone slabs attached for 'sleeking'

could operate the machine. In fact, a single *mazdūr* could sleek multiple skins by managing two to four drums simultaneously (*M'adnī*, 182–183).

In his book *A Monograph on Tanning and Working in Leather,* Walton highlights the distinction between leatherworkers and tanners (Walton, 1903, 27). In contrast, Imdad Ali's manuals do not explicitly differentiate between leatherworkers and tanners. However, the *kārīgars* mentioned earlier, were considered to possess a 'learned' or 'taught' skill. Conversely, the sources of hides and skins were associated with two 'traditional' castes, namely the *chamārs* and the *qassābs*. Imdad Ali matter-of-factly states that the 'skill' of flaying the skins should be executed in the manner practiced by the *chamārs* and the *qassābs* (*M'adnī*, 27). Further, Imdad Ali noted that in rural areas, there were ample *chamārs* available who could be employed for this purpose.

Although in this context, Imdad Ali assumed, much like colonial officials and planners of technical education in India, that *chamārs* should be considered an obvious choice for leather work, he went further to elaborate on the 'craft' of the *chamār* as a *fann-e latīf* (fine art) rather than a *fann-e-kasīf* (dirty work). Imdad Ali explained this subtle distinction by recounting an anecdote about the son of a *chamār* who possessed exceptional abilities and skills in taxidermy, the art of mounting animal skins to give them a lifelike appearance. This young talent secretly practiced this 'art' in his free time and, upon discovery by a local British official, was generously rewarded for his ability to bring animals 'back to life' (*M'adnī*, 16–19). Imdad Ali likened the 'art' of the taxidermy to the *fann* of musicians, portraying the *chamār* as an artist and a practitioner of a *fann-e latīf*. This extended anecdotal account of the *chamār's* artistic prowess was Imdad Ali's effort to underscore the crucial role of the *chamār* in the prospects of the rural and local tanning industry. However, despite these anecdotal accounts, the model of the organizational structure that Imdad Ali proposed for the rural tanning industry conspicuously omits the *chamārs* and the *qassābs*. This absence reflects how the discourse on chrome-tanning-based leather industry assigned these occupational castes their 'traditional' roles, beyond which they do not feature in the new hierarchies of skills associated with the modern industry.

Conclusion

This chapter examined two Urdu manuals that focused on the development of chrome tanning as a rural trade during the late colonial period. These manuals, authored by Imdad Ali, shared the pedagogical vision of their publishers, the Anjuman-e Taraqqi-e Urdu. Together with intellectuals at Osmania University, they aimed to promote Urdu as a medium for imparting new scientific technologies and technical knowledge. This effort was intended to contribute to the advancement of industries for the emerging nation. Imdad Ali's manuals were part of a larger body of texts that sought to translate and re-conceptualize Western science and technologies into Urdu.

A careful analysis of these manuals highlights the underlying tensions within the broader vision of the Anjuman. It also provides insights into the challenges of disseminating technical knowledge beyond the limited scope of industrial schools, as well as the difficulties in establishing chrome-based tanneries in rural areas outside industrial cities. Imdad Ali's manuals primarily targeted a new readership composed of rural individuals interested in undertaking the practical aspects of setting up a tannery. These manuals were not particularly intended for artisans or members of the working class. Instead, their audience comprised individuals seeking to establish tanneries, students desiring to acquire tanning skills, or those aspiring to become a *māhir-e fann* – the master craftsman crucial to the tanning industry, possessing the practiced and perfected skills associated with the *fann-e dabāğat*.

Imdad Ali's distinction between the *māhir-e fann* and the scientist or chemist offered a unique perspective on the tanning industry, categorizing it as a craft, in contrast to some of the technical education frameworks proposed by government industrial institutes. His proposed organizational structure for rural tanning was based on an apprenticeship model, which involved the familiar *ustad-shāgird* (master-apprentice) relationship found in other traditional Indian industries.

In this model, the *māhir-e fann*, functioning as an *ustād*, had the capacity to impart a 'new' set of essential skills to the *shāgird*. These skills were pivotal in an industry that was gradually transitioning from being export oriented, producing raw or semi-tanned hides, to catering to a local demand-driven market for finished leather goods using chrome-based tanning methods. Imdad Ali's manuals primarily focused on these contemporary transformations within the leather industry. They did not perceive technological change through the lens of 'religious heritage' (Lanzillo, 2021). Instead, they highlighted the evolution of skills associated with modern chrome-based tanneries and the creation of a new hierarchies within them. In Imdad Ali's manuals, the roles of scourers and shavers, considered 'skilled' wage employees in leather goods factories, were acknowledged. However, the traditional roles of *chamār* and the *qassābs* were conspicuously absent beyond their 'traditional' function of supplying raw materials to tanneries and factories.

Imdad Ali's emphasis on the *practice* and *process* of tanning reflected the concerns of hides and skins merchants who sought improvements in hide quality. For example, they raised issues regarding marks on hides due to butcher's flaying, which diminished their quality. Imdad Ali repeatedly elaborated on these skills and their practical application in his manual. In his proposal for the development of chrome tanning as a rural trade, Imdad Ali addressed the concerns of a network of native capital, including hide and skins merchants, contractors, tannery owners, traders, and exporters. These stakeholders had benefited from the expansion and commercialization of the hides and leather industry in the past decades.

This chapter illustrated the utilization of Urdu as a medium for translating and disseminating scientific knowledge through popular writing. However, this endeavour was undertaken by elite individuals who were deeply involved in the nexus between science and capital. They saw the advancement of native industries as crucial for the progress of the nation. In pursuing this objective, they emphasized the importance of traditional artisanal industries like tanning and leather, adopting modern methods and processes, leading to the evolution of new hierarchies of skills and labour. Given the challenges in practicing these methods in rural areas, figures like Imdad Ali, who had the practical experience in Indian factories, advocated for the apprenticeship workshop model to promote a concept of skill centred around the pivotal role of the master craftsman, disregarding any notions of community or caste-based skills in the process.

Note: All images used in this chapter are from the Urdu text, Ali, I. 1940. *M'adnī Dabāgat,* Delhi: Anjuman Taraqqi Urdu (Hind). This text was published 85 years ago and is copyright free; available in libraries across the world as well as online repositories.

Notes

1 National Policy for Skill Development and Entrepreneurship, 2015, https://www.msde.gov.in/sites/default/files/2019-09/National%20Policy%20on%20Skill%20Development%20and%20Entreprenurship%20Final.pdf.

2 See, the ITI programme of the Maulana Azad National Urdu University in Hyderabad, which provides technical education in Urdu medium, https://manuu.edu.in/University/ITI/ITI-Hyderabad/Profile, or the National Council for the Promotion of Urdu Language (NCPUL) efforts at translating the curricula and textbooks of ITI's to Urdu, https://www.milligazette.com/news/1-community-news/3948-translation-of-iti-syllabus-into-urdu/.

3 Scholars have critiqued the use of the term 'vernacular' to denote non-English or regional languages in colonial India, as they point out that the term connotes a hierarchy between English and the vernacular languages. Here I use the term not to denote a hierarchy but rather to emphasize difference.

4 Imdad Ali, *M'adnī Dabāg̱at*, Delhi: Anjuman Taraqqi Urdu (Hind), 1940 and Imdad Ali, *Nabātī Dabāg̱at*, Delhi: Anjuman Taraqqi Urdu (Hind), 1946. The transliteration of Urdu terms in this article follows the Platts Urdu dictionary with some exceptions, to minimize diacritics. Various letters that have the same sound in Urdu (particularly s, t and z) have not been differentiated. The Urdu letter *'ain* has been noted with an apostrophe and the letter *nun ghunna* has been approximated with the letter *ṇ*; the *izāfā* is denoted with –e. I do not transliterate names of people and authors of various texts.

5 The basic idea to study the action of chromium salts on hides was first investigated by the German scientist Frederick Knapp in 1858. However, it was only in 1881 that Eitner from Vienna used iron and chromium salts to commercially tan hides from what came to known as the chrome tanning process. Further development of the chrome-tanning process was initiated by the chemist Augustus Schultz from USA, who in 1884 patented the 'two bath' process for chrome tannage using bio chromate salts. In 1897 the English scientist Procter demonstrated the 'one bath' process which began to be practiced in colonial India as well. For more on the early evolution of the chemistry of leather manufacture, see Procter (1903).

6 In some instances, the use of chemicals in some stages of the pre-tanning processes gradually evolved, such as one instance where sodium sulphide was used for liming (Gaitonde, 1930, 18).

7 Government of India, *Report of the Hides Cess Enquiry Committee, 21st October 1929–18th February 1930*, Vol. I, Calcutta: Government of India, 1930, 27.

8 Government of India, *Report on the Marketing of Hides in India and Burma*, Shimla: Government of India Press, 1943, 28.

9 Government of India, *Report on the Marketing of Hides in India and Burma*, Shimla: Government of India Press, 1943, 29.

10 Government of India, *Report on the Marketing of Hides in India and Burma*, Shimla: Government of India Press, 1943, 95.

11 Mukhtar, 1946, 58.

12 Mukhtar, 1946, 10–11.

13 Abdul Haq claimed that *M'adnī Dabāġat* was the first such writing on the *fann* of *dabāġat* in any Asian language and the first such work in Urdu (*M'adnī*, 2).

14 See footnote 27.

15 For Hindi, see Singh (2022a); for Marathi, Gujarati, see Raina (2000, 59).

16 The term *fann* is an Arabic term which connotes art, but its usage in Persian and Urdu has evolved into multiple meanings which can refer to craft, as well as science, even skill or technique or technology. See Platts (1884, 784).

17 *Hirfa* refers to craft, but it generally also connotes a trade or profession undertaken for livelihood (Platts, 1884, 476). Here I stress on the connotation of *hirfa* as craft, while in other places I translate it as trade.

18 I translate *māhir-e fann* as master craftsman following Tirthankar Roy's discussion of master artisans in colonial India where he uses the term 'master' not only

to refer to the highest form of skill, but also to an individual who functions as an innovator; see Roy, 2007, 963–991.

19 The texts he wrote carried his full name on the cover title as Janab Sayyid Imdad Ali Sahab 'Dabbag' Sailanvi. Sailana State was a princely state in Malwa region which was annexed by the Gwalior Estate in the nineteenth century.

20 Ali I, *M'adnī Dabāġat*, Delhi: Anjuman Taraqqi Urdu (Hind), 1940 and Ali, I. *Nabātī Dabāġat*, Delhi: Anjuman Taraqqi Urdu (Hind), 1946. Henceforth cited as *M'adnī* and *Nabātī*.

21 The subtitle of both the manuals was the same – *chromī dabāġat bahaisīyat ek dehī hirfā* (Chrome tanning as a rural trade).

22 In the 30 years from 1917 to 1947 the *Darul Tarjuma* had translated, compiled, and wrote a total of 457 books, out of which 426 books were translations from a number of languages, English, Arabic, German, and French (Datla, 2013, 65). Imdad Ali was in close collaboration with some of the intellectuals associated with the Osmania University; he thanked Mohd Usman Khan, professor at the *Darul Tarjuma* and Professor Muhammad Nasir Ahmad Usmani, Department of Tibbiyat, who urged Imdad Ali to write his manual, (*Nabātī*, 5).

23 See Hasan, 1925; Haq, 1939; Dehalvi, 1933–1944.

24 See Samiullah, 1919; Beg, 1936.

25 The title page of the manuals mentions their number in the series published by the Anjuman-e Taraqqi-e Urdu. *M'adnī Dabāġat* was the 123rd publication while *Nabātī Dabāġat* 239th publication. Several chapters of both manuals were published in different issues of *Science – Fann-e Dabāġat kī Tārīkh*, Vol. 10 (39), July 1937; *Thal Charbī Godām*, Vol. 11 (41), January 1938; *M'adnī Dabāġhat*, April 1938; *M'adnī Dabāġat*, October, 1938; *Nabātī Dabāġāt*, January, 1939; *Chand Darakhtoṇ kī Chāleṇ*, Vol. 9 (33), January 1936; *Fann-e Dabāġat*, Vol. 9 (34), April 1936.

26 The word tanning has its root in *tan*, the bark of a tree.

27 H.R. Proctor, an English scientist based at the University of Leeds in 1885, published a book titled *A Textbook of Tanning*, which was used in the leading tanning schools in Vienna, Leeds, London, Copenhagen, Berlin, and elsewhere. In 1898 he published *Leather Industries Laboratory Book*, dealing with the purely chemical side of tanning. In 1903 he published *The Principles of Leather Manufacture*, with several revised editions released subsequently. In its preface, Proctor says that he intended to appeal to both the chemist and the practical tanner (Proctor, 1903, vi). Another English 'leather workers manual' was H.C Standage 's manual, which was published in 1899. Standage, like Imdad Ali, had written articles giving instructions on how to dye leather in a leather trades journal and after receiving a lot of interest from readers compiled his writings into a manual. The manual comprised mainly of instructions for preparing all kinds of leather goods, detailing several practical processes as well as a chapter on Chrome Tanning as well (Standage, 1903).

28 All translations from Urdu are mine, unless otherwise specified.

29 The formula for this solution included 16 lbs of chrome alum, 4 lbs of soda crystal or 1 lb of soda ash, 80 lbs of water and bichromate of soda or potash that is *siyāh* or *zard phitkarī*. Imdad Ali provides the Urdu name for each of these compounds. See Procter, 1903.

30 However, the divisions of labour characteristic of modern tanneries of Calcutta or Kanpur, such as the scourer, scudder, glazer, or shaver among others, and who were paid wages according to their skills, were not specifically named by Imdad Ali, who only described the 'skill' involved in the various labour tasks performed by the generic term *kārīgar*. For a detailed list of wage employees at the tanneries and leather goods factories, see Mukhtar (1946).

References

Ali, I. 1940. *M'adnī Dabāgaat*. Delhi: Anjuman Taraqqi Urdu (Hind).

Ali, I. 1946. *Nabātī Dabāgat*. Delhi: Anjuman Taraqqi Urdu (Hind).

Amstutz, A. 2023. 'New Perspectives on Science, Medicine, and Language in Modern South Asia', *East Asian Science, Technology and Society: An International Journal*, 17(2): 266–272.

Amstutz, A. M. 2017. *Finding a Home for Urdu: Islam and Science in Modern South Asia*. PhD Diss. Cornell University.

Beg, A. Q. 1936, *Tālīmī Dastī Kām*, Tr. Alfred H. Jackson, Hyderabad: Aazam Steam Press.

Bhattacharya, S. 2013. 'Rotting Hides and Runaway Labour: Labour Control and Workers Resistance in the Indian Leather Industry, c 1860–1960', in R. Ahuja (ed.), *Workers Lives and Worker Militancy: The Politics of Labour in Colonial India*, pp. 47–96. Delhi: Tulika Books.

Bhattacharya, S. 2018. 'Transforming Skin, Changing Caste: Technical Education in Leather Production in India, 1900–1950', *The Indian Economic and Social History Review*, 55(3): 307–343.

Chandra, R. 1904. *Tanning and Working in Leather in the Province of Bengal*. Calcutta: Bengal Secretariat Press.

Chatterton, A. 1904. *Monograph on Tanning and Working in Leather in the Madras Presidency*. Madras: Superintendent, Government Press.

Dehalvi, Z. R. 1933–1944. *Farhang Istilāḥāt-e Peshevarāṇ*, vol. 1–8, New Delhi: Anjuman-e Taraqqi-e Urdu.

Datla, K. 2013. *The Language of Secular Islam: Urdu Nationalism and Colonial India*. Honolulu: University of Hawaii Press.

Gaitonde, V. R. 1930. *Report on the Village Tanning Industry in the Bombay Presidency*. Department of Industries: Bulletins. Bombay: Government of Bombay.

Garde, M. B. 1936. *A Handbook of Gwalior*. Gwalior: Alijah Darbar Press.

Government of India. 1930. *Report of the Hides Cess Enquiry Committee, 21st October 1929–18th February 1930*, Vol. I. Calcutta: Government of India.

Government of India. 1943. *Report on the Marketing of Hides in India and Burma*. Shimla: Government of India Press.

Haq, A. 1939. *Farhang Istilāḥāt-e Kīmiyā*, New Delhi: Anjuman-e Taraqqi-e Urdu.

Haq, A. 1951. *Urdu behisyat zariya'h-yi tālīm-i-science*. Karachi: Anjuman-e Taraqqi-e Urdu, Pakistan.

Haq, A. 1969. *Urdu Zabān Meṇ Ilmī Istilāḥāt kā Masla*. Karachi: Anjuman-e Taraqqi-e Urdu, Pakistan.

Harris, J. R. 1992. 'Skills, Coal and British Industry in the Eighteenth Century', in *His Essays in Industry and Technology in the Eighteenth Century*, pp. 167–182. Ashgate: Variorum.

Hasan. M.S. 1925. *Farhang Istilāḥāt-e I'lmīyāh*, Aurangabad: Anjuman-e Taraqqi-e Urdu.

Lanzillo, A. 2021. 'Writing Industrial Change in Urdu: Artisanship, Islam and Technology in Colonial India', *South Asia: Journal of South Asian Studies*, 44(4): 666–683.

Martin, J. R. 1903. *A Monograph on Tanning and Working in Leather in the Bombay Presidency*. Bombay: Government Central Press.

Menon, M. 2021. 'Indigenous knowledges and colonial sciences in South Asia', *South Asian History and Culture* 13(1): 1–18.

Mukhtar, A. 1946. *Report on Labour Conditions in Tanneries and Leather Goods Factories*. Simla: Government of India Press.

Platts, J. T. 1884. *A Dictionary of Urdu, Classical Hindi, and English*. London: W.H. Allen & Co.

Procter, H. R. 1903. *The Principles of Leather Manufacture*. London: E and F N Spon.

Rai, S. K. 2022. 'Communities of Skill in the Age of Capitalism: Handloom Weavers in Twentieth-Century United Provinces, India', *Modern Asian Studies* 56(4): 1183–1221.

Raina, D. 2000. 'Lamenting the Past, Anticipating the Future: A Chronology of Popular Science Writing in India (1850–1914)', in N. K. Sehgal, S. Sangwan and S. Mahanti (eds.), *Uncharted Terrains: Essays on Science Popularization in Pre-Independence India*, pp. 54–64. Delhi: Vigyan Parisar.

Raina, D. 2011. 'Travelling Both Ways: The Adaptations of Disciplines, Scientific Textbooks and Institutions', in F. Günergun and D. Raina (eds.) *Science between Asia and Europe: Historical Studies on the Transmission, Adoption and Adaption of Knowledge*, pp. 165–176. Dordrecht: Springer.

Raina, D., & Irfan Habib, S. 1993. 'The Unfolding of an Engagement: "The Dawn" on Science, Technical Education and Industrialization: India, 1896–1912', *Studies in History*, 9(1), 87–117.

Roy, T. 1994. 'Foreign Trade and the Artisans in Colonial India: A Study of Leather', *The Indian Economic and Social History Review*, 31(4): 461–490.

Roy, T. 2007. 'Out of Tradition: Master Artisans and Economic Change in Colonial India', *The Journal of Asian Studies*, 66(4): 963–991.

Samiullah, S. 1919. *Hirfatī Kām*, Tr. Edward F. Worst. Hyderabad: Aazam Steam Press.

Singh, C. 2021. 'Science and Its Publics in British India', in A. Goss (ed.), *The Routledge Handbook of Science and Empire*, pp. 218–227. London: Routledge.

Singh, C. 2022a. 'Science in the Vernacular? Translation, Terminology and Lexicography in the Hindi Scientific Glossary (1906)', *South Asian History and Culture*, 13(1): 63–86.

Singh, C. 2022b. 'The Shastri and the Air-Pump: Experimental Fictions and Fictions of Experiment for Hindi Readers in Colonial North India', *History of Science*, 60(2): 232–254.

Smith, P. H., Meyers, A. R. W. and Cook, H. J. 2014. *Ways of Making and Knowing: The Material Culture of Empirical Knowledge*. Ann Arbor: University of Michigan Press.

Standage, H. C. 1903. *Leather Worker's Manual: Being a Compendium of Practical Recipes and Working Formule for Curriers, Bootmakers, Leather Dressers, Blacking Manufacturers, Saddlers and Fancy Leather Workers*. London: Greenwood Scott.

Walton, H. G. 1903. *A Monograph on Tanning and Working in Leather in the United Provinces of Agra and Oudh*. Allahabad: Government Press.

Watts, G. 1908. *The Commercial Products of India*. London: John Murray.

PART II

Skill as making, producing, doing

5

SKILLS, CASTE AND CLASS IN AN EASTERN INDIAN STEEL TOWN, 1950S–2000S

Christian Strümpell

Introduction

On one afternoon in March 2008, Mahadeb, a man in his late 50s working in a repair shop of a large steel mill in the town of Rourkela in the eastern Indian state of Odisha, took great care to make me understand that he has a 'worker's *buddhi*', or 'brains'. To illustrate what this means, he told how once a machine from the rolling mills was brought to his department for repair, but that none of the engineers grasped what was wrong with it. The problem was that these well-educated engineers were reluctant to grasp the machine literally, to touch it, and – as always – instead tried to solve the problem by staring, hand in pocket, alternatively at the machine and at the drawings. He, by contrast, without any technical training and with only few years of school education, ran his hands over the steel plates, and thus realised that the problem was that some plates were much thinner than specified in the drawings and had to be replaced. "This is", he explained, "a workman's *buddhi*!" or a form of knowledge that does not come with bookish education, but with an attitude to do things, not merely to contemplate them, and with a work practice, that involves brain and brawn. He was so emphatic about his *buddhi* because he knew that the engineers and other executives in the steel plant looked down upon him as an uneducated manual labourer.

Mahadeb's expression and concern closely resemble discussions among construction workers in the central Indian town of Bhopal, which Arnaud Kaba describes (2022: 318–321). Experienced workers there make it a point that their work involves a lot of *dimag ka kam* ('brain work') and, Kaba argues, they do so to counter the claims of college-educated engineers that they are just uneducated manual labourers. The way the steel worker Mahadeb

DOI: 10.4324/9781003604846-7

as well as construction workers in Bhopal talk about the contrasting kinds of knowledge in their work environments reminds us of the distinction between the ancient Greek concepts *metis* and *techne* that James Scott (1998: 309–341) has brought into social science debates in his famous monograph *Seeing Like a State*. While *metis* refers to contingent practical knowledge that is required to deal with complex ever-changing environments and that can only be acquired through experience, *techne* refers to supposedly universal theoretical knowledge that is based on clearly spelled out deductive principles and acquired through learning them. Despite their broadly convergent views on different kinds of knowledge and on the value of their practical knowledge and skills, the respective working and employment conditions Mahadeb and Bhopal's construction workers face differ starkly. Construction workers are quintessentially precarious and poorly paid informal-sector workers in a labour-intensive industry (at least in Bhopal and Rourkela, where large construction machinery is still rare). Mahadeb, by contrast, works in the Rourkela Steel Plant, a quintessentially modern, capital-intensive industry in the public sector that offers regular company workers like Mahadeb secure employment and – relatively speaking – very good wages (Parry 2013; Strümpell 2018). Furthermore, it is important to know that for Mahadeb his *buddhi* was also what distinguished him from other workers who had received their skills in formal technical training – not only executives – and who, Mahadeb was convinced, usually look down upon 'uneducated' people like him in the same manner as executives do. This difference among workers overlapped to a significant degree with caste. His haughty, educated workmates usually had an upper-caste background; Mahadeb and others who were considered uneducated were usually Adivasi; that is, they belong to one of several supposedly 'primitive' tribes, although especially among the younger cohort of workers Adivasis had higher levels of formal education and vocational training, too.

In this chapter, I discuss notions of skill and practices of skilling prevailing in the Rourkela Steel Plant, or RSP. My aim is to show how the scope and meaning of different skills required for working in RSP have been shaped by the complex interplay between the company, its workforces, the central and regional state, as well as wider global forces, that is, by the 'skill ecology' (see Maitra, Maitra and Schwecke, this volume) that emerged in Rourkela. Moreover, I highlight the transformations and recalibrations the scope and meaning of industrial skills have undergone during the 50 years since the 1950s, when the steel plant was established, and the 2000s, when I conducted ethnographic research in Rourkela.[1] In particular, I will focus on the changing role ethnicity and caste, or the caste-tribe divide, played in this process. In the first section, I will briefly place the foundation of the steel plant in its historical context of Nehruvian nation-building and import-substituting industrialization. In the second section follows an account of skills and skilling among the first generation of steel workers in a region that had until then been an 'internal periphery'. In the third section, I show how the nativist agenda of the regional state and widespread upper-caste notions on the otherness of the 'tribes' or Adivasis early on lend an ethnic as well as casteist tinge to notions of skills and claims to skilled positions in the industry, with which also came better pay and more authority. In the fourth and fifth sections, I discuss the transformations that RSP and its workforces have undergone in the wake of India's economic liberalisation since the late 1980s and focus especially on the growing number of contract workers working alongside company workers since then, but under very different, much less secure and badly paid conditions. I will show that this bifurcation reflects in the self-understanding of both kinds of workers and of their skills, that it divides them economically, socially and politically and supersedes the earlier ethnic and/or caste divides within the workforce. As I further show, the bifurcation ultimately rests on the inequalities the skill ecology in Rourkela has produced since the coming of the steel plant in the 1950s.

The steel plant in the 'periphery'

The construction of RSP started in 1957, a few years after Independence and almost simultaneously with two other steel plants in Bhilai and in Durgapur, roughly 450 km southwest and northeast of Rourkela in Odisha's neighbouring states of Chhattisgarh and West Bengal respectively (a fourth one was set up in Bokaro in the early 1960s in then Bihar).[2] Like RSP, the other steel plants were public sector undertakings, and these steel plants were to form a cornerstone in Nehru's vision of an economically autarkic, modern, secular, industrial nation-state with a 'socialistic pattern of society' (cf. Parry 2020: 3; Khilnani 2003 [1997]: 61–106; Deshpande 1993). The steel plants were to make India independent from imports from advanced industrial countries and to buttress its hard-won political independence. As public sector undertakings they were to act as model employers providing their workforces with comparatively high wages, high job security and substantial fringe benefits; and they were to provide such employment on a mass scale. RSP was supposed to employ a workforce of approximately 15,000 in total. In comparison, steel works of the same size in capitalist western Europe would run with a workforce of less than half that strength at that time (Röh 1967: 151). Furthermore, actual recruitments soon surpassed initial manpower plans. In 1962, RSP employed roughly 15,000 workers, but that figure rose to 23,000 in 1966, rose to 35,000 in 1974 and reached its peak in 1989 with an overall workforce of 39,000. These large workforces were supposed to include workers from a multitude of castes, religious communities and ethnic-linguistic groups. By working together in modern industries irrespective of caste, religious and regional ethnicity it was expected that public sector steel workers would inevitably transcend the allegedly divisive 'traditional' identities they brought into these places. They would thus form 'mini Indias' and as such stand as a model for the citizenry at large (Roy 2007: 155).

The steel plants were established in a belt stretching across central-eastern India from the southern parts of West Bengal via Jharkhand, northern and western Odisha to Chhattisgarh that had abundant reserves of iron ore and coal, among other resources. The industrialist Jamshedji Tata had established India's first steel plant in this region in the early twentieth century and opened up a few mines and quarries feeding it, but the region was otherwise a rural backwater without major urban centres and industries. The location of the three new steel plants in 'internal peripheries' also was to integrate them closer into the emerging nation-state. Since these regions were only sparsely populated the upcoming industrial complexes had to attract and to bind labour to these 'wildernesses', as elder migrants described the Rourkela region of the 1950s to me (Strümpell 2017), which was another reason for the relatively privileged employment conditions steel workers were offered.

The peripheral location also made the construction of full-fledged company townships with all kinds of state-of-the-art urban amenities adjacent to the steel plants necessary to attract workers and executives and to make them stay – just as the Tatas had done in the model company town Jamshedpur (Sanchez 2016: 6, 13–15). Like the steel plants, these steel towns were supposed to become melting pots where engineers and workers from all caste, religious and regional backgrounds would meet and mingle together with their families to form 'mini Indias', and where the next generation of model working-class citizens was to be raised in well-funded above-standard schools, vocational training centres and colleges.

Skilling labour in an internal periphery

Since the Government of India lacked the capital and the expertise for constructing the steel plants, it sought collaboration with foreign partners. The steel plant in Bhilai was constructed in collaboration with the Soviet Union (Parry 2020: 76–79), the one in Durgapur with British aid and the one in Rourkela in collaboration with a consortium of around 30 steel manufacturers from West Germany. This constellation quickly turned into a competitive Cold War-race to prove to India and the developing world the superiority of their respective socialist and capitalist approach to industrial development (Unger 2015: 158, 182–187).

Krupp and DEMAG, two major West German steel manufacturers, and an array of smaller largely West German companies, sent personnel to Rourkela to survey the ground, to supervise and engage in the construction and to set the plant into operation. For that purpose, several hundred, at peak times almost 2,000 West Germans worked in Rourkela; were supposed to train Indian counterparts in the operation of their machines. In the case of prospective executives, this often took place during internships in West Germany, while foremen and skilled workers were supposed to be trained during assembling and commissioning the plant in Rourkela (Röh 1967: 152, 306).[3]

Several first-hand accounts of the plant's construction describe in detail the many difficulties that marred the project from the start, prolonged its construction and multiplied its costs. Major delays occurred in the shipment of material to the port in Kolkata, and from there to Rourkela; the lack of heavy machinery caused further delays in the unloading of goods in Rourkela, and in preparatory works, all of which led to exorbitant delays in assembling the different plants. West German authors, such as Sperling (1963, 1965) who headed the German Social Centre at Rourkela between 1958 and 1962, and Röh (1967), an economic analyst who investigated the successes and shortcomings of RSP's construction in the early 1960s, attribute several difficulties to the kind of technology transferred. The RSP was to produce steel with the basic oxygen process, the most modern and sophisticated production process at that time, which required special knowledge and maintenance, which – the Germans state – was often not followed leading to frequent breakdowns. Difficulties were aggravated by the inexperience of Indian planners and engineers and – as Sperling and English journalist Taya Zinkin (1966: 97–102) describe – the inexperience, widespread ignorance and in many cases outright arrogance of the West German partners. West German executives had no doubt that the state is unlikely to be a good industrialist, that it is too bureaucratic, giving too much room to political interference, and too overburdened with additional responsibilities, such as company housing; and they frequently ridiculed Nehru's socialist ambitions behind the project.

West German engineers and workers found the work ethic of their Indian counterparts in Rourkela wanting and they held India's traditional 'culture' responsible for it. Indian executives and workers alike, they say, do not full-heartedly embrace modern 'functional-practical thinking' but cling to a traditional 'status thinking' which allegedly manifested itself most distinctively in an aversion against dirtying one's hands with any kind of manual labour (cf. Röh 1968). Relationships between West Germans and Indians were often strained, and this also hampered the skilling of Indian personnel. The Indian engineering students sent as interns to Germany actually rarely came to practice at the machines, because they lacked sufficient prior technical knowledge as well as interest, as West German companies complained (Röh 1967: 306–308), but also – as they admit – because of warranty issues and the protection of trade secrets (Röh 1967: 311). Similarly, the skilling of Indian technicians in Rourkela remained insufficient. The whole project was enormously lagging behind in time, and the West German manufacturers were desperate to fulfil their turnkey contracts with RSP. Hence, they often did not spend as much time on training Indian personnel as would have been necessary, as Sperling (1965: 172) writes. Quite tellingly, eyewitnesses in Rourkela told me during my research in the 2000s that *raus* ('get out') was one of the few German words everybody soon learned in Rourkela, others being *kaputt* ('damaged').

The Indian state and RSP not only relied on West German collaborators for skilling the workforce. An agreement was also reached with the private steel manufacturers Tata Iron and Steel Company (TISCO) as well as the Indian Iron and Steel Company (IISCO) for skilling workers at their respective plants in Jamshedpur and Burnpur, which were just a few hours train journey northwest of Rourkela (Röh 1967: 306). On their return, the trainees were to be employed on grade 3, the first grade of supervisory workers, not on grades 1 and 2, as unskilled and semi-skilled workers (*khalasi* and helpers) were. The 'passed-out trainees' were also supposed to train other workers in RSP subsequently.

Furthermore, for skilling workers now and in future, the Government of Odisha established an Industrial Training Institute (ITI), a vocational school, at Rourkela in 1960, and the central government an engineering college in 1961. Admission to the trainee positions as well as the educational institutions was only open for applicants who had completed schooling, that is, who had passed the matriculation exams in class 11. According to RSP executives of that time as well as workers with a 'matric', this was a small minority among a RSP workforce they describe as largely illiterate. Although that depiction is almost certainly an exaggeration, the large majority of RSP workers of that generation I had talked to indeed had at best just a few years of schooling to their credit, but had not graduated from school. This suggests that skilled workers had a rather elevated class background than most other workers of that time. However, I also came across individuals among the first generation of workers who had a matric and were from modest backgrounds. Michael Dudhray is case in point. He came from a family of smallholders from a tiny village in the remote hinterland of Rourkela, but managed to complete primary school in his village, then also the secondary school in a nearby small town and passed the matric in Rourkela in 1961. There, he went then to the ITI where he learned the skills of a fitter.

Although the emphasis was on the formal, institutionalised acquisition of certified and standardised technical skills, I also came across several workers who had learned their skills informally on the job, from other skilled workers or who taught it themselves. Thus, Prakash Sahoo had left his village in coastal Odisha on his own after he had heard from a brother-in-law who was already in Rourkela that there are plenty of work opportunities. He arrived in Rourkela in 1957 when constructions started in earnest and when the contractors employed by the West German companies and the large Indian civil engineering companies in charge of construction were constantly in search of workers. Having been used to hard work outside the house as a farmer's son, to carrying and digging, he had no qualms to work for a contractor engaged in setting up the poles for the electrification of the emerging township. He was also shown then how to install electric connections and was taken on by another contractor engaged in electrical works, this time as a skilled worker. When RSP started recruiting the workforce for running the plant, he became an electrician in RSP's township department. Others I met in Rourkela had learned their skills on the job after having been recruited by RSP. Santosh Singh, for example, came to Rourkela from a nearby village in the early 1970s after finishing his matric to register at the local employment exchange, the state government institution from where RSP was obliged to draw applicants for vacancies in manual positions from 1968 onwards. He then took up the unskilled job of breaking stones in a lime stone quarry on the outskirts of the town, until RSP eventually called him for an interview a few months later. He passed and was recruited in 1973 for the Repair Construction and Maintenance department. There, as he told me, an elder worker took him under his wings and taught him welding and gas-cutting, two of the major skills required in the department. That elder worker had learned welding and gas-cutting informally, on the job, in his native town Jamshedpur while the TISCO plant was modernized in the late 1950s. After that was complete and his contractor retrenched him, he came down to nearby Rourkela in search for new work. Since his skills were rare in Rourkela then, he was employed immediately as a skilled worker, first on the construction sites and a little later in RSP.

As these stories demonstrate, skills were recognised in the formal structure of RSP even if they had not been formally acquired. The stories of Prakash and Santosh further show that they consider their upbringing in rural farm households essential for their ability to acquire skills, similar to notions of the self among the South Indian artisans Venkatesan (2006: 74) writes about. However, they both also emphasise the newness of the skills they learned on their jobs, which sets them apart from their rural backgrounds. In Prakash's and Santosh's stories skill is also passed on through intimate personal relations, in the latter's case from *guru* to *chela*, as they told me. In fact, in Prakash's and Santosh's narratives skills appear bestowed on them as gifts from experienced, skilled workers, akin to the informal master-apprentice relations between steelworkers and their junior helpers in the derelict Victorian tool factory in Sheffield Mollona (2005) analyses. It is also important to note that these personal relations cut across ethnic and caste boundaries, much as Nehru had dreamed. Prakash Sahoo is from a Hindu caste in the middle of the caste hierarchy and learned his skills from a Muslim from Maharashtra while the skilled worker from Jamshedpur from whom the Adivasi Santosh learned his skills was a Bihari Brahmin.

Skills, ethnicity and caste (or 'tribe')

Despite these 'cosmopolitan' accounts, there was also an ethnic dimension to 'skill'. RSP recruited workers from the construction sites, like Prakash and the Bihari welder, as well as among newcomers who constantly poured into Rourkela (as well as out if they did not find a job). These workers came from the wider region around Rourkela, from the state Odisha but also from all over the country. The workforce thus indeed epitomised the ethnic heterogeneity the planners had aimed for. Most of the workers taken on as trainees in the TISCO and IISCO steel plants in Jamshedpur and Burnpur, as indeed skilled workers in general, were migrants from other states than Odisha, especially from Bengal, Punjab and the southern states Tamil Nadu und Kerala. This did not go down well with local workers working under their supervision, many of whom thought, I was often told, that they had acquired enough skills on the RSP's construction sites or during earlier stints as migrant workers in factories in Kolkata to occupy themselves skilled positions in RSP. In a similar fashion, Mohanty (1953: 67–68), a civil servant in the Industries Department of the Government of Odisha in the 1950s, claimed that there were enough skilled and unskilled workers available in Odisha to operate a steel plant in the state. He estimated that more than one million people from Odisha were working in industries in Kolkata and elsewhere in India then, also in the existing private steel plants in Jamshedpur as well as in Kulti and Burnpur, and he assumed that many of them would return to Odisha as soon as a steel plant is established in Rourkela.[4] The German economist Röh (1967: 124) calls the report in which Mohanty makes these claims utterly euphemistic especially with regard to its alleged reserve of skilled workers. And he speculates whether this euphemism was motivated by the desire to convince the central government that Rourkela is the site 'par excellence' for India's first public sector steel plant.

However, many Odia I had met not only claimed to have enough industrial skills to take up the jobs the prestigious new industry on their 'home turf' in Odisha offered but they also doubted whether the 'foreigners' from Bengal, Punjab and South India had been as skilled as they claimed. Some also suspected that the school and industrial training certificates they had allegedly lost when fleeing from East Bengal and West Punjab in the wake of Partition – as many Bengali and Punjabi workers in Rourkela had done – in fact had never existed. Even more frequently, I was told that the foreign workers anyway did not require such certificates to make it onto skilled positions. Executives, even on departmental level, had a large say in postings then. These executives were overwhelmingly Bengali, Punjabi and other foreigners, too, and they liked to see supervisory positions staffed with their co-ethnics. Thus, in the eyes of my elderly Odia interlocutors, holding skilled positions in RSP indicated good relations with executives rather than skills. Furthermore, such relations allowed these workers also to delegate their tasks to lower-grade co-workers and to get by without many technical skills. As this shows, 'skill', what constitutes it and who has the power to recognise it and to get it recognised, was a major bone of contention in RSP, and this contention had a strong ethnic tone.

The sense of disentitlement among Odia RSP workers was aggravated by the problems Odia allegedly faced already when applying for RSP jobs. RSP workers earned higher wages, enjoyed better fringe benefits and had securer employment than workers in the much smaller ancillary and downstream industries that came up locally after the establishment of RSP. People in Odisha (as well as the state government) have had big expectations that a large share of the relatively privileged employment RSP offered would also go to locals, especially because the public sector steel plants held the promise of regional development. To their frustration, however, the arbitrary power to decide over who is going to get the jobs, not only which positions in RSP, lay with the foreign RSP executives, too.[5]

The situation began to change in the late 1960s when the central government made it compulsory for public sector undertakings to recruit workers through employment exchanges. Since these are under the jurisdiction of state governments, this legal change gave the state of Odisha control of access to employment in RSP. Unlike in some other Indian states, such as Madhya Pradesh, where RSP's 'sister' undertaking, the Bhilai Steel Plant (BSP), is located (Parry 2020), state politics in Odisha was driven by a strong nativist current. In order to boost their political standing ministers in Odisha clandestinely ordered the state civil servants at the Rourkela employment exchange, I was told, to reserve upcoming jobs to 'sons of the soil'. When RSP expanded production in the late 1960s and again recruited workers in large numbers, the large majority of them were Odia. In RSP, they took on positions of semi-skilled or skilled workers, because these new recruits usually had completed school as well as vocational training, thanks to the proliferation of industrial training centres in Odisha and also because the executive heading RSP's personnel department then was a staunch Odia nationalist, too, as several old and now retired workers from various ethnic backgrounds told me. In due time, Odia nationalists gained also clout on RSP shop floors and in the major unions. As argued elsewhere (Strümpell 2022, 2024), in the late 1960s, connections to the regional state, not only to plant management, became significant for making it into RSP, for one's position in the production process and in the shop floor hierarchy. This includes the recognition of one's skills.

Many locals continued being employed in unskilled positions. These were Adivasis who were widely said (by others) to have been *jangli* ('wild'), almost untouched by any kind of formal education, lacking not only proper clothes and diet but in fact civilisation. These disparaging descriptions resemble nineteenth-century colonial notions of the primitive otherness of the 'tribes' or 'aboriginals' that distinguished them not only from the British or Europeans but also from Indians of caste society. Their primitive characteristics rendered them the perfect 'coolie nation' the colonial state and planters had long sought after for staffing the tea plantations in Assam (cf. Ghosh 1999; Mohapatro 1985; Varma 2016). As argued in detail elsewhere (Strümpell

2022, 2024: 159–223), these notions of a 'tribal' otherness prevailed widely in Rourkela during my extended research visits in the 2000s. Judging from what my interlocutors told, this was also the case back in the 1950s. As in the colonial context, also in Rourkela the Adivasis' otherness pertained centrally to 'labour'. Sperling (1963: 24), for example, states that many German engineers and technicians in Rourkela praised the labouring prowess and straightforwardness of Adivasis, and alleged that this is rooted in their 'raw' nature 'unadulterated' by education and civilisation. For that reason, the German engineers Sperling had talked to claimed, Adivasis would actually make much better steel workers than the already trained migrant and upper-caste workers.

As under colonialism, the alleged otherness of Adivasis informed the way work processes were organised in Rourkela, and thereby entrenched it. Already during the construction of RSP Adivasis were employed in large numbers, and in contrast to migrants both men and women. But they were employed exclusively for digging the excavations, levelling the ground and laying rail tracks. Only little heavy machinery was available for this work, and hence contractors largely relied on manual labour with hatchets and winnows, which Adivasis used to perform since generations (Sperling 1963: 22). Many of these Adivasis were retrenched when preparatory work was complete and the assemblage of the plant started, but many continued to work as unskilled labourers also then and RSP also continued to employ Adivasis in numbers when the plant's different departments went into operation between 1959 and 1962. According to estimates of erstwhile personnel officers and unionists RSP employed at least several thousand Adivasis as regular workers. However, they were distributed unevenly along the labour process. They were almost exclusively employed for unskilled jobs and most commonly also in the so-called hot shops, the coke ovens, blast furnaces and steel melting shops, where high heat, fumes and dust rendered working conditions notoriously bad. If they were posted in other, cleaner and 'cooler' departments, such as the rolling mills, they were employed for *mati kamo*, 'earth work' or 'work on the ground', that is, for cleaning the floors from dust and grease, or they were posted in maintenance shops, as slingers for lifting heavy machinery.

As this shows, despite the planners' intentions, the division of labour in RSP displays, at least when it comes to the 'tribes', a pronounced caste bias. Furthermore, the stories about Adivasi workers also show that the skills they practice at work are not in fact considered skills at all. Akin to the widespread managerial 'nimble fingers' discourse on women in export industries in the Global South (Elson and Pearson 1981: 93; Beechey 1982: 65; Akgöz 2023), in Rourkela Adivasis are described as a 'natural' fit for rough manual labour, especially in the hot shops, because their innate 'tribal' nature equips them with brawn, but not much brain; and because it also equips them with a strong inclination for drinking, which allegedly helps to clean the throat from dust and to better bear the heat (Strümpell 2024: 166–174).

However, as these Adivasi workers themselves or their children told me, they possessed some practical industrial skills already prior to the arrival of RSP. It was quite common for them to seasonally take up wage work in the mines and quarries that had been opened up in the region in the early twentieth century with the arrival of the TISCO steel plant in Jamshedpur. In Rourkela and its surrounding areas lay several lime stone quarries feeding the TISCO plant, while the company sourced iron ore from large mines in the nearby Mayurbhanj district, from where Adivasi from the Santal 'tribe' had travelled to Rourkela in numbers in the 1950s to find work on the construction site and later on in the plant. Furthermore, in contrast to their widespread stereotyping as 'uneducated', some Adivasis had visited school and a few had undergone vocational training as well. Although they were employed on semi-skilled positions, they nevertheless also ended up in the hot shops. A case in point is Michael Dudhray, the ITI-educated fitter introduced earlier. He was certainly qualified enough for skilled positions in a variety of departments in RSP but he ended up in the coke ovens, one of the 'hot shops', and it was obvious to him when we talked that he worked there because he was an Adivasi (from the Munda 'tribe' to be precise). As his Adivasi neighbours explained to me, unlike others with his technical background, Michael Dudhray was also not promoted during his more than 30 years of working in RSP. In his case, this had a lot to do with frequent disciplinary actions he faced because he of his active engagement in a small far-left splinter union. However, Adivasis in general were rarely promoted further up the labour hierarchy and instead remained in the unskilled or at best semi-skilled grades throughout their working lives. Promotions depended on vacancies in the next higher grade as well as on merit and skills, that a promotion committee assessed in interviews and tests. However, Adivasi workers rarely passed these interviews and tests – if they were called for them at all. Given the stereotyping of Adivasis, it does not come as a surprise that for most non-Adivasis the reason for the fact that Adivasi RSP workers very often remained at the bottom of the ladder during their working lives was obvious; Adivasis were simply too uneducated to acquire any skills that made them eligible for promotions. Adivasi interlocutors, by contrast, and a few sympathetic non-Adivasis I met emphasised that this was the case rather because they had few advocates among the executives sitting on the promotion board who would recognise their skills.

As is obvious, Adivasis occupy the positions they do not only or in several cases even not primarily because they are 'unskilled' but because of the arbitrary power the largely upper-caste executives enjoy over them. Only this position of power allowed them to inscribe the stereotypes of Adivasis they cherish into the labour process. As is also obvious and as I have shown elsewhere (Strümpell 2022, 2024: 166–174), Adivasis nevertheless tried to reassert themselves and to renegotiate their positions and at the same time the very meaning of being an Adivasi. Like Santosh or Mahadeb, whom I introduced at the start of the chapter, they emphasised that they had acquired skills on the job. Frequently, Adivasi workers also boasted that they work in the 'mother departments' of RSP, where the whole process of making steel starts and where work means heavy slogging which others, especially the Odia shirkers (*kam chor*, literally 'work thieves'), are incapable of. In contrast to upper-caste executives and co-workers, they did not conceive their Adivasiness as innately given, but as a product of their upbringing in Adivasi communities with their particular sociability and values. This Adivasiness was re-produced in RSP due to their lack of connections to the regional state, not only to management. State government officers did not hinder their recruitment, as in the case other non-Odia workers, because they consider Adivasis as belonging to Odisha, too, not only the Odia. However, the upper-caste Odia nationalists in the personnel department obviously shared with upper castes of other ethnic backgrounds that Adivasis are best posted in the hot shops. Furthermore, unions did not offer much remedy either. The major ones were dominated by upper-caste Odias. For establishing a new one as a viable alternative required backing not only from sizeable sections of the workforce, but also from the state government and administration, which Adivasis in particular lacked (Strümpell 2022). Consequently, they lacked union support for claiming better jobs in RSP and for claiming recognition of their skills, akin to women workers in other parts of the world (cf. Beechey 1982: 65).

The bifurcation of the RSP workforces

When I started my ethnographic research in Rourkela in 2004, Michael Dudhray was already retired, Mahadeb was on his last leg and Santosh had ten years left until he was to reach retirement age at 60. The majority of Adivasi RSP workers I met and socialised with were much younger, in their 30s and 40s, and had been recruited in the 1990s. In that decade, RSP and Rourkela were going through some drastic changes that were the direct outcome of wider structural changes. These wider structural changes were most notably a partial liberalisation of the Indian economy that accelerated since the late 1980s, that explicitly broke with Nehruvian developmentalism in 1991 and that was ultimately driven by global forces of neoliberal capitalism that had gained an upper hand in the last quarter of the twentieth century (cf. Nayar 2004 [2001]; Münster and Strümpell 2014; Neveling 2014). Unlike in many parts of the world (cf. Kofti 2018; Trevisani 2018; Soul 2017), in India the break with state-led industrialization did not lead to the privatization of public sector steel plants. However, also in the Indian case profitability topped the agenda now, not employment provision anymore. Thus, from the late 1980s to 2004, the workforce in RSP dropped from 39,000 to 22,000. By 2009, when I ended my extended visits to Rourkela, the number was down to 19,000 and on my last short visits in early 2014 and late 2019 to 15,000. Downsizing was achieved by voluntary retirement schemes and, more effectively, by natural attrition. In the 1990s, the first generation of RSP workers recruited in the 1950s and 1960s reached their age of retirement, and in their place, RSP recruited a smaller workforce.

It was not only RSP that reduced its relatively securely employed and well-paid workforce during this time, but public sector industries or formal sector industries in India in general. In the Bhilai Steel Plant, a 'sister' undertaking of the RSP in the neighbouring state Chhattisgarh, the workforce was reduced from 64,000 in 1986 to 28,500 in 2013 (Parry 2020: 163). Indian Telephone Industries, to give another example of a public sector undertaking, reduced the workforces in its several plants from altogether 30,280 in 1992 to 19,600 in 2003 (Subramanian 2014: 89). Moreover, as was the case in Bhilai and in many other Indian industries, too, in the early 1970s, RSP started to employ a growing number of contract workers in addition to its regular 'company workforce'.[6] Contract workers were employed through a chain of contractors and subcontractors, and hence not directly by RSP. The Contract Labour Regulation and Abolition Act, 1971, actually prohibited the deployment of contract workers in all activities that are permanent and perennial to the production process of a company. As public and private sector undertakings in India in general practiced since then (Parry 2013), RSP circumvented these restrictions by claiming certain jobs to be temporary, even if they were repeated on a constant basis, such as the cleaning of shop floors or the repair and maintenance of machinery (cf. Patnaik 1990: 57–58). For RSP, outsourcing or externalising jobs to contractors and contract workers had the advantage that these workers were exempted from several legal provisions enforcing the terms of employment and working conditions of company workers. The minimum wage contract workers earned was far below the one of company workers, and few of the former in fact were paid the minimum wage. They also did not receive incentive bonuses; they rarely had paid holidays, and only meagre (if at all) claims to compensations in cases of work-related injuries or deaths, to name some important differences. Furthermore, contract workers *de facto* lacked any form of job security; they could be fired any time, which made it even more difficult for them to organise and confront their employers.

Some former executives in junior ranks told me that many of their senior colleagues were keen on such a 'contract labour system' because it offered a good way to earn extra money by taking commission from contractors winning the tender for jobs in their department. The much more important overall benefit for management was that this externalisation of labour created an additional, peripheral workforce in RSP that was not only cheaper than company workers, but that it could more readily deploy for menial jobs that regular company workers could refuse to do. That also applies to Adivasis among the company workers who were routinely put to menial work in harsh working environments, but who – thanks to their employment status as company workers – could afford to skip workdays without risking their jobs, as it is said many of them did, especially after paydays.

Hence, in the 1970s, two kinds of workforces got established in RSP, set apart from each other in quite stark ways in terms of their respective employment relation with the company, which in turn set them apart economically to a degree that amounts to a class division, not only in Rourkela, but also in Bhilai, as Parry (2013, 2020: 61–70) has shown. Furthermore, the ratio between company and contract workers changed drastically over the decades. While in the early 1970s, around 4,000 contract workers were working on RSP's premises, ten years later their number had risen to 8,000, and by the late 1980s, when the company workforce counted 39,000, to 10,000 (Sengupta 1983: 51). By 2014, when the company workforce was down to 15,000 workers, contract workers numbered 15,000, and hence the two workforces stood numerically at par.

The two workforces were set apart not only economically. In terms of ethnicity and caste, the company workforce was predominantly Odia with a sizeable Adivasi minority (amounting to one-third, as several well-informed unionists estimated). Since the Odisha state continued with its nativist agenda, Bengali, Bihari, Punjabi or south Indian workers appeared only in ones or twos, if at all, in the different work groups on which I gathered data. These were exclusively workers who were employed on 'father's ground', that is, as compensation to their father's work-related disabilities. Others left the town for industrial centres in their anyway industrially more developed native states. Contract workers were largely Adivasis, from Odisha or from the adjacent state Jharkhand, but there were also a few Odia from various caste backgrounds among them, and even fewer Bengali, Bihari, Punjabi and South Indians (Sengupta 1983: 75). Contract workers lived in self-built houses or huts in *basti* ('settlements'), dispersed across Rourkela or at its fringes. Several also lived in so-called resettlement colonies at the fringes of Rourkela, which the Odisha state government established in the 1950s for the 13,000 people who lost their land and homestead to RSP and the urban-industrial complex around it, and who in their large majority had also been Adivasis. In resettlement colonies, many (though not all) residents had legal titles over their plots, but the *basti* were usually encroachments on company land or municipality land, in which residents were under the risk of eviction. Although the residents of resettlement colonies also enjoyed somewhat better civic amenities in their neighbourhoods than those in the *basti* (e.g. proper electric connections, not self-constructed illegal ones) both spaces compared poorly to where company workers lived (Strümpell 2018, 2024: 234–312). The latter lived in the company township RSP built alongside the steel plant and that offered company quarters endowed with electricity connection, running water and indoor plumbing in spaciously laid-out neighbourhoods, further endowed with public parks, sports grounds and an array of good schools.

The spatial distance between company and contract workers entrenched the economic gap between them. As argued elsewhere (Strümpell 2018, 2024: 234–312) company workers actively seek to distance themselves from the labouring poor, the 'labour class', as they call them. Until the 1990s, most Adivasi company workers had indeed lived in *basti* and resettlement colonies together with contract workers and other informal-sector labour. Michael Dudhray was among the few who settled in the township. Santosh or Mahadeb, for example, lived in resettlement colonies, despite the fact that they came from surrounding villages and had not been displaced by RSP. The township had only 24,000 quarters for a workforce ranging between 35,000 and 39,000 in the 1970s and 1980s. Hence, in contradiction to the initial plans, the township could not accommodate the entire workforce, and among those who put up beyond it, Adivasi RSP workers ranked prime. Given the discrimination they experienced at the hands of upper-caste executives and workmates in RSP they had no interest to live among them in the township (Strümpell 2018, 2024: 234–312). The Adivasi RSP workers recruited since the 1990s, by contrast, almost all choose to settle in the township (that was of course large enough to do so after manpower reduction). The reason for their choice of residence was, they told unanimously, that it is difficult to educate one's children in the uneducated 'labour-class' environment of *basti* and resettlement colonies. As I discuss in the following section – formal education and standardised skills had become increasingly important for aspirations to formal employment.

Skill and the bifurcation of the RSP workforces

Already RSP workers recruited since the 1990s were bound to be more educated than the first generations of workers. In the mid-1980s, RSP had made a 'matriculation' compulsory for employment, but it actually considered only applicants who had completed vocational training or college. According to executives, higher levels of schooling and training were necessary because RSP had modernised production in the 1990s, closed down some outdated departments, such as the iron foundry, and newly constructed others, such as a new steel melting shop in which the technically more sophisticated continuous casting process was installed to produce more and better-quality steel than in ingot casting. Consequently, RSP stopped recruiting workers for the unskilled ranks S1 and S2. Recruits with completed vocational training were taken on in rank S3 while college-educated ones on S6. However, the large presence of contract workers in RSP obviously shows that the changing recruitment policies were not only about sophisticated labour-saving technologies and superior skills required for operating them but also simply about the reduction of the regularly employed company workforce.

Although, as mentioned earlier, Adivasis in general were still regarded as uneducated almost all those working in RSP also had visited ITIs or colleges and were employed on the corresponding ranks. They were posted again overwhelmingly in the hot shops and the reason for that still was their supposedly 'natural' ability to cope with the working conditions there. However, since RSP's technical modernisation in the 1990s these shops were not as hot or not as dusty anymore as before and, most importantly, contract workers, not company workers now did the most menial tasks there. When talking to Adivasi company workers, they still frequently complained about the casteism of upper-caste Odia workmates and executives. But they also boasted that upper-caste co-workers and executives did not dare anymore to humiliate them because of the 'gravity' they had gained on the shop floors and because of their *buddhi*, that is their 'brains' or 'smartness', required for getting along in RSP, for avoiding being taken for a ride by colleagues. Just like Mahadeb does in the vignette at the start of this chapter, here, too, *buddhi* refers to a *metis*-like form of knowledge or ability that goes beyond the *techne* knowledge taught in formal education and training, and that one acquires by exposure to the ways things 'really' work. This usage can be read as a critique of the emphasis that is put on formal education and that they – as Adivasis in general – are said to lack (see Strümpell 2022: 1706, 2024: 174–183). This critique often goes beyond the critique of purely technical knowledge Mahadeb expresses in the vignette at the start of this chapter, and in fact encompasses all kinds of bookish knowledge, from the running of machines to the running of government institutions.

Given all the emphasis Adivasi RSP workers frequently put on their innate distinctiveness from Odia – and vice versa – it is surprising at first sight that technical skills never came to the fore in that regard. Perhaps, one reason why skills did not seem to matter much in the relation among RSP workers of whatever caste and ethnic background was that they did not affect their position in RSP very much. In the late 1980s, RSP introduced a so-called cluster promotion scheme according to which every RSP worker is up for promotions every four years regardless of their skills – unless they faced serious disciplinary action. Furthermore, at the same time, RSP merged positions of different trades into composite positions, for example, to turn the position of a fitter in the maintenance department into the position of a 'fitter-cum-welder-cum-mechanic-cum-technician'. Some workers of that time (already retired when I talked to them), like Prakash Sahoo, for example, criticised the multi-skilling scheme as debasing their particular skills.

However, workers were aware that this 'multi-skilling' had not much to do with skilling in different trades but with reducing the number of sanctioned posts in RSP and hence with reducing the number of the regular workforce.

As Mahadeb's explanations at the beginning of this chapter show, company workers did take pride in their skills in our conversations, but this happened in different contexts. The emphasis Mahadeb put on his practical skills in that moment was directed against the stuck-up college-educated engineers in his department. More commonly, RSP company workers emphasised their skills when our conversations turned to the difference between them and the contract workers. In these moments, company workers regularly claimed (regardless whether Odia, Adivasis or from any other ethnic and caste background) that thanks to their education they understand their jobs and the technical processes behind their work much better than the uneducated contract workers do. Furthermore, they also emphasised that they, as 'educated' workers, differ from contract workers in terms of their commitment to their jobs and the company. They take their jobs seriously and do not bunk off, and they claimed that this relates to their general educated outlook on life, which reflects also in their sobriety and thrift. These notions of their selves should of course not be taken at face value. As I regularly witnessed, skilled workers bunked off quite regularly, usually in connivance with their line managers, the lowest-ranking executives on departmental level. Nevertheless, these notions of the self RSP workers nowadays cherish are telling because they refer more to class than to ethnicity and caste (or 'tribe'), unlike earlier.

Few contract workers denied that company workers have better technical education than they do. Many of them indeed had just a few years of schooling to their credit. However, contract workers frequently claimed to have more practical skills than company workers and also to understand the production process better. Company workers, they said – and which is basically true – usually spend their entire working lives in one single department where they are engaged in the very same production steps. They, by contrast, constantly shift workplaces in RSP, are engaged for some weeks in the maintenance and repair of parts of the coke ovens, followed by some weeks in the blast furnaces. Thus, Adivasi contract workers speak back against their depiction as the unskilled, uneducated antipode of the company worker, similar to the much less subaltern Adivasi RSP company workers of today.

It is important to note, of course, that contract workers were a heterogeneous group in several regards, also in terms of skill. Depending on the arbitrary power of the contractors employing them rather than on levels of formal education, they are differentiated into official categories unskilled, semi-skilled, skilled and high-skilled workers and they are supposed to receive a minimum daily wage of 90, 103, 116, and 129 rupees, respectively in 2009. On top of that they are further supposed to receive monthly allowances for housing, travel and canteen that amount to 390 rupees, independently of their skill category. In reality, many contract workers receive their minimum wages only on the papers they have to sign, but in fact much less. This is especially the case for the unskilled among them. Among the latter, a substantial part were women who made up almost 30% of the contract workers working in RSP, and who were all employed as unskilled workers regardless how many years of work experience they had. The male contract workers I knew well were usually semi-skilled or skilled. Most of them also worked in RSP for long, some up to ten years with only minor interruptions, and had acquired their skills over the years on their jobs and had worked their way up from unskilled workers. I also met one contract worker who had learned the trade of a fitter at an ITI. He earned a substantially higher monthly wage of 5,000 rupees and in fact had been promised twice as much by the middleman who fixed him the job. Although that contract worker was the only one who had completed vocational training, I met several others who had started but discontinued their training after some years, and I was told that there were many more working in RSP. This shows that in terms of skill or even formal, certified technical education at least many male contract workers are not as different from company workers as the latter routinely suggest and that their employment relation with RSP constituted the dividing line between them.

It also shows the extent to which the situation of the first decades had changed since the 1990s. In fact, the situation had almost been reversed. When RSP recruited its first workforce in the 1960s, levels of skill among RSP workers often starkly differed, but RSP offered all of them proper company jobs. Since the 1990s, RSP offers such jobs only to a selected few formally trained workers but in addition it draws on a large pool of precariously employed contract workers with varying degrees of skills, which they acquired informally, on the job, but in some cases also formally. The difference is in line with the global tendencies of a formalization of labour in the decades following World War II and its subsequent precarisation since the 1970s (see Breman and van der Linden 2014; Mayer-Ahuja 2017). The difference also relates to the larger availability of industrial skills in India. Engineering colleges and vocational training institutes had proliferated in all regions. Already by the 1960s, the state government had established ITIs in all major towns and in most districts of the state. With economic liberalisation in the 1990s, privately run industrial training centres further mushroomed, of which several hundred exist all over the state and seven in Rourkela alone. This suggests that the difference also relates to the fact that Rourkela by then was not any more an internal periphery but an industrial town of more than 500,000 inhabitants where such a pool of workers with different skills required for the steel industry was available in a stable manner and did not need to be attracted to the place as in the 1950s. Without such a stable pool of workers with sufficient industrial skills, learned formally or informally, it would have been more difficult for RSP to externalise labour to such an extent.

Conclusion

Shortly after Independence, the Government of India embarked on a program of rapid state-led industrialization, especially the establishment of steel plants (as well as large dams), to attain economic autarchy from the capitalist countries of the West, national integration and a modern secular and socialistic society. The steel plants and their attached townships were to become 'special places for special people' who would act – enabled by their benevolent public sector employer – as 'models for, not of the nation' (Roy 2007: 135). People were attracted to the internal peripheries where these places were located because of the job opportunities they offered on a mass scale, and also out of the excitement to become part of the new India (cf. Zinkin 1966: 127). However, workers and engineers had not only to be attracted to the peripheries, but they had to stay and form a stable workforce. That was especially so since the industrial skills that were required for running the steel plants were actually scarce then (a fact exacerbated by the almost simultaneous construction of other steel plants in nearby regions). Workers were supposed to learn the skills necessary for operating the steel plants through training provided by foreign collaborators, by the existing steel industry elsewhere in India and by industrial training institutes that were established in different towns and cities across India, also of course in the steel towns themselves. As I have shown, many workers had acquired their skills also informally, at work in RSP, on the construction sites, or already earlier in other industries. Very often, these workers had been rural migrants without any prior experience of industrial work, and this was the case not only in Rourkela but also in Bhilai (Parry 2020: 80–85).

Whether informal, non-standardised skills were recognised depended upon the executives who allocated workers their tasks in the labour process and who had a considerable say in their recruitment, too. Sons of the soil suspected that shared ethnic bonds between these executives who in the first decades were largely from industrially more advanced regions in India such as Bengal, Punjab or the South, were more decisive in their attaining skilled positions in RSP than the actual possession of skills. The strong nativist currents prevailing in Odisha's politics then emboldened these sentiments and lend claims to the recognition of skills and to authoritative skilled positions in RSP an ethnic tinge. Moreover, Odia nativism succeeds when the Odisha state government gains control of the recruitment process in RSP in the late 1960s and manages to reserve jobs for sons of the soil. Many of the latter by then had not only also undergone formal technical training, but thanks to the leverage of Odia nationalists in executive positions in RSP and elsewhere in Rourkela, many of these new recruits also ended up in skilled positions. Thus, one requires not only skills but also good relations to management and/or the state to get these skills recognised and posted on a skilled position. Other sons of the soil, the Adivasis, lacked both, relations to the management and to the regional state. Hence, they ended up in menial positions in the plant's hot shops (or in maintenance shops), which is legitimated with reference to prevailing upper-caste stereotypes of 'tribals' as natural manual labourers, able to cope with physically demanding work in hazardous conditions but untouched by civilization, education and formal technical skills. Adivasis in and around RSP struggled to re-imagine themselves and their skills as well as to attain educational qualifications and vocational training. It is important to note that this trajectory stands in contrast to Bhilai, another steel town in the neighbouring state Chhattisgarh. There, the regional state never showed any compulsion to defend sons-of-the-soil interests against ethnic others and a melting pot indeed developed in the local steel plant (Parry 2020: 294–296; Parry and Strümpell 2008). The nativist and casteist tinge of the skill ecology in Rourkela is thus not a defining characteristic of public sector industries *per se*.

During the time of my research in the 2000s, Adivasis nevertheless still overwhelmingly staffed the hot shops. However, they only had to engage in the menial tasks there when they were also only temporarily employed contract workers, not permanently employed company workers. In the wake of India's turn to economic liberalization, RSP retained only a core workforce with relatively high technical skills and outsourced especially the most menial and arduous tasks to privately operating labour contractors who then largely informally employed contract workers to execute them. The bifurcation of labour in RSP introduced a class divide among the workforce that overlay – but did not erase – the ethnic and caste-tribe divides. It was also more emphatically than earlier framed in terms of formally acquired technical knowledge and skills, or their lack.

Moreover, the bifurcation of labour in RSP thrived on inequalities in the specific skill ecology the company and Odisha state produced in Rourkela in the first decades. Contract workers were from villages of the region but often also they were sons (and daughters, since many contract workers are women) of Adivasi RSP workers who had lived in the *basti* surrounding or laying dispersed within Rourkela, but not in the township. The skills they required as contract workers in RSP they had learned informally, at work on their jobs in the plant, and since the 1990s some also formally, in vocational training courses, but usually without completing them, which excluded them from formal employment. By contrast, those who had grown up in the township – and even more so those who grew up there during the 2000s – more often attained high levels of formal education and technical training offered there, and could realistically aspire to formal employment, often successfully judging from talk in Rourkela. However, they sought and found this employment not in Rourkela and in the public sector, but elsewhere in India, preferably in metropolitan places like Delhi, Mumbai and Bangalore, and in a large range of private sector industries in the IT or the automobile sector. Thus, the inequalities that were produced in Rourkela's specific skill ecology since the 1950s not only allows RSP to outsource labour but also offers private sector industries a formally high-skilled workforces to tap into.

Notes

1 My ethnographic research extended over roughly 32 months conducted intermittently between 2004 and 2014, during which I lived among and talked continuously and extensively to steel plant workers, unionists and executives, as well as to many of the town's other inhabitants. I gratefully acknowledge the support of the German Research Council (DFG), the Max-Planck-Institute for Social Anthropology, Halle, Germany, and the research centre Work and Human Lifecycle in Global History at Humboldt University Berlin.
2 A fifth public sector steel plant was built much later also in the port city Vishakhapatnam in Andhra Pradesh. Although planned already in 1970, it went into operation only in 1982, and it belongs to a different public sector holding company, to Rashtriya Ispat Nigam Ltd, not Steel Authority of India Ltd, as the first four plants.
3 For further details on the skilling of Indian personnel by West German companies in Rourkela and in Germany, see Josefine Hoffmann, Training as a Gatekeeper at the Indo-German Factory, in: *TRAFO – Blog for Transregional Research*, 16.04.2021, http://trafo.hypotheses.org/28070.
4 The steel plants at Kulti and Burnpur, both situated close to the Raniganj coalfields in the Asansol region of West Bengal, were established much earlier in the late nineteenth and early twentieth centuries respectively by British and Indian industrialists (Brush 1952), while the steel plant at Bhadravathi was established by the princely government of Mysore in also in the early twentieth century. After many ups and downs, they were turned into public sector undertakings in 1972, and since 2006 both are units of the Steel Authority of India Ltd. (SAIL), the public sector holding company to which also RSP belongs.
5 The sense of disentitlement among the Odia elite of landlords and urban educated intelligentsia especially towards the Bengalis is in fact much older and goes back to British colonialism. Since the early nineteenth century large tracts of present-day Odisha were part of the Bengal Presidency and Bengali soon came to monopolise positions open to Indians in the Presidency's colonial administration. They are said to not only have blocked the careers of aspiring British-educated Odia and bought up large tracts of land in Odisha but also to have ridiculed Odia culture and language (Mohanty 1982: 20) and to act like an 'intermediary ruling race' in the colonial power structure (Bailey 1998: 32). Although Odisha was established as a separate province in 1936 in the last years of colonial rule, Frederick Bailey still noticed a remarkable thinness of skin among educated Odia towards Bengali and other Indians when he conducted ethnographic research in the state capital Bhubaneswar in the late 1950s.
6 There are important variations in this regard, however. Thus, Sanchez (2016: 8) shows that Tata Motors, another industry of the Tata Corporation located in Jamshedpur, casualised labour not by employing contract workers, but trainees and apprentices on fixed-term contracts on a large scale. Thus, at the time when he undertook long-term ethnographic research in the plant, three-quarters of the 11,000 workers Tata Motors employed belonged to either of these two categories of workers. By contrast, in the case of the factories of Indian Telephone Industries, the number of contract workers remained negligible despite the large-scale reduction of company workers (Subramanian 2010: 22–23).

References

Akgöz, G. 2023. 'Metaphorical Machines or Mindless Consumers: Young Working-Class Femininity in Early Postwar Turkey', *International Labor and Working Class History* 104: 32–54.

Bailey, F. G. 1998. *The Need for Enemies: A Bestiary of Political Forms*. Ithaca: Cornell University Press.

Beechey, V. 1982. 'The Sexual Division of Labour and the Labour Process: A Critical Assessment of Braverman', in S. Wood (ed.) *The Degradation of Work? Skill, Deskilling, and the Labour Process*, pp. 54–73. London: Hutchinson.

Breman, J. and M. van der Linden. 2014. 'Informalizing the Economy: The Return of the Social Question at a Global Level', *Development and Change* 45 (5): 920–940.

Brush, J. E. 1952. 'The Iron and Steel Industry in India', *Geographical Review* 42 (1): 37–55.

Deshpande, S. 1993. 'Imagined Economies: Styles of Nation-Building in Twentieth Century India', *Journal of Arts and Ideas* 25–26: 5–35.

Elson, D. and R. Pearson. 1981. '"Nimble Fingers Make Cheap Workers": An Analysis of Women's Employment in Third World Export Manufacturing', *Feminist Review* 7 (1): 87–107.

Ghosh, K. 1999. 'A Market for Aboriginality: Primitivism and Race Classification in the Indentured Labour Market of Colonial India', in G. Bhadra, G. Prakash and S. Tharu (eds.) *Subaltern Studies X*, pp. 8–48. Delhi: Oxford University Press.

Kaba, A. 2022. 'Between Construction Yard and Village: Changing Relations of Caste and Hierarchy among Madhya Pradesh's Labouring Classes', *Journal of Agrarian Change* 23 (2): 307–326.

Khilnani, S. 2003 [1997]. *The Idea of India*. London: Penguin Books.

Kofti, D. 2018. 'Regular Work in Decline: Precarious Households, and Changing Solidarities in Bulgaria', in C. Hann and J. Parry (eds.) *Industrial Labor on the Margins of Capitalism. Precarity, Class, and the Neoliberal Subject*, pp. 111–133. New York: Berghahn.

Mayer-Ahuja, N. 2017. 'Die Globalität unsicherer Arbeit als konzeptionelle Provokation: Zum Zusammenhang zwischen Informalität im Globalen Süden und Prekarität im Globalen Norden', *Geschichte und Gesellschaft* 43 (2): 264–296.

Mohanty, H. B. 1953. *Location of Steel Plant in Orissa: Rourkela*. Cuttack: Orissa Government Press; Government of Orissa: Industries Department.

Mohanty, N. 1982. *Oriya Nationalism: Quest for a United Orissa, 1866–1936*. New Delhi: Manohar.

Mohapatro, P. 1985. 'Coolies and Colliers: A Study of the Agrarian Context of Labour Migration from Chota Nagpur, 1880–1920', *Studies in History* 1 (2): 247–303.

Mollona, M. 2005. 'Gifts of Labour: Steel Production and Technological Imagination in an Area of Urban Deprivation, Sheffield, UK', *Critique of Anthropology* 25 (2): 177–198.

Münster, D. and C. Strümpell. 2014. 'The Anthropology of Neoliberal India: An Introduction', *Contributions to Indian Sociology (n.s.)* 48 (1): 1–16.

Nayar, B. R. 2004 [2001]. *Globalization and Nationalism: The Changing Balance in India's Economic Policy, 1950–2000*. New Delhi: SAGE Publications.

Neveling, P. 2014. 'Structural Contingencies and Untimely Coincidences in the Making of Neoliberal India: The Kandla Free Trade Zone, 1965–1991', *Contributions to Indian Sociology (n.s.)* 48 (1): 17–43.

Parry, J. P. 2013. 'Company and Contract Labour in a Central Indian Steel Plant', *Economy and Society* 42 (3): 348–374.

Parry, J. P. (in collaboration with T. G. Ajay). 2020. *Classes of Labour: Work and Life in a Central Indian Steel Town*. Delhi: Social Science Press.

Parry, J. P. and C. Strümpell. 2008. 'On the Desecration of Nehru's "Temples": Bhilai and Rourkela Compared', *Economic and Political Weekly* 43 (19): 47–57.
Patnaik, A. K. 1990. *Formation of the Working Class: A Study of the Labour Force of the Rourkela Steel Plant*. Unpublished PhD Thesis. Jawaharlal Nehru University, New Delhi, India.
Röh, K. 1967. *Rourkela als Testfall für die Errichtung von Industrieprojekten in Entwicklungsländern*. Hamburg: Verlag Weltarchiv Gmbh.
Röh, K. 1968. Zum Arbeitsverhalten der indischen Belegschaft in Rourkela. *Mitteilungen des Instituts für Asienkunde* 24. Hamburg.
Roy, S. 2007. *Beyond Belief: India and the Politics of Postcolonial Nationalism*. Durham: Duke University Press.
Sanchez, A. 2016. *Criminal Capital: Violence, Corruption and Class in Industrial India*. New Delhi: Routledge.
Scott, J. 1998. *Seeing Like a State: How Certain Schemes to Improve the Human Condition Have Failed*. New Haven: Yale University Press.
Sengupta, N. 1983. *Contract Labour in the Steel Region: Rourkela*. Rourkela: Asian Workers Development Institute.
Soul, J. 2017. 'Workers' Responses to Corporate Restructuring: Working Class Disorganization/Reorganization Processes in Argentina's Steel Industry', *Sociologia del Lavoro* 146: 122–138.
Sperling, J. B. 1963. *Rourkela: Sozio-ökonomische Probleme eines Entwicklungsprojekts*. Bonn: Eichholz Verlag.
Sperling, J. B. 1965. *Die Rourkela-Deutschen*. Stuttgart: Deutsche Verlags-Anstalt.
Strümpell, C. 2017. 'A Steel Town in the "Wilderness": Industry, State and Empire in Western Odisha', in U. Skoda and B. Pati (eds.), *Highland Odisha: Life and Society beyond the Coastal World*, pp. 241–264. Delhi: Primus.
Strümpell, C. 2018. 'Precarious Labor and Precarious Livelihoods in an Indian Company Town', in C. Hann and J. Parry (eds.), *Industrial Labor on the Margins of Capitalism: Precarity, Class, and the Neoliberal Subject*, pp. 134–154. New York: Berghahn.
Strümpell, C. 2022. 'Struggles about Class and Adivasi-Ness in an Eastern Indian Steel Plant', *Modern Asian Studies* 56 (5): 1691–1714.
Strümpell, C. 2024. *Steel Town Adivasis: Industry and Inequality in Eastern India*. London: Routledge (South Asian edition 2023, New Delhi: Social Science Press).
Subramanian, D. 2010. *Telecommunications Industry in India: State, Business and Labour in a Global Economy*. New Delhi: Social Science Press.
Subramanian, D. 2014. 'From Monopoly Power to Deregulated Markets: The Travails of a State-Owned Firm (ITI Ltd)', *Contributions to Indian Sociology (n.s.)* 48 (1): 73–102.
Trevisani, T. 2018. 'Work, Precarity, and Resistance: Company and Contract Labor in Kazakhstan's former Soviet Steel Town', in C. Hann and J. Parry (eds.) *Industrial Labor on the Margins of Capitalism: Precarity, Class, and the Neoliberal Subject*, pp. 85–110. New York: Berghahn.
Unger, C. 2015. *Entwicklungspfade in Indien: Eine internationale Geschichte 1947–1980*. Göttingen: Wallstein Verlag.
Varma, N. 2016. *Coolies for Capitalism: Assam Tea and the Making of Coolie Labour*. Berlin: De Gruyter.
Venkatesan, S. 2006. 'Shifting Balances in a "Craft Community": The Mat Weavers of Pattamadai, South India', *Contributions to Indian Sociology (n.s.)* 40 (1): 63–89.
Zinkin, T. 1966. *Challenges in India*. London: Chatto & Windus.

6

HAPTIC KNOWLEDGE

Artisanal skills, labour, and embodied knowledge practices

Pankhuree R. Dube

Introduction

A man was admiring the objects on display at a glass-blower's studio in Canada. He turned to his wife and said "God, these things are beautiful. I just don't know where these people get the time to make them." His wife responded, "Well, they don't work" (Flanders 1981). Potential buyers like these express a common, although contradictory, reaction to artisanal handicrafts: admiring the skills while denying that it is skilled labour. Soumhya Venkatesan, an ethnographer of handicraft, relates a similar instance from an encounter she had in Delhi with a buyer who wanted the fixed price of a product to be lowered. He turned to Venkatesan who was translating for the craftspersons and said, "Oh come on, after all they just do this while they are sitting around with nothing else to do." The man, Venkatesan explains, had "clearly bought into the rhetoric of craft being a way of life, not work, and was using it to get a better price" (Venkatesan 2003: 238–239). The reactions of these buyers to craftsmen in the marketplace suggest ways in which skill as a form of labour and time in artisanal production is routinely discounted. Treated as the result of ritual work or a way of life, the artisan is simultaneously anonymized, and the fruits of her skills made available for appropriation. This rhetoric of craft is activated especially when the community that engages in artisanal production is already marginalized.

How should we analyse the skill of the Indian artisan in a modern economy? Skill has been theorized as adjacent to but not overlapping with knowledge. The discourse of skill is worth parsing so we can better appreciate how the binary between skill and knowledge has proved detrimental to recognizing artisanal skills as a form of knowledge. Edwin Layton articulates this

DOI: 10.4324/9781003604846-8

distinction: "Technique means detailed procedures and skill and their application. But complex procedures can only come into being through knowledge. Skill is the ability to use one's knowledge effectively" (Layton 1974: 31–41). Other scholars also mark the difference between skill and knowledge, often demoting skill in relation to knowledge. For J.K. Feibleman, skill is simply the "proficiency in the use of artefacts" (Feibleman 1966: 318–328). To David Pye, skill is a "particular application of dexterity" which Pye contrasts with "know-how." According to Pye, it is "know-how" that enables the craftsman to imagine the final form of his labour before it can take shape in his hands (Pye 1964). Perhaps the most apt definition of skill with regard to artisanal labour is social anthropologist Tim Ingold's, which incorporates how artisans speak about their own work. The artisan works to a "design that is inscribed within the [natural and divine] order, . . . revealed in the raw material rather than superficially imposed upon it." The world, Ingold argues, "*opens itself out* [emphasis in original] to the traditional artisan" and his skill involves acting on the world in accord with its temporal rhythms and forms (Ingold 2000: 326). Ingold's definition of artisanal skill suggests how the artisan works in tune with their environment, and their work rhythms are seasonal, sidereal, rather than in accord with a mechanized regulation which overrides the body's own circadian clock.

Departing from the binary between skill and knowledge, the present argument calls for a reconfiguration of these two in describing how artisans rely on haptic knowledge. Haptic knowledge is an embodied knowledge. Therefore, we cannot annex it within the Western logocentric bias as there are aspects of embodiment that are beyond the reach of language. Though this inexpressible feature of haptic knowledge may be construed by other scholars as a sign of its lower place within a hierarchy of knowledges, that is not a hierarchy I impose here. Haptic knowledge is not pre-verbal or unconscious because it is not language-based, it is simply a different kind of knowledge which partially defies the grasp of language. Touch and knowing the world through touch remain undertheorized, particularly when compared to vision; however, it is our capacity as a human species to make something by hand which distinguishes human labour from the work of the machine (Ratcliffe 2008: 77–102). Artisans create handicrafts and so much of their skills are passed down by observing how their bodies move, what the apprentice can mimic which even the master craftsman cannot or does not explain in words, and the particular rhythms and gestures of the craft that animate the workspace (Herzfeld 2003).

In this chapter, I will argue that the skills of the South Asian artisan contain an array of haptic knowledges and pre-capitalist labour practices that cannot be subsumed by the industrialization of labour. Through the term "haptic knowledge," I gesture to the history of artisanal production as an entire episteme in South Asia which colonial authorities sought to dismantle discursively and materially. By denoting a particular labourer an artisan, the colonial capitalist demoted the recognition of the skills of that worker. My conceptualization of artisanal skill as haptic knowledge, then, marks a distinction from colonial tropes which recognized the skill of artisans while simultaneously effacing the trace of their labour. A contradiction in those colonial tropes (continued into the present) was that recognition of artisanal skill as a form of mastery and craftsmanship was simultaneously involved with reification of artisanal knowledge to erase the labour inherent in the work of art. Our failure to sufficiently understand the particular skill ecology within which artisans operate in India has impoverished our understanding of the Indian labour force as a whole. Following historian Pamela Smith, it is imperative to situate our discussion of art or *ars*, with a pre-colonial, early modern sensibility in mind. The *artista* of seventeenth-century Europe, Smith explains, "connoted a student of the liberal arts in a university and 'art' continued to refer to manual operations. Thus, the early modern connotations associated with the term 'art' are much more tied to what we would call 'craft' today, and those to whom we refer today as artists would generally have been viewed as artisans" (Smith 2004: 27). Without conflating artist and artisan here, I will examine how these two terms bear a historical relation to each other.

Artisanal skills are embedded within the nationalist discourse in India, which means that any scholar of South Asian craft must contend with government institutions and their patronage of handicrafts. The persistence of the term "artisan" into our present has to do with the appropriation of craft by nationalism. Historians and art historians of South Asia have examined, in some depth, the intersections between nationalism and artisanal skill in a particular narrative of the Indian nation-state (Sarkar 1973; Mitter 1995; Guha-Thakurta 1992; Pinney 2004; McGowan 2009; Brown 2009). Artisanal labour has been located largely within debates about deindustrialization. The historiography of deindustrialization had the following key propositions: pre-colonial prosperity, competition, loss of occupation, and dispersion of artisanal communities into the countryside as landless labour. By the 1960s, the Indian state had begun to enshrine craft. Within the broader framework of nationalist discourse surrounding artisanal crafts, these state-directed initiatives particularly affected relations between government bodies and minoritized indigenous communities known as *adivasis*. The present argument, therefore, will move between a more generalized discussion of South Asian artisans and the specific case of *adivasi* Pardhan Gond artisans, a community whose history I have delineated for the past two-and-a-half decades. Since the implicit presumption of nationalist discourse was that the *adivasi* artisan could not know or understand their own skills, it fell to the state to mediate and serve as the patron of an always dying craft tradition.

Although we must resist the tendency to idealize the figure of the artisan, *adivasi* artisans' skills reveal the complex history of Indian labour, indigenous knowledges, and nationalism in important ways. The historiography of Indian labour has been preoccupied with the question of Indian factory workers and their urban settings. With the publication of Dipesh Chakrabarty's *Rethinking Working Class History* and his contributions to Subaltern Studies as a provocation, Indian labour historians began to critique the teleological Marxist argument about the emergent Indian working class. Chakrabarty's attention to cultural identity among the jute mill workers of Kolkata challenged labour historians to stop treating class as a totalizing basis of workplace unity. His research signalled a shift from the singular focus on institutions such as trade unions by labour historians at the expense of histories of workers themselves (Chakrabarty 1989, 1983, 1984). Rajnarayan Chandavarkar's research on Bombay cotton mill workers disrupted the binary between the formal and the informal sector as the industrial worker coexisted with (and relied upon) a network made up of an informal, casual workforce (Chandavarkar 1994, 1981, 1985). Chitra Joshi's work on Kanpur textile mill workers synthesized the interventions of Chakrabarty and Chandavarkar while critiquing both how Chakrabarty reified culture and how Chandavarkar failed to acknowledge agency amongst the workers themselves (Joshi 2018, 1981, 1985). Samita Sen's study of women in Bengal jute mills drew attention to the production of gendered identities (Sen 1999). Both Sen's and Joshi's research paved the way for scholarship examining a more expansive view of politics among workers, and how identities are fluid, not impermeable or bound by binary logics of free/unfree labour or formal/informal sector work. With the fragmentation of factory labour and the casualization of the Indian labour force, recent scholarship has attended to more dispersed sites of labour analysis (van der Linden and Mohapatra 2009: *ix*). As these influential labour histories show, the common theme within Indian labour history and locus from which theorizations on Indian labour emerge are urban mill workers.

The importance of the pre-colonial in my discussion of haptic knowledge is that its practitioners retain traces of pre-colonial skills and through these, some vestigial forms of un-alienated labour escape the ruthless taxonomy of capitalism. Tirthankar Roy foregrounded the dynamism of a new artisan class in the colonial period (Roy 1993). Following Roy, historians searched for ways this group emerged and survived the exploitations of the colonial economy. Douglas E. Haynes' monograph is recognized as a major intervention in the historiography of South Asian artisanal labour. Haynes departed from conventional histories of artisans in which they were relegated to a stereotypical position of attacking machinery, victims of the relentless march of capitalism or pre-industrial throwbacks. Like Roy, he explored how cloth producers actively shaped the capitalist economy. Haynes' tracking of cloth producers in Western India revealed the interlocking of capitalist and pre-capitalist economic forms, the delicate negotiations between artisan-producers and workshop owners, and the ways in which new technologies and innovations were adapted by a *karkhana* (glossed as factories or workshops) otherwise run on pre-capitalist lines. Haynes' exhaustive survey of the field of artisanal labour in Western India also illuminated the penumbra around the figure of the *adivasi* artisan. Through interviews with *adivasis*, Haynes recorded the way artisan-made cloth was a desired commodity in *adivasi* communities; *adivasi* women needing a new sari would add it to their loans with the local moneylender. The women expressed certain preferences for design and colours (Haynes 2012). These intriguing mentions of *adivasis* as consumers and *adivasi* taste raised questions about the absence of *adivasis* as artisan-producers – of cloth and other handmade goods.

The methodology of this chapter comprises seven years of fieldwork in North and Central India, in particular the cities of Delhi and Bhopal, and ethnography and oral history interviews conducted during fieldwork together with archival research. Another method utilized in this study is philological: delving into terms in Hindi-Urdu vernaculars associated with artisanal production and tracking how these words changed in meaning. This philological method is in conversation with other studies by South Asianists and Africanists which attempt to decolonize theoretical concepts and identify traces of theory in pre-colonial texts (Wakankar 2021; Mudimbe 1988); key to this theorization is the recognition that some vernacular terms remain untranslatable (Apter 2013). Finally, there is an effort, albeit embryonic, to craft a method to document a domain of knowledge that I am calling "haptic knowledge."

Traces of pre-capitalist labour practices in vernaculars

Though haptic knowledge exceeds articulation in language and a discursive analysis does not exhaust the potential of haptic knowledge, there are linguistic traces of haptic knowledge that are worth noting. Artisanal labour as a haptic knowledge is articulated in vernacular terms by artisans. These vernacular terms deserve philological analysis; in particular, the terms bear traces of pre-capitalist labour practices that continue into the present day. Moreover, a philological analysis of vernacular terms used by artisans suggest that these labourers understand their own labour in ways that are not entirely broken by capitalist modernity. Here one finds a constellation of pre-capitalist labour practices that function as the backbone of the Indian economy; yet their lineage and its epistemology remain opaque to all but the initiated.

In regional South Asian case studies, historians look for terms that described the pre-colonial organization of artisans like the *karkhana* system in the metropolitan areas, or *jajmani* system in the rural areas; we may find words for "artisan" like *karigar* that earlier referred to artists and artisans without distinguishing between either but now refer only to the latter (while *kalakar* is used for the privileged artist) or *shilpa*, which, as a form of labour, encompassed the range of creative expression, skill, design, ability, ritual, and innovation yet now denotes "craft" only. Arcane terms such as *chatera* in Hindustani or *karmi* in the Newari language made no distinction between artisan, artist, or worker (AsiaInCH Encyclopedia; Jorgensen 1995: 35).

The term "artisan" is at once amorphous and yet bounded by seemingly common-sensical limitations. No one, for instance, would refer to a mechanic as an artisan even though the term "mechanic" originally denoted the artisan in a pre-industrial era and has today been repurposed to mean someone who fixes one of the most recognizable industrial machines. Historians of artisanal production and craft struggle with the vagueness of this category. Abigail McGowan asks: "Are crafts particular objects, a means of production, or a sector of the economy? Could they be all three?" (McGowan 2009: 13). For labour historians and ethnographers of work who employ our contemporary academic language, the terms of a profession are generally transparent. The scholar undertaking an ethnography of a call centre, for example, may continue to complicate the parameters of the job description but would begin their analysis by providing a consensus on what a particular job in the call centre entails. Parameters of each profession are laid out in labour contracts, defined and revised by institutional bodies and broken down into a set of skills that the worker will demonstrate, and the employer will regulate. However, one recent labour history has shown that even the modern nineteenth-century British factory largely operated beyond formal contracts (Steinfeld 2001). Workers in colonial India, according to another labour historian, never enjoyed legally bound labour contracts with employers (Anderson 2004: 422–454).

The ad hoc nature of work characterized factory labour in colonial Britain and colonized India and this ambiguity extended to the so-called informal sector where most Indian artisans work. For colonial and post-colonial authorities alike, there was an idealization of the modern industrial worker working under a formal contract even though such workers occupied only a small niche. Left unexamined or relegated to the domain of pre-industrial relic were the informal workers who till today continue to enjoy a marginal status with little or no labour rights and recognition.

This imprecision in delimiting the labour of the artisan has not in any way detracted from the ubiquity of artisanal labour. Language is continually mutating and adapting to a world in flux, neologisms are coined, objects or concepts rendered obsolete fall into disuse and are either discarded or redefined. Why has the inadequacy of the term "artisan" not been superseded by a more precise term? It is a problem that transcends the particularity of idiom; the vagueness of "artisan" in English mirrors the ambiguous lineaments of "artisan" in South Asian languages such as Hindi, Urdu, and Newari. Like "mechanic," our common-sensical, everyday terms which could historically refer to a range of artisanal labour have latterly been repurposed to suit only certain professions; for instance, the Hindi/Urdu word *mistri* was once a term for artisans. Its contemporary usage, for educated speakers of Hindi and Urdu alike, is as a reference to a supervisor of a range of manual professions from carpentry to construction to electronic repair and tailoring. As one ethnographer of contemporary labour in Bhopal, Arnaud Kaba, points out, *mistri* can mean "mason" or "foreman" in North Indian vernaculars yet in South India, *mistri* designates the foreman subcontracting the labour or, in some cases, the contractor (Kaba 2022a: 3). To the initiated, the designation *mistri* is never vague and always denotes authority and skill and commands better pay. The historical signification of artisanal practice has not disappeared from the term *mistri* amongst the workers themselves.

For a closer attention to the linguistic repertoire of artisans in the vernacular, we need to delve into the language world of Hindi-Urdu and social class of labourers in the oldest parts of two cities where Hindi-Urdu language, largely uninterrupted by English, is omnipresent. Two cities that span the spectrum of urbanization, Delhi and Bhopal, offer us some lessons from how artisans understand their own labour. For the homeless day labourers of Delhi's Sadar Bazaar, work is divided into lines based on perceived skill: at the higher end are *karigar* lines for a job like plumbing or carpentry. Like other craft professions, the *karigar* line is broken down into master craftsman and apprenticeship. The *karigar mistri* is considered an expert who supervises the mixing of cement and is paid accordingly anywhere from 175 to 250 rupees per day; the *beldaar* is his understudy and the *mazdoor* is paid at the lowest rung from 150 to 80 rupees a day and expected to follow the orders given by more skilled workers (Sethi 2011: 13–14). In the older part of the city of Bhopal, metalworkers aspire to government jobs or *naukri*; lacking the requisite qualifications and contacts to obtain such jobs, they continue to train apprentices from age 8 upwards. The teachers, for whom the young apprentices are expected to bring tea, are known as *mistri*. The *mistri* commands 500 rupees a day and will refuse to work for a lower wage (Kaba 2022b).

How much the artisan does, in the Indian context, is instructive. Artisanal production accounts for 64% of firms and serves as the most common form of production. Artisanal production is referenced by adjacent terms such as petty commodity production, craft, handicraft, cottage industry, homework, microenterprise, own account enterprise, simple or small sector enterprise, tiny sector, and village industry. Barbara Harriss-White provides a working definition of artisanal labour; in her analysis, there is an inextricable connection between artisanal work and industrialized labour. Contrary to the assumption that artisanal labour is a by-product of leisure time, Harriss-White argues that artisans' survival is dependent on this form of work. Even though artisans enjoy some measure of autonomy over the production process, she shows that they cannot retreat into subsistence farming and are in fact incentivized to exploit their own quotas as they earn their dividends through self-exploitation (Harriss-White 2014). This shadowy realm of artisanal production exists in the informal sector that, by 2004–2005, accounted for over half of the Indian workforce, not working for a direct employer (Ghosh 2009: 37). Economist Jayati Ghosh explains that the problem with studying the informal sector is not only of defining it but also of "identifying and quantifying it" (Ghosh 2009: 52). Ghosh explores how the Indian labour force that operates within the informal sector is increasingly a workforce made up of women. Harriss-White flags growing percentages of Scheduled Castes' and Scheduled Tribes' incorporation into the participation index of the non-farm economy within the informal sector (Harriss-White et al. 2013).

The delicate choreography between master craftsman, journeyman, and apprentice on a construction site or a workshop gets buried in the capaciousness of the generic term *mistri* in Hindi/Urdu or artisan in English. Once again, the term has been freighted with such an assortment of meanings that the way pre-colonial labour practices are nested within present-day sites of labour gets obscured. Returning to these defunct terms from an earlier ecumene may help to revivify our understanding of the flattening out of "artisan" in the current ecumene. By tracing these terms, we may come to an understanding of how certain figures and their attendant discourses were superseded by the language of capitalism. But in pursuing this methodology, the historian is confronted with the problem that these indigenous terms have acquired certain colonial accretions: for instance, literature on the *karkhana* system cites European observers who equated it with corruption and exploitation; similar connotations attend other terms (among others, see Bernier 1891). Nonetheless, in paying scrupulous attention to vernacular terms and concepts, we can excavate a pre-capitalist language that has not been superseded entirely by capital logic.

The artisan's signature as a mark of haptic knowledge

In pre-colonial South Asia, the signature was a mark of haptic knowledge. Remnants of the pre-colonial conception of the signature indicate ways the signature was part of haptic knowledge: inviolate, a non-alphabetic bodily trace left on the work which the discerning eye could not mistake for the work of another. Even an illiterate artisan could leave their bodily trace on what they had created through a non-alphabetic iconographic symbol. Conversely, an alphabetic signature could be recognized by the unlettered as an inviolable iconographic sign. The work of pre-colonial artisans was not received as un-individuated, anonymized. In the context of an edited volume on India's skill economy, it is imperative to foreground the historical processes by which colonialism devalued the skills of artisans. The devaluation was especially acute when the work did not have an alphabetic signature.

One common misconception is that the signature is the distinguishing feature of the artist whereas the artisan remains anonymized. This is belied by evidence of signatures by pre-colonial artisans. Along the walkway to Ghiyas ud-Din Tughlaq's fourteenth-century mausoleum in Tughlaqabad (now the southern part of Delhi NCR), one may notice inscriptions in Brahmi script on the paving stones. Historian Narayini Gupta considers these to be masons' marks that would have been used to distinguish the paving stones one mason supplied from another for the purpose of being paid.[1] By the thirteenth century we see the appearance of an ornately stylized signature for the sultan of the Ottoman empire designed by the court calligrapher. This was the *tughra* and it travelled to the Mughal empire to serve as the royal seal on *firmans* (decree issued by a ruler). The *tughra* had a recognizable form – three vertical slashes in the middle with two loops on the left side. The name of the sultan would be at the bottom and the writing within the shape would be honorifics and laudatory titles. What I want to emphasize here is that in a pre-literate society, this signature was both an alphabetic sign and an iconographic sign. The shape of this signature could not be mistaken for anything else. Its uniqueness was inviolable.

The skill of artisans in Mughal *karkhanas* was so highly regarded by their royal patrons that even when the work was not signed to indicate individuated skill, a discerning patron could distinguish each artisan's identity based on their individual skill. According to his memoir *Tuzuk-i-Jahangiri* Mughal Emperor Jehangir (1569–1627), upon viewing a painting from his *karkhana*, could determine which of them had painted an eyebrow or an eye:

> As regards myself, my liking for painting and my practice in judging it have arrived at such a point that when any work is brought before me, either of deceased artists or of those of the present day, without the names being told to me, I say on the spur of the moment that it is the work of such and such a man. And if there be a picture containing many portraits, and each face be the work of a different master, I can discover which face is the work of each of them. If any other person has put in the eye and eyebrow of a face I can perceive whose work the original face is, and who has painted the eye and eyebrows.[2]

Jehangir's claim to be able to distinguish skill indicates that for pre-colonial artists, their work was not received as un-individuated, anonymized.

To appreciate the steady devaluation of the artisan, we must examine the colonial movement devoted to preserving Indian artisanal manufactures. The Arts and Crafts movement was deeply influential for the administrators, anthropologists, and missionaries concerned with *adivasi* artisanal production. Originating in the mid-nineteenth century, the Arts and Crafts Movement was a moderate response to the immiseration of British artisans during the Industrial Revolution. The Great Exhibition of 1851 at the Crystal Palace in London brought the variety and intricacy of Indian design to the notice of the British public.

The ensuing popularity of Indian crafts, as one scholar argues, "rendered Indian skills ethnographic, not industrial" (McGowan 2009: 62). Industrial labour and the skills associated with it, in other words, were classified as distinct from the cultural skills of the artisan which would be henceforth recorded in ethnographies of tribes and castes. This movement was not simply a set of ideas transmitted to the colony from the metropole; instead, it was a response in the metropole to artisanal objects from the colony. Any discussion of the Arts and Crafts Movement, therefore, must contend with it as an intellectual movement as well as an archive of material culture (Brantlinger 1996: 466–485).

The artisan's signature was a significant feature within an emerging nineteenth-century legal framework that included copyright, patents and trademarks. Indian handicrafts dominated the Great Exhibition of 1851 and it was in the wake of that momentous exhibition that British officials built institutions which would administer artisanal production in the metropole and the colony as well as inculcate "taste" among the public. Drawing was recognized under copyright law which, as scholar Arindam Dutta explains, is why architects still sign their drawings. The artisanal production of the Indian colony was the motor for the delineation of these legal frameworks, and yet Indian artisans were anonymized and denied access to these rights claims. Dutta argues the artisan, especially the aboriginal artisan was "an interruptive, unruly figure" whose exclusion from modern employment contracts would make more susceptible to direct super-exploitation. He writes, "Although the artisan occupied the center of aesthetic discourse in the nineteenth century, he or she could not access the liberal legal framework on his or her own terms. What remained for the artisan was the inevitable downward mobility into informal labor (Dutta 2007: 154–155)." The artisan's signature, then, had a direct bearing on their access to legal recognition for their labour, and British colonialism in India had a vested interest in systematically obscuring the pre-colonial traces of artisans' signatures even as it championed traditional Indian handicrafts.

The idealization of the skill of the South Asian artisan was driven by British colonial officials' agenda of creating a division between European industrial modernity and Indian pre-industrial economic decline. Prominent followers of Arts and Crafts ideas in India included Sir George Birdwood, William Morris, E.B. Havell, Ananda Coomaraswamy, and Rudyard Kipling's father John Lockwood Kipling; incidentally, Kipling was "among the first to advocate the revival of Indian handicraft based on training in native techniques" (Tarapor 1980: 53–82). Birdwood was the most active of these men in terms of formulating policies, arranging exhibitions, and writing accounts of the Indian craftsman. Birdwood's *Industrial Arts of India* (1880) presented an idealized picture of the Indian village craftsman:

> But of late these handicraftsmen, for the sake of whose works the whole world has been ceaselessly pouring its bullion for 3000 years into India, and

> who, for all the marvellous tissues and embroideries they have wrought, have polluted no rivers, deformed no pleasing prospects, nor poisoned any air; whose skill and individuality the training of countless generations has developed to the highest perfection, these hereditary craftsmen are being everywhere gathered from their democratic village communities in hundreds and thousands to the colossal mills of Bombay, to drudge in gangs at manufacturing piece goods, in competition with Manchester, in the production of which they are no more intellectually and morally concerned than the grinder of a barrel organ in the tunes it turns out.
>
> *(Birdwood 1880: 58–59)*

Notably, Birdwood's celebration of the Indian artisan's "skill and individuality" was accompanied by the value in terms of "bullion" that skill commanded in the global marketplace over "3000 years." Certain features of the Arts and Crafts movement are evident in this passage. First, the weaver overshadows all other forms of Indian craft. Second, the craftsman was associated with the call for a revival of the pre-industrial. Sustained attention to the plight of artisans may have provoked a critique of industrialism. Rather than an engaged critique of industrial capitalism, this set of responses from the intellectuals of the Arts and Crafts Movement encapsulated a co-optation of any such insurrectionary impulse. Birdwood's response was pernicious in its own way, building the argument for the consumption of artisanal production as a form of nostalgia.

The notion that he was a disinterested champion of Indian artisans was proven false in 1910, when Birdwood was tasked with chairing the Indian section of the annual meeting of the Royal Society of Arts and summarily dismissed it (much like Thomas Babington Macaulay's dismissal of non-Western literature in 1835). When shown a sculpture of the Buddha, he delivered his judgement that India had no fine arts: "This senseless similitude, in its immemorial fixed pose, is nothing more than an uninspired brazen image . . . A boiled suet pudding would serve equally well as a symbol of passionless purity and serenity of soul." The implication was that Indian art was unoriginal, lacking in any disruptive iconoclastic skill which would distinguish the signed work of Western fine art. The Buddha sculpture was actually Javanese and not Indian, a fact that speaks more to Birdwood's lack of discernment than to the skills of the sculptor. It was the colonial expert's inability to read the sculptor's signature that he represented as "senseless" and "uninspired." If 30 years prior he had acknowledged the hereditary craftsmen "whose skill and individuality the training of countless generations has developed to the highest perfection," he later reversed himself to consign them all to being "uninspired" copies of traditional crafts. This dismissal of craft as a mechanical rendition of traditional templates was a way to distinguish European fine art as a higher intellectual pursuit; it was the European mind which could produce art, the South Asian artisan merely produced artefacts (Gell 1992: 56; Coleman 1988: 7). In Birdwood's remark, there was a latent misogyny which equated low-paid artisanal skills as a step above unpaid domestic labour. Yet we should ask why the skill of a cook who delivers the dish according to the recipe (in this case a boiled suet pudding) is somehow inferior or uninspired when compared to an original, innovated recipe.

Scholars have argued that the signature is an indelible mark that differentiates the labour of one skilled artisan from an unskilled labourer. Deepak Mehta suggests that "the worker . . . is characterized by a signature. This signature is not available to the bride who cures yarn in everyday life because as a worker she can be substituted. Her conjugal household may financially contract the labour, a contract that is denied when cloth for the shroud is woven" (Mehta 1997: 21). The metaphor through which women artisans describe their own signatures is the *lal kitab* (red book). Elsewhere in his research on Muslim Ansari weavers of North India, Mehta documents how women artisans describe their skills in quilting. Each woman engaged in quilting can provide a genealogy of each scrap of cloth, almost akin to an archive with its own protocols for recording and knowing history. The quilter, Mehta notes, carries within her head a *lal kitab*: "The book is notional and operates on the basis of a woman's recapitulation of past and remembered events" (Mehta 1997: 161). For such women, often barred from formal education and constrained by patriarchy from claiming recognition for their skills of quilting as on par with the male domain of weaving, this *lal kitab* is the internal redoubt that cannot be wrested from them.

The work itself bears its own signature as does the quilter's mobilizing of a repertoire of motifs with her accompanying interpretations of their auspicious or unfavourable qualities. Mehta describes the convivial nature of the exchange among women quilters:

> Usually there is a discernible difference between the "traditionalists" and "modernists," with the former arguing for geometric designs and the customarily used colours of white and green. The latter prefer a variety of bright colours, with numerous flowers, petals and plants as motifs. At this point most women reveal their *lal kitab*, citing precedents for embroidering specific designs or cautioning against others. The *lal kitab* becomes important because someone will provide an example of how a design of flowers was represented on an embroidered quilt and the consequent breakup of the marriage. Another provides a counterexample of how the same design blessed the woman for whom it was made with innumerable male children.
> *(Mehta 1997: 164–165).*

Much like Birdwood's analogy with suet pudding or Mehta's reference to the bride's task of curing yarn, the work of quilting is unpaid domestic labour. However, it is incontrovertibly de-anonymized and no one quilt is like another.

The parallelism between handicraft and domestic labour becomes a way to differentiate or denigrate the skill of the artisan. Is the bride's labour easily substituted according to her fellow quilters? Surely, each woman who cures yarn does so in her own way with varying levels of skill; the bodily technique and gestures might be mimicked but never exactly reproduced by another. Among these women sharing in the work of curing yarn there would be constant comments about how one's technique is superior to another's. The social worker Anis Kidwai claimed that in her overseeing of rehabilitation schemes for Partition refugees, Hindu Punjabi women refugees lacked the careful attention to detail and skill in their stitchwork when compared to Muslim women whose "sewing was neater, more delicate and superior" but who worked much less efficiently (Kidwai 2011: 165–166). Indeed, scholars have shown that women's skills are routinely devalued (Grugulis et al. 2004). The linkages between artisanal skill as a step above domestic labour or the presumption that women artisans lack a signature and, by implication, are not skilled in relation to their male counterparts has direct repercussions on their wage-earning capacities. Furthermore, certain forms of labour, especially the work of care which maintains the everyday and is usually termed "women's work," is not within the money economy and is therefore devalued.

Adivasi artisanry

This chapter has referred to several marginalized communities within the larger pool of artisans: Muslim women quilters, Partition refugees, and sub-contracted daily wage labourers. The final section examines, in more depth, haptic knowledge within one specific marginalized community: Pardhan Gonds are one of India's *adivasi* communities (glossed as indigenous, an umbrella term that literally means original *adi* inhabitant *vasi*). Pardhan Gonds historically served as the bards and genealogists of the larger Gond community; within the pre-capitalist social ordering, the term *jajmani* system encapsulated certain ritual caste obligations between feudal patron and service caste. In this instance, Gonds were the *jajmans* with the Pardhans as the service caste who would annually visit to exercise their ceremonial feudal obligation of singing. Pardhan Gond bardic recitations were accompanied by a *bana* instrument (fiddle or stringed lute) the Pardhan had crafted himself, thus combining the knowledge work of the genealogist with the labour of the artisan. The subalternity of the Gond community can be gauged from census reports of their poverty level. Gonds are one of the 645 Scheduled Tribes recognized in the Indian Constitution. They are the second most numerous Scheduled Tribe in Madhya Pradesh. The economic status of the Gond community is either subsistence farming or landless labour. About 89% of the Gonds of Madhya Pradesh are registered as cultivators or agricultural labourers.

The late *adivasi* Pardhan Gond painter Jangarh Singh Shyam (b. 1964–d. 2001) built on the bardic traditions and artisanal production of his community, aspects which were obscured in the heroization of Shyam as iconoclastic artist. Shyam performed low-paid and unpaid labour like his forebears, itinerant minstrel during one period and a member of a road construction gang or begging during another. His style of painting was indebted to village women whose art included wall paintings, floor patterns, and tattoos. Even as Shyam's fame continues to grow and the price of his paintings appreciate in the global art market, there is not a recognition of Shyam's skills as bridging both art and artisanry. Shyam brought artisanal modes of production (i.e. shared canvases, borrowed techniques, apprenticeships) into his labour as artist. It was precisely this mode of work that reflected his artisanal antecedents.

According to the artist Gulammohammed Sheikh, Gond art straddled a major shift in mode of production. In its early stages this art form inhabited the realm of use-value "since making pictures or reliefs on walls of houses is a community act in most tribal societies" and "the practice does not involve monetary transactions between the 'maker' and the 'user.'" Sheikh questioned how an object produced for use could function when it was transplanted into an economy of exchange. Would the pre-commodity form of production change in its very essentials or would it continue to retain its intrinsic use-value even while being put into circulation as the product of Gond labour for sale? In Sheikh's words: "How would such works, removed from the site of their genesis, function when put for sale as commodities?" (Sheikh 1998: 18).

The problem as Sheikh saw it concerned the hierarchy of modernities within which the *adivasi* was always placed in opposing relation to the modern through the category of folk or tribal art. Sheikh's point implies that tribal art troubles the borders between those goods that are recognizably modern versus other objects that enter the circuit of exchange while being clearly marked as belonging to another time. It is in this persistently uneven collision between the time of capital and what it sees as an impediment to its flow that we can glimpse a fragmented and discontinuous series of Pardhan Gond attempts to adapt themselves to the regimes of modern work. In the same moment of transforming themselves into producers of goods the Pardhan Gond artists also try to remake the human relations between artisan and community, men and women as producers, worker and owner in ways that are not subsumed within the goal of maximum extraction of surplus but instead give the producer a measure of control and self-determination over their conditions of work.

Haptic knowledge is capacious enough to enable us to think about Shyam's many forms of manual labour on a continuum. By examining Shyam's art within the framework of haptic knowledge, we do not need to discount the labour or skills of women whose art inspired his paintings but who would not themselves be considered artists, or even artisans. For the Indian government, only certain forms of labour were identified as handicrafts. A pamphlet issued by the All-India Handicrafts Board in 1969 for Bastar District farther south in the same state (then Madhya Pradesh, now Chhattisgarh) claimed, "This study of tribal crafts of Bastar district has revealed a rather striking feature that except for minor woodwork and basketry, the tribals do not pursue any handicrafts" (Duke Library and Archives South Asia Pamphlet Collection 1969: 11). This meant that the labour that inspired Shyam's art would not even be classified as artisanal skills. Such an omission primarily affected women artisans whose artisanal skills included painting on mud walls (*bhittichitra*) or tattooing (*godna*) as well as the aforementioned work by men in creating the instrument (*bana*) which Pardhan Gond men used to accompany their bardic recitations for patronage from upper-caste Gonds. Shyam's nephew Rajendra Shyam, himself an artist, explained that there were links between their painting and the blue designs that his wife had tattooed on her ankles prior to marriage (Author Interview: Bhopal, 2011).

There is a direct conflict between the demand for individuated artistic work and the pre-colonial traditions of cooperative artisanal labour. Artisanal production relies on several hands, generally apprentices overseen by a master craftsman, whereas contemporary artistic production is seen as the work of one creative genius. Raymond Williams considers the decisive moment artist and artisan were rent asunder to be the exclusion of engravers from the newly established Royal Academy of late eighteenth-century England, where the so-called "fine arts" of painting, drawing, and sculpture would be showcased. Of relevance for the present argument, Williams explains that this separation drew upon other foundational binaries of mind and body, intellectual versus manual labour (Williams 1976: 33). For one prestigious and large-scale project, Shyam organized a team of Pardhan Gond men from Patangarh village and elsewhere to assist him. Embodying the role of a master craftsman establishing a guild, Shyam mentored these young artists, providing them material help, even hosting them at times in his own home in the city. Some had assisted Shyam before with colouring in or finishing up his larger works. For many of them (such as Bhajju Shyam), this was their first introduction to a career they made their own.[3] Although the mural was the work of an artisanal community, the responsibility of paying everyone fell solely on Shyam who paid each rupees 3,000 to 5,000 according to the work they had done from Shyam's own payment of rupees 7 lakh for the project.

Modernity launched the process of stripping the signature from the artist's work. As Walter Benjamin expounded in his essay "The Work of Art in the Age of Mechanical Reproduction," the mechanical copy diminished the aesthetic value of the original (Benjamin 1935). The signature, for indigenous artisans who aspire to be recognized as named artists, is hardly the guarantee of their artistic "presence" in the artwork, rather market logics predetermine the perception of artistic skill. Present-day indigenous artisans are discursively produced as place-based, rooted in a culture of region. Since much of artisanal production in indigenous communities is done collectively and does not bear the mark of a single signature, it lends itself to appropriation by designers. The signature, then, is a marker of un-substitutable, individuated labour that escapes anonymization. It is the signature that designates artistic work as unique whereas the unsigned artisanal craft is treated as something which is part of a larger repertoire of cultural traditions held in common.

While in the instance cited earlier Shyam relied on cooperative artisanal labour, in another (detailed in the following) he demanded recognition for his signature as an individuated artist. The contradiction between these two moments shows how the monetary value the artwork commands determine how the artist positions his identity – paying young artists and mentoring them or struggling against other artists' effort to supplant his work by copying it. Neither the artist nor the artisan faces this problem, perhaps, but it is one which Shyam, the artist-artisan, confronted. In the summer of 2013 when I was in Bhopal, I met with the artist Akhilesh who has been associated with Bharat Bhavan Museum from its inception. Akhilesh knew the late Pardhan Gond painter Jangarh Singh Shyam very well and has coined the term "Jangarh Kalam" to describe Gond art. Akhilesh argues that it was Jangarh who developed Gond art into the form we have now come to expect and before he became famous, there were several different styles of painting that the Gonds working for Bharat Bhavan were experimenting with. Other artists like Doobi, a young girl, and Narmada Prasad Tekam came to work in Bhopal for Bharat Bhavan at the same time as Shyam. They saw that his pieces were successful, and he was attaining more of a reputation than they were, so they began to copy his style. This led to heated conflicts and Shyam made them promise that they would distinguish their work from his by not incorporating his signature – certain motifs that could only be found in his work. This carried on for some years and one can identify the artist of paintings in this period from a characteristic signature motif in their work (Author Interview with Akhilesh, Bhopal, 2013).

Forty-four Gond artists were asked to reflect on the signatures that defined their own work in *Signature: Patterns in Gond Art* published by Gita Wolf of Tara Books. Wolf began by contending that "the singular, most striking thing about these patterns – or 'detailing' as it is known among the Gonds – is the fact that each artist has invented his or her own particular design." This pattern is their "signature . . . We would like this individual pattern – the signature – to be a marker, a trope which gathers together, links, and opens out the genius of Gond art" (Wolf 2010: Introduction, no pagination). The signatures range from fish scales, twisted rope to dancers and marriage processions. The adoption of a signature then appears to be an attempt to individualize a collective artform that was developed by an individual; thus, it is a mark of authenticating but is itself a replication of the original gesture by Shyam that sought to separate his work from the copies.

The proliferation of copies and appropriations by designers attest to the erosion of artisans' rights within a capitalist economic system that overwrites their labour and skills as cultural traditions held in common, and thus, belonging to no one in particular. Saurabh Gupta of Manthan Design has uploaded a series of videos on YouTube entitled "Making a Gond Art Brush," in which he shows viewers how to disassemble the key motifs of Gond paintings into commands for a computer program which can then reproduce a generic Gond painting. Of course, the very act of disassembling presumes to render Gond painting generic, but this is not something the designer acknowledges (Gupta). Aditi Prakash, owner of Pure Ghee Designs, advertises herself as a designer who "believes in creating products with a soul, products that are powerful antidotes to the big hollow brands of commerce." For Samode Safari Lodge in Madhya Pradesh's Bandhavgarh National Park, Prakash provides "Gond paintings" of a tiger on the walls of a bathroom to "bring out the mood of the jungle." "Oh! The jungle can be such fun!" Prakash exclaims (Prakash 2011). The paintings are a copy of a wall mural made by Shyam although his name features nowhere in the credits or as a citation in Prakash's blog. At issue here is not the designer taking uncredited inspiration from another artist or even attributing the work of one artist (Shyam) to a generalized tribal identity. Prior to Shyam's garnering institutional support from Jagdish Swaminathan, Pardhan Gond artists received 5 rupees for their work; at Bharat Bhavan Museum, Swaminathan helped these artists receive upwards of 500 rupees (Tully 1991). By ignoring the signature of Gond artists and demoting their artwork to cultural ethnographic skills freely available to inspire anyone, designers and entrepreneurs threaten the livelihood of Gond artists struggling to carve a niche in the global art market for their particular skills.

Much of Shyam's life and his formative experience was as an indigent artisan farmer who took on menial jobs to supplement his meagre income. Shyam's father had worked for the British anthropologist Verrier Elwin as a *khansamma* (man of all work), leaving Patangarh village to accompany Elwin to Shillong. According to my interview with Shyam's eldest brother, the village suffered indebtedness and extreme poverty 40 years ago and it was through remittances sent by Shyam's father and eventually Shyam himself that circumstances improved (Author Interview with Shyam family, Bhopal, 2011). One of his five brothers in Patangarh told me they grow rice, lentils (*masoor* and *makka dal*), grains (wheat or *gehun*), legumes like soybeans (*soya*) and chickpeas (*chana*), and the millets (*kodo* known by the same name in English and *kutki* or little millet). There were, in 2012, roughly

1,500 people in the village within 150 houses and of these, about 40 families made art (Author Interview with Shyam family, Patangarh village, 2012). As I learned from the local Hindi writer Vijay Chaurasia, much of the artwork in the village is done by women as they are the ones who recall the stories of gods and goddesses within the artwork (Author Interview with Dr. Vijay Chaurasia, Garha Serai, 2012).

We can glean Shyam's self-representation of his shift from manual to skilled labourer in the interview Shyam gave to BBC journalist Mark Tully. Before Shyam was recognized as an artist, he worked as a day labourer. Shyam revealed in conversations with Tully that he attended school till age 13 when his father died (Tully 1991: 268). From his youthful chores of being a cowherd and getting into mischief by throwing stones at birds roosting in the trees, Shyam now faced adult responsibilities (Author Interview with Shyam family, Bhopal, 2011). When Tully asked him why he worked when he had land of his own, Shyam explained that there were 50 to 60 people in his family sharing a plot that was about 10 to 12 acres. So, the road construction gang was preferable although it kept him away from his village for months at a time. "I lived alone," Shyam told Tully, "and used to sleep under trees in the hot weather. When it rained or got cold, we used to put up some sort of shelter. The jobs used to last a few months at a time, and then we went back home" (Tully 1991: 277). Shyam's elder brother (now deceased) would sculpt statues to sell in the village (Author Interview with Shyam family, Bhopal, 2011). In order to support his wife and one of his sisters, Shyam quit government school and started working. He described the types of work he found as a subsistence labourer: carrying loads of wood to the bazaar to sell, working with a road construction gang carrying baskets of mud on his head and digging up mud to fill other people's baskets, or working in the fields. This last option, augmented with money he made from collecting firewood from the jungle and selling it to the village schoolmaster, was only taken as a recourse when Shyam was unemployed from the road gang.

Most journalistic accounts of Shyam frame his entry to the city of Bhopal with the talent scouts of Bharat Bhavan as part of what we may call a narrative of discovery where art was conferred onto him through the museum and its representatives. Although such accounts of Shyam's art present a linear trajectory for his acquisition of artistic skills, this does not accurately represent the dialogic aspect of the labour itself. Shyam, in his own accounts, did not denigrate his earlier work or deny the earlier self whose struggles informed his current work. In Shyam's own narrative, however, art was something he practiced before he was "discovered." He began painting by secretly copying his elder brother and other Patangarh artists not by copying urban artists. If we recognize Shyam's developing of Pardhan Gond art on canvas as a dialogic and self-reflexive act, then we begin to understand how the concept of haptic knowledge enables a more expansive view of all the labours that inform the knowledge housed in the body of the artist at any given moment. At most we can say that Shyam's transition from destitute artisan-farmer to recognized artist occurred in 1981 when Shyam was 17. He met students working for the artist and activist-curator Jagdish Swaminathan who were traveling through Madhya Pradesh looking for Gond wall paintings for Swaminathan's Bharat Bhavan arts complex in Bhopal (Swaminathan 1987: 9). The students saw one of the paintings Shyam had done on the walls of a neighbour's hut in the village of Patangarh. When I interviewed his eldest brother, he said the painting was of Hanuman Bajrang Bali depicted in reds and browns as there were no artificial paints available to them in the village (Author Interview with Shyam family, Bhopal, 2011). The students and later Swaminathan were impressed with the paintings. Shyam was working in the fields at the time and was called for. After speaking with Swaminathan, Shyam asked to be enrolled into Bharat Bhavan.

While enrolling in an institution was a crucial first step in the transition from rural artisan to globally recognized artist, the next important turning point was a shift in Shyam's materials of production. He switched from charcoal and traditional vegetable dyes on mud walls and mineral paints to acrylics on paper and canvas. Within five years, the artisan had become an acclaimed artist, awarded the Madhya Pradesh government's highest award, the Shikhar Samman. He went on to exhibit his work in Kolkata, Paris, and Tokyo. But the subaltern artist's life ended tragically in 2001. Elsewhere I have analysed the circumstances of Shyam's death in greater detail and how his death is mourned and commemorated. Certainly, the denigration of his identity as both artist and artisan contributed to his death.

The economic protectionist model launched by Verrier Elwin in the Nehruvian era treated artisanal industry across India in the 1950s and 1960s as part of the burgeoning vocational training sector; by the 1970s, Tribal Research Institutes were established to monitor tribal development policies. Institutions like the Kendra Lalit Kala Akademi (National Academy for Fine Arts) launched an ethnographic survey of folk craft traditions in 1956 under the supervision of Marxist poet Bishnu Dey. Within a decade, the Warli painting tradition of Maharashtra and the Mithila painting tradition of Bihar began to receive institutional support. Whereas Elwin's own practice admitted room to refine and alter policies, the vast bureaucratic apparatus of the post-colonial Indian government bolstered itself with its own data generated through annual reports and administrative experts who could not move beyond the inherent assumptions that relegated artisanal industry to a folk past as India focused resolutely on modern and large-scale industrialization at the level of national policy.

For this bureaucracy, *adivasis*' artisanal skills were patronized as part of universal education and health care as well as more forms of empowerment or skills development that located rural and *adivasi* poor in a small-scale livelihood sector which lay in some relation to agriculture and allied industries. By the 1960s, the Indian state had begun to enshrine *adivasi* craft. Through the combined efforts of Kamaladevi Chattopadhyay, L.C. Jain, and others, a number of institutions and co-operative societies were set up to organize the production and marketing of Indian handicrafts. In Chattopadhyay's characterization, the *adivasi* artisan was an "intimate child of nature" guided by "intuition" (Chattopadhyay 2000: 4). The state would serve as mediator for and judge of *adivasi* craft, and *adivasi* artisans would rely on state patronage.

Touch and knowing the world through touch are an integral part of haptic knowledge. The academic task of defining haptic knowledge has its early curatorial counterpart in Jagdish Swaminathan's chosen title for the Roopankar Collection catalogue *The Perceiving Fingers*. Notable in Swaminathan's innovative collection strategies for Bharat Bhavan was the idea that *adivasis* had talents which talent scouts should be trained to identify; this was a sharp contrast from prior government policies which reduced *adivasi* artisanal production to skills that any of them might perform and whose worth any bureaucrat might judge. Swaminathan described how 30 boys and girls from art colleges in the state of Madhya Pradesh were chosen as talent scouts, given an orientation and training, divided into groups, and sent into rural Madhya Pradesh to identify promising *adivasi* artists after completing a stay of two months in their assigned districts. Their collection would become the core of the folk and *adivasi* wing of Bharat Bhavan's Roopankar Gallery (Hacker 2014: 191).

Swaminathan's own incipient concept of Bharat Bhavan as a space of haptic knowledge meant that he actively worked to help artisans explore new methods, materials, and mediums. This was in marked contrast to the sort of vocational training they would receive where they were restricted to traditional methods and a set of motifs deemed culturally appropriate by the state expert. Swaminathan encouraged Shyam to switch from traditional vegetable dyes and mineral paints to acrylics on paper. Whereas Elwin would have fought to preserve traditional methods, Swaminathan conceived of Bharat Bhavan as a space where the traditional Gond artist could experiment with modern materials and subject matter as it inspired him and there was no restriction placed on his artistic expression. Shyam initially worked as an attendant in Bharat Bhavan's graphic studios where he quickly mastered printmaking techniques. He moved beyond making simple screen-printed copies to experiment with serigraphy and, through "multiple impressions, textures, stencilling, splashing inks, and scraping, and scratching the silkscreen itself," he essentially created unique impressions in each screen-print or a "mono-print" (Karode and Jain 2018). Aside from its art workshops where artists like Shyam learned print-making techniques, Bharat Bhavan hosted international art biennales and world poetry festivals to stimulate the imagination of artists.

We may interpret Shyam's artist statement in the catalogue for the *Magiciens de la Terre* with the curator's own preoccupations and mediations in mind. Shyam began by saying "I am from the Pardhan Gond community" and went on to describe what inspired him as an artist:

> I passed my childhood in the company of the mountains, forests filled with trees, birds, animals, insects, and terrifying deities. I was both frightened and amazed. My people had to rediscover this forest on the walls of their houses, with clay and colours. This with the intention of calling the deities on to the hearth. This practice is still in use. I was so scared of these deities that I thought I should try to represent them in forms that would be personal to me. I was trying to crystallize fear in forms of beauty. This is how I could feel my fright in the form of raw vibrations – the tiger, the bushy banyan, the multi-coloured poisonous insects, all charged with the fluid of fear, love and beauty: I imagine them and I paint them. My ancestors painted black and white squares in our courtyards. Me, I use colours. I want to draw the figures of my desires and want to charge them with my desire. For me, art and life are continuous silences. Art penetrates life like a dancing explosion. I remember the forests. This memory makes me paint what I paint.
>
> *(Martin et al. 1989,* translation mine*)*[4]

Shyam's phrase "raw vibrations" describes his own artistic techniques, which he would develop further over the course of his career, and which distinguished his work from his contemporary Gond artists. By the 1990s, Shyam had developed his pen and ink drawings with a Rotring pen bought on his trips abroad; the pen and its jet-black ink enabled his "experimentation with the graded tonality of each stroke of the pen attained by varying levels of pressure exerted" and Shyam's version of a chiaroscuro pattern with this experimentation yielded what art critics call a "radiant sunburst" (Karode and Jain 2018). Here we may recall Shyam's own phrase of "raw vibrations," which evokes the technique he was yet to develop. Far from performing the role of naïve, self-taught *adivasi* artist, Shyam's self-reflection revealed his understanding of the creative process at work in bringing his art to life. He was not discussing the transmission of an unchanged tradition; rather, he was articulating his conception of modernity in relation to his ancestor's techniques versus his style and vision.

Conclusion

The artisan serves as a heuristic device to open up a set of questions regarding how labour was named and evaluated. Scholars Nandini Gooptu and Rangan Chakravarty examine how the Indian Government's skill development initiatives "overlook and undervalue [. . .] pre-existing or traditional skills and artisanal forms of apprenticeship" (Gooptu and Chakravarty 2018: 294–295).

In terms of both academic research and the drafting of development policies, the neglect of the artisan means that a whole episteme of pre-colonial labour is cordoned off and therefore cannot serve as a way to marshal, draw insights from, and theorize about conditions of Indian labour now. Inherited colonial categories overdetermine our scholarly understanding of Indian labour today. A reliance on these colonial categories threatens our ability to comprehend the perspectives of Indian labourers themselves. As a corrective, the argument of my chapter emphasizes pre-colonial concepts in various vernaculars and the lived practice of artisanal work. De-skilling, according to one political economist, is central to capital-labour relations under advanced capitalism (Braverman 1974). To excavate the traces of pre-colonial skills within artisanal communities, then, is to draw lessons for the future from the past. Since our written histories bear the indelible stain of their encounter with colonialism, the stakes in charting the domain of haptic knowledge are to imagine forms of labour which defied and exceeded the taxonomy of the colonial archive.

Acknowledgements

The author would like to thank the editors Saikat Maitra, Sebastien Schwecke, Srabani Maitra, and the family of Jangarh Singh Shyam, Gyan Pandey, Akhilesh, Dr. Vijay Chaurasia, Sohail Hashmi, Leslie Dick, Rashmi Dube Bhatnagar, Douglas E. Haynes, Milind Wakankar, Justine "Ellie" Smith, Arnaud Kaba, and Pamela H. Smith and all participants and convenors of the International Institute for Asian Studies-Leiden Summer School titled "Reading Craft: Itineraries of Culture, Knowledge, and Power in the Global Ecumene" at Chiang Mai University (2014) and the Association Jeunes Études Indiennes (French-Indian South Asianist Organization) Workshop titled "Labour, Mobility and Mobilization" at Jawaharlal Nehru University in New Delhi (2014).

Notes

1 I am grateful to Sohail Hashmi for this reference.
2 *Jahangir, Tuzuk-i-Jahangiri or Memoirs of Jahangir*. 1914. Volume 2. Translated by Alexander Rogers, Edited by Henry Beveridge, Project Gutenberg, 21.
3 Among the notable names were Ram Singh Urveti, Narmada Prasad Tekam, Suresh Dhurve, Sumer Singh Kushram, Subhash Vyam, Bhajju Shyam, Anand Shyam, Kalavati Shyam, Mohan Singh Shyam, and Bhagat Singh. Jain, *Conjuror's Archive*, 45.
4 I am grateful to Leslie Dick for scans of the exhibition catalogue.

References

Anderson, M. 2004. "India 1858–1950: The Illusion of Free Labour," in D. Hay and P. Craven (eds.), *Masters, Servants and Magistrates in Britain and the Empire*, pp. 422–454. Chapel Hill, NC: University of North Carolina Press.

Apter, Emily. 2013. *Against World Literature: On the Politics of Untranslatability*. Verso.
AsiaInCH. *Encyclopedia: The Encyclopedia of Intangible Cultural Heritage*. www.craftrevival.org/Glossary [Stable URL].
Benjamin, Walter. 1935. "The Work of Art in the Age of Mechanical Reproduction," in Hannah Arendt (ed.), German by Harry Zohn (trans.), *Illuminations*. New York: Schocken Books, 1969.
Bernier, Francois. 1891. *Travels in the Mogul Empire, A.D. 1656–1668*. Trans. from French by Archibald Constable. London.
Birdwood, Sir George. 1880. *The Industrial Arts of India*, pp. 58–59. London: Chapman and Hall.
Brantlinger, Patrick. 1996. "A Postindustrial Prelude to Post-Colonialism: John Ruskin, William Morris and Gandhianism," *Critical Inquiry* 22: 3 (Spring), 466–485.
Braverman, Harry. 1974. *Labor and Monopoly Capital: The Degradation of Work in the Twentieth Century*. New York, NY: Monthly Review Press.
Brown, Rebecca M. 2009. *Displaying Time: The Many Temporalities of the Festival of India*. University of Washington Press.
Chakrabarty, Dipesh. 1983. "Conditions for Knowledge of Working-Class Conditions: Employers, Government and the Jute of Calcutta, 1890–1940," in Ranajit Guha (ed.), *Subaltern Studies II: Writings on South Asian History and Society*. Delhi: Oxford University Press.
Chakrabarty, Dipesh. 1984. "Trade Unions in a Hierarchical Culture: The Jute Workers of Calcutta, 1920–50," in Ranajit Guha (ed.), *Subaltern Studies III: Writings on South Asian History and Society*. Delhi: Oxford University Press.
Chakrabarty, Dipesh. 1989. *Rethinking Working Class History: Bengal, 1890–1940*. Princeton.
Chandavarkar, Rajnarayan. 1981. "Workers' Politics and the Mill Districts in Bombay between the Wars," *Modern Asian Studies* 15, 603–647.
Chandavarkar, Rajnarayan. 1985. "Industrialization in India before 1947: Conventional Approaches and Alternative Perspectives," *Modern Asian Studies* 19, 623–668.
Chandavarkar, Rajnarayan. 1994. *The Origins of Industrial Capitalism in India: Business Strategies and the Working Classes in Bombay, 1900–1940*. Cambridge University Press.
Chattopadhyay, Kamaladevi. 2000. *India's Craft Tradition*. Govt. of India, Publications Division, Ministry of Information and Broadcasting.
Coleman, R. 1988. *The Art of Work: An Epitaph to Skill*. London: Pluto Press.
Dutta, Arindam. 2007. *The Bureaucracy of Beauty: Design in the Age of Its Global Reproducibility*. Routledge.
Feibleman, J. K. 1966. "Technology and Skills," *Technology and Culture* 7: 318–328.
Flanders, J. 1981. *The Craftsman's Way: Canadian Expression*. Toronto: University of Toronto Press.
Gell, Alfred. 1992. "The Technology of Enchantment and the Enchantment of Technology," in J. Chattopadhyay, Coote and A. Shelton (eds.), *Anthropology, Art and Aesthetics*, pp. 40–63, 56. Oxford: Clarendon.
Ghosh, Jayati. 2009. *Never Done and Poorly Paid: Women's Work in Globalizing India*. Women Unlimited.
Gooptu, Nandini and Rangan Chakravarty. 2018. "Skill, Work and Gendered Identity in Contemporary India: The Business of Delivering Home-Cooked Food for Domestic Consumption," *Journal of South Asian Development* 13: 3, 293–314.
Government of India, All India Handicrafts Board, Planning Section. 1969. *Report on Tribal Crafts of Bastar District, Survey Report No 119*. Duke Library and Archives South Asia Pamphlet Collection.

Grugulis, I., Warhurst, C. and E. Keep. 2004. "What's Happening to Skill?," in C. Warhurst, I. Grugulis and E. Keep (eds.), *The Skills That Matter*, pp. 1–18. Basingstoke, UK: Palgrave Macmillan.

Guha-Thakurta, Tapti. 1992. *The Making of a New 'Indian' Art: Artists, Aesthetics and Nationalism in Bengal.* Cambridge University Press.

Gupta, Saurabh. *Manthan Designs.* YouTube. http://www.youtube.com/user/manthan design/videos.

Hacker, Katherine. 2014."A Simultaneous Validity of Co-Existing Cultures: J. Swaminathan, the Bharat Bhavan and Contemporaneity," *Archives of Asian Art* 64: 2, 191–209.

Harriss-White, Barbara. 2014. "Self-Employment/Petty Production: Labour Theory and (Im)practical Politics," Paper Presented at JNU, New Delhi for AJEI Workshop.

Harriss-White, Barbara, Elisabetta Basile, Anita Dixit, Pinaki Joddar, Aseem Prakash, and Kaushal Vidyarthee. 2013. *Dalits and Adivasis in India's Business Economy: Three Essays and an Atlas.* Gurgaon: Three Essays Collective.

Haynes, Douglas E. 2012. *Small Town Capitalism in Western India: Artisans, Merchants and the Making of the Informal Economy, 1870–1960.* Cambridge University Press.

Herzfeld, Michael. 2003. *The Body Impolitic: Artisans and Artifice in the Global Hierarchy of Value.* First Ed. University of Chicago Press.

Ingold, Tim. 2000. *The Perception of the Environment: Essays on Livelihood, Dwelling and Skill.* Routledge.

Jahangir, Tuzuk-i-Jahangiri or Memoirs of Jahangir. 1914. Volume 2. Trans. Alexander Rogers. Ed. Henry Beveridge. Project Gutenberg.

Jorgensen, Hans. 1995. *A Dictionary of the Classical Newari* (original publication date 1936). Second Ed. New Delhi: Asian Educational Services.

Joshi, Chitra. 1981. "Kanpur Textile Labour: Some Structural Features of Formative Years," *Economic and Political Weekly* xvi, 1823–1828.

Joshi, Chitra. 1985. "Bonds of Community, Ties of Religion: Kanpur Textile Workers in the Early Twentieth Century," *Indian Economic and Social History Review* 22, 251–280.

Joshi, Chitra. 2018. *Lost Worlds: Indian Labour and Its Forgotten Histories.* New Delhi: Permanent Black.

Kaba, Arnaud. 2022a. "Between Construction Yard and Village: Changing Relations of Caste and Hierarchy among Madhya Pradesh's labouring classes," *Journal of Agrarian Change*, 1–20.

Kaba, Arnaud. 2022b. "Beyond the Disaster: Communities of Practice and Statuses of Labor among Bhopal's Metalworkers," *Samaj Issue 28: Subalternity, Marginality, and Agency in Contemporary India*, p. 16 Based on "The 'Precariats' Cultures: Values at Work and Work's Value amongst Metal Workers in Madhya Pradesh," Paper Presented at JNU, New Delhi for AJEI Workshop, 2014.

Karode, Roobina and Jyotindra Jain, curators. 2018. *Jangarh Singh Shyam: A Conjuror's Archive* Exhibition. Kiran Nadar Museum of Art, New Delhi, Attended: December 18, 2018.

Kidwai, Anis. 2011. *In Freedom's Shade.* Trans. Ayesha Kidwai. New Delhi: Penguin.

Layton, E. T. 1974. "Technology as Knowledge," *Technology and Culture* 15, 31–41.

Macaulay, Thomas Babington. 1835. "Minute on Education" in Henry Sharp (ed.), *Selections from the Educational Records, Bureau of Education, India*, I. Calcutta, Superintendent, Government Printing, 1920.

Martin, Jean-Hubert, Mark Francis, et al. 1989. *Magiciens de la Terre.* Exhibition Catalog. French. Paris: Editions du Centre Georges Pompidou.

McGowan, Abigail. 2009. *Crafting the Nation in Colonial India.* Palgrave Macmillan.

Mehta, Deepak. 1997. *Work, Ritual, Biography: A Muslim Community in North India*. Oxford University Press.
Mitter, Partha. 1995. *Art and Nationalism in Colonial India 1850–1920: Occidental Orientations*. Cambridge University Press.
Mudimbe, V. Y. 1988. *The Invention of Africa: Gnosis, Philosophy, and the Order of Knowledge*. Bloomington: Indiana University Press.
Pinney, Christopher. 2004. *Photos of the Gods: The Printed Image and Political Struggle in India*. Reaktion Books.
Prakash, Aditi. 2011, February 13. *Kalamkari Designs for Samode Safari Lodge*. Pure Ghee Designs blog. http://puregheedesigns.blogspot.in/2011/02/kalamkari-paintings-for-samode-safari.html.
Pye, David. 1964. *The Nature of Design*. London: Studio Vista.
Ratcliffe, Matthew. 2008. "The Phenomenology of Touch," in *Feelings of Being: Phenomenology, Psychiatry, and the Sense of Reality*, pp. 77–102. Oxford University Press.
Roy, Tirthankar. 1993. *Artisans and Industrialization: Indian Weaving in the Twentieth Century*. New Delhi: Oxford University Press.
Sarkar, Sumit. 1973. *The Swadeshi Movement in Bengal, 1903–1908*. New Delhi: People's Publishing House.
Sen, Samita. 1999. *Women and Labour in Late Colonial India: The Bengal Jute Industry*. Cambridge University Press.
Sethi, Aman. 2011. *A Free Man: A True Story of Life and Death in Delhi*. Random House India.
Sheikh, Gulammohamed. 1998. "The World of Jangarh Singh Shyam," in Jyotindra Jain (ed.), *Other Masters: Five Contemporary Folk and Tribal Artists of India*. New Delhi: Crafts Museum and The Handicrafts and Handlooms Exports Corporation.
Smith, Pamela H. 2004. *The Body of the Artisan: Art and Experience in the Scientific Revolution*. University of Chicago.
Steinfeld, R. J. 2001. *Coercion, Contract and Free Labour in the Nineteenth Century*. Cambridge University Press.
Swaminathan, Jagdish. 1987. *The Perceiving Fingers: Catalogue of Roopankar Collection of Folk and Adivasi Art from Madhya Pradesh, India*. Bhopal: Bharat Bhavan.
Tarapor, Mahrukh. 1980. "John Lockwood Kipling and British Art Education in India," *Victorian Studies* 24: 1 (Autumn), 53–82.
Tully, Mark. 1991. *No Full Stops in India*. London: Viking.
Van der Linden, Marcel and Prabhu P. Mohapatra, eds. 2009. *Labour Matters: Towards Global Histories, Studies in Honour of Sabyasachi Bhattacharya*. New Delhi: Tullika Books.
Venkatesan, Soumhya. 2003. *Craft Matters: Artisans, Development and the Indian Nation*. Orient Black Swan.
Wakankar, Milind. 2021. *On Deities: The Aesthetics of Concretion*. Routledge.
Williams, Raymond. 1976. *Keywords*. London: Fontana.
Wolf, Gita. 2010. *Signature: Patterns in Gond Art*. Eds. Gita Wolf, Bhajju Shyam, and Jonathan Yamakami. Tara Books.

7

SKILLING AS A MODE OF DOING

Techniques and trajectories of street vending in Delhi's weekly bazaars

Samprati Pani

Introduction

The practice of street vending – plying a trade in a commodity or service on the street through a temporary structure or by being on the move – is among the oldest and most ubiquitous forms of work across the world. The term 'street vendor', however, has a more recent origin, becoming a part of public discourse with the coining of the term 'informal economy' by the anthropologist Keith Hart in the 1970s and its subsequent adoption by the International Labour Organization (ILO) (Chen and Carré 2020). Hart's study (1973) of 'unskilled' migrants in Accra, Ghana, performing non-wage forms of employment, including petty trading and street vending, spawned a growing interest in the informal economy and informal workers. Modernist discourses have viewed forms of street trade as a disorderly, unproductive, and parasitical activity, which, with planned urban development, would/should be replaced by the organized distribution networks of capitalism (Bromley 2007). Far from disappearing, street vendors have a pervasive presence in cities, with scholars arguing that it is a global urban practice and not limited to the 'Global South' (Chen and Carré 2020; Cross and Morales 2007; Graaff and Ha 2020).

With cities across the world becoming a 'strategic frontier zone for global corporate capital' (Sassen 2014: 8), public space is increasingly commoditized, exclusionary, and under surveillance. Consequently, harassment of street vendors is a common phenomenon across the globe. Street vendors the world over primarily belong to marginalized groups, with the precarity of plying a trade on the street being exacerbated by their ethnic, religious, racial, caste, class, and/or gender positionalities. The continued existence and proliferation of street vending has been explained in terms of the shift from

DOI: 10.4324/9781003604846-9

manufacturing to services in the wake of globalization and neoliberal policies, and the resultant shrinking of formal-sector jobs. The attack on street vendors is viewed as driven by the collusion of the state with big business to acquire urban public land for world-class infrastructure projects. Given this structural context, it is not surprising that a bulk of the literature on street vending in the last two decades or so has centred on spatial politics around the highly contested arena of the street and the power relations between various stakeholders (e.g. Bayat 1997; Bhowmik 2010; Cross 1998). This literature highlights the challenges faced by street vendors in dealing with processes of neoliberal regulations aimed at formalizing, restricting, or outright banning their operations.[1]

In the Indian context, policy-oriented studies have highlighted the plight of vendors suffering from harassment and evictions, mapped the demography of street vendors, and assessed the contribution of street vending to the economy (Bhowmik 2007, 2010; Bhowmik and Saha 2012; Kumar and Bhowmik 2010). These studies argue for a disaggregated view of the informal sector to understand street vendors as a workforce facing distinct problems. Since these studies focused on the mobilization of street vendors, including lobbying for a national street vendor policy and the subsequent promulgation of the Street Vendors Act 2014, they highlighted conditions and issues common to all street vendors in India, inadvertently glossing over the diverse activities and skills that come under the rubric of street vending. Anthropological studies on street vending in India, like studies from other parts of the world, have focused on spatial politics, highlighting how states govern vendors through ambiguity and arbitrariness, the mobilization of street vendors as a form of subaltern politics, and the negotiations and claim-making that vendors are engaged in (Anjaria 2016; Bandyopadhyay 2016; Rao-Cavale 2019).

The construction of street vending as low-skilled work

Across different studies and policies, as well as in documents from street vendors' associations, street vending is represented as a relatively easy, unskilled, or low-skilled form of employment in Indian cities.[2] On one hand, the low levels of formal education and lack of training (vocational or technical) among street vendors is taken as an indicator of low skills; on the other, street vending as a form of work is believed to require little or no skills (Meher et al. 2021; Sekhania et al. 2019). In the absence of skills and formal employment opportunities, street vending is viewed as work that people 'settle for' (Bhowmik and Saha 2012: 6).

The idea that street vending is low skilled is echoed in the National Classification of Occupations (NCO) put together by the Ministry of Labour & Employment, Government of India.[3] The first NCO in 1946 was industry based, but it has gradually evolved to consider types of work irrespective of industry. The latest NCO of 2015 places more emphasis on the nature of work performed, rather than formal education, in determining occupational skill levels. It also recognizes the significance of 'informal skill (acquired through informal training and experience)' in the Indian context (GoI 2016: 10). Notwithstanding these nuances, informal skills are taken into account, in combination with or in lieu of ten years of formal education, only at the lowest skill level of the NCO (Level I). This level has occupations characterized by 'the performance of simple and routine physical or manual tasks' (GoI 2016: 6). Except for cobblers/shoe-makers and street food vendors, all other types of street vendors are placed in Level I of the NCO hierarchy. These two exceptions are placed in Level II, which is defined as occupations involving 'tasks such as operating machinery and electronic equipment, driving vehicles, maintenance and repair of electrical and mechanical equipment, and manipulation, ordering, and storage information tasks' (GoI 2016: 6),[4] possibly because in these categories there is a visible use of tools and the vendors are engaged in not only a trade but also making a commodity.

This perspective of street vending as low skilled/unskilled aligns with the global literature, where the existence and expansion of street vending is seen as a marker of deskilling in the economy. In fact, the informal sector as a whole is conflated with low skills. The ILO (1998: 167) points out that the production processes in this sector, whether of the self-employed or small enterprises, are characterized by 'relatively high levels of working capital as against fixed capital, which in turn reflects the relatively low level of technology and skills involved'. Here, fixed capital is not understood in terms of limited or unequal access to resources but rather as reflective of skill levels. There is a similar bias in *Peddlers and Princes*, where Geertz (1963: 29) compares a Western capitalist economy with the bazaar economy of Indonesia. He points out that while impersonally defined social institutions organize production and distribution in the former, the latter comprises an incredible volume of fragmented and '*ad hoc* acts of exchange' (Geertz 1963: 29, emphasis added). Geertz saw the lack of dynamism and of organization as inherent to the bazaar economy, with vendors having no interest in expanding their businesses or competing with each other. For peddlers, according to him, 'the idea is not so much to create or stimulate a market for whatever you have to sell; rather it is to be present when the chance to sell appears' (Geertz 1963: 35). Even as Geertz has been criticized by scholars working on street vending,[5] the widespread assumption that street vending requires little or no skill forecloses an understanding of vendors' work and how they do it. Moreover, the preoccupation with viewing street vending primarily through the lens of spatial politics (the power dynamics of occupying space) inadvertently presents an image similar to that of Geertz: that the primary activity of a street vendor is to occupy a place.

Street vending, while being precarious, is also characterized by stability in terms of its continuity and expansion as well as individual vendors continuing to operate from the same spots over extended periods of time. It is a marginalized activity in terms of the low status of its practitioners and the continuous harassment they deal with; yet it is an activity that is central to the social, economic, and everyday life of cities. The embeddedness of street vending in the local politics of cities through the payment of bribes and vendors being adept at negotiating regulation are factors that only partially explain the stability and centrality of street vending. The continuity of street vending, I argue, relies more significantly on the ability to viably carry out a trade, that is, make available commodities and services that draw in and satisfy customers. Some studies within India and globally are moving beyond a focus on the structural landscape in which street vending operates to the aspects of this form of work. They engage with the entrepreneurial spirit and strategies involved in street vending, the social and affective connections of street vendors with their customers and their work, and the intertwining of street vending with the everyday life of cities (Anjaria 2016; Cross and Morales 2007; Stillerman 2006; Stillerman and Sundt 2007). The conflation of street vending with low skills is also being challenged by a few studies that draw attention to various kinds of skills (e.g. business, communication, trade) that vendors deploy (Graaff and Ha 2020; Pilz et al. 2015; Sharma and Konwar 2014).

Foregrounding street vending as a form of work and not just a form of politics, this chapter provides an ethnography of street vending in the periodic markets, colloquially known as *hafta* (weekly) bazaars, of India's capital city, Delhi. It seeks to understand the practices street vendors engage in and the techniques involved in these practices. Technique refers to a way of doing, that is, the dexterity and skills involved in bodies working with materials in any practice. It is 'effective' and 'traditional' (Mauss 1973), effective in that it has to work in the context of the materials being used and combined, and traditional in the sense that it is learnt through training, education, or imitation. This chapter explores the techniques involved in specific kinds of street vending and the processes through which vendors learn and hone these. It also engages with vendors' perception of their work as well as the relationship between customers and vendors in the weekly bazaars of Delhi. In doing so, the chapter not only challenges the conceptualization of street vending as unskilled or low-skilled but also reimagines skills beyond an ability or expertise derived from formal education and formal training.

This chapter is based on 18 months of fieldwork conducted across 12 weekly bazaars in different neighbourhoods of Delhi from 2016 to 2018, as part of my doctoral research, with subsequent follow-up visits to the field sites undertaken in 2022–23. Walking in the bazaar, from the time vendors set up their shops to the time the bazaar is dismantled, and observing the activities of vendors through the course of bazaar day forms a part of the research. Given the labour-intensive nature of street vending, unstructured interviews were conducted with vendors during lulls in activity. The research also involved following about ten vendors as they moved from one bazaar to another through the week and tracing the improvisations in this movement. In addition, the research included walking with bazaar customers as they went about their routines of shopping and other activities, interviews with customers at their homes, and participant observation as a bazaar customer.[6]

The making of weekly bazaars

Almost every neighbourhood of Delhi has makeshift bazaars held on a fixed day of the week for a couple of hours, named after the day on which the specific bazaar is held (Monday bazaar, Tuesday bazaar, and so on). Half of Delhi's 300,000 street vendors ply in its 1,000-odd weekly bazaars. Typically, bazaar vendors set up shops in at least five different neighbourhoods,[7] moving from one locality to another through the week.

The weekly bazaar is marked by various hierarchies and differences. The majority of street vendors in Delhi, including in its weekly bazaars, are from Other Backward Classes (OBCs), followed by Scheduled Castes and Muslims (Bhowmik and Saha 2012). They are mostly poor migrants who have come to the city in search of opportunities for livelihood and mobility. The majority are men, while women usually enter bazaar vending if they are the primary breadwinners of their families.[8] Women vendors face greater harassment from state officials as well as hostility from male vendors, which act as barriers to their entry. However, many women contribute labour and skills indirectly to bazaar trade through the support they provide to male vendors in the family. This ranges from managing storage and inventory, to preparing ingredients and components of street food, and even making products (e.g. garments, trinkets) which are sold by male vendors. Apart from caste, religion, place of origin, and gender, street vendors are also differentiated in terms of commodities or services they trade, with some commodities (e.g. cloth, readymade clothes) being regarded as more respectable in the perception of vendors. They are further differentiated by income from vending and period of operation in the bazaar. Some of these differentiations are spatially reflected in the bazaar's architecture, with recent entrants and poor vendors squatting at the periphery of the bazaar, while long-standing and well-established vendors have lucrative spots and larger spaces within the bazaar.

While weekly bazaars reflect and reproduce certain social hierarchies, they are also places where people of diverse backgrounds come into close proximity and where some norms of social interaction are relaxed. Being open street markets, with multiple entry/exit points, there is no restriction on who can use these bazaars for shopping, hanging out, or just passing by. Both low-income and middle-class residents frequent these bazaars. The casual intimacy between customers of different socioeconomic backgrounds and vendors and among customers is what makes the public character of the weekly bazaar. This is particularly significant in the context of Delhi, where public places are increasingly becoming exclusionary through devices such as ticketed entry to public parks and heritage sites, the construction of architectural elements such as walls and gates in thoroughfares in posh localities, and barring people who 'look poor' from entering parks in affluent localities, malls, and restaurants. Even as the gender composition of vendors is overwhelmingly male, weekly bazaars are especially popular among women customers, who consider these bazaars safe and as places to engage in both individualistic and social rituals of shopping, eating a snack, meeting people, or just loitering.

Weekly bazaars are the locus for the movement of an amazing diversity of goods and services such as fresh produce, grains and pulses, spices, shoes, clothes, jewellery, cosmetics, utensils, fast-food, knife-sharpening, mending of zips and bags, and repair of kitchen implements, which draws in diverse customers. The bazaar, however, is not just a site where the movements of economic transactions are located. It takes shape and is continuously made through various other movements, as the following description of bazaar day in a Delhi neighbourhood illustrates:

> It's around eleven on a Monday morning. The otherwise bustling permanent market in Madhu Vihar in east Delhi is quieter today, with most of its shops closed. There are stacks of folding tables on both sides of the street. Further down the street, a few men are unloading and dropping off more such tables.
>
> Around three in the afternoon, the streets around Madhu Vihar have more traffic than at this time on other days of the week. The nature of the traffic is also different. Wares of different kinds, some invisible in their packaging and others peeking out of cloth bundles, gunnysacks, cartons, and crates, along with aluminium and bamboo poles, string, tarpaulin, and cots are being ferried on foot or by different modes of transportation such as *thela*s (pushcarts), cycles, cycle rickshaws, auto rickshaws, and tempos.
>
> The market in Madhu Vihar is closed on Monday, making way for the weekly bazaar. The people ferrying the wares and materials are street vendors on their way to different spots on the street, where they will create their makeshift shops. Vendors who are done with unloading are sitting on the stacks of folding tables, resting, chatting, smoking, or eating a snack. In about an hour, the movement of wares and materials into the street peter out and give way to another set of movements. Vegetable and fruit

> vendors are unpacking, cleaning, and neatly arranging their produce on their *thela*s or on plastic sheets on the ground. Other vendors are unfolding tables, joining them together, and pitching bamboo poles. Readymade clothes are being put on mannequins and hangers, glass bangles are being laid out in rows, artificial jewellery is being hung on strings, ceramic cups are being arranged in colourful plastic baskets. At his cycle parked against a wall, the tea-seller is busy making batches of tea, which he serves to the vendors in small disposable glasses.
>
> By five in the evening, most shops have been set up, while a few are getting finishing touches. The shops are set cheek by jowl with no space between adjoining ones, yet care has been taken that there is a clear pathway between rows of shops for customers to move. The *chole bhature* (a snack) shop is heating oil in the pan. The *bantawala* (soda seller) is ringing his bell. The repair handyman is laying out his tools on a tarpaulin sheet. A few early customers are trickling into the bazaar.
>
> As darkness falls, the shops look bright and colourful with their displays and signage lit up with LED lights. There's a cacophony of overlapping, sing-song cries from the vendors: 'Twenty rupees, twenty rupees', 'Four for a hundred, four for a hundred', 'For twenty, for twenty, it's a steal, it's a steal', 'The sale is on in your city; the stock is for grabs for five and ten rupees'. The trickle of customers has grown over the hours to form a dense swarm of moving bodies: walking, eating, chatting, touching things, checking out wares, haggling, buying.

This description provides a glimpse into how the street transforms, spatially and temporally, movement by movement, into a bustling marketplace on bazaar day. A report on Delhi's weekly bazaars describes these bazaars as 'English gardens where elements interact with each other organically' and as 'spontaneously emerging systems' (Narang 2022: 51, 53). The description is in line with the conceptualization of informal spatial forms, including Indian streets, as 'organic' or 'unintended' (Edensor 2006; Sen 2001) and of street vendors as 'wizards in making a virtue of necessity' (Naik 2015).[9] While drawing attention to the creativity of street actors, such conceptualizations underplay the intentionality, planning, labour, and techniques, not to mention the processes of learning, involved in making informal spatial forms such as the bazaar.

The practices of bazaar vendors send out tentacles linking the bazaar associatively with places, entities, and processes beyond its physical boundaries, which include wholesale markets in the city and other parts of the country; national and global production, distribution, and supply chains; and kinship ties, relationships, and connections that are forged or enacted in the bazaar but not bounded within it. The combination of people, materials, and activities folding into the bazaar as well as these connections extending beyond the site of the bazaar form a field of relations, constituting, what I refer to as the 'associative milieu' of the bazaar. An understanding of the practices of street vending and of the skills entailed in these practices need to be understood through their relationality and embeddedness within this associative milieu rather than just a category of informal work or a shared political position derived from the insecurities of working on the street.

What distinguishes weekly bazaar vendors from daily vendors is that they set up their shops anew every day of the week in a different neighbourhood. Bazaar shops do not sprout up spontaneously. They are part of an intricate system, involving a combination of planned and improvised activities, with a large cast of supporting characters. A simple shop comprises a tarpaulin sheet spread out on the ground or on a *thela*, with the goods laid out in different ways. An elaborate shop comprises tables or cots, placed next to each other in different arrangements, with a frame created by pushing the bottom ends of bamboo poles into holes in the ground and tying the upper ends with strings and thinner pieces of bamboo. This is a tricky process and requires patience and dexterity – if too little pressure or too much pressure is applied in pitching the poles or tying the strings, the whole frame can collapse. Vendors do this slowly and carefully, manoeuvring around dug-up roads, construction debris, broken patches, or pools of water.

Vendors not only modify the range of their wares and prices as they move across neighbourhoods but also continuously improvise their shop designs, paring down or adding elements according to the space available. If there appears to be an ease with which vendors set up and dismantle their shops, it does not imply that these are natural, spontaneous, low-skilled, or unskilled activities. The ease comes from the continuous *doing* of the practice, what vendors refer to as *karte, karte rehna* (doing repetitively), whereby they improve and adapt their techniques through repetition, becoming more adept at problem-solving in the process.

Repetition is often conflated with manual, low-skilled work. For instance, the broad criterion that the NCO-2015 uses to make its classification is whether a job is 'of administrative, managerial, and supervisory nature' or 'of a subordinate/repetitive nature' (GoI 2016: 11), the latter being at the bottom of the skills hierarchy. This neat dichotomy fails to take into account the complexities of all kinds of work, where even managerial jobs have repetitive elements or seemingly repetitive tasks involve applying the mind. The philosophy and anthropology of practice has underlined that repetition is not necessarily mindless or mechanical; it can be a mode of engagement imbued with potentiality, where thinking and feeling are inseparable from a way of doing, and 'difference' is built into the repetition (de Certeau 1988; Ingold 2013; Lefebvre 2014; Ravaisson 2008; Sennett 2008). Even as bazaar vendors repeat the activities of sourcing, setting up shops, making displays, dealing with customers, and so on, the conditions of these repetitions do not remain the same. The space available and the surfaces of the street continuously change, weather conditions change through the year, different customers demand different interpersonal skills, and tastes and fashions keep transforming. Vendors get better at handling these differences with experience and through the 'tacit knowledge' (Sennett 2008) acquired in the doing of their work. Tacit knowledge may be invisible, yet it is learnt and embodied. In his study of auto-mechanic workers in Darjeeling, Barber (2004: 134) refers to this tacit knowledge as 'mechanics feel' and shows how workers develop it in the course of informal practical training. Similarly, Pilz et al. (2015) point to how street food vendors in Delhi and Coimbatore acquire a tacit knowledge of marketing, sales, and pricing in the course of informal learning activities. This tacit knowledge is not acquired at one moment and mechanically applied subsequently – it is continuously realized in time through the continuation of a practice. The following section explores trajectories of learning processes in the bazaar by focusing on two interrelated practices that vendors engage in: *dukaan lagana* (setting up a shop) and *dukaan chalana* (running a shop).

Practices and techniques of vending

Ajay,[10] a middle-aged clothes vendor, who sets up his stall in five weekly bazaars, tells me that many hours of labour and different activities go into his work – from loading, transporting, unloading, and setting up the shop, to manning the shop without a break for six to seven hours, all the while keeping an eye out for pickpockets and attracting and managing customers, dismantling the shop, and packing up. There is bodily effort not only in the seemingly physical tasks of setting up and dismantling shops but also in the performative and interactive tasks of engaging with customers, which requires paying attention, saying the right things, remembering return customers, and so forth. All of these tasks involve techniques, ways of doing, which are learnt and embodied with practice.

The two days of the week when Ajay is not vending in the bazaar, he spends doing inventory, sourcing, helping out the family with chores, and, if possible, catching some rest. He explains,

> Trading in the bazaar is not like a *naukri* (job) that I can take leave from. And it's not like every day is good for business. . . . The thing with this work is that sometimes it's on track and sometimes it's not, but you have to keep at it.

A key component of keeping at it, whether you are a new entrant or a seasoned vendor, according to vendors is *karte, karte seekhna* (learning by doing), and *dehkte, dekhte seekhna* (learning by observing). This section elaborates on how vendors enter into and continue to operate in the bazaar through the learning processes they engage in.

According to the ILO (2020: 1), the context and processes of learning in the informal economy are extremely diverse, but a significant proportion of informal economy workers 'get their skills from the informal economy itself', acquiring it through family, community, at the workplace, apprenticeships, 'learning by doing', or 'self-teaching' (ILO 2020: 2; see also Bonnet et al. 2019). This is not a one-time training but a 'lifelong' process (ILO 2020). While this chapter focuses on forms of informal learning that take place within the bazaar, it is important to note that many vendors also use skills derived from prior formal/informal education, training, and work experience. Vendors use numeracy skills learnt at primary school levels in *hisaab-kitaab* (maintaining accounts) to calculate prices, profits, money owed to wholesalers, and so forth. In the course of my fieldwork, I have come across street food vendors who were previously helpers or cooks in restaurants, *dhaba*s (roadside eateries), or private homes. A zips and bags repairman in one weekly bazaar had previously worked in a garment factory. A section of cloth vendors I interviewed hailed from Uttar Pradesh and had apprenticed in their family's (permanent) shops in their hometowns. They source their wares from back home through long-standing business connections and have chosen to expand the family business by selling in Delhi's weekly bazaars, where they can sell at higher prices and save on paying rent for a permanent shop. There are certain caste-based traders in the bazaar, for instance, Churihars, who sell bangles, and Garhia Lohars, who sell iron tools and utensils that they make themselves. In these cases, the techniques of the trade are learnt and passed on within the community. These examples challenge the idea that those with little or no skills 'settle for' street vending. Some vendors enter the bazaar with skills that they then adapt to trading in the bazaar, while others pick up and hone skills by learning in the bazaar itself.

The calibration of skills merely on the basis of formal education and formal training devalues forms of work and practices involving other modes and trajectories of learning. The NCO defines skill as 'the ability to carry out the tasks and duties of a given job', pointing out that it has two dimensions: (i) skill level, that is, 'the range of tasks and duties involved'; and (ii) skill specialization, that is, 'the field of knowledge required, the tools and machinery used, the materials worked on, and the kinds of goods and services produced' (GoI 2016: 5). Yet, the hierarchization of occupations in the NCO conflates each of the four skill levels (arranged in ascending order) in its classification with a level of formal education: primary education, secondary education, first university degree, and post-graduate university degree respectively, with the exception that primary education can be substituted or complemented with informal training. Skill in this classification is viewed as the end product of formal learning, or at the lowest skill level, the end product of informal training.

As discussed earlier, vendors have dexterity across a range of tasks. They also have knowledge about the commodities or services they work with, as well as knowledge of how to trade within the specific context of the weekly bazaar. Moreover, they do not simply trade *in* the bazaar but also *make* the bazaar, transforming a street into a public place and marketplace that is open and inviting to people, both through the shops they create from scratch every week and through the customer experiences they provide. On all these counts, their work is skilled even within the framework of the NCO definition. The calibration of skills is discursively and socially constructed, recognized, and valued (Bryson 2017), and while this chapter challenges the construction of street vendors as low skilled, it is not aimed at consigning a higher skill level to street vending. It instead reimagines skills beyond a hierarchy and beyond an end product of formal, or for that matter informal, learning. This chapter makes a shift from skills as a fixed, measurable state to skilling as a *process* of learning, a mode of doing, involving continuous commitment and judgement, which is perhaps common to all kinds of work and not just informal work. It unravels some aspects of this process in the context of specific kinds of street vending and within the field of relations of the bazaar.

Inheriting a shop in the bazaar

Prakash sells imitation jewellery, nail paint, and other 'ladies items' across five weekly bazaars. His nephew is training under him, just as Prakash had with his father. Prakash tells me that he was still in school and around 14 when he started accompanying his father to various weekly bazaars. He would help with the packing and unpacking of the wares and laying them out in the shop. His father taught him how to arrange the wares neatly in the small space of their shop.

Vendors learning with a family member often start by learning how to set up a shop. This is not because it is an easier or less significant task than handling customers or sales but rather a way of familiarizing oneself with commodities: what is the range of wares being sold and how to make them attractive and easy for customers to peruse. For a couple of years, in addition to setting up the stall, Prakash's job was to stand behind the back frame of the shop, making sure no one stole from the shop and observing his father conduct business. After finishing school, he started accompanying his father to Sadar Bazaar in the old city,[11] doing the rounds of the wholesalers from whom his father had been sourcing his wares for years. A large segment of weekly bazaar vendors sources its wares from Sadar Bazaar, cultivating long-standing relationships with wholesalers, with whom payments are settled within a month or longer, depending on the duration of and trust involved in the relationship. Prakash tells me:

> It was a while before my father allowed me to do the sourcing by myself, but I got good recommendations and prices from the wholesalers because they knew my father. It was even longer before I was allowed to handle money and interact with customers. I was good with calculation but shy when it came to handling customers . . . they were all women and I didn't know what to say to them. If someone asked me to show them something or asked the price of something, I would do it but that was it.

He adds:

> My father had a knack for engaging with customers. He would invite customers into the shop, saying 'At least, check it out once. There's no charge for seeing'. If a customer asked for something, my father would show it to her but also show other things, saying, 'There's this too. See this also – it's a rage these days', or, 'This will look nice on you'. I learnt over time that it isn't about showing anything or everything to a customer but assessing what she might like, whether she is likely to make a purchase, and how much she will spend.

Assessing customers, which often also translates into charging different prices, is crucial to bazaar vending. It also involves adopting different strategies with customers: cajoling, bargaining aggressively, arguing, flattering, dismissing. What strategies are deployed and how they are deployed is never completely identical from one vendor to another and is often imbued with the individual styles of vendors. Yet, it is not simply about having a knack for engaging with customers. The literature on embodied work in organized retail and the hospitality industry shows how there is nothing natural about the sociability or vitality of service workers in their customer interactions – it is cultivated through training (Maitra and Maitra 2018; Witz et al. 2003; Wolkowitz 2006). This argument holds true for bazaar vendors as well, even though they do not undergo training within an organizational set-up where they have to conform to a style of service or a brand image. The sociability and casual intimacy that vendors display in customer interactions is not natural or innate – it is learned through observing customers minutely and through the course of interactions with customers.

It took Prakash a while to get over his shyness with customers and he cannot pinpoint when it happened: 'By continuing to run the shop, I don't know when I learnt to actually run the shop'. His statement underlines how tacit knowledge develops through the repetition of a practice. When Prakash's father fell ill some years ago, Prakash took over the shop but found it difficult to manage all the work involved. That is when he asked his nephew to join him. Prakash is keen to now pass on his knowledge of *dukaan chalana* to his nephew: 'Whatever I know, now I'm teaching him [the nephew]'. The reason bazaar vendors pass on a spot and a shop to a (male) family member is because of the time, labour, skills, and negotiations embedded in it. Along with the shop, they pass on knowledge of running the shop and networks of relationships with wholesalers and other bazaar actors.[12] The shop, thus, is more than just a physical site or infrastructure for trading but a site of learning and a conduit for the reproduction of skills and of a mode of (informal) learning over generations, making possible the continuity of street vending as a form of work and of the weekly bazaar as a spatial and marketplace form in the city.

Establishing a shop in the bazaar

Mantu has been running a clothes stall in various weekly bazaars in south Delhi for about ten years now. He started afresh in the bazaar rather than 'inheriting' a shop. He had run away from his village in Bihar to come to Delhi, and is reluctant to talk about his family back there. On arriving in Delhi, he contacted his uncle (mother's brother), who had a tea shop in a neighbourhood in south Delhi, and started living with him. He spent a couple of years doing odd jobs: helping his uncle, working as a parking attendant, and being a delivery boy for a grocery store. He says, 'Somehow, I couldn't stay put in one work. I was restless . . . and wanted to do something of my own. I didn't want to work for someone'. At some point, Mantu's uncle introduced him to his contacts among the clothes vendors in the Tuesday Bazaar of the neighbourhood to whom he supplied tea. Mantu spent several months understanding the clothes trade, tagging along with the vendors for their sourcing trips and doing odd jobs for them, especially during the festival season when they required extra hands. The Street Vendors Act 2014 bans street vendors from hiring employees, only allowing assistance from family members. This rule is widely flouted because working as a helper is a key route of entry into the bazaar. Moreover, the only way well-established traders can expand, however minimally, is by hiring help.

While working as a daily-wage helper, Mantu became familiar with Azad Market, the largest wholesale market in Delhi for second-hand clothes. Taking a loan from his uncle, he bought a clothes-stand, a tarpaulin sheet, and his first lot of second-hand clothes from Azad Market,[13] setting up his shop on the periphery of the Tuesday Bazaar, a spot he was able to get through his uncle's connections.

Second-hand clothes sourced from Azad Market come pre-sorted by type: ladies tops, shirts, T-shirts, jackets, and so forth. These come in sealed bundles sold by weight or tied together in a set number of pieces. Mantu started his clothes trade by getting sealed bundles of T-shirts, shirts, and trousers. He explains to me that while the sealed bundles are cheaper, there is much variation in the quality and size of clothes. He would spend time re-sorting these clothes into price categories, getting some of them altered, repaired, and ironed. He hung up the good-quality ironed clothes on his stand, while making a pile of the low-quality ones on the ground. Though Mantu did not have a lucrative spot in the bazaar, it worked out for him because customers often wandered to the periphery of the bazaar looking for cheaper alternatives. He says:

> Business was up and down. Much depended on what I would find on opening the [sealed] bundle. Sometimes, I would be left with many odd pieces that just wouldn't sell . . . and sometimes I managed to sell most [clothes] in a lot. But over time, I figured out what sells.

The precarity of being a bazaar vendor is bound within the structural context of informality, in which vendors have to negotiate daily harassment from state officials and resident welfare associations (RWAs) of middle-class neighbourhoods, not to mention the lack of access to formal loans or state support in the day-to-day running of the bazaar. However, in their narratives, vendors often explain precarity as a condition of doing business in general and not specific to the bazaar, pointing to examples of (permanent) shops in the neighbourhood that have gone out of business for various reasons. They also understand precarity as a condition of the times and of all forms of work, arguing that there is no such thing as a permanent job and that one day you might have a job, and the next day you could be on the street fending for yourself. Vendors consider learning to be patient, to wait, to keep at it, and to adapt as central to their work. Among recent entrants to the bazaar, there are people who give up and try something else (e.g. daily wage work), while others tide over difficult periods by making do with less earnings, taking loans, or taking on additional work outside the bazaar.[14] Learning in the bazaar is never a seamless and linear process – it is marked by breaks, losses, trial and error, cycles of despair and hope. Vendors sometimes change the commodities they sell or diversify them, taking a chance on improving their earnings.

Mantu took a chance and added second-hand jackets, sourced in sets of 20 pieces, in the winter months. It paid off and he managed to make better profits. In the first two years of vending clothes, Mantu set up a shop only in the Tuesday Bazaar, spending the rest of the week helping his uncle and doing odd jobs. But he also spent time making contacts in the bazaar and persuading the *pradhan* (market head) to give him a spot in other weekly bazaars in south Delhi. He tagged along with vendors of new clothes to Gandhi Nagar,[15] trying to understand the options available and getting introduced to wholesale dealers. Taking a loan again from his uncle, Mantu bought his first lot of jeans from Gandhi Nagar. By this time, he had also managed to find a better spot in the Tuesday Bazaar.

Mantu is reluctant to share how much he earns, but he says that he has no debts and has managed to rent a place of his own. He considers himself lucky that he had his uncle's support, but he also takes pride in his hard work and perseverance. He believes he made a smart move by switching to jeans, because they sell through the year and are never out of fashion. He continues to spend time roaming wholesale clothes markets to understand *kya chal raha hai* (what's trending) and assess options to diversify his clothes trade.

Weekly bazaar vendors are diverse, with different durations of and unique biographies of entering the bazaar. What is common, however, is the intertwining of their practices with a process of learning and skilling. This process includes a 'training' period of working for a vendor on daily wages or 'apprenticing' with a family member. The process, however, does not end here but continues through practices of independently running a shop.

Who is a skilled vendor for a customer?

While the preceding section traced trajectories of learning in the bazaar, this section will examine how vendors' skills are perceived by customers. The customer–vendor relationship is central in the field of relations constituting the bazaar. Attracting, retaining, and expanding a customer base creates feedback loops in vendors' tacit knowledge of what sells and how to sell, being central to sustaining bazaar trade.

No two vendors in the bazaar, even if they deal in the same commodity, are identical. Vendors distinguish themselves through shop designs, prices, quality, and, more significantly, customer engagement. Some wait quietly for customers to come to their shops; others loudly shout out their prices and deals in rhymes. Some do not entertain bargaining, while others engage in elaborate, long-drawn bargaining tactics. It is the diversity offered by the bazaar, including the idiosyncrasies of individual vendors, that makes the bazaar an alluring place for its customers. Bazaar regulars have preferences for specific vendors, but there is nothing fixed about what specific skill draws a customer to a particular vendor. Let us look at two encounters to illustrate this.

I am accompanying my interlocutor Neelam, a middle-aged schoolteacher, to the Friday Bazaar in Trilokpuri, which caters to the low-income residents of the neighbourhood. Neelam, who lives in a middle-class apartment complex about 3 kilometres from the bazaar, has a love for weekly bazaars and she likes checking out different ones across neighbourhoods.

At the entrance point of the bazaar, we come across an elderly woman bangle seller,[16] plying from a *thela*. Neelam asks her, 'Do you have [bangles] in my size?', 'Of course' she replies. Neelam moves from one end of the *thela* to the other, checking out bangles. Every now and then, she asks the vendor if a particular design is available in her size. A number of women customers are milling around the bangle shop, and they refer to the vendor as Mataji (Mother). They are checking out bangles and chatting, and seem to be in no hurry to leave. One customer tries to convince Neelam to go for a set of green bangles: 'They'll look good on you'. The other women murmur in agreement.

'Will you put the bangles on me?' Neelam asks Mataji, pointing to the green bangles. 'Of course!' she responds. Neelam extends her left hand forward and Mataji presses her wrist and puts on a set of four bangles first, two of which break, and then another four. Neelam contorts her face in pain as Mataji squeezes the bangles on. Neelam tells Mataji that she wants just six bangles, which she wants to wear on her left hand. Mataji is offended: 'That's not how it is done! No one wears bangles on one hand!' Neelam tries to tell her that she can't work with glass bangles on both hands. Mataji shakes her head vehemently and pushes a set of six bangles onto Neelam's right wrist, even as their argument is ensuing.

The women are amused over the argument. Some reassure Neelam that the bangles indeed look good. Neelam pays Mataji, pleased with the purchase but not about having bangles on both hands. 'How will I work now?' she mutters as we are leaving. 'Has work ever stopped because of wearing bangles?' Mataji retorts loudly. As we are leaving the shop, we notice broken bangles around the *thela*. Neelam tells me that it is a sign of Mataji not being a skilled bangle seller. 'Then why did you buy bangles from her?', I ask her. 'Did she leave me with a choice? And it was fun, right?' she says.

As we walk away from Mataji's *thela*, we come across another bangle seller, an elderly male Muslim vendor. He is a man of few words, and he quietly attends to customers in the order they have arrived at his shop. Neelam points to some designs and asks him if they are available in her size. He softly says 'Yes', but continues to attend to a woman who was there before us. When our turn comes, I choose blue ones for myself, and tell the old man that I want only four bangles. He does not get into any argument about the number of bangles. He simply puts six bangles on one wrist, then gently takes my other wrist and puts six on the other. He does the same with Neelam, after removing the bangles she already has on. No bangles break in the process. 'You can easily remove these ones; they aren't like the ones you were wearing', gently making a point about his skill in choosing the right size. Neelam later tells me that she did not feel a thing when the old man put on the bangles, unlike the sharp pain she experienced when Mataji put the bangles on her.

As we walk through the bazaar, Neelam recounts an encounter she had with a bangle seller in her neighbourhood market:

> The shopkeeper refused to put the bangles on my hand. He said, 'You do it yourself'. He even offered to give me cream, so I could put the bangles on myself. I walked away in a huff, saying, 'You should shut your shop if you don't know how to put bangles on a customer'.

Women customers in different weekly bazaars have told me that you never buy bangles without trying them and that it goes without saying that the bangle seller will put them on your wrists. *Chudi pehnana* (lit., putting on bangles on someone) is viewed as a skilled activity, and neither customers nor vendors prefer that customers try on glass bangles themselves to avoid damage. Neelam is well versed in these codes, and she found it difficult to digest the blasé attitude of the bangle seller in her neighbourhood market.

Being engaged in a practice does not inevitably result in being well versed in its techniques and codes, as we see in the case of the bangle seller in Neelam's neighbourhood market. More significantly, as seen in the encounters with the two bangle sellers in the Trilokpuri bazaar, there is nothing fixed about what clinches a purchase for a customer. Even as Mataji is not skilled in the technique of *chudi pehnana*, she did not ask customers to try on the bangles themselves and abided by the code of selling bangles. She makes up for the lack of this particular skill through her persuasive techniques, the ability to simultaneously hold the attention of different customers, and also create an atmosphere of intimacy around her *thela* for women to hang out, chat, and engage in banter and laughter. The old male vendor, on the other hand, did not display his skills through the performance of casual intimacy and sales talk typically associated with bazaar vendors but through his no-nonsense demeanour and the grace with which he performed *chudi pehnana*.

Mataji's interpersonal skills and that of the old male vendor in *chudi pehnana* are not commensurable, and these two distinctive skills achieve the same instrumental end: attracting customers, providing an experience to them, and making sales. So, it would probably not be accurate to say that Mataji is a less skilled vendor than the male vendor. However, it is important to understand the gendered aspects of these differences. The extent of the sociability of a vendor and the creation of an atmosphere that is conducive to women hanging out around a shop is not related to the gender of a vendor. Bazaar vendors are primarily male and most perform different forms of sociability with women customers. The atmosphere around Mataji's shop is something I have observed in shops run by male vendors as well.

Access to learning opportunities in the bazaar is, however, clearly gendered. Women daily-wage helpers/trainees are non-existent in the bazaar. In family-based apprenticeships, it is sons or male relatives who get the opportunity to learn the trade. A shop in the bazaar is also passed through the male line. Only the widow/daughter of a deceased street vendor is likely to inherit a shop in the bazaar. This is never the same as a man inheriting a shop, because a woman is usually not familiar with all aspects of the trade or her husband/father's connections with other bazaar actors. For women vendors (like Mataji) who start from scratch in the bazaar, learning is a slow and patchy process, involving learning by yourself, by observation, and by trial and error. If the bazaar reproduces skilling and modes of learning, facilitating the entry of new vendors, this applies primarily to male vendors. The bazaar simultaneously reproduces barriers to the entry of women and to their skilling and learning processes.

Conclusion

The weekly bazaar does not spontaneously emerge with vendors occupying a space. A street transforms into a bazaar when diverse materials, objects, activities, and exchanges are set into motion through the bodily efforts, dexterities, and techniques of vendors' practices. This chapter illustrates how these practices are neither innate abilities nor mechanical tasks but rather developed through lifelong learning processes. The dynamic potential of the practices unfolds over time: over the course of bazaar day, over every week, and over extended periods of time, whereby daily wage work for another vendor or 'apprenticing' with a family member could potentially transform into a shop of one's own. Learning in the bazaar does not end with informal training; it is continued through ongoing vending and through the passing on of skills to new entrants and generations.

By tracing the trajectories of vendors' work, how they enter the bazaar, what they do in the bazaar, and how they do it, this chapter reveals street vending to be a complex, dynamic practice encompassing a multiplicity of activities involving diverse skills. These trajectories challenge the construction of street vending as a relatively easy form of work or as something people 'settle for' in the absence of skills or formal-sector jobs. Notwithstanding the structural reasons for the proliferation of informal work, vendors also choose, learn, and keep at this work with intentionality, hope, and tenacity. They display care and commitment in performing their tasks. They take pride in their work and make continuous endeavours to improve.

Recognizing the presence of skills in informal settings such as the bazaar is, however, possible only by moving beyond the limited conceptualization of skill as derived from formal education and training and as being an end product. This chapter instead draws attention to other modes of learning and to the processual nature of skilling, in which *doing* becomes a mode of continuous learning. It also underlines the relationality of skilling, with its trajectories and experiences being constituted in relation to specific commodities, trades, biographies and positionalities of vendors, perceptions of customers, and the associative milieu of the bazaar, including its inequalities and hierarchies.

Notes

1 For an overview of the literature on street vending as a global practice, see Aliaga-Linares and Roever (2019) and for the Indian context, see Naik (2015).
2 See, for instance, Bhowmik and Saha (2012), Bhowmik (2010), and the website of the National Association of Street Vendors of India (NASVI): http://nasvinet.org/overview-of-street-vendors-a-little-history/.

3 The NCO maintains standards of employment through a 'scientific and hierarchical approach' (GoI 2016: i), corresponding with the ILO's International Standard Classification of Occupations. It is used in data collection, policy formulation, and employment exchanges.
4 Skill Level III in the NCO-2015 involves 'complex technical and practical tasks that require an extensive body of factual, technical, and procedural knowledge in a specialized field' and Level IV involves 'tasks that require complex problem-solving, decision-making, and creativity based on an extensive body of theoretical and factual knowledge in a specialized field' (GoI 2016: 6).
5 Cross and Morales (2007) argue that if street vendors were indeed inefficient, they would not pose a threat to big businesses such as supermarkets. It is precisely because street vendors successfully compete with modern retail outlets that businesses in league with politicians use the police to drive out vendors (Cross and Morales 2007: 7).
6 For details on using walking as a technique of research, see Pani (2023).
7 Customers and vendors refer to street vending units in the weekly bazaar as 'dukaan' (shop), using the same term for permanent shops in permanent markets. This chapter thus uses 'shop' in the generic sense as a physical site of economic transactions.
8 Delhi has one weekly bazaar with only female vendors: the *mahila* bazaar at Tagore Road. It was established in 2008 by street vendors belonging to the Self-Employed Women's Association (SEWA), a trade union, with permission from the Municipal Corporation of Delhi. This bazaar is not part of my research.
9 This quote is from the title of an article by Naik (2015), which in turn is taken from a quote in Walter Benjamin's *The Arcades Project* (1999) to underline the improvisational abilities of street vendors. The analogy with wizards, however, takes away from the effort and skills involved in street vending. There is nothing innate or magical about the ability to improvise; it comes with the doing of a practice.
10 Names of interlocutors have been anonymized.
11 Sadar Bazaar is Delhi's biggest wholesale market of household items.
12 In the context of Indian markets, Vidal (2003) argues that if a trader's son becomes a trader, this cannot be understood in terms of a simplistic determination of caste codes. It has to be understood in terms of the passing on of an opportunity – 'immediate access to business know-how, social and trading networks, and material facilities' (Vidal 2003: 1348).
13 Second-hand clothes trading in India is part of a complex, global chain of charity collections, commercial recycling, importing, sorting, repairing, dealing, and trading involving legal and illegal commodity flows, and formal and informal actors (Norris 2015).
14 The rules related to the issuance of a certificate of vending under the Street Vendors Act 2014 bans moonlighting, completely disregarding the precarious conditions of this trade.
15 Gandhi Nagar in east Delhi is among the largest wholesale markets for readymade garments in the world.
16 This was the first time I encountered a woman bangle seller in Delhi. Bangle sellers, whether in specialized bangle markets in the Old City or across weekly bazaars, are usually male and belong to the community of Churihars, a Muslim OBC community.

References

Aliaga-Linares, L., and Roever, S. 2019. 'Street Trade', in A. M. Orum (ed.), *The Wiley Blackwell Encyclopedia of Urban and Regional Studies*. https://doi.org/10.1002/9781118568446.eurs0324.

Anjaria, J. A. 2016. *The Slow Boil: Street Food, Rights and Public Space in Mumbai*. Stanford: Stanford University Press.

Bandyopadhyay, R. 2016. 'Institutionalizing Informality: The Hawkers' Question in Post-Colonial Calcutta', *Modern Asian Studies*, 50(2): 675–717.

Barber, J. 2004. 'Skill Upgrading within Informal Training: Lessons from the Indian Auto Mechanic', *International Journal of Training and Development*, 8(2): 128–139.

Bayat, A. 1997. *Street Politics: Poor People's Movements in Iran*. New York: Columbia University Press.

Benjamin, W. 1999. *The Arcades Project*. Cambridge: The Belknap Press of Harvard University Press.

Bhowmik, S. K. 2007. 'Street Vending in Urban India: The Struggle for Recognition', in J. Cross, and A. Morales (eds.), *Street Entrepreneurs: People, Place and Politics in Local and Global Perspective*, pp. 92–107. London: Routledge.

Bhowmik, S. K. 2010. 'Introduction', in S. K. Bhowmik (ed.), *Street Vendors in the Global Economy*, pp. 1–19. New Delhi: Routledge.

Bhowmik, S. K., and Saha, D. 2012. 'Street Vending in Ten Cities in India', Study Report by School of Management and Labour Studies, Tata Institute of Social Sciences, Mumbai, for National Association of Street Vendors of India, Delhi.

Bonnet, F., Vanek, J., and Chen, M. 2019. *Women and Men in the Informal Economy: A Statistical Brief*. Manchester: Women in Informal Employment Globalizing and Organizing (WIEGO).

Bromley, R. 2007. 'Foreword', in J. Cross, and A. Morales (eds.), *Street Entrepreneurs: People, Place and Politics in Local and Global Perspective*, pp. xv–xvii. London: Routledge.

Bryson, J. 2017. 'Disciplinary Perspectives on Skill', in J. Buchanan, D. Finegold, K. Mayhew, and C. Warhurst (eds.), *The Oxford Handbook of Skills and Training*, pp. 17–35. Oxford: Oxford University Press.

Chen, M., and Carré, F. 2020. 'Introduction', in M. Chen, and F. Carré (eds.), *The Informal Economy Revisited: Examining the Past, Envisioning the Future*, pp. 1–27. London: Routledge.

Cross, J. C. 1998. *Informal Politics: Street Vendors and the State in Mexico City*. Stanford: Stanford University Press.

Cross, J. C., and Morales, A. (eds.). 2007. *Street Entrepreneurs: People, Place and Politics in Local and Global Perspective*. London: Routledge.

de Certeau, M. 1988. *The Practice of Everyday Life*. Berkeley: University of California Press.

Edensor, T. 2006. 'The Culture of the Indian Street', in N. R. Fyfe (ed.), *Images of the Street: Planning, Identity and Control in Public Space*, pp. 201–216. London: Routledge.

Geertz, C. 1963. *Peddlers and Princes: Social Change and Economic Modernization in Two Indonesian Towns*. Chicago: The University of Chicago Press.

Government of India [GoI]. 2016. 'National Classification of Occupations-2015 (Code Structure)', Vol. I, Ministry of Labour & Employment, Directorate General of Employment, Government of India, New Delhi.

Graaff, K., and Ha, N. 2020. *Street Vending in the Neoliberal City: A Global Perspective on the Practices and Policies of a Marginalized Economy*. New York: Berhgahn.

Hart, K. 1973. 'Informal Income Opportunities and Urban Employment in Ghana', *The Journal of Modern African Studies*, 11(1): 61–89.

Ingold, T. 2013. *Making: Anthropology, Archaeology, Art and Architecture*. London: Routledge.

International Labour Organization [ILO]. 2020. 'Lifelong Learning in the Informal Economy', ILO Research Brief, International Labour Organization, Geneva.

International Labour Organization [ILO]. 1998. *World Employment Report*. Geneva: International Labour Organization.
Kumar, S., and Bhowmik, S. K. 2010. 'Street Vending in Delhi', in S. K. Bhowmik (ed.), *Street Vendors in the Global Economy*, pp. 46–68. New Delhi: Routledge.
Lefebvre, H. 2014. *Rhythmanalysis: Space, Time and Everyday Life*. London: Bloomsbury Academic.
Maitra, S., and Maitra, S. 2018. 'Producing the Aesthetic Self: An Analysis of Aesthetic Skill and Labour in the Organized Retail Industries in India', *Journal of South Asian Development*, 13(3): 1–21.
Mauss, M. 1973. 'Techniques of the Body', *Economy and Society*, 2(1): 70–88.
Meher, S. R., Ranjan, A., Shukla, P., and Atram, Y. 2021. 'Effect of COVID-19 Lockdown on the Livelihood of Street Vendors in Maharashtra, India', *International Journal of Community Medicine and Public Health*, 8(11): 5297–5303.
Naik, A. 2015. '"Wizards at Making a Virtue of Necessity": Street Vendors in India', *Socio-Legal Review*, 11(1): 1–60.
Narang, P. (ed.). 2022. *Hafta Bazaar: Walking through Delhi's Corridors of Commerce*. New Delhi: Centre for Civil Society.
Norris, L. 2015. 'The Limits of Ethicality in International Markets: Imported Second-Hand Clothing in India', *Geoforum*, 67: 183–193.
Pani, S. 2023. 'Making Paths and Doing Bazaar: Rhythms and Techniques of Walking as Dwelling', *City & Society*, 35(2): 112–120.
Pilz, M., Gengaiah, U., and Rengan, V. 2015. 'Skills Development in the Informal Sector in India: The Case of Street Food Vendors', *International Review of Education*, 61: 191–209.
Rao-Cavale, K. 2019. 'The Art of Buying Time: Street Vendor Politics and Legal Mobilization in Metropolitan India', in G. Rosenberg, S. Krishnaswamy, and S. Bail (eds.), *A Qualified Hope: The Indian Supreme Court and Progressive Social Change*, pp. 151–183. Cambridge: Cambridge University Press.
Ravaisson, F. 2008. *Of Habit*. London: Continuum International Publishing Group.
Sassen, S. 2014. 'Who Owns the City?', *Urban Age Governing Urban Futures Conference*, New Delhi, 14–15 November.
Sekhania, R., Mohan, D., and Medipally, S. 2019. 'Street Vending in Urban "Informal" Markets: Reflections from Case-Studies of Street Vendors in Delhi (India) and Phnom Penh City (Cambodia)', *Cities*, 89: 120–129.
Sen, J. 2001. 'The Unintended City', *Seminar*, 500. Available online at https://www.india-seminar.com/2001/500/500%20jai%20sen.htm (downloaded 14.10.2023).
Sennett, R. 2008. *The Craftsman*. London: Penguin.
Sharma, A., and Konwar. D. 2014. 'Struggles for Spaces: Everyday Life of a Woman Street Vendor in Delhi', *The Delhi University Journal of the Humanities & the Social Sciences*, 1: 48–59.
Stillerman, J. 2006. 'The Politics of Space and Culture in Santiago: Chile's Street Markets', *Qualitative Sociology*, 29: 507–530.
Stillerman, J., and Sundt, C. 2007. 'Embeddedness and Business Strategies among Santiago, Chile's Street and Flea Market Vendors', in J. Cross, and A. Morales (eds.), *Street Entrepreneurs: People, Place and Politics in Local and Global Perspective*, pp. 180–200. London: Routledge.
Vidal, D. 2003. 'Markets', in V. Das (ed.), *The Oxford Companion to Sociology and Social Anthropology*, pp. 1342–1360. New Delhi: Oxford University Press.
Witz, A., Warhurst, C., and Nickson, D. 2003. 'The Labour of Aesthetics and the Aesthetics of Organization', *Organization*, 10(1): 33–54.
Wolkowitz, C. 2006. *Bodies at Work*. London: Sage Publications.

PART III

Skilling at the margins of the skill ecology

8

THE SKILLS OF 'CITY-MAKERS'

Waste-work in small-town India

Advaita Rajendra[1] *and Barbara Harriss-White*[2]

Introduction

In his 2016 book, Indu Prakash Singh bestows the name 'city-makers' on the labourers who directly build India's cities and provide the cities' essential services (Singh 2016). Singh is concerned with the contrast between their work in the urban economic base and the brutal oppression and criminalization they face when unable to find shelter in those very urban centres. Here we focus on one of these essential urban services, waste disposal, without which towns and cities would rapidly become uninhabitable.

In India, waste-work is an activity that exemplifies Deliège's paradox of marginalization and is entwined with the condition of untouchability. On the one hand, for Deliège (1999/1995), untouchables are reviled yet ritually indispensable; on the other, as has long been established, waste-workers are stigmatized while also being materially indispensable, for they make the city. Both kinds of indispensability coalesce when, as is commonly the case, workers self-identifying as ex-untouchables – *Dalits*[3] *Dalit-Bahujan*, from Scheduled Castes (SCs) and Scheduled Tribes (STs), dominate in waste disposal. However, while Ilaiah (2009), celebrating the productive life – the cultural and scientific knowledge – of *Dalit-Bahujan* castes, invokes knowledge and skills classified in ways familiar to their practitioners, he omits mention of waste and so, it seems, do they.

In rectifying this omission here, we imagine that in Ilaiah's *Dalit-Bahujan* society, the waste created was organic and biodegradable, like human faecal material, human and animal bodies, and food and agricultural waste. However, the quantities and composition of waste materials are now rapidly changing (Kaza et al. 2018, 2021). Even village panchayats, overwhelmed by

DOI: 10.4324/9781003604846-11

the 'public bad' of their waste, fly-tip and dump great piles dominated by plastic on the outskirts of urban territories. Clearing such waste-scapes – public or common land – and their networks of waste – verges and drains – has been socially naturalized as work for *Dalits*. In public spaces that involve the 'impure' mingling of castes, waste is left 'to fester until someone of the right caste comes by to clean up' (Doron and Raja 2015: 195). Dalits who break free from ritually polluting work are nonetheless devoid of choices to leave roles closely related to their caste-related tasks (Harriss-White 2003; Harriss-White et al. 2013; Thorat and Neuman 2012). And whether or not waste-workers are from ex-untouchable castes (for backward castes and occasionally Muslims are reluctantly forced by poverty to enter the labour force), by virtue of the oppressive conditions in which they work, they identify politically as *Dalit*.

All economies and societies produce waste, making waste one of the fastest growing sectors of India's economy. The Urban Development and Local Government Unit of the World Bank estimates that India's 'peak waste' – the point beyond which resource efficiency will drive a decline in absolute waste generation – lies approximately a century into the future (Hoornweg, Bhada-Tata and Kennedy 2013). Information about waste is inexact. One official estimate suggests that India produces about 960 million tonnes of solid waste each year, roughly a third each from agriculture, industry, and consumption (Centre for Environmental Education (CEE) 2014: 4). Government estimates suggest that municipal solid waste alone contributes 54.8 million tonnes per year (Ministry of Urban Development, Government of India (MoUD, GoI) 2013)[4] Regardless of totals, the contribution of waste to the material imbalances of the economy is expected to do nothing but rise.

Though it is never centrally addressed as a sustainable development goal, waste has become a 'development problem'. It is elliptically referred to in goals – 6: sanitation, 9: infrastructure, 11: sustainable cities, and 12: responsible consumption (United Nations (UN) 2020). While there is no waste-work without waste, the development of sub-fields of waste[5] and waste-work are practically distinct. The former is dominated by technology, land-use planning, and engineering solutions to problems of bulk and toxicity. The latter is a field of social science primarily pre-occupied with the life worlds of certain kinds of waste-workers who handle materials imbued with stigma in conditions that are hazardous, notably rag-pickers (waste-gatherers) and manual scavengers (cleaners of faeces from dry toilets, shit-workers, usually women, and workers who manually unclog sewers by entering them, typically male (see Harriss-White 2018). As a development field that slips between SDG cracks, waste is the object of projectized Solid Waste Management (SWM) technologies such as incineration, composting, biowaste-to-energy, plastic to energy (pyrolysis), mass sanitation, and integrated Information Technology (IT)–powered infrastructural plans for smart cities.[6]

It is rare that the costs of labour (as opposed to engineering and management costs) or the costs of redeploying waste-workers displaced or evicted by these technologies are internalized in this technical literature (Luthra 2017). But, due to the widespread failure to recognize and formalize the army of unregistered and/or incompletely contracted waste-workers, a growing number of experiments are focused on improving the work conditions of waste-workers: first, through illegalizing the most stigmatized forms of work like manual scavenging in 1993 and again in 2013 (Government of India (GoI) 1993, 2013; Wilson and Singh 2017), de-reserving the grade 4 category of public servants (2006), putting an end to recruitment for municipal sanitation jobs, and criminalizing verge-side migrant gatherers of waste (Chikarmane and Narayan 2000), second, through discursively sanitizing and relabelling sanitation jobs as 'green' jobs and re-skilling (Bozkurt and Stowell 2016; Skill Council for Green Jobs 2016).

Official skill categories in India are based on composite components of level, specification, tools, and educational attainment. The different official categorizations include the Minimum Wages Act (Department of Labour and Employment (DoLE) 2020), International Standard Classification of Occupations (ISCO) – 08 (ILO 2012: 42), and the National Classification of Occupations (NCO), 2005 (GoI 2016). While some focus on tools used (ILO 2012),[7] other may focus on the deployment of 'independent judgement' (DoLE 2020)[8] and/or on educational attainment (GoI 2016). The official categories may often contradict each other. For example, in the case of education, while NCO-2005's four levels of skills map onto educational qualifications (GoI 2016: 6), a Right to Information (RTI) request, asking for the definition and the basis of skills classifications, pointed instead to the criteria that were absent. It read: 'It may be seen that classification is not based on the mental or physical nature of work. The classification is also not based on the post and education qualification' (Ministry of Labour and Employment (MoLE) GoI 2019).

However, while the composition and recycling possibilities of waste and their implications for work change continually, most waste-work, whether recycling or refuse sweeping, is considered at the lowest level of skill. They are often bureaucratically categorized as 'unskilled', assumed to have a simple routine, needing limited training and autonomy. Policies that seek to 'skill' further assume that it happens in a social vacuum and that skilling leads to better wages (Maitra and Maitra 2018). However, what is categorized as 'skilled' or 'unskilled' is deeply political and based on bold assumptions about forms of work that contribute to economic growth and historical, social structures that devalue the labour of some bodies (Carswell and De Neve 2018). This chapter interrogates the category of 'unskilled' work through a systematic analysis of waste-work. What skills does it take to do 'unskilled' waste-work? And how does the state skill waste-workers?

Framing waste-work: methods, concepts, and their field contexts

Following the pioneering work of Lave (1993), skill is framed here as a process of tacit learning that is not acquired in formal educational institutions. Instead, facts and problem-solving strategies form knowledge systems cognitively developed through practical engagement. What Lave calls situated practice is embedded in the social world of workers, undergoing reorganization as the work environment changes and as different forms of knowledge collide in social interactions. Situated practice may be developed outside formal work hours as competences are transmitted and adapted from one generation to another (Roman 2008).

This frame has implications for the design of field research on skill. First, learning and skilling must be assumed to occur throughout the waste system and not confined to the sector recognized and managed by the state. Second, the social and physical contexts of learning are vital to the acquisition of competences. Third, for Lave, there is no boundary between the practice of skill and the feelings and values that confer meaning on these practical actions. In this case, meaning is affected by the capability of waste-throwers not to notice the work of waste-workers, just as they avoid registering physically and socially dirty public space (Rodrigues 2009). Fourth, the study of practice, praxiography, involves the likelihood that workers' categories, actions and meanings differ from those of 'experts'. Hence, workers' accounts need critical juxtaposition with, and translation to, those from official sources. Let us elaborate on the four implications of Lave's frame by introducing the life world of waste in which skill is practised.

Waste system

First, waste is part of an open system of materials and energy that has to be closed for practical tractability. In the literature, the system is closed by taking a type of waste (e.g. e-waste or plastic) (Bhaskar and Turaga 2018; Corwin 2018; Gill 2010) or a kind of worker (e.g. waste-gatherers or manual scavengers) (Chikarmane and Narayan 2000; Darokar 2018) or a place of waste (e.g. a leather-working street or dump yard) (Chatterjee 2019). We have taken as analytical units two towns with 100,000 to 200,000 people, one in Chhattisgarh (N)[9] and one in Tamil Nadu (S).[10]

Town (N) has radically reformed the municipal sanitation workforce (MSW) based on groups. In the reorganization of waste-work in 2015, over 450 new workers were brought to N, organized as a federation of self-help groups (SHG workers) involved in the doorstep collection of consumer/household waste. These workers are primarily *Adivasi* rural women who had earlier not worked with waste materials. They partly replaced and partly worked parallel to the older bureaucratic system, predominantly employing

Dalit men as sanitation workers (*safai karamcharis*) (197 workers). Their work included cleaning streets, unclogging drains, evacuating septic tanks, and moving household waste to recycling centres and landfill. The formalization of waste flows meant that self-employed waste gatherers had primarily been pushed out of the public urban spaces and landfills to neighbouring rural and urban areas (Rajendra and Sarin 2024).

Town (S), struggling with revenue scarcity, is forced to subcontract ever more of its streets to private companies and tolerate a hardly visible army of self-employed gatherers to help dispose of waste (Harriss-White 2019a, 2019b, 2020). S. generates about 35 tonnes of solid waste a day, of which half is worked over by wage labour of private firms sub-contracted to the municipality and an army of unregistered self-employed workers. Both segments of the workforce supply recyclable raw material – about half the waste – to a hierarchy of bulkers, while the wage-workers take the residue by cycle carts and trailer to the dump yard. MSW manages the other half directly (with 115 MSWs). Of this waste, 20% is said to be processed experimentally for compost and plastic for pyrolysis, the MSW privately sells 30%, and the remaining 50% is deposited in the dump-yard outside town.

In our extended field research, we had over 300 respondents in S and N; from whom we studied the skilling and skills of 46 workers interviewed in September–November 2019. These workers pick, sort, clean, sell, and dispose of different materials categorized as waste – varying from recyclables to human faeces.

In S., in 2015 and 2016, we researched the life worlds of 120 workers and officials working with waste throughout the urban circuits of capital. Respondents handled waste generated in productive and distributive economic activity, waste from consumption, waste from the physical metabolism of labour, and medical waste from the health-care sector which ensures the long-term reproduction of urban society (Harriss-White 2017a, 2017b). We returned in 2019. A further 22 waste-workers, two-thirds of whom were women, niched throughout the urban system, spoke to us about our 'official' concept of 'skill' and their experience of learning and practice. Research in N. was conducted over 2018–2019 (Rajendra 2022), which relies on conversational interviews with 180 workers and officials. In 2019, 20 workers were interviewed, discussing various aspects of their skills.

Our method is not comparative; instead, it combines insights about skills from both sites.

Context and environment

In S., the context for waste is changing rapidly in ways that affect work. Two dimensions to this dynamism are particularly relevant to situated practice.

Supply

The first is the supply of waste. In S., waste in the twenty-first century has increased fourfold, while the number of MSWs has declined by half. Technological change that increases productivity is one response to this imbalance. The cycle-trailers of 2015 are being replaced by three-wheelers, autos, and tractor-trailers – and lorries by electric trailer-vans.[11] Small fleets of septic tankers are multiplying for the inadequately sized septic tanks installed in most residential buildings under the Government of India's *Swachh Bharat* (Clean India) Programme. The supply radius of waste-gatherers' routes has increased, penetrating local villages. In turn, villages generate waste and dump it on their peripheries and urban streets. Meanwhile, the final demand for products made from recycled waste is reported not to be increasing proportionately. 'Consumers recognise recycled plastic, demand is declining, and prices of finished products are lowering. So much for the circular economy', said one separator in S.

The second response to the mismatch between the supply of waste and the constraints of the municipal budget and MSW involves creeping privatization. But private companies bidding for municipal contracts at lower rates than it costs the municipality to carry out this work directly must take profit at the expense of wages and work conditions. 'Contract labour is paid very low salaries (around Rs 7,000/month in 2019) and works in terrible conditions' (S). Increasing volumes of waste affect work in contradictory ways in different parts of the system. The working day is informally lengthened for MSW's declining force to be able to cope. In the informal waste economy, there are more jobs. For both, competition for recyclables intensifies, alongside greater disinclination to do dump-yard work.

Contrast this with the response to pressures of increasing waste and national programs like the *Swachh Bharat* in N. First, petrol-fuelled autos have been replaced by rickshaws drawing energy from the muscles of *Adivasi rural* women. Second, while the Urban Local Body (ULB) claims to have shifted away from privatization, it relies on grossly underpaying SHG workers, paying them less than minimum wages (Rs. 5,000 in 2018–19). Further, the returns to selling recyclables were not additions but were subsumed in the salaries paid to SHG workers.

Composition

The second source of contextual change is the composition of waste. Since 2015 in S., new kinds of waste have appeared. Because the municipal water supply is increasingly 'not trusted' (also perhaps influenced by TV advertising), plastic water bottles have witnessed a 'massive increase'. For the first time in S.'s history, electronic items have become obsolescent and are being thrown out: 'from computers to tube lights, they go to the private scrap yard'. Further, a new wave of disposable medical equipment (Hodges 2013) has generated a rapid rise in infectious waste – syringes, disposable bottles and tubes, drips, bandages – not all of which enter a special sub-circuit for incineration. Construction waste proliferates as bungalows and houses are demolished for blocks of apartments.

While much of the 'written' policy focuses on the segregation of waste materials, 'mixed' waste is a novel term imposed by officials upon MSWs. Despite a new cadre of local house-to-house animators and TV messaging, very few households segregate their waste in both S. and N.

User fees imposed by both municipalities are widely evaded and, if enforced,[12] perversely incentivise non-compliance. Urban elites assume that dealing with waste is someone else's job. 'If they [waste generators] pay, they then think they have a right to throw mixed waste' (S). 'Educated high caste people are disdainful and don't co-operate'. . .'Most homes have no space to segregate' (S). 'You would think it is the slums that are dirty, but let me tell you, they are the ones who segregate and they also pay on time', a mid-level bureaucrat emphasizes (N). N's policy documents and public discourse claim that households segregate all their waste. So the work of segregating mixed waste – something that was never specified in the roles of the workers – is rendered invisible.

The experience of segregation has changed some perceptions of waste materials. For example, one plastic segregator commented about an effect of learning by doing: 'Before I did this work, I didn't know the value of waste and just threw it. Now I segregate the valuable waste in my home' (S). Mixed waste complexifies the waste classification before segregation by workers – with implications for shift length, waste quality, purity, and price formation. The routes followed by substances also become more complex and have to be discovered by workers.

The third aspect of the changing composition of waste is its toxic filth. The 'dirty waste', expanding rapidly since 2015, is a whole life cycle's worth of foul disposables: nappies/diapers, sanitary pads, incontinence pads – 'complicated and horrible waste' (S) – thrown with other household consumption waste onto verges and into drains. Not only is more time required than exists in a formal shift to un-mix filthy waste and to inspect clean recyclable components before segregation, but incentives to spend time on this filthy 'extra' work also vary. MSWs have a heavy incentive to dump because although, since 2018, MSWs can legally sell recyclables. A MSW worker (S) says:

> We might get Rs 30 for much work after our extended shift has ended. For contract labour on wages that are half or a third of ours, Rs 30–40 means much more than it does to us. Still, many MSWs do this after-work work.

Actions and values/meaning

The tasks of 'retrieving, collecting, sorting, dismantling, breaking down, and sometimes washing that convert the collected materials into commodities that can be sold as raw material to manufacturing industries' (Chikarmane 2012: 3) are frequently listed as though such tasks were not differentiated by status. In S. and N., waste substances associated with these tasks confer or deny status. Unclaimed human and animal corpses, body parts, and all other work involving human faeces (such as the public toilets) have the lowest status, and dump yard gathering and drain-clearing are hardly higher. Broom-work has a higher status than shovel-work while the collection, segregation, and classification of waste metals (though it is associated with crime) and paper and the operating of waste machinery (tractor-trailers, vans, plastic shredders, JCBs) have the highest status of all.

Tasks in these different forms of waste-work cannot also be dissociated from sites. Sewer-pit cleaning and repair and dump yard surface combing are putrid and physically dangerous places abhorred by all but destitute waste-workers with no other option for work. None of S's human waste is treated. Half enters the general system of open drains and *gulleys*, coating general consumption waste. Other work sites are notoriously dangerous for brawls involving alcohol and broken glass, criminal scapegoating, and/or sexual harassment. In 2019, N. set up a new Faecal Sludge Treatment Plant (FSTP), which had begun to process the human waste collected from the clearing septic tanks. However, the human faecal waste flowing into drains went untreated into lakes and other water bodies.

This status hierarchy, combining tasks, substances, and sites, affects its social meaning. 'They don't have to reserve these jobs', said an ST *Kattunaickers* (KN) worker of drain-clearing, 'because this is stinking work and no-one else will do it'. Yet, while in the eyes of waste-throwers who practise disrespect, adverse difference, or outright discrimination (Harriss-White and Rodrigo 2016), waste-work and workers lack dignity, the waste-workers we interviewed showed no dearth of personal dignity. However, unless they conceal their work, they cannot escape the effects of waste-work on their social identity.

Gender

Waste reproduces the social order, and waste-work is gendered. In S. and N., property ownership in the waste economy is male. Men manage all public property. They control and direct the corporate, private company formally subcontracted to the municipality and the ownership of all the officially registered but informally operated wholesale and warehouse recycling businesses. Supervisory and administrative work is overwhelmingly male, as is very 'heavy' work. In private clinics, men do 'high' work requiring stretching, cleaning of lifts, and waste disposal from kitchen carts. In gendered teams, men drive vehicles and clear wet waste. Shit work, which used to be manual scavenging for the lowest-status women, has become work for men over the years. The faecal waste which men clear is deposited in septic tanks or dribbles and oozes into drains and gullies, which further mixes with wet consumption waste. Women sweep and sift dry waste and are well represented in segregation work. In clinics, women still clean toilets and wards; they wash soiled walls and bend for 'low' work. Conversations around the gendering of work often pointed to assumptions of what women could (not) do. For example, in N., a supervisor, explaining the allocation of workers across city administrative units says, '. . . each ward has 1 man and 2 women. The cleaning of the open drain cannot be done by women, so we [men] have to do that'.

Overall, workforce participation in waste is comparatively feminised. Whether in the formal or informal waste economy, women's work is arduous to combine with childcare and household reproductive work. Their returns to work are significantly lower than men's, and they face more harassment and stigma. Further, there is little to no provision made in the workplace for women's biological and social needs – no changing places or bathrooms for female MSWs (Harriss-White 2019b). In the waste economy, gender was inextricably intertwined with age and caste in a structure of disadvantage.

Age

Although waste is a new sector, its workforce is ageing. Trapped parents want an exit for their children, and the security of inherited jobs has long been abandoned. Young people refuse the worst work. So waste-workers labour on into their 60s, and the MSWs in S. know the statistic from Human Rights Watch (2014) that 90% of India's sanitation workers die before retirement age. 'In future shit-workers will be *Dalit* drop-outs from far-off villages' (said a Muslim 'housekeeper' in a private clinic). 'As sweepers, we are denied education, so we will be confined to sweeping. It starts in school where Dalit children clean the building and the lavatories but are not allowed to learn', said a 47-year-old *Dalit* sanitation worker. Yet, in the complex ecosystem of waste, there are niches for young women for whom the alternative is agricultural labour. One, in her 20s, sorting plastic for the private depot in S., put it this way: 'As we are all SCs and BCs, we are not under pressure at home to conform. This work gets us out of our homes and gives us incomes. It is regular, while agricultural work and NREGA are unpredictable'.

Caste and ethnicity

While in India, *Dalits* (SCs) and *Adivasis*[13] (STs) together form 25% of the population, in S. they are 70% of the formally employed and unionised municipal sanitation workforce, the remaining being drawn from backward castes. Forward caste engineers man the administrative and managerial work in the municipal office. Meanwhile, unregistered waste-work, which may generate over a thousand livelihoods in and around S. alone, is dominated by SC *Dalits* and ST *Adivasis* (with a few Muslims, *Naickers*, and *Nadars*). *Dalits* and *Adivasis* are further differentiated in their socially regulated positions in waste-work and their prospects of exit – for we heard no waste-worker wanting their children to follow them. While SC *Paraiyars* work in all kinds of waste-work, some with a few years of education are upwardly mobile (e.g. the lorry and septic tanker owner who is also a construction labour contractor and site manager). 'Waste shops and depots are the only ones in town not screening for your education and caste background. Waste is liberating!' said a rural *Paraiyar* migrant.

But ST KNs, also known as Telugu *Arundathiars*, are less educated and economically mobile than *Paraiyars* as a social group and more confined to the lowest status work. 'We have no hope of promotion! Even those of us with ST certificates don't get college entrance or government jobs' (KN association president). Pig-rearing has become their supplement to waste-work (with a constant demand for pork from Chennai restaurants and 5% of S.'s population). By contrast, most ST *Irulars* sifting the dump yard and the outer roadside verges have no schooling, nor do their children. They are actively evicted from both sites of work and lodging. Rather than social exclusion, they face social expulsion. So also do 'permanent transients' trapped in the process of destitution in which the social right to be dependent has been forfeited. Meanwhile, other status groups structure different niches in the expanding waste system. Muslims dominate new second-hand markets for reusable goods; the commanding heights of recycling (the scrap yard monopoly and gunny bag depot) are defended not by *Dalits* but by enterprising *Nadar* migrants. Thus, work affects identity, identity affects work options, and path-dependent options reinforce identity.

In N., waste-work was done by different STs and SCs. The door-to-door collectors of waste were predominantly local rural ST *Oraon* women. MSWs often belonged to the local SC *Mehtar* caste, migrant ST groups like *Ghasia and Bhunia* and local *Adivasi* groups like *Oraon*. We came across no cases of formal promotions or moving to supervisory roles. Even third-generation workers were stuck as workers, and third-generation supervisors continued to work as supervisors. On being asked about prospects of promotion to government official ('*afsar*') positions, a supervisor remarked, laughing, 'we only get to here'.

Overall, in N., caste affinity and group solidarity formed contrasting axes of sociability at work. For example, sanitation workers (predominantly Dalit males) and the newly formed self-help groups (predominantly Adivasi females) often informed each other about surprise visits by senior government officials or discussed wage delays. There were also some scattered efforts to include the self-help group workers with existing unions of which the sanitation workers were a part. These efforts were largely unsuccessful due to pressures of the ULB.

Concepts for the practice of skill

Waste is not simply a physically disordered field; it is a meeting place of different knowledge forms and bristles with epistemological incoherence. The official national Total Sanitation Campaign classified waste through many management technologies, while the World Bank stresses it as being unwanted after productive use. Yet others classify waste through sites and spaces, economic sectors and subsectors, institutions, physical form, and its potential for recycling, degradability (and origins – whether plant or animal derived) (CEE 2014: 9).

For N.'s consumption waste, SHGs are organised into hierarchies of tasks and classifications. Recyclable waste is distinguished from dump yard waste at the first, 'doorstep' level. Amid recyclables, there is a further classification into organic and inorganic, clean and dirty. At the second level, the segregation point, clean waste is classified as dry and wet. Dry waste is further divided into up to 12 categories. Meanwhile, dirty waste is further classified as potentially recyclable if washed, further sorted and dried. Or it is assembled into consignments for the dump yard. At the top level of the hierarchy, fine-grained classifications are organised.

This diversity is not confined to official classifications. In S., both formal and informal waste-workers distinguish waste according to a bewildering range of categories.

1. 'general' versus 'recyclable' (e.g. in public buildings);
2. liquid and solid (to all intents and purposes, gaseous waste does not exist);
3. hazardous versus non-hazardous, poison and toxicity;
4. wet and dry (forming the basis of the gendered division of tasks for MSW;
5. by origins (e.g. medical waste, meals, hotels, wedding halls, streets);
6. by significant recyclable/re-processable materials (e.g. glass, paper, cardboard, plastic, metals in which there is specialization);
7. by site (e.g. the Indian Railways, the government hospital);
8. by whole commodities (e.g. motherboards, glass bottles);
9. by types of degradability (e.g. edible (by animals): and further, by desirable fodder for cattle, pigs, goats, domestic fowl, and so forth; by biodegradability (and suitability for composting) vs. non-biodegradability);
10. by human versus non-human waste (animal waste in S. being no longer composted or deposited onto flooded pastureland, it enters general consumption waste streams);

11 human and non-human disposal (animals, nature);
12 by the kind of exchange involved (gathering, barter, sharing, selling and buying, public expenditure, gifting for second-hand re-use and sale (clothing), recycling or disposal) – and a lot of abandoning.

Disposal by abandoning is not necessarily the final resting place of useless waste. Waste would burn or decompose to enter the bio-physical restitution processes of socially and physically produced 'nature' because dump yards are sites of further human or animal agency.

Workers' concepts of skill are mapped onto this conceptual complex. But workers express their experience of learning and skilling using a range of near substitute words. In S. in Tamil, these were the following: *thiramai* (skill, mostly rarely used); *velai* (job); *arivu* (knowledge), *nutpam* (competence), *pani* (task). In N., workers laughed, giggled, or looked blankly at the use of terms like *Kaushal* (skill), *kushalta* (deftness, skilfulness), and *hunar* (skill or mastery) for skill. The phrases we relied on included 'what do you need to know to do this work' (Hindi: *ye kaam karne se kya janna zaroori hai hai*/Tamil: *intha velai seirathukku ungalukku enna theriyanum*?); 'what do you need to learn to do this work' (*ye kaam karne ke lie kya seekhna padta hai/intha velai seirathukku neengal enna kaththukkanum*?); 'What did you learn, how much time it took to learn?' (*Kya seekha kaise seekha, kitna time laga. seekhne mei/Neenga enna katthukiteenga?/Ithai kaththukka evvalavu kaalam eduthathu?*). These phrases elaborated the 'practice' of the work, as opposed to an abstract labelling of tasks as skills. In the case of waste-work there is little distinction between the skill needed and the practice of work (see Saikat Maitra and Sebastian Schwecke, this book for a case of retail).[14]

The wide range of principles and the incoherence of the terms defeat the concept of a 'system' of waste. Yet, in practice, there is a system of waste, even if it is conceptually and physically disordered and governed in many ways: state and market categorizations of waste regulate how and which forms of waste are recycled. Waste-workers understand it, and a path-dependent coherence is derived from the regulatory and socially embedded knowledge systems, the livelihoods and the agency activated by waste.

Workers' descriptions of skills and situated practice are also inseparable from the work conditions in which their skills are deployed. Chief among these in S. is the dramatic deterioration between 2015 and 2019.

Agrarian distress has pushed agricultural labourers into town. For self-employed gatherers, 'new gangs of bonded waste-workers are kept at the buyers shop and invade our routes and territories. They are wealthier than us, with wrist watches and chains. They threaten us. The shopkeepers have withdrawn loans, advances and bonded carts', said itinerant gatherers in S. In 2019, MSWs were much more actively concerned about their competitors in the informal economy than they were in 2015, aware that contract wage labour for private companies and self-employed have longer days and far lower wages. Meanwhile, 'our pensions are being made insecure, our payments are delayed, the contracts of people replacing workers who have died are ad hoc ones hardly different from those in private companies' (S). In N. SHG, waste-workers had to endure six months without wages, pay slowly creeping towards minimum wage with endemic delays. In waste-generating public and private services (railways, hospitals, colleges, clinics, schools), private companies are subcontracted for waste, and permanent contracts are in the process of extinction: increasingly verbal, increasingly without benefits (S).

Across the board, this deterioration in conditions and contracts affects the duration of, and returns from, the working day. It affects the skills needed to cope.

Skills and skilling of the unskilled

Learning processes: 'see, do, make mistakes, and learn'

While some tasks such as cleaning are socialised domestically by parents to children and passed across generations to people who will never earn wages from cleaning, except for manual scavenging and composting, the volume and composition of most urban waste are new. Urban waste is a first-generation modern sector in which 'teachers' and supervisors lack experience with work they will never carry out themselves.

In both N. and S., municipal corporations/local governments provide occupational training to the relatively small labour forces they employ directly, including some engineering managers. 'I went on a World Bank composting course in Singapore, but it was useless – not appropriate to conditions in S.', said one. Infectious medical waste classified as dangerous to health (needles and sharps; plastic syringes; blood transfusion equipment, blood products, bloody and septic waste; soiled cotton and cloth; drug bottles; saline and glucose bottles; body parts) is, at least on paper, strictly regulated in a separate system of segregation, collection, incineration and burial handled by specialized 'government servants' with 'a year of training' (S). Even so, some such waste surfaces on the dump yard and the apex private scrap yard. In S., a local government composting hangar with fermenting pits, in the throes of inauguration in 2019 and subcontracted to a private company, had labour teams of SC women who 'met for a week with an official' to learn to compost. Working subsequently on unwritten contracts, 'there are no facilities, and we have to use common land' (S). In N. SHG, members were given 15 days' training; in S. MSWs have three days training every year. 'It's never different' (S).

Workers emphasized the discrepancies between formal learning and their work practices. Although the trainers described waste flows and familiarized 'trainees' with tasks, MSWs knew more about both than did their teachers. Official terms, which changed over the years, did not match the local labels used by the buyers niched in the hierarchy of bulking and segregation for recycling. Official categories needed translation to the terms vital to price negotiations and incomes from selling useful waste. Detailed categories of plastic and polythene, some of which are illegal and so not taught about, are crucial for recycling.

The pure substances used in practical classes contrasted dramatically with real-life waste's mixed nature and dirtiness. In N., we meet a 56-year-old *Oraon* tribal woman, working in collecting consumption waste door-to-door for five years, who contrasts the waste used in training with the waste they ended up handling, explaining, 'When they taught us, the waste was very clean. They only gave us peels of vegetables and fruits, but here there was food waste with water and diapers. They never showed us how to deal with that'.

In both N. and S., throughout the system, whether formal or informal, knowledge was acquired and/or relearned not by orders from bosses but through watching, shadowing, on-the-job learning, learning by doing, making mistakes, and setting them right. Most waste-work tasks require between 15 and 30 days of unpaid learning. 'We talk about what we observe, and we share information and sometime pool what we collect', said an *Irular* gatherer (S). Kindness, help, and sharing among workers are among the collective preconditions for competitive gathering – qualities needed for gendered work teams and gangs and especially for migrant workers ignorant of local languages, who suffer social ostracization.

Protection from toxicity

Waste-work is physically hazardous, biologically infectious, and offensive to the senses. It combines repetition and surprise. Close contact cannot be avoided. Where not acquired privately by workers, tools and protective equipment are frequently experienced as inadequate, and some cleaning materials (acid for cleaning public toilets) are chemically dangerous. Commodities handled may be dangerous in a very different way – some are stolen goods. So a wide range of knowledge and practices that protect the self from these hazards is central to the work.

Prime among these is bodily cleanliness. 'An important skill is to remain clean when we are working in dirt. We come back from collecting waste – wash our hands – some take a bath – then we eat and take rest – then we segregate the waste, then clean the centre and then leave', says an SHG door-to-door collector in N. One of the greatest ironies of waste is the lack of washing, bathing, or lavatory facilities in municipal offices. In 2019 in S., 'there are still no toilets. No changing room. No drinking water. No soap. No cleaning facilities. Nowhere for menstrual cloths or pads. What an irony! If we need it, we have to shit on the verges'. 'Women with periods have to beg permission to use private lavatories' and/or work short shifts, for which they report abuse from roadside households (S).

Waste-workers often demanded equipment from their supervisors and government officials but received little response. In both N. and S., municipal workers were given gloves, boots, and so forth, once a year. 'Useless chappals pick up mud. Masks are far too hot. Gloves? How can you separate tampons and napkins wearing those thick gloves? They might give sarees, but they show your waist. We want jackets. We have had a 15-year campaign without success to have jackets (S). Workers complained of bad quality gloves, ill-fitting shoes, and boots: 'the gloves melt, disintegrate, putrefy when we wash them. They then do not give new ones', an SHG worker says in N. Workers even resorted to bricolage for their protection. Waste plastic bags could be tied to the wrist with the help of a bangle or a rubber hairband. 'It is easier to segregate wearing bags than wearing gloves', she adds. Handkerchiefs and long pieces of cloth (*dupattas*) served as masks. Waste itself may be fashioned into tools: twigs and branches, even a broken badminton racket are fashioned into claws (*panja*) and rakes. Roadside water or mud is used to clean hands while working or after work. In a new composting depot subcontracted from the municipality in S., the workers make their own rakes and brooms.

Disciplining the working body: 'Getting used to waste-work': **aadat** *(Hindi),* **pazhahi porathu** *(Tamil)*

Mental disciplines

Though some tasks like sweeping require little cognitive capacity, others require compendious knowledge. In N., for instance, official dry waste is subdivided into 111 categories. At the same time, in S. at the apex private scrap yard, over 200 raw materials are segregated for re-processing in Chennai, and the male manager keeps track of all their prices. Even edible waste is sorted before some of it becomes fodder for backyard animal rearing.

Identifying, classifying, sorting, purifying, and drying recyclable raw material is carried out at speed and needs intense and sustained concentration. To make them tractable, sets of tasks are often divided among the workforce. Plastic in S. provides a model. Instead of sitting on stools and working on a bench, six local women of all ages (and with none to 9th standard schooling) plus 4 young migrant men sit cross-legged on the floor in segregated groups picking 4 each of 40 kinds of plastic from the winnowing trays full of plastic debris passed down the line[15] and throwing them in 41 bins. At the end is a special skip for the waste-waste, which includes bits of metal having to be disentangled from plastic objects thrown to the verge to be collected for the dump yard. Figure 8.1 uses examples in N. to show variations in the spatial arrangements of this process.

It takes 10 to 14 days to learn segregation without disrupting the flow of winnowing trays. The pace is fast, the waste is dirty, the ordering is idiosyncratic, some components (used syringes) are potentially infectious, the work 'doesn't require literacy; it needs intense 'eye-brain-hand' concentration and coordination' (S). Workers' bodies are crunched painfully, and shifts are nine hours long, counting toilet breaks. 'I've sat in this position on this concrete for ten years', says a woman recycler. 'Ankle pain is very common'. 'Every so often after several weeks we change positions and categories to stop being bored'. 'This is not a job in which you can age gracefully'.

The purity of segregated waste material, Gidwani and Chaturvedi (2011) remark, is where much of the 'artistry in arbitrage, and assorting' lies. The distribution of income from waste-work depends on this purity. 'A trader who deals only in PET bottles will underpay or cut advances if he finds the bottle caps on. A cardboard dealer will do the same if he finds bits of paper in the bales' (55).

Incomes, profits, and costs require granular knowledge of materials, qualities and 'prevailing prices', cognitive skills and experience at bargaining, and risk-taking in being bonded by debt or borrowed equipment. One illiterate *Irular* gatherer lamented, 'We are easily fooled. Cannot bargain' (S). Tied to their buyer through interlocked contracts, their prices were reported to be down to half those obtained by a canny, un-indebted segregator.

Physical discipline

The smells, textures, weight, and sight of waste need speedy interpretations, which have to be learned. For instance, sight, touch, and taste are deployed to test the quality of plastic and paper. Sight and smell are mobilised for decomposing waste, festooned in flies and crawling with maggots. Yet, at the same time, the senses also have to be numbed, especially that of smell. 'It smells a lot. It took two weeks. I would feel uneasy (*ghabrahat*) in the beginning. (pauses) It happens in any work. But at first, the smell pervades the body (laughs). Later nothing smells' (N).

But for others, in S.: 'we never *ever* get used to the smell'.

Coping with the assault of waste on the senses requires bodily discipline. The tendency to wretch must be subdued. 'We don't eat properly', said a woman MSW in S. Most waste-workers reported that they have nothing but tea before their shifts. 'CCTV everywhere inhibits you from urinating' (S). Because they minimise the need to expel body waste until their shift has finished, the lengthening of shifts challenges their daily metabolism.

Unclaimed human bodies require more skill than simply controlling the impact of seeing them on workers' feelings. The corpse needs teamwork to lift and must not be cremated; burial must be at a depth preventing stray dogs

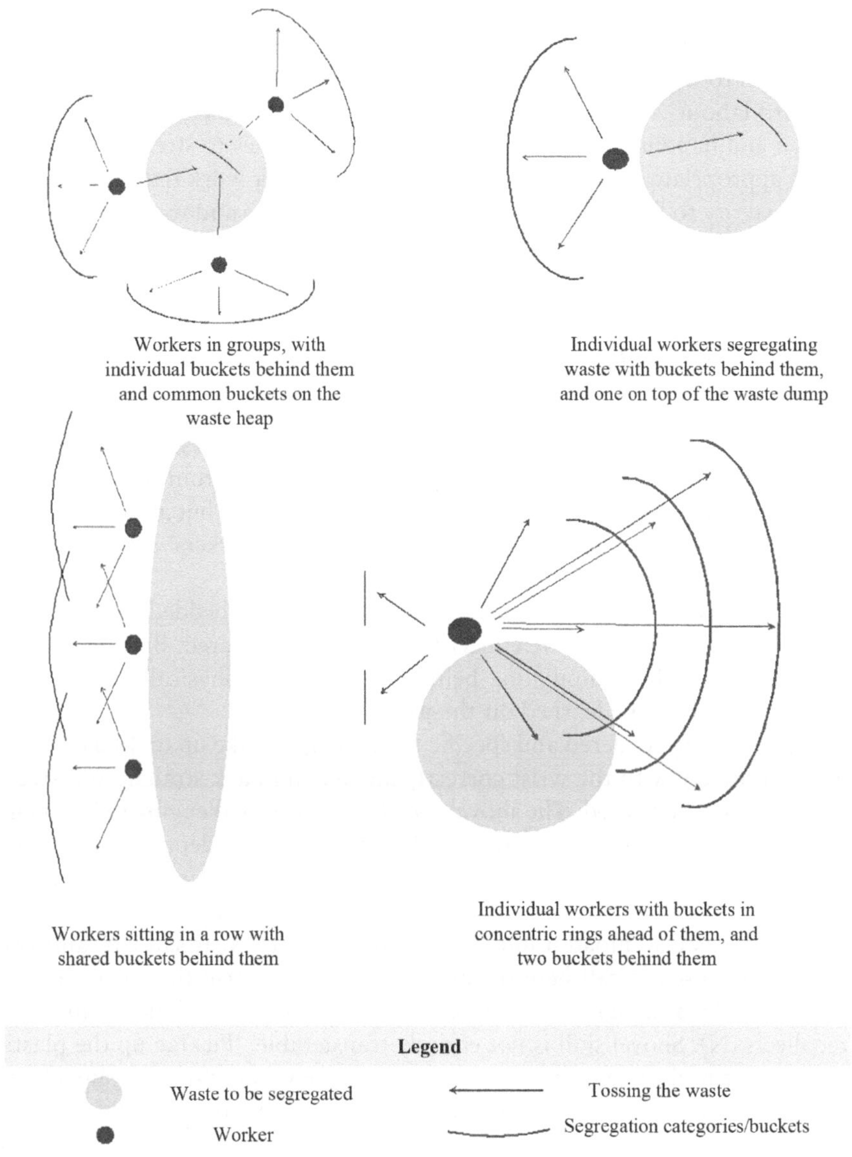

FIGURE 8.1 Examples of different spatial arrangements of workers while segregating in N

Source: Authors

from exhuming the body. The site requires careful recording in case relatives emerge later and demand identification. In both N. and S., alcohol is liberally consumed to dull the effects of work with corpses.

'Hard labour' – pulling manual rickshaw-trailers in the door-to-door collection and handling tools – needs practice for muscles to strengthen, which needs appropriate and adequate food. Cart and trailer work requires strength and dexterity to load, compress and assess the balance and weight of various kinds of segregated waste. 'We need stamina and strength to deal with what we find' (S).

Instruments of learning

While the social practices of waste cannot be performed without hands, tools – baskets, shovels, pickaxes, claws, iron rods, brushes – serve essential dual functions of increasing productivity and protecting workers from hazardous and contaminating substances. Often, they are not only simple but also of such low quality – mainly supplied by the municipality – that workers' substitute their privately-owned tools.

These tools are not just simple technology but also embedded in social relations. For instance, some are collectively owned and shared. Brooms require stooping to swish – humiliating behaviour. The least physically demanding deployment has to be learned on-the-job.

Brooms come gendered and specific to tasks. They take up to 30 days to be used intuitively with the wrist correctly angled and back straight and swept so that dust is not raised. The shovel (*belcha*) is more challenging to learn and takes 30 to 60 days to operate intuitively. 'It was my first deputation. It could turn and cut the hands, and there would be blood all over, so it was difficult in the beginning and fellow workers used to help. I also didn't know how to lift the waste and load it into the tractor. I used to wear sandals, and half the garbage used to fall here (laughs). So slowly, I learnt the work. It took time. Then I was assigned other work . . . . and now I'm back here', an MSW recollects (N). Shovel skill is not entirely transferable. 'Picking up the plastic was new. It took time to learn how to gather the waste. Both the shovel and the foot have to be used' (N). A former construction worker in N. explains: 'what was difficult was handling and loading of plastics. That I did not know earlier. I would work as a construction labourer earlier with soil and mud to load. But plastic flies. The other type of waste is when people demolish their homes. They put water over it, and it sticks to the ground. We cannot pick it up. The shovel cannot be shoved into this waste'.

Women's e-rickshaw trailer driving takes a month to learn, relying on prior familiarity with scooters. Men's JCB and tractor-driving take three to four months to master, bit by bit on the job with the help of other drivers and accelerated by prior experience. It is not simply a question of driving; it is also a matter of negotiating cramped spaces, steep gradients and rough surfaces with heavy machinery and coordinating with teams on the ground. But 'while waste-work develops transferable skills, it is hard to exit' (S).

Street wisdom

To identify and protect the exclusivity of routes and consignments, both the formal workforces and the unregistered ones require an intimate knowledge of urban streets, layouts, bin sites (if any), households' seasonal and festival peaking waste-throwing habits, and new sites and large campuses as the town expands. They must develop mental maps of the locations of recycling shops and depots, and then the dumping spaces, riverbeds, forests (where faeces can be tipped into hidden holes) and water bodies that the various kinds of waste will pollute, distinguishing the public from private ownership on which they may encroach. They must memorize details of infrastructure that are invisible to most urban residents: networks of drains, tunnels, holes, chambers, entrances and the quality of covers, tanks and syphons. They must know the routines of vigilance forces with whom they may have to engage – the police and supervisory staff from public or private organizations – and the habits of (other) illegal actors whom most waste-workers wish to avoid. Most waste administrators have no idea about any of this vital information; indeed, they actively distance themselves from situations requiring it.

Conclusion: unskilled city-makers

City-making waste-work, learned so that it is practised intuitively, seems effortless – 'in some sense invisible' (Lave 1993: 10). Through this chapter, we have tried to make explicit and visible the daily practices, skills, and effort it requires. We are not constructing a case that waste-work is very skilled. Instead, we argue that when the state classifies waste-work, it is not 'unskilled' because it does not require learning. The complex urban waste ecology we describe is also a skill ecology. It involves social practices requiring a range of cognitive skills, physical stamina and strength, and extreme disciplining of the body and its processes, with scope for ingenuity and bricolage.

Our evidence from small towns (N. and S.) in north-central and south India confirms Deliege's paradox of marginality. Whether through ignorance or contemptuous disregard, urban society depends on this work. 'Without us the town would become dangerous very quickly', remarked a worker in S. Pauperized (often migrant) city-makers, overwhelmingly *Dalit* and *Adivasi*, are developing essential skills to dispose of and recycle the rapidly commodifying waste-scape. Indeed, a perverse imperative operates in which an army of labour, working and living in relations of pauperization and discrimination, is indispensable to India's economy and society.

In a further paradox, this modern, rapidly expanding sector is adopting old practices akin to those of agriculture (Ilaiah 2009) to develop appropriate competences. Formal training is thin on the ground and rarely appropriate, and we found no record of apprenticeships. Most forms of work were informally learnt, on-the-job by 'seeing and learning' and learning by doing. Workers described several skills at work: 'paying attention', 'segregating', the least punitive way to wield instruments like the spade, claw, and so forth, negotiating access to public spaces, and mediating their engagement with vigilance forces. These skills are unrecognized by society at large, not respected by employers and not taught in training institutes. Private sector profit and the public sector's diminishing budgets ride on this cheaply skilled labour. Just as Roman (2008) found in silk weaving, the acquisition of these competences spreads among groups of workers while public and private employers are ignorant of the means their labour uses to achieve the ends they mandate.

Lave's theory (1993) that learning is encouraged by opportunities for social interaction and that innovation springs from the engagement of multiple actors and perspectives is not confirmed here. This is because the work environment is far from cosmopolitan, and few self-employed workers can exercise agency. The imposition of formal knowledge with little relevance and inappropriate equipment creates perverse incentives to perpetuate the informal economy of waste together with its modes of learning.

The resulting collision of knowledge systems reinforces these perverse incentives. The state's official categorizations of work and waste materials are often embedded in unrecognized but discriminatory social structures of caste and gender and clash with the knowledge systems of waste-workers. The latter aspire to this knowledge's being a one-generation phenomenon in which they are trapped at the foot of the social order. Very few children of waste-workers wish to enter the waste economy even as the work (segregating plastic) signifies liberation from domestic conformity and control over their incomes for a minority of young rural women.

Workers found it difficult to discuss work skills as distinct from their physical and economic working conditions – often alluded to as 'getting used to' the work while the conditions they are getting used to deteriorate constantly. While there is formal recognition of some forms of waste-work, workers are simultaneously being displaced by privatization and contractualization and by the growing informal economy. Permanent positions are being replaced by ad hoc/casualized/informalized ones in local municipal labour forces. Throughout the waste economy, the terms and conditions of waste-work are converging in the opposite direction to arrangements that would reflect the significance of waste to the economy and public health. 'Waste disposal should be organized through the Government of India like the police and army and not through arbitrary schemes like *Swachch Bharat*, or cash-starved municipalities, let alone self-help groups', said a woman MSW trade union leader in S. But the state, embodying upper-caste interests, is part of the problem, not the solution. Meanwhile, 'I love the Irulars', said an upper-caste business association official in 2015, who couldn't care less about waste, 'For Rs 100 a day each [£1; $1.6], they clean our town'!

Notes

1 Assistant Professor, Indian Institute of Management, Sirmaur. I am thankful to Praful Lakra for his help during the fieldwork and all workers and officials who spent time with me and helped understand their work. I would like to thank Ankur Sarin, Ajay Pandey, Vipul Paikra, and Harsh Mittal for guidance and conversations during and after the fieldwork.

2 Emeritus Fellow, Wolfson College, Oxford University. I am very grateful to Gilbert Rodrigo with whom I carried out fieldwork in 2015, 2016, and 2019.

3 *Dalit* is an identity meaning 'oppressed' (as in the *Dalit* Panthers movement, which is active in S.) and covers several scheduled castes and tribes working in waste. Here we use this overarching concept in contexts recognized by our respondents.

4 The amount of waste generated is often difficult to capture, with estimates varying widely. There could be two potential reasons: different categorizations used in different estimates. For example, solid waste estimates usually consider only municipal solid waste or household waste, while others might include industrial waste. Second, materials can take different forms, and the weight estimate may vary. For example, industrial waste may often have significant water content, and other assessments could use dry or wet weight, leading to very different numbers (see Liboiron 2016).

5 A *Scopus* search for 'waste' shows 39% of total studies in environmental science, 27% in engineering, 3% in social sciences, and 0.6% in arts and humanities.

6 In 2021, Hyderabad won three awards at the Smart City Expo, one under the Smart Waste Disposal Project category (7th Smart Cities India Expo, 2021). *Telangana Today* reported on the initiative that received the award in a way emphasizing technology and excluding workers. It reads, 'The Fleet that has been deployed is based on large capacity (35 GVW) Benz vehicles with fully integrated IOT sensors, telemetry and advanced safety systems such as Driver Awareness System and numerous other safety and efficiency innovations. This is the first time such smart vehicles, coupled with 20 cubic meter capacity Portable Self Compactors (PSCs); and 24 cubic meter capacity hermetically sealed waste containers, are being used for secured waste conveyance in India' (Telangana Today 2020).

7 Skill grade 1 in ISCO – 08, vary in the type of tools one used: 'hand-held tools, such as shovels, or simple electrical equipment . . . that may require physical strength and/or endurance' (ILO 2012: 12).

8 'An unskilled employee is one who does operations that involve the performance of simple duties, which require the experience of little or no independent judgment or previous experience although familiarity with the occupational environment is necessary. His work (sic) may thus require in addition to physical exertion familiarity with variety of articles or goods' (Department of Labour and Employment, Government of Himachal Pradesh 2020).

9 N. has approximately 150,000 people according to the 2011 census. It is the district headquarters and surrounded by industrial mining activities. The town has a high proportion of Adivasis (~40%) and ~5% people from scheduled caste backgrounds.

10 S. had about 63,000 people according to the 2011 census. An administrative, transport, and retail hub, 16% were from scheduled castes compared, with 26% in the surrounding taluk. Adivasis accounted for only 1.5%.

11 Battery-operated trucks and trailers are too small – half the size of diesel tractor trailers so needing two circuits to replace what one did before. There is not enough room for a team of 3 to sit, no there is protection from rain/sun, and more work is needed separating wet and dry waste before tipping it into the truck.
12 In N., official estimates suggested that 70% of the households paid the user fee.
13 *Adivasis* are tribal people considered indigenous to South and Central India. *Kattunaickers* (self-identified as 'pigmen' [rearers] and migrants from Andhra to the north) are one such 'forest people'. *Irulars* are another. *Oraon* is an indigenous group in central India spread across Jharkhand, Odisha, and Chhattisgarh.
14 In other forms of work, skills may be separate from the work that needs to the done. For example, in the case of writing a manuscript, the skill of writing and research have been acquired separately from the work of writing the manuscript. This often also translates into a perception of a given task as needing little skills (Carswell and De Neve 2023).
15 For example, a woman in position 10 selects plastic thread, water cups, larger cans, and toothbrushes.

References

Bhaskar, K., and Turaga, R. M. R. 2018. 'India's E-Waste Rules and Their Impact on E-Waste Management Practices: A Case Study', *Journal of Industrial Ecology*, 22(4): 930–942.

Bozkurt, Ö., and Stowell, A. 2016. 'Skills in the Green Economy: Recycling Promises in the UK E-waste Management Sector', *New Technology, Work and Employment*, 3(2): 146–160.

Carswell, G., and De Neve, G. 2018. 'Towards a Political Economy of Skill and Garment Work: The Case of the Tiruppur Industrial Cluster in South India', in C. Hann, and J. Parry (eds.), *Industrial Labor on the Margins of Capitalism: Precarity, Class and the Neoliberal Subject*, pp. 309–335. New York: Berghahn Books.

Carswell, G., and De Neve, G. 2023. 'Training for Employment or Skilling up from Employment? Jobs and Skill Acquisition in the Tiruppur Textile Region, India', *Third World Quarterly*, 45(4): 715–733.

CEE. 2014. *Sourcebook on Solid and Liquid Waste Management in Rural India.* Centre for Environment Education, Ahmedabad.

Chatterjee, S. 2019. 'The Labors of Failure: Labor, Toxicity, and Belonging in Mumbai', *International Labor and Working-Class History*, 95: 49–75.

Chikarmane, P. 2012. 'Integrating Waste Pickers into Municipal Solid Waste Management in Pune, India', *Women in Informal Employment: Globalizing and Organizing (WEIGO) Policy Brief (Urban Policies)*, 8: 1–12.

Chikarmane, P., and Narayan, L. 2000. 'Formalising Livelihood: Case of Wastepickers in Pune', *Economic and Political Weekly*, 35(41): 3639–3642.

Corwin, J. 2018. *Circuits of Capital: India's Electronic Waste in the Informal Global Economy*. PhD dissertation, University of Minnesota, Minneapolis.

Darokar, S. 2018. 'Manual Scavengers: A Blind Spot in Urban Development Discourse', *Economic and Political Weekly*, 53(22): 1–13.

Deliège, R. 1999/1995. *The Untouchables of India* (N. Scott, tr.). London: Berg Publishers.

DoLE. 2020. *Notification: Department of Labour and Employment, Government of Himachal Pradesh, No. Shram (A) 4-2/2018-L.* Department of Labour and Employment, Government of Himachal Pradesh, Shimla.

Doron, A., and Raja, I. 2015. 'The Cultural Politics of Shit: Class, Gender and Public Space in India', *Postcolonial Studies*, 18(2): 189–207.

Gidwani, V., and Chaturvedi, B. 2011. 'Poverty as Geography: Motility, Stoppage and Circuits of Waste in Delhi', in J. S. Anjaria, and C. McFarlane (eds.), *Urban Navigations: Politics, Space and the City in South Asia*, pp. 50–78. New Delhi: Routledge.

Gill, K. 2010. *Of Poverty and Plastic Scavenging and Scrap Trading Entrepreneurs in India's Urban Informal Economy*. New Delhi: Oxford University Press.

GoI. 1993. *The Employment of Manual Scavengers and Construction of Dry Latrines (Prohibition) Act, 1993*. Government of India, New Delhi.

GoI. 2013. *The Prohibition of Employment as Manual Scavengers and Rehabilitation Act, 2013*. Government of India, New Delhi.

GoI. 2016. *National Classification of Occupations – 2015 (Code Structure)*. Ministry of Labour and Employment, Directorate General of Employment, Government of India, New Delhi.

Harriss-White, B. 2003. *India Working: Essays on Society and Economy*. Cambridge: Cambridge University Press.

Harriss-White, B. 2017a. 'Formality and Informality in an Indian Urban Waste Economy', *International Journal of Sociology and Social Policy*, 37(7/8): 417–434.

Harriss-White, B. 2017b. 'Matter in Motion: Work and Livelihoods in India's Economy of Waste', in E. Noronha, and P. D'Cruz (eds.), *Critical Perspectives on Work and Employment in Globalising India*, pp. 95–111. Singapore: Springer.

Harriss-White, B. 2018. 'India's Informal Waste Economy and Urban Informality: An Illustrated Tour of the Epistemological Horizon', *Work in Progress Paper*, Contemporary South Asian Studies Programme, School of Interdisciplinary Area Studies, Oxford University.

Harriss-White, B. 2019a. 'Waste, Social Order, and Physical Disorder in Small-Town India', *The Journal of Development Studies*, 56(2): 239–258.

Harriss-White, B. 2019b. 'Formal, Informal, Social and Unsocial Economy: Waste and the Work and Politics of Women', in S. Ray, N. Choudhury, and R. K. Kumar (eds.), *Theorizing Cohesive Development: An Alternative Paradigm*, pp. 142–173. New Delhi: Routledge.

Harriss-White, B. 2020. 'Waste and Public Policy Problems for Equitable Development – Micro-Level Insights', in R. Saleth, S. Galab, and E. Revathi (eds.), *Issues and Challenges of Inclusive Development*, pp. 233–257. Singapore: Springer.

Harriss-White, B., Prakash, A., Dixit, A., Joddar, P., Basile, E., and Vidyarthee, K. 2013. *Dalits and Adivasis in India's Business Economy: Three Essays and an Atlas*. New Delhi: Three Essays Collective.

Harriss-White, B., and Rodrigo, G. 2016. 'Discrimination in the Waste Economy: Narratives from the Waste Workers of a Small Town', *Journal of Social Inclusion Studies*, 2(2): 3–27.

Hodges, S. 2013. 'Medical Garbage and the Making of Neoliberalism in India' *Economic and Political Weekly* 48 (48): 112–119.

Hoornweg, D., Bhada-Tata, P., and Kennedy, C. 2013. 'Waste Production Must Peak This Century', *Nature*, 502: 615–617.

Human Rights Watch. 2014. *Cleaning Human Waste: 'Manual Scavenging,' Caste, and Discrimination in India*. Human Rights Watch, New York.

Ilaiah, K. 2009. *Post-Hindu India: A Discourse in Dalit-Bahujan, Socio-Spiritual and Scientific Revolution*. New Delhi: Sage Publications India.

ILO. 2012. *Resolution Concerning Updating the International Standard Classification of Occupations*. International Labour Organization, Geneva.

Kaza, S., Shrikanth, S., and Chaudhary, S. 2021. *More Growth, Less Garbage*. World Bank Publications, Washington DC.

Kaza, S., Yao, L., Bhada-Tata, P., and Van Woerden, F. 2018. *What a Waste 2.0: A Global Snapshot of Solid Waste Management to 2050*. World Bank Publications, Washington, DC.

Lave, J. 1993. 'The Practice of Learning', in J. Lave, and S. Chaiklin (eds.), *Understanding Practice: Perspectives on Activity and Context*, pp. 3–34. Cambridge: Cambridge University Press.

Liboiron, M. 2016. 'Municipal versus Industrial Waste: Questioning the 3–97 Ratio', *Discard Studies*.

Luthra, A. 2017. 'Waste-to-Energy and Recycling', *Economic and Political Weekly*, 52(13): 51–58.

Maitra, S., and Maitra, S. 2018. 'Producing the Aesthetic Self: An Analysis of Aesthetic Skill and Labour in the Organized Retail Industries in India', *Journal of South Asian Development*, 13(3): 337–357.

MoLE, GoI. 2019. *Right to Information Response – MLABE/R/2019/80658*. Ministry of Labour and Employment, Government of India, New Delhi.

MoUD, GoI. 2013. *Advisory on Improving Municipal Solid Waste Management Services*. Central Public Health and Environmental Engineering Organization (CPHEEO), Ministry of Urban Development, Government of India, New Delhi.

Rajendra, A. 2022. *Governing by (In)visibilising: A Case of Waste Materials, Infrastructure and Work*. PhD dissertation, Indian Institute of Management, Ahmedabad.

Rajendra, A., & Sarin, A. 2024. 'Worker, Owner, Volunteer, Employee or Worse? Registers of Work in Organising Waste Work in India', in A. Stowell, J. Gutberlet, F. Valenzuela, P. Zapata, and M. J. Zapata Campos (eds.), *Waste Research from the Social Sciences and Humanities Perspectives*, pp. 115–132. Newcastle: Cambridge Scholars Publishing.

Rodrigues, V. 2009. 'Untouchability, Filth, and the Public Domain', in G. Guru (ed.), *Humiliation: Claims and Context*, pp. 108–123. New Delhi: Oxford University Press.

Roman, C. 2008. *Learning and Innovation in Clusters: Case Studies from the Indian Silk Industry*. PhD dissertation, University of Oxford, Oxford.

Roy, T. 1999. *Traditional Industry in the Economy of Colonial India*. Cambridge University Press.

Singh, I. P. 2016. *CityMakers: Tribulations and Triumphs – a Saga of Heroic Struggle of the Homeless Residents of India*. New Delhi: Mukul Prakashan.

Skill Council for Green Jobs. 2016. 'Solid Waste Management (SGJ/Q6102, Version 1, Level 3)'. Available online at https://sscgj.in/solid-waste-management/ (downloaded on 04.11.2022).

Telangana Today. 2020. 'Hyderabad Now Has India's Most Advanced Waste Management System: KTR', *Telangana Today*, Hyderabad, 12 November.

Thorat, S., and Neuman, K. S. 2012. *Blocked by Caste: Economic Discrimination in Modern India*. New Delhi: Oxford University Press.

UN. 2020. *The Sustainable Development Goals Report*. United Nations, New York.

Wilson, B., and Singh, B. 2017. 'The Long March to Eliminate Manual Scavenging', in *India Exclusion Report 2016*, pp. 298–319. New Delhi: Yoda Press.

9

BEYOND THE ALGORITHM

The significance of skill in platform work

Ujjwal Kango

Introduction

The emergence of digital platforms, particularly in the last decade, has dramatically altered the nature of work in the contemporary global economy, leading to fundamental shifts in the organization and management of labour. The adoption of digital platforms for work allocation has resulted in a move away from traditional employment models to a system that directly allocates work to independent contractors. While platform workers of different kinds vary in their experiences and conditions of work, it is notable that a significant proportion of platform work exhibits common characteristics such as low levels of job security, low pay, minimal skill requirements, and a lack of union representation. Moreover, digital platforms employ algorithmic management systems to manage these distributed workers (Kellogg et al. 2020; Lee et al. 2015; Rosenblat and Stark 2016). These algorithms monitor workers, dictate worker behaviour, evaluate performance, and even automatically discipline workers, with little human oversight (Chai and Scully 2019; Kaine and Josserand 2019; Veen et al. 2020). As a result, workers are subjected to a form of control that is both pervasive and invisible. Numerous scholars have posited that the proliferation of algorithms has resulted in heightened levels of monitoring and regulation over the actions of workers (Kellogg et al. 2020: 388). Some scholars have likened this phenomenon to an 'algorithmic cage' (Faraj et al. 2018; Rahman and Thelen 2019) in which platform workers are deprived of any semblance of autonomy. Consequently, the nature of work in these on-demand platforms is often misrepresented as low skilled, mindless labour. This misconception has led to a devaluation of the work and the workers who perform it. In this chapter, I challenge this notion by

DOI: 10.4324/9781003604846-12

exploring the complexities of food delivery work and the skills required to perform it effectively. The chapter presents the results of an ethnographic study that examines the practices and experiences of food delivery workers in two Indian cities, Delhi NCR and Dharamshala, conducted as part of the author's doctoral research. Data collection involved the author undertaking participant observation by assuming the role of a food delivery worker for Food-delivery Company One (FCO) in Dharamshala, as well as conducting semi-structured interviews with food delivery workers using FCO and Food-delivery Company Two (FCT) in Delhi NCR.[1] Participant observation enabled first-hand experience and exploration of various themes, including engagement with the digital application, access to worker conversations, and the challenges of managing deliveries in adverse weather conditions without the support of a traditional office setting. By engaging in participant observation, the study could delve deeper into the habitual and mundane practices that may otherwise remain unexplored, offering a more comprehensive understanding of the multifaceted nature of food delivery work.

This chapter presents three key arguments. First, findings from the study challenge deterministic accounts of algorithmic control in the context of work by highlighting the partial nature of 'algorithmic control' on food delivery platforms. Contrary to assumptions of invasive monitoring and strict control over workers' activities (Kellogg et al. 2020; Rosenblat and Stark 2016), the findings suggest that algorithms used by food delivery platforms provide significant space for worker autonomy. This study highlights the complex interplay between algorithms and human agency in shaping work practices. While algorithms are designed to guide and coordinate food delivery operations, workers actively negotiate and shape these processes to suit their own needs and preferences. In fact, food delivery platforms often depend upon workers' creative problem-solving capabilities to navigate unforeseen challenges that arise during the food delivery process. Second, this chapter takes a nuanced perspective on the notion of skill within this work context. Contrary to its common portrayal as low-skilled work, this research demonstrates that local platform work (gig work) demands a diverse skill set, encompassing cognitive abilities, practical proficiencies, and adaptability. To successfully perform food delivery work, workers must be able to deftly balance the demands of the algorithmic system with the contingencies of the real-world environments they operate in, often having to make decisions and devise strategies in real time to optimize their earnings while delivering food safely and efficiently. This requires workers to demonstrate adaptability, resourcefulness, and commitment to ongoing learning. Third, this chapter emphasizes the significance of reimagining skill from the perspective of workers. I argue that in understanding skill at work, it is critical to consider the meaning and significance of skills from the perspective of those who acquire and use them, going beyond dominant approaches to skill development as a strategy to enhance employability, productivity, and economic benefit. Skill cannot be understood solely from a utilitarian perspective as a freely deployable asset acquired through new forms of organized training, leading to enhanced employability and economic mobility. Rather, skill must be seen as a social and cultural phenomenon shaped by the context in which it is acquired and used.

The chapter is structured as follows. The opening section examines different types of platform work and sheds light on the various levels of skill that are associated with platform work. Continuing, I address how food delivery work has become commonly associated with low-skilled labour in public discourse. The subsequent section presents the findings from the fieldwork and argues that despite the perception of algorithmic control as leading to high levels of restriction, food delivery work provides significant discretionary space for workers. In the next section, we explain how food delivery workers utilize this discretionary space to engage in work games to achieve their daily incentive targets. Due to the absence of extensive training and rapid onboarding processes, workers play these learning games to improve their skills in navigating the ever-changing urban landscape and comprehending the platform's functionalities, resulting in the accumulation of skills. The following section analyses how workers leverage these skills to develop various strategies to complete tasks within a minimal timeframe. Finally, the chapter concludes by summarizing the findings and arguing that any conception of skill should be informed by the experiences and perspectives of those who acquire and employ them, highlighting the importance of centring workers' experiences in the conceptualization of skill.

What is platform work?

Digital platforms offer a new mode of organizing work, providing labour as an 'on-demand service'. While digital labour platforms can be owned by various entities, such as corporations, start-ups, or individuals, it is important to note that these platforms do not employ the workers who provide the on-demand services. The platform acts solely as an intermediary between workers, who engage with the platform to perform services in exchange for payment, and customers, who make payments to the platform in exchange for goods or services delivered by the workers. These platforms 'onboard' independent contractors instead of hiring employees and present themselves as digital marketplaces where 'peers' meet in order to exchange goods or services (Schmidt 2017; De Stefano 2016). Independent contractors are also responsible for providing the capital assets required for the job, unlike traditional firms, which own/provide the capital assets required for work. According to Srnicek (2017: 76), what distinguishes digital labour platforms from other platform models is their 'hyper-outsourced model, whereby workers are outsourced, fixed capital is outsourced, maintenance costs are outsourced, and training is outsourced.

All that remains is a bare extractive minimum – control over the platform that enables a monopoly rent to be gained'.

Platform work encompasses various types of platforms, as demonstrated in Table 9.1. Common features of digital labour platforms include hiring workers as independent contractors, a tripartite arrangement (platform, worker, and customer), and the disintermediation of human managers through the use of algorithms for work allocation and evaluation (Howcroft and Bergvall-Kåreborn 2019: 23–24). One notable example is the ride-hailing platform Uber. Uber operates by hiring drivers as independent contractors who use their own vehicles to provide transportation services. The tripartite arrangement involves Uber as the digital online platform, drivers as workers, and passengers as customers. Uber's algorithm determines which driver is assigned to a particular ride based on factors such as proximity and driver ratings. The algorithm also evaluates driver performance and customer ratings to ensure quality control and accountability. Consequently, platform-mediated work makes it possible to avoid responsibilities that come with an employment contract for both parties to the contract. This alleviates regulatory requirements and shifts the major risks, such as lack of work and maintenance of capital equipment, onto workers. Furthermore, the activities and performance of service providers associated with the labour platform are monitored and evaluated digitally via algorithms. As a result, direct managerial oversight of work is replaced with algorithmic management (Lee et al. 2015). Most labour platforms use feedback rating systems (Rosenblat and Stark 2016), which allow the platforms to track productivity/efficiency and, hence, link payments to performance.

Platform-mediated work has been categorized into two broad types: online platform work and local platform work (Schmidt 2017; De Stefano 2016; Vallas 2019). These two conceptual categories (as shown in Table 9.1) differentiate between jobs that are executed, monitored, and paid for online and those that are allocated, monitored, and paid for online but executed physically 'in-person'. The first type of platform work is carried out entirely online, through digital platforms, and typically involves performing tasks or services remotely. Examples of online platform work include freelance platforms such as Upwork and Amazon Mechanical Turk. The second type of platform work is carried out physically, usually on-demand last mile service delivery in a specific location or setting.[2] Examples of local platform work include ride-hailing services, food delivery, and local professional services. Platform work comprises a broad spectrum of workers, ranging from highly skilled freelancers to those engaged in low skilled activities such as data entry or last-mile service delivery. In this study, we choose to focus on a particular group of workers who have come to epitomize platform work in public discourse: food delivery workers. Food delivery platforms in India are one of the largest labour platforms in both economic and geographical terms.

TABLE 9.1 Types of platform work

Characteristics	*Local platform work (gig work)*			*Online platform work*	
	Ride-hailing platforms	*Food delivery platforms*	*Local professional services*	*Freelance platforms*	*Crowd-work platforms*
Examples	Uber, Lyft, Ola	UberEATS, Zomato, Deliveroo	Urban Company, appJobber	Freelancer	Amazon Mturk
Job Duration	Shorter Duration	Shorter Duration	Shorter Duration	Longer Duration	Shorter Duration
Skill	Low Skill	Low Skill	Medium Skill	Medium-High Skill	Low Skill

Source: Adapted from Vallas (2019).

Is local platform work low skilled?

Food delivery work is commonly categorized as low skilled work in the existing literature (Vallas 2019; Wood et al. 2019; Goods et al. 2019). Food delivery work is described as simplistic and routine, with workers following predetermined routes and protocols when collecting food orders from restaurants and making deliveries to customers. Moreover, food delivery platforms utilize algorithmic management to determine task assignments and regulate work organization, ostensibly reducing the skill demands of the work environment. As the platform retains decision-making power over crucial aspects of the work, such as task assignment and organization, worker autonomy and discretion are assumed to be limited. Moreover, food delivery workers do not require any formal education or previous experience and are not typically provided with on-the-job training (potentially because platforms seek to preserve the perceived self-employment status of their workforce). Collectively, these factors contribute to the perception of food delivery work as being low skilled.

However, there exists a deeper problem with the existing frameworks used to define 'skill', which predominantly rely on a positivist understanding. According to this view, skill is a function of the complexity and range of tasks and duties to be performed in an occupation (Attewell 1990; Spenner 1990). It is indirectly measured using the formal education levels required for a particular job, the level of worker wages, and the amount of informal on-the-job training and/or previous experience required for competent performance of tasks and duties. This poses a conundrum for the conceptualization of skill in the gig economy. While food delivery workers require no formal education to join the platform and are not provided with any on-the-job training, my findings highlight the substantial skill and elaborate working knowledge that food delivery workers require and employ in their daily work. These workers operate in immensely complicated settings and skilfully engage with urban and digital landscapes on a daily basis (Briziarelli 2019). For Spinney and Popan (2020: 141–142):

> Working for Deliveroo or Uber Eats, for example, requires a host of often overlooked practical and safety-related mobility skills for navigating the complexity of road systems, including negotiation of other road users, whilst in interaction with or directed by digital media, defined by Richardson and Bissell (2019) as 'digital skills'. Being able to juggle such complex tasks, while also running red lights, avoiding a dangerous area, rejecting an order from a restaurant with long waiting times and still delivering an undamaged pizza on time, makes the difference between a successful and respectable messenger and a less effective one, and contributes implicitly to building and maintaining a strong street capital.

Despite the skill level required, these jobs are categorized as low skilled and, in turn, have lower pay scales and societal standing. Thus, such a conception of skill does not accurately consider the actual complex manoeuvring and strategic decision-making required by food delivery work. To address this limitation, it is crucial to broaden the conceptualization of skill within the context of platform work. This expanded perspective should encompass not only traditional notions of formal education or explicit training, but also the diverse array of cognitive, practical, and adaptive skills that workers demonstrate in their daily tasks. By acknowledging the complexity and significance of these skills, a more comprehensive understanding of skill in platform work can be fostered, leading to a more equitable evaluation and recognition of workers' contributions.

Incomplete control of the algorithmic boss: space for autonomy in food delivery work

To explore the issue of skill in food delivery work, it is necessary to closely examine the labour process that takes place on food delivery platforms. Understanding the specific tasks, interactions, and relationships that constitute such a process is crucial to discerning the skill requirements and work practices of food delivery workers. This section does just that, focusing specifically on the role of algorithms and their shortcomings in managing the labour process.

The rise of algorithmic management in the gig economy has brought significant changes to the way work is organized and managed, diverging from previous modes of management that relied on more traditional hierarchical structures and human decision-making processes. One of the most significant changes is the rise of algorithmic management, whereby workers are managed by digital platforms that rely on algorithms to assign tasks, monitor work, and evaluate performance (Kellogg et al. 2020). Scholars such as Kellogg et al. (2020) argue that algorithmic management cannot be viewed as a mere evolutionary development in technical control as it possesses unique characteristics that set it apart from traditional forms of control. They highlight the technical capabilities of algorithmic systems, such as comprehensiveness, instantaneity, interactivity, and opacity, which distinguish them from technologies of control that have been deployed in the past (Kellogg et al. 2020: 388; Curchod et al. 2020) and allow for a novel form of rational control.

While algorithmic management has brought significant efficiency gains to food delivery work, it has also raised concerns about its impact on worker autonomy. Many critics argue that algorithmic management strips workers of control, leaving them powerless in the face of an algorithmic boss. In the current era, platforms have leveraged modern technology to develop algorithms that enable the effective management and evaluation of work processes. This has been achieved through the use of artificial intelligence, which enables the forecasting of service delivery times and real-time tracking of worker movements through GPS surveillance (Aloisi 2015). Such technological advancements have led to the capture of detailed data on worker actions, enabling a more invasive form of monitoring. Scholars argue that these digital technologies facilitate the capturing of even the most minute of worker actions, allowing for a more refined labour process that ensures workers carry out their roles as expected in the most efficient way (Kellogg et al. 2020; Shapiro 2020; Woodcock 2020). As a result, algorithmic control has been compared to the development of an 'algorithmic cage' (Faraj et al. 2018; Rahman and Thelen 2019), which is 'more encompassing, instantaneous, interactive, opaque, and disintermediating than the historical regimes of control that employers have used over the past two centuries' (Kellogg et al. 2020: 388).

However, a closer look at the realities of food delivery work suggests that the situation is more complex. In reality, the degree of control that algorithmic management has over food delivery workers is not absolute. While the algorithms used by delivery companies do play a central role in determining which jobs workers receive and how much they are paid, they do not dictate every aspect of the work. In fact, workers often have a significant degree of autonomy over how they perform their tasks, which can provide them with a sense of agency and control (Galière 2020). During the fieldwork, I observed that the food delivery labour process contained several points at which workers use their discretion, such as when to leave for the restaurant, whether to agree to additional customer requests,[3] and navigating parking. For example, when a food delivery worker reaches a restaurant to collect an order, one of the first challenges they may face is finding a suitable place to park their bike. Depending on the location of the restaurant and the historical meal preparation times, workers must find a safe and secure place to park, ensuring that the bike is not in the way of pedestrians or other vehicles, or where it is not towed away by the police. For workers in Delhi NCR, this is a source of constant anxiety. This is especially true when collecting from restaurants located inside shopping malls, where finding a secure parking space can be time consuming and costly. Parking fees can even result in workers making a loss on deliveries. Facing this problem, food delivery workers develop strategies such as locating free parking spots, negotiating with the restaurant to provide a parking space or waive parking fees, or making informal arrangements with other food delivery workers to help them park their bikes while they pick up food orders. During my fieldwork, I found that workers in Saket, a locality in Delhi, congregate and wait outside the cinema hall (PVR Anupam) and ask their fellow workers to keep an eye on the bikes parked at the roadside to prevent them from being towed away. However, such solutions are not fool proof and not available to all food delivery workers. There were instances when bikes were towed away from no-parking zones outside restaurants in Delhi. Moreover, it was observed that algorithmic instructions are not taken at face value by the workers. Workers follow their own heuristics to determine the pace and method of work in the labour process, demonstrating their relative autonomy.

Additionally, managerial agency at crucial points is an important element within each step of direction, evaluation, and discipline on food delivery platforms. Both FCO and FCT employ fleet managers who play a key role in the labour process. It is common practice for fleet managers to create a WhatsApp group of all delivery workers in each locality, where they provide instructions and help to 'solve issues'. Moreover, workers can also contact fleet managers or the remote support team if they get stuck during the food delivery process. Sometimes unforeseen situations arise making the delivery impossible as per algorithmic instructions – for example, if a worker receives a large bulk order and the items cannot fit inside the delivery bag or cannot be stacked on top of each other. In such cases, workers typically contact the remote support team or fleet manager for support. The fleet manager generally asks the rider to hire a taxi/auto rickshaw to complete the delivery. The fleet manager later manually adds the cost of the taxi/auto rickshaw to the worker's weekly pay-out. There are also other non-routine scenarios that can occur – for example, a bike is impounded by the police, a road accident, order snatching, a closed restaurant, or customer violence – for which the algorithms are not adequately designed. Thus, human managers play an essential role in directing work in such cases, complementing and completing the algorithmic instructions. These managers polish and maintain algorithmic control while also acting as intermediaries between workers and higher management, directly engaging with workers to accomplish certain tasks and helping to resolve worker grievances that arise from algorithmic misinterpretations/errors. In some cases, the fleet managers also manually override algorithmic decisions and make a more informed and appropriate assignment based on factors such as the worker's location, availability, and weather conditions. For example, during rainy weather conditions, there is usually an increase in demand for food delivery services. In response to this surge in demand, the food delivery app may activate a 'rain surge' feature that offers incentives to workers who complete orders during rainy weather. However, we observed that in both FCO and FCT, the rain surge feature was not automatic. The food delivery platforms relied on human managers to manually activate the rain surge feature based on their knowledge and understanding of the duration and intensity of rain and demand-supply trends. This example shows how human managers play a crucial role in managing and optimizing the food delivery platform in response to changing external conditions and demand patterns.

Therefore, I highlight that while research on algorithmic control tendentiously assumes algorithms to be 'unsupervised' or 'automated', in practice, these algorithmic systems are heavily networked and supervised systems. In other words, algorithmic directions are incomplete – workers routinely make autonomous decisions to complete food delivery. Therefore, the notion of standardizing and closely regulating workers seems irrelevant (if not contradictory) to the reality of food delivery work. In the next section, we discuss some of the tactics that food delivery workers employ to be successful in their work tasks.

Work games in food delivery

Engaging with work as a game is the first major piece to the puzzle of labour control on food delivery platforms. Work games can be described as a phenomenon whereby workers use a range of tactics and strategies within the defined set of rules of their job to achieve uncertain outcomes (Burawoy 1979). The 'outcomes' can range from raising one's pace of work (Sherman 2005) to enhancing one's tip money (Mears 2015; Sallaz 2002), to earning monetary bonuses (Burawoy 1979). Drawing on Michael Burawoy's study of labour processes at a manufacturing unit, we can see how the use of piece rate pay and limited monitoring provided workers with the flexibility to construct games and continually surpass the expected production quota. This enabled workers to self-organize the production process and transform it into a game that regulated the conditions of work (Burawoy 1979: 51). In the context of food delivery platforms in Dharamshala and Delhi, a similar dynamic is observed, with workers developing 'platform games' based on the system of earnings.[4] As food delivery platforms pay piece wages, the faster the workers deliver, the more money they can make. Food delivery platforms exercise control over payment terms and associated conditions while simultaneously allowing workers a degree of discretion over the labour process. Within this discretionary realm, workers have the opportunity to construct a dynamic work game with strategies designed to enhance the number of deliveries they make in a day and facilitate the attainment of the daily incentive pay (Burawoy 1985: 38). However, in contrast to Burawoy's characterization of factory work, where work games serve as a veneer to mask the monotony of the job, food delivery workers engage in the form of play that is intrinsic to their profession. This spontaneous and innovative behaviour is not incidental but rather constitutes an essential element of food delivery work.

The playful nature of work can also be observed in the social interactions between food delivery workers. Workers often engage in playful banter or competition with each other, such as eagerness to complete orders or comparing the number of deliveries made in a day. When workers ran into each other in the mornings at the notional office,[5] they asked, 'How many orders did you hit yesterday?' or 'When did you return home?' During the day, the usual salutations were, 'How many orders have you completed?' or discussions about customers/restaurants wasting their time. The eagerness to maximize and reach targets was seen as almost compulsive behaviour. A worker in Delhi described feeling addicted to accepting incoming food orders:

> Being a food delivery worker, the anticipation of incoming orders is always present in my job. It's like waiting for my turn, and when the order buzzes, it's an immediate rush to press the accept button.

A skilled food delivery worker has an absolute understanding of their speed, intricate knowhow of the urban landscape, knowledge of available parking places, a comprehensive understanding of the food delivery application, and a precise idea of the time it would take to reach a customer's doorstep. A telling example can be found in my field notes from 2 April 2021.

> Today, while I was stuck in traffic at a busy intersection in Delhi, I noticed a food delivery worker manoeuvring his way through the chaos on his bike. The traffic was gridlocked, and the pedestrians were swarming, but he seemed to glide between them effortlessly. He was finding gaps and spaces that I couldn't even see. Despite the apparent chaos and danger, he moved with purpose and precision. Watching him, I couldn't help but be impressed by his skill and agility on the bike. It is a reminder of the unique challenges that food delivery workers face in India's congested cities and the incredible effort and skill that they bring to their work every day.

Mastering the learning game

Upon joining food delivery platforms, new workers undergo a brief online onboarding process. However, this one-hour process leaves them inadequately equipped to deal with the challenges they encounter while on the job. As a consequence, food delivery workers engage in what Sallaz (2015) refers to as 'learning games'.[6] These games require workers to continuously learn and master new challenges on a daily basis. Therefore, despite the significant learning that occurs after workers join the platform, their lack of preparation during onboarding leads to ongoing learning games as they strive to navigate the difficulties that arise in the course of their work.

The work of food delivery involves a series of challenges that must be mastered in order to reach their daily targets. These challenges include navigating the delivery application, getting familiar with the locality, and developing effective delivery strategies for meeting daily order targets. As a result, food delivery workers engage in an absorbing learning game as they seek to succeed in their work. During the initial period of working as a food delivery worker with the FCO platform in Dharamshala, I experienced a sense of disorientation and anxiety in navigating the city and interpreting algorithmic instructions, despite being a resident of the city. Additionally, I found myself relying on my fellow workers to help me navigate the challenges of the job. When facing difficulties, I would even return to the notional office to seek assistance from other workers in completing the delivery successfully.

To encourage workers to participate in the learning game, FCO offered a substantial joining bonus of Rs. 2,000 to those who successfully delivered 100 food orders within their first 20 days of work. The joining bonus served as an incentive for the new workers to continue to participate in the learning game and acquire the skills needed to master the complexities of their work. The impetus or incentive to participate in learning games is especially significant as it is crucial for workers' learning process and skill enhancement. This involves establishing a rapport with their bike and smartphone, gaining a comprehensive understanding of the food delivery application, and acquiring an in-depth knowledge of the locality.

During my fieldwork, on 16 January 2021, a new worker Vishal joined FCO as a delivery partner in Dharamshala. On his first day as a food delivery worker, he messed up his first order of the day. As he rode to the restaurant, he struggled to find it due to his lack of familiarity with the GPS. When he tried to contact the restaurant for assistance, he accidentally cancelled the order on the application. Such issues with navigating the application interface were common for new workers. While the application instructions are displayed in the worker's preferred language, many new workers are not very comfortable handling a smartphone, with some being first-time smartphone users. Thus, for most new workers, learning the application interface and its functionalities is also a major task during the first few weeks.

Through trial and error, sharing of experiences, and even videos or blogs on the internet, workers learn about the application and various strategies for consistently and quickly earning daily incentives. On my second day at work with FCO, I was advised by a fellow worker: 'Never return home without completing at least the first target. Try to work during the dinner peak. You will get back-to-back orders during that time'. Co-workers helped newer workers with addresses, application issues, phone charging, bike parking, optimal work schedules, working in rainy conditions (where to wait for orders and obtain waterproof covers for phones), shortest routes to restaurants, and so forth.

Ultimately, the learning games played by food delivery workers highlight the dynamic and complex nature of their work and the significant role that continuous learning and adaptation play in achieving success. Moreover, these learning games not only showcase the intricate nature of food delivery work, but also debunk the misconception that platform work requires no training. By actively engaging in these learning games, workers are able to improve their skills and adapt to the constantly changing environment, ultimately leading to greater success in their work. Indeed, workers who are unable to keep up with the learning games and adapt to the evolving demands of the platform are more likely to leave the platform. The high turnover rate among food delivery workers further highlights the importance of continuous learning and adaptation in platform work and the need for platforms to provide adequate training and support to their workers.

Developing strategies to play the game

Playing work games required workers to develop (a combination of) particular strategies (Burawoy 1979: 38), such as carefully managing of their work schedule, maintaining good relations with restaurant staff and fleet managers, and acquiring extensive knowledge of the spatio-temporal character of city localities. While most of these tactics were individual, workers also used collective strategies to 'make out' (Burawoy 1979) in the work games. Burawoy (1979) put forth the concept of making-out which refers to a situation where workers in a piece-rate system competed with each other to surpass their expected production quotas, effectively transforming work into a sort of game. The workers who made out were eligible for a bonus in their wages. However, according to Burawoy (1979), their motivation stemmed from the sense of accomplishment, and personal pride, rather than solely from the financial incentives. In the context of food delivery platforms, food delivery workers employed various strategies to reach maximum targets in the minimum time possible. These included avoiding orders from restaurants which had long meal preparation times (especially during peak hours), calling customers to ascertain their location before leaving the restaurant (minimizing travel time), maintaining good relationships with restaurants and even helping to pack orders, and developing detailed knowledge of the locality (e.g. congested routes, parking spots, shortcuts) that would assist in hitting daily targets.

I will examine two of the strategies delineated here in further depth. The research findings revealed that food delivery workers often need to invest in specialized equipment (e.g. rain gear) to enable them to work in adverse weather conditions, and certain paraphernalia (e.g. power banks, mobile holders, more comfortable seat covers) that helped them to endure extended shifts and meet delivery targets. This demonstrates that knowledge of and investment in the means of production needed for food delivery work (accessories, in this case) was an essential precondition to 'make out' at the platform games. Second, it was found that extensive knowledge of the locality was also crucial for acing platform games. While digital maps and GPS coordinates streamline the information needed to reach customers, these abstract representations of the city are often misleading due to missing information (e.g. internal roads, entry/exit gates to residential complexes, parking spots), inaccurate GPS markup by customers, and inaccurate GPS locations caused by signal failure (due to the high density of buildings and mountainous terrain). It is noteworthy that, although the public at large tends to concentrate on the speed at which food delivery personnel traverse city streets, a considerable portion of their labour occurs within buildings, as they take lifts, stand in lobbies, wait at security check-in desks, and walk up and down staircases. A food delivery worker based in Gurgaon revealed that the quantity of orders fulfilled, and thus a worker's earnings, has more to do with speed inside, rather than outside, buildings. This sort of speed primarily derives from the worker's familiarity with building layouts and policies – for example, whether building security requires entry in registers and checking of bags, if there are stairs in addition to lifts, guest parking policies – and workers' ability to swiftly tackle problems, for instance by persuading or evading security personnel or quickly spotting a wrongly marked GPS address.

> As a food delivery worker, my earnings depend on more than just my speed on the road. Navigating the ins and outs of each building, from security procedures to parking policies, is just as important as getting the food to the customer on time. Being quick on my feet and adapting to any situation is what truly sets me apart.

Furthermore, food delivery workers develop skills not only to efficiently complete their work tasks, but also to disentangle their physical movements from the data collected by platform surveillance systems, allowing them to maintain a degree of control over their work and avoid excessive monitoring by the platform. They achieve this by strategically disentangling their physical movements from the data collected by these systems, thereby maintaining a semblance of control over their work environment and, concurrently, evading the potentially intrusive scrutiny of the platform. For instance, some workers engaged in strategically switching on and off their GPS, to control when and how their locations are shared with the platform. This allows them to selectively disclose their whereabouts only when it suits their workflow or personal preferences. In addition, during my fieldwork in Delhi, I encountered instances where workers employed fake GPS applications to deceive the algorithms, creating a simulated location that does not accurately reflect their actual position. Such subversive tactics exemplify the adaptive strategies employed by workers to manipulate the algorithmic monitoring systems.

Therefore, the analysis suggests that the use of 'platform games' serves as a crucial mechanism for establishing control over food delivery platforms. Through a complex system of rewards and low piece earnings, workers are incentivized to attain and surpass their target pay, leading them to employ various strategies to complete tasks within minimal time. As new workers are onboarded onto the platform without formal training, they must learn to navigate the system and devise methods to maximize their earnings, resulting in an engrossing process of continuous learning and adaptation that could be described as a 'learning game', as theorized by Sallaz (2002, 2015). Furthermore, the agency and strategic decision-making displayed by workers in their pursuit of maximizing their earnings has significant implications for redefining the notion of skill within the context of food delivery work.

Conclusion: rethinking skill

In this chapter, we argue that contrary to assumptions of invasive monitoring and strict control over worker activities, algorithms used by food delivery platforms provide significant space for worker autonomy. In other words, food delivery platforms exert a relatively *loose* control mechanism. As a result, food delivery workers establish considerable control over the labour process and retain the knowledge necessary for executing work tasks. While our analysis underscores the substantial autonomy wielded by food delivery workers in navigating algorithmic structures, it is imperative to recognize the nuanced dynamics at play. Platforms have the ability to continuously intervene in the game by implementing changes to the rules of the game, such as the quantum of bonuses and the conditionalities for earning bonuses, making it possible to drive work games and orient them according to what works for an individual worker. In fact, platform games emerge as a means to impose directions on a party (delivery workers) in the absence of any legally enforceable and contractually specified obligations. Thus, work games, at least partially, come under the influence of platforms and exhibit a somewhat top-down character.

Overall, this chapter highlights the importance of skill in food delivery work and underscores the importance of worker subjectivity in achieving work outcomes. Thus, the notion that such work is low or unskilled is challenged by a counter-narrative that contests the devaluation of gig work and underscores the significance of skill in negotiating and succeeding in the food delivery sector.

Indeed, this research advocates for a more nuanced perspective on food delivery work. The designated responsibilities of a food delivery worker may appear unskilled based on classifications such as the International Standard

Classification of Occupations (ISCO) or popular perceptions. However, it is important to recognize the ways in which specific utilization of embodied skill to navigate the hybrid space of the city challenges such a classification. This chapter underscores the complexity of the challenges faced by food delivery workers, which demand a range of sophisticated skills and expertise. Despite being subjected to algorithmic control and surveillance, food delivery workers nonetheless exercise considerable autonomy in the course of their work. Through engagement in learning games, food delivery workers develop an embodied skill that enables them to efficiently navigate the city, interpret algorithmic instructions, and fulfil customer demands. This research suggests that workers must deftly balance the demands of the algorithmic system with the contingencies of the real-world environments in which they operate, often having to make decisions and devise strategies in real time to optimize their earnings while delivering food safely and efficiently. Food delivery work thus requires workers to be adaptable, resourceful, and capable of continuous learning. Therefore, food delivery work cannot be seen as low skilled, as it demands autonomy, discretion, and a range of cognitive and practical skills beyond mere technical or mechanical ability.

As exemplified by the case of food delivery work, this research problematizes traditional definitional frameworks for understanding 'skill' and challenges narrow conceptions that often overlook the complexity and nuance of workers' embodied expertise. Indeed, drawing on the ethnomethodological understanding of skill as an embodied construct (Attewell 1990), the multifaceted nature of skill development in the context of food delivery work is highlighted. By emphasizing the situated and practical nature of skill acquisition, our research underscores the importance of recognizing the embodied knowledge, adaptability, and problem-solving abilities that food delivery workers develop through their engagement in learning games and dynamic interactions within their work environment.

This research further demonstrates that in exploring the nature and significance of skills at work, it is crucial to account for the experiences and viewpoints of those who acquire and use them. This requires moving beyond conventional approaches that view skill development solely as a means of enhancing employability, productivity, and economic gains. By the same token, skills must be understood as more than just utilitarian assets that can be acquired through formal training programmes. In fact, skill development is often deeply intertwined with the personal experiences and learning cycles of workers themselves – as demonstrated by the case of food delivery workers in the platform economy. Indeed, by adopting a more nuanced perspective on skills at work, we can gain a deeper understanding of the challenges and opportunities faced by workers in the platform economy. This can inform the design of policies that are better aligned with the needs and experiences of workers, ultimately leading to improved outcomes for both workers and platforms alike.

Notes

1 Platform names are pseudonyms.
2 An on-demand service is called as such because services are provided by platforms as soon as a customer experiences a need for the service and the demand for the service is sensitive to delay (Taylor 2018).
3 As a food delivery worker, requests to buy additional items such as cigarettes or cold drinks en route are not uncommon, and deciding whether to accept such requests can be a challenging decision. On the one hand, accommodating these requests may lead to higher customer satisfaction and potentially better tips. On the other hand, it may lead to delays in completing other deliveries or increase the complexity and time demand of the original order. There is also an added risk that the customer will refuse to pay for the additional items. Food delivery workers may also need to consider their own safety and well-being, especially if requests involve potentially risky or dangerous situations. As a result, food delivery workers develop their own logics to help them make quick and effective decisions.
4 On both food delivery platforms, delivery workers are paid according to a piece rate system, that is paid for each food order delivered. The applicable piece rates are displayed on the application in the form of a rate card. Rate cards differ between cities, as was the case for Dharamshala and Delhi NCR. The rate card can be divided into order pay, target pay, and minimum guarantee pay. The order pay is earnings that a worker earns on a per-order basis. Target pay is awarded when a worker successfully completes a certain pre-defined number of orders or reaches pre-defined total earnings. However, a number of conditions must be met to unlock target pay, such as zero order cancellations, one denial per day, and compulsory log-in during certain times (4 hours between 7 pm and 11:59 pm in Delhi NCR). The minimum guarantee pay is the minimum income assured to workers if they log in a certain number of hours (typically 10–12 hours) and meet a number of associated conditions.
5 During the fieldwork, it was observed that workers gathered at a public place, which served as their 'notional office' while they waited to receive food orders. In Dharamshala, the 'notional office' was a public place just outside a police building, which was proximate to most restaurants listed on FCO and had free parking spaces for bikes. On some days, the police hosted various tournaments which the workers enjoyed watching while waiting for orders to come in. Even the fleet managers (supervisors) used to conduct their field visits at these 'notional offices' when they wanted to monitor and meet the delivery workers.
6 The term refers to the process through which workers engage in activities that enable them to acquire skills and knowledge necessary for their work, and which are not explicitly taught in formal training. These games are characterized by the dynamic and complex nature of the work and the need for workers to continuously learn and adapt in response to the changing demands of the job.

References

Attewell, Paul. 1990. 'What Is Skill?' *Work and Occupations* 17(4): 422–448. https://doi.org/10.1177/0730888490017004003.

Briziarelli, Marco. 2019. 'Spatial Politics in the Digital Realm: The Logistics/Precarity Dialectics and Deliveroo's Tertiary Space Struggles'. *Cultural Studies* 33(5): 823–840. https://doi.org/10.1080/09502386.2018.1519583.

Burawoy, Michael. 1979. *Manufacturing Consent: Changes in the Labor Process under Monopoly Capitalism*. Chicago: The University of Chicago Press.

Burawoy, Michael. 1985. *The Politics of Production: Factory Regimes Under Capitalism and Socialism*. London: Verso.
Chai, Sunyu, and Maureen A. Scully. 2019. 'It's about Distributing Rather Than Sharing: Using Labor Process Theory to Probe the "Sharing" Economy'. *Journal of Business Ethics* 159(4): 943–960. https://doi.org/10.1007/s10551-019-04210-y.
Curchod, Corentin, Gerardo Patriotta, Laurie Cohen, and Nicolas Neysen. 2020. 'Working for an Algorithm: Power Asymmetries and Agency in Online Work Settings'. *Administrative Science Quarterly* 65(3): 644–676. https://doi.org/10.1177/0001839219867024.
Faraj, Samer, Stella Pachidi, and Karla Sayegh. 2018. 'Working and Organizing in the Age of the Learning Algorithm'. *Information and Organization* 28(1): 62–70. https://doi.org/10.1016/j.infoandorg.2018.02.005.
Galière, Sophia. 2020. 'When Food-Delivery Platform Workers Consent to Algorithmic Management: A Foucauldian Perspective'. *New Technology, Work and Employment* 35(3): 357–370. https://doi.org/10.1111/ntwe.12177.
Goods, Caleb, Alex Veen, and Tom Barratt. 2019. "Is Your Gig Any Good?' Analysing Job Quality in the Australian Platform-Based Food-Delivery Sector'. *Journal of Industrial Relations* 61(4): 502–527. https://doi.org/10.1177/0022185618817069.
Howcroft, Debra, and Birgitta Bergvall-Kåreborn. 2019. 'A Typology of Crowdwork Platforms'. *Work, Employment and Society* 33(1): 21–38. https://doi.org/10.1177/0950017018760136.
Kaine, Sarah, and Emmanuel Josserand. 2019. 'The Organisation and Experience of Work in the Gig Economy'. *Journal of Industrial Relations* 61(4): 479–501. https://doi.org/10.1177/0022185619865480.
Kellogg, Katherine C., Melissa A. Valentine, and Angèle Christin. 2020. 'Algorithms at Work: The New Contested Terrain of Control'. *Academy of Management Annals* 14(1): 366–410. https://doi.org/10.5465/annals.2018.0174.
Mears, Ashley. 2015. 'Working for Free in the VIP'. *American Sociological Review* 80(6): 1099–1122. https://doi.org/10.1177/0003122415609730.
Rahman, K. Sabeel, and Kathleen Thelen. 2019. 'The Rise of the Platform Business Model and the Transformation of Twenty-First-Century Capitalism'. *Politics and Society* 47(2): 177–204. https://doi.org/10.1177/0032329219838932.
Richardson, Lizzie, and David Bissell. 2019. 'Geographies of Digital Skill'. *Geoforum* 99: 278–286. https://doi.org/10.1016/j.geoforum.2017.09.014.
Rosenblat, Alex, and Luke Stark. 2016. 'Algorithmic Labor and Information Asymmetries: A Case Study of Uber's Drivers'. *International Journal of Communication* 10: 3758–3784. https://doi.org/10.2139/ssrn.2686227.
Sallaz, Jeffrey J. 2002. 'The House Rules: Autonomy and Interests among Service Workers in the Contemporary Casino Industry'. *Work and Occupations* 29(4). https://doi.org/10.1177/0730888402029004002.
Sallaz, Jeffrey J. 2015. 'Permanent Pedagogy'. *Work and Occupations* 42(1): 3–34. https://doi.org/10.1177/0730888414551207.
Shapiro, Aaron. 2020. 'Dynamic Exploits: Calculative Asymmetries in the on-Demand Economy'. *New Technology, Work and Employment* 35(2): 162–177. https://doi.org/10.1111/ntwe.12160.
Sherman, Rachel. 2005. 'Producing the Superior Self'. *Ethnography* 6(2): 131–158. https://doi.org/10.1177/1466138105057546.
Spenner, Kenneth I. 1990. 'Skill: Meanings, Methods, and Measures'. *Work and Occupations* 17(4): 399–421. https://doi.org/10.1177/0730888490017004002.
Spinney, Justin and Cosmin Popan. 2020. 'Mobilising Street Culture: Understanding the Implications of the Shift from Lifestyle Bike Messengers to Gig Economy Workers'. In Routledge Handbook of Street Culture, edited by J. I. Ross, 137–146. London: Routledge.

Srnicek, Nick. 2017. 'The Challenges of Platform Capitalism: Understanding the Logic of a New Business Model'. *Juncture* 23(4): 254–257. https://doi.org/10.1111/newe.12023.

Taylor, Terry A. 2018. 'On-Demand Service Platforms'. *Manufacturing & Service Operations Management* 20(4): 704–720. https://doi.org/10.1287/msom.2017.0678.

Vallas, Steven P. 2019. 'Platform Capitalism: What's at Stake for Workers?'. *New Labor Forum* 28(1): 48–59. https://doi.org/10.1177/1095796018817059.

Veen, Alex, Tom Barratt, and Caleb Goods. 2020. 'Platform-Capital's "App-Etite" for Control: A Labour Process Analysis of Food-Delivery Work in Australia'. *Work, Employment and Society* 34(3): 388–406. https://doi.org/10.1177/0950017019836911.

Wood, Alex J., Mark Graham, Vili Lehdonvirta, and Isis Hjorth. 2019. 'Good Gig, Bad Gig: Autonomy and Algorithmic Control in the Global Gig Economy'. *Work, Employment and Society* 33(1): 56–75. https://doi.org/10.1177/0950017018785616.

Woodcock, Jamie. 2020. 'The Algorithmic Panopticon at Deliveroo: Measurement, Precarity, and the Illusion of Control'. *Ephemera. Theory & Politics in Organization* 20(3): 1–20. www.ephemerajournal.org.

10

"LEARNING COMPUTERS"

Skilling, working, and waiting in Seelampur

Sreela Sarkar

Introduction

In early 2020, India witnessed a growing swell of protests against the Citizenship Amendment Act (CAA) and the National Register of Citizens (NRC). In December 2019, the Indian nationalist government enacted the CAA (Citizenship Amendment Act) and proposed the NRC (National Register of Citizens) that together would further persecute Indian Muslims without valid legal documents and effectively strip them out of their "citizenship." This move was followed by several protests in India and globally and resulted in violent clashes between the state and protestors. In Seelampur, women came out in large numbers to stage sit-in protests near the Jaffarabad metro station.

Located in the north-eastern border of the capital city of Delhi, Seelampur is a diverse but primarily a Muslim dominated working-class neighborhood with a long history of state violence. From December 2019 to the middle of January 2020, women residents of Seelampur had campaigned door to door and initiated candlelight marches against the CAA and the NRC that Indian Muslims feared would be used to persecute and disenfranchise them (ANI 2020; The Caravan Magazine 2020). By mid-January, the protests had turned into a round the clock sit-in. The sit-in grew to hundreds of women who called themselves the Seelampur-Jaffarabad protestors. On February 23, 2020, Kapil Mishra, who belonged to the ruling Hindu Nationalist Bharatiya Janata Party, gave a speech demanding that the protestors be removed. Police violence followed this speech and it was reported that mostly Hindu mobs brandishing weapons and saffron flags entered the north-eastern part of Delhi including Seelampur (Daniyal 2020). Women protestors returned to sites of protest in Seelampur, gaining less recognition in media coverage than

DOI: 10.4324/9781003604846-13

the internationally recognized Shaheen Bagh protestors.[1] This relative lack of visibility for Seelampur women follows a longer history of media representation of the locality as the "capital city's social underbelly" (Kumar 2013), containing "lumpen elements" (Pathak & Katiyar 1993), and a "rampaging mob" (The Hindu 2006).

For Seelampur residents, this was not their first encounter with state sanctioned violence. During the National Emergency years of 1975–77, Indian Muslim men whose homes were destroyed by the Delhi Development Authority (DDA) were given small plots of land in exchange for sterilization under the infamous sterilization initiative of the state (Tarlo 2003). Muslim men "volunteered" to be sterilized often as an attempt to prevent homelessness and keep their families together (Tarlo 2003). Over the decades, the Delhi government has razed homes and businesses in the area to enact its slum clearing policies and its controversial laws on "polluting industries" related to denim manufacturing in the area. In the 2006 protests that were in reaction to the shutdown of "illegal" manufacturing units in the locality dealing with jeans, iron and timber goods, incense, and lathes, the police opened fire on several denim workers. In her work on slum clearances and environmental issues in Delhi, Baviskar (2003) argues that such "bourgeois environmentalism" in Delhi includes a convergence of upper-class concerns about aesthetics, health, and safety and the interests of the disciplinary state in creating spaces deemed appropriate for the investment of modern capital. In 2006, Seelampur residents who protested against these actions that threw an estimated two million people out of work were deemed as "lumpen" (Rediff 2006) as they were during the CAA protests (OpIndia 2019; Kumar 2020).

Seelampur women had been in the news before as constituting ideal citizens as the recipients of computer skills training programs for well over a decade. In 2003, G-Tech Foundation, an arm of the Indian IT corporation G-Tech, in partnership with UNESCO started the ICT center in Seelampur in a small room in the basement of the local Madrasa with the permission of Maulana Aamir Ahmed, who exercises considerable political and religious power in the locality. Madrasa means "school" in Arabic but occupies a prominent place in the Western imagination as a "breeding ground of Islamic terror." In 2006, G-Tech Foundation partnered with the Delhi government and moved out of the Madrasa into the Gender Resource Center (GRC) housed in a small building in Jaffarabad next to denim production units. In 2008, the ICT skills center was brought under the umbrella of the new public-private partnership of the Delhi government called Mission Convergence or Samajik Suvidha Kendra that introduced two changes to the Seelampur initiative. One, other skills training programs started for women at the GRC, including Cutting, Tailoring, and Dress Designing and Beauty Culture. Second, the skilling programs at the GRC were brought under Mission Convergence program in 2008. This program sought to provide marginalized residents a smooth interface for accessing social services through the GRCs and also to train urban poor citizens in employable "skills." The Chief Minister of Delhi from the "secular" Congress Party championed this program that claimed to reach "vulnerable and most vulnerable sections of the society" (Government of NCT of Delhi 2015). In 2015, Narendra Modi inaugurated his signature Skill India Mission soon after taking office as the Prime Minister. The Skills Mission focused on training youth who constitute over half of the population; 22% of India's youth, classified as individuals 15–24 years, have been unemployed over the last decade in 2021 (Statista 2021). In his Independence Day address to the nation in 2014, Modi referred to dismantling the "archaic system" to create an employable labor force. The Seelampur ICT program was considered to be an early exemplar of skilling interventions.

From 2008 to 2017, I studied the Seelampur skills program through sustained, ethnographic work as part of a larger project on the institutional and cultural politics of ICT and development programs in India. Following the work of feminist and critical ethnographers of globalization and media (Abu-Lughod 2005; Mankekar 1999; Mazzarella 2003; Rajagopal 2001), my multi-method study of the Seelampur initiative includes in-depth participation observation, interviews, and textual analysis of publicity materials to study interconnected institutions, markets, and communities. All names of organizations and individuals are changed according to Institutional Review Board (IRB) guidelines to preserve confidentiality.

In this chapter, I study the ICT-skills program located in the Gender Resource center in Seelampur. Instead of active, politicized subjects, the skills initiative considered "Muslim women" as passive recipients of a development mission that used technology to "leapfrog" (Steinmueller 2001) them into modernity. I locate the ICT skilling program in the ecology of economically productive activities in Seelampur such as denim manufacturing units and home-based industries. I point out that Seelampur was already a vital node of the global economy and the GRC students participated in a number of these occupations, belying the assumption that they were in a state of prolonged suspension in the contemporary economy and society. Second, I follow the daily lives of the ICT participants both inside and outside the training center. The skilling program promised economic and social mobility for participants in India's "new" economy. Program staff encouraged Seelampur women residents to enroll in the computer training initiative by pointing to the possibility of jobs in lower – end call centers, ticketing stations at the Delhi Metro, entry level data entry positions, customer service positions at malls, ground staff at airlines, and other positions. Seelampur women perceived these positions as enabling them to support their families and paving the way for mobility. Despite the promise of rapid advancement by the ICT skills program, most participants did not find formal employment after the program or worked in precarious and exploitative occupations at the lower end of the information economy. Third, the Mission Convergence program promised smooth access to social services through deployment of technology. However, the program often resulted in more confusion, tedious processes, and delays in receiving entitlements for residents who found themselves at the receiving end of skilling politics. As we will see, Seelampur computer students inadvertently became the representatives of the state under Convergence and felt called on to provide care to residents. The contradictions that the women experienced as messengers of the state led them to occasionally criticize its role in the provision of social goods and services. Despite the promise of rapid inclusion through technological interfaces of the state, the women at the Seelampur center experienced much lingering and waiting both inside the space of the center and away from the doorsteps of the center. Their wait for employment, mobility, and access to social services was amplified by their participation in the skilling program that demonstrated deep limitations in the promise of economic and social ascension.

The ecology of skill in Seelampur: waiting to be "modern"

One of the most popular images associated with the computer training initiative in Seelampur, according to prominent project staff members, has been its aim to "empower women straight from the Madrasa." Seelampur was located relatively close to G-Tech Foundation's office in north-east Delhi and this constituted a major reason why they chose this location for the computer centers. The Foundation subsequently opened "multimedia centers" in other parts of north-east Delhi such as Khichripur and Sunder Nagri that are also diverse working-class neighborhoods with a significant proportion of Muslim residents like Seelampur. The Seelampur center was the only one that came under the aegis of the state run GRC program.

Seelampur project documents revealed "culturalist" assumptions about modernizing Islam (Afshar & Maynard 1994) that have a longer history in the development discourse in India. Project initiators framed Seelampur in policy documents as a place with "towering minarets of numerous mosques in the area" that indicated the powerful influences of the clergy and religion in the area, and claimed that "traditional customs" played a powerful role for women. Thus, project visionaries associated Seelampur women with "tradition" and conservatism rooted in Islam and Seelampur as a place outside modernity.

From the start, the leaders of the ICT skills project framed technology access as breaking down political, economic, and cultural barriers (Sarkar 2016). According to an early project document:

> The lack of access to ICT reinforces gender inequalities whether economic (for instance, the ability to earn), political (for instance, participation in

key political processes), or cultural (for instance changing existing social hierarchies).

When the Millennium Development Goals in 2000 emphasized access to ICTs as a basic right, India emerged as a poster child of ICT for Development (ICTD) initiatives. In policy discourse, ICTs hold the promise of "leapfrogging for developing countries" (Steinmueller 2001: 195). Societies no longer need to be confined to the "waiting room of history." The e-governance Mission Convergence program and the associated ICT skills training project promised an end to waiting for rapid economic and social mobility.

Several of the publicity pictures for the ICT skilling project showed side shots of women wearing veils, sitting in front of desktops. Thus "Muslim women" were rendered faceless and Islam was juxtaposed with the veil and modernity with computers. "Learning computers" would lead the women to cross over to modernity. Feminist scholars have critiqued the construction of the "Muslim woman" as the quintessential "other" who is waiting to be liberated by the West or liberal feminism (Ahmed 1993; Mohanty 2003). Through an empirical survey, Hasan and Menon (2004) conclude that Indian Muslim women are not disadvantaged because of religious conservatism but because of the trinity of being economically marginalized, of being women, and of being a religious minority in India. In a parallel vein, publicity pictures for the Skills India Mission show young people working at their computers in a row. The faces of the individuals are obscured in the pictures and the computers are in sharper focus. These pictures reinforce the popular representation that large numbers of individuals are passive participants of tech-focused, modernization projects that have the power to be emancipatory.

Though the representation of Seelampur placed the residents as "backward" and outside the modern economy, the skills ecology in the locality contradicted that portrayal. IT professionals have been upheld as iconic figures in India in popular discourse, especially since the 1990s liberalization of the economy and the Silicon Valley burst that led to diasporic returnees (Saxenian 2002). Billboards in Seelampur advertised computer training courses by private companies such as NIIT, Aptech, and Wadhwa Computer Training. Many young women could not afford the privately run computer courses and a few of them had completed short-term programs at these institutes. Seelampur women enrolled in the G-Tech/Delhi government program because it was free of charge and it promised a better future. The promise of a better life through computer training trickled down through popular culture representation but in the case of the Seelampur women, that promise was somewhat amorphous. Most women enrolled in the program to financially support their families and perceived the program to lead to employment and social mobility. However, they remained unclear about the exact positions and the work and compensation associated with those jobs after graduation.

The GRC was located in a narrow alley, a short rickshaw ride from the metro station. The street housed houses, cattle sheds, and small denim manufacturing units that provided both work and living space for several workmen. Below the small GRC building, migrant laborers from the states of Bihar and Uttar Pradesh worked in the denim unit. About eight men lived and slept overnight at this small denim workshop. Some of these men used computer-aided designs in the workshop that received no mention when policymakers mapped the locality for skilling initiatives. Both the denim workers and the ICT students were unaware of each other's work.

Project representations of Seelampur women as not participating in the modern economy were flawed. Women were the invisible labor force of denim factories, working on hammering metal buttons on jeans from within their homes. Each tack was called a "repeat" and required a hammer. This was a painstaking task and their wages were calculated according to each "repeat." About 20–25 jeans earned the women workers about 250 rupees a day or less than $6. This work for the denim industry paralleled an extensive informal economy of work among Seelampur women that is often concealed behind the closed doors of houses. This labor included sewing, embroidering, giving private tuitions at home, working in beauty care, and making pickles and chocolates for sale. Several of these small businesses earned the family more income than that from male members. The women also contributed significantly to small-scale family businesses in the area through informal positions such as managing accounts and keeping records. However, the varied skills and expertise of the women went without acknowledgement in policy literature and project documents. Work done within the confines of the home was equated with other household labor performed by women such as cooking and caretaking for large families and dismissed by project leaders. A major emphasis of the Seelampur project was to lead women to work outside the home as part of the formal economy, especially positions in call centers and other customer care enterprises. These positions were recognized as needing expertise and "skills" versus work done at home for the manufacturing industry and the informal economy.

One of the largest waste cloth markets was located in narrow alleys of Seelampur right next to the Carrefour Mall. Leftover and rejected cloth from export shipments to Asia, United States, and Europe are traded in this market. Buyers from export and design companies frequented the narrow alleys. Construction workers from the neighborhood were hired to build the new Carrefour Mall that mostly catered to elite shoppers and denied entry to the majority of Seelampur residents. Although Seelampur residents were represented as primitive in project documents, they participated in a range of occupations that were part of the modern global economy. In the locality, billboards advertised "air-conditioned condominiums" built by Parsvnath Developers. Parsvnath is a real estate conglomerate that builds Special

Economic Zones (SEZs) and gated apartment complexes for India's urban elite. The computer students lived outside these gated complexes and were denied access to the Carrefour shopping mall, built by the French conglomerate, that catered to members including families from embassies. Their family monthly incomes ranged US$100–200 that were often inadequate for daily sustenance, and the students experienced the unequal impacts of the "new economy" in their everyday lives.

The "computer girls": waiting inside/outside the center

Inside the computer skilling center

The GRC building was approximately 700 square feet and consisted of two floors. The first floor included a central helpdesk that also functioned as a window for information and paperwork about the state's social service schemes under Mission Convergence. The adult literacy class was held on the first floor of the GRC building. The first floor also had a small room with doors that was mainly used as a free clinic on Wednesdays from 9 am to 2 pm and as a free legal advice center on Thursday afternoons. The clinic was staffed by a doctor who worked in the state health-care system. Volunteers from the GRC kept stock of commonly prescribed drugs that were given free of cost to Seelampur residents. A Delhi high court lawyer worked for a few hours weekly at the GRC and gave legal counseling mainly related to property and divorce matters. The legal center was popular among Seelampur residents and the clinic attracted long queues every week.

On the second floor of the GRC building, the small room was informally divided into three separate spaces. A group of 15 young women usually sat on rugs on the floor working with sewing and embroidery as part of the Tailoring and Cutting class. The Tailoring course taught participants pattern drafting for clothes, cutting and tailoring of clothes, and embroidery. Next to the Tailoring class, another group of 20 young women sat on the floor as part of the Beauty Culture class that taught young women to work in beauty salons. They were given lessons in facial bleaches, hair-cutting, applying make-up, and giving manicures and pedicures.

The two groups were separated from the ICT class by a partial screen. The ICT center occupied a small corner of this room and had eight computers, chairs, and a desk. The ICT center taught basic skills to its participants. Learning computers was free of cost and the minimum qualification for admission was passing grade ten. The courses were for a duration of six months. The syllabus included programs such as MS Word, design and page layout software like e PageMaker and Dreamweaver, basic languages such as HTML, and graphics editor programs like CorelDraw and Photoshop. Students from the tailoring and crafts classes called the ICT students "computer ki ladki" or the "computer girls" (Sarkar 2016). The computer girls had a special status in the center that distinguished them as a group from other young women at the center. Students from the other training courses looked up to the computer girls because they often had more education and familiarity with English. Significantly, the familiarity with computers afforded these women a higher status among GRC students.

The instructors emphasized discipline and timeliness that were meant to be crucial in "learning computers." This narrative was unique to the computer classes at the GRC. At the dress designing classes, students mostly worked slowly in groups sewing by hand. At the Beauty Culture class, practicum sessions were fast paced but these were few in number and students mostly spent time in talking to each other. There was an informality that characterized these programs and teachers focused on technical direction. The computer classes were more tightly structured and the instructors emphasized efficiency and self-discipline.

During lessons, the Seelampur women were told that they will have to work in a fast-paced environment at a call center or at a large department store, and it is essential to cultivate the ability to work efficiently and under pressure. The computer girls were given lessons on discipline such as arriving on time to class, paying attention to the instructor, and not running home to have lunch or to help family during the day. Significantly, there was an onus on disciplining the self and the students were told that they were solely responsible for improving their life conditions. Outside the walls of the ICT center, there lay a competitive, fast-paced world of work at technology and service industries and the women were meant to be ready to enter that domain.

The focus on the self-disciplined and regulated individual forms a crucial part of an "enterprise culture" that emerged in opposition to the Keynesian welfare state in the United Kingdom and United States in the 1980s (Douglas, Heap & Ross 1992: 1; Peters 2001: 58; Rose 1992: 141). The declining welfare role of the state was diverted by placing the onus on "entrepreneurial" individuals. This new enterprise culture rests on cultivating future selves through skills training and technological literacy (Gooptu 2009; Peters 2001). As critical scholars have demonstrated, these trends create new risks of exploitation that function through deception and opportunism (Gooptu 2009; Neff 2014; Irani 2019).

In contrast to the narratives of project staff about fast paced and productive days that prepared the women for the "new" economy, a usual day at the center moved very slowly often interrupted by power outages. Women spent a lot of time waiting at the center for classes to start or for their friends from other classes. For Shabnam Ansari and Shahnaz Ali and other computer girls, this was an opportunity to get individual time from the ICT instructor who would resolve their "doubts" from previous lessons. However, most days were spent waiting for "Sir" who taught in other GRCs and private institutes and had to leave right after the class. GRC staff described lab sessions as important where students had to do homework and learn to think on their feet while solving problems. However, Seelampur women worked slowly on their own during most lab sessions without clear directions or progress. Fatima had worked on creating her resume on Word using a few headers like Education, Hobbies, and Address. She felt stuck after that exercise and did not know how to improve her resume. She and her friend Saalima shared that they had spent the morning sitting at their computers waiting for help from their peers. Saalima further explained that, "We do not know what else to do so we play with the mouse or the keyboard and wait." Similarly, during Photoshop exercises, most women felt that they only worked with a few images and spent most of the lab time talking to their friends or feeling bored. Only one computer occasionally had internet access and the girls waited to use that computer to check email or to go on to chat sites.

For some students, coming to the GRC each day provided a sanctuary. Vahida came to the center each morning after finishing her chores and sending her children to school. She regarded the GRC as a space where she could get away from her extended family for a while and attend the ICT class on certain days. Tabassum had a conflicted relationship with her husband's family and had lied to them that her class was held daily. However, most women said that they came to the GRC because they urgently needed to find a well-paying job to support their families.

Project leaders emphasized that time spent at the center was highly productive in young women acquiring skills that would lead to promised advancement. However, some young women spoke of lab sessions and time spent inside the center as "time pass." In his work with unemployed young men in Northern India, Jeffrey (2010) finds that "time pass" or "passing time" have several connotations – imagining time as something that needs to be "passed" or "killed," hanging out in street corners and tea shops, boredom and disengagement from studies, or the feelings of being left behind. While the Seelampur women attended their classes and hoped for a better future, they also felt that they were merely passing or killing time as they waited for deeper learning and also an indeterminate future.

For the computer girls, skill acquisition was promised as a form of "permanent deferral" (Alhassan & Chakravartty 2011) for subjects who would have to become enlightened enough to enjoy associated rights and benefits. The Founding Trustee of G-Tech Foundation Meeta Mishra claimed, "These girls are very good with the skills they have inherited from their ancestors. But they are not very good at learning computer skills that require hard work and aptitude." In Mishra's hierarchy of skills, "modern" skills like technology skills could only be acquired when the young women had innate abilities. The staff often lectured the women on cultivating independence and efficiency. As we will see, most Seelampur women had held jobs outside the home and successfully navigated multiple responsibilities on a daily basis. Being at the center however involved waiting for the instructor, waiting and wading through muddled exercises, and contradictorily waiting to be perceived as "efficient," "disciplined," and "modern."

Away from the doorsteps of the center

The everyday lives of the computer girls had parallels inside and outside the doorsteps of the ICT center. The majority of the graduates did not find employment related to their ICT program even after successfully completing the skilling certification. Shahnaz Ali had created a poster that hung in the ICT classroom behind the makeshift screen. It described S-t-u-d-e-n-t as Social Worker, Truth, Understand, Discipline, Education, Natural, and Try. She identified herself as being a hard worker with a commitment to "social work." She said, "I work hard day and night. My only priority is to help my family." Shahnaz's family was relatively privileged in the locality. Her family income of INR 20,000 (about $300) a month was considerably higher than most of the other computer girls. However, this income did not translate into economic and cultural resources for her family. Her brothers had to leave school after grade ten because of lack of resources (Sarkar 2016). Shahnaz had trained as a nurse for three years after acquiring a bachelor's degree through a state-run distance education program. She had to leave her hospital job that paid her about INR 3000 ($40 approximately) a month because she had not felt adequately protected during night shifts as a young woman. Reflecting on her classes at the ICT center that emphasized self-reliance, she said, "we are told to be independent because I think Muslim women are generally thought to stay at home. But most of us have had jobs." A year and a half after completing the program, Shahnaz was still waiting to find an appropriate job. She had applied to many call center positions and for teaching computers in schools in the neighborhood. But she had been told by some employers that her GRC certification was not enough to qualify her for the work. The women had little contact with previous computer training participants and did not know much about their attempts to find employment after graduation.

Shahnaz's situation paralleled that of Rabeena Siddiqui. Rabeena was known to many Seelampur residents as "Doctor Sahiba." She had trained as a local doctor's assistant for a couple of years and performed routine blood pressure checks and patient care. Her dream was to actually go to medical school. However, she hoped that the ICT course would give her access to medical imaging jobs. After finishing the GRC program, she realized that the GRC class only taught basic skills and that she would need to raise a significant amount of money to take a specialized program in medical imaging that ranged from a short course of a few weeks at a private institute or a bachelor's degree program at an accredited college in Delhi.

A year after the program, she was back in her old position as a medical assistant and was still looking for opportunities for advancement.

Seelampur women, who did find work in the formal economy, performed precarious pink-collar labor. Many of the computer girls considered these jobs as gathering "experience" and waiting for better opportunities. These positions were located at the bottom rung of the information economy and brought in very little economic and social mobility contrary to the promises made by the state and project initiators. Some graduates found work as ticketing assistants at Delhi metro stations. The Delhi metro subcontracted the hiring workers to different private sector companies, and insisted that they monitored these firms for appropriate labor practices. However, the nature of this contract work translated into an unorganized labor force that had short-term contracts, less benefits, unstable working conditions, and precarious employment (Sarkar 2010). Seelampur women considered these jobs as "safe" and also glamorous because of access to air-conditioned offices. However, they found that male customers misbehaved with them. Officers at the DMRC (Delhi Metro Rail Corporation) asserted that they maintained their rights as principal employers and regularly monitored these companies for appropriate labor practices.

Some of the Seelampur students found work in large shopping malls as customer service assistants. They were attracted to these jobs because of the incentives that would be provided based on the number of successful sales. However, they often did not get these promised incentives. Shabnam shared, "I am still waiting to get my bonus from two months back. I met the target for the sales and my supervisor said that I will get my extra money but I am still waiting." A few of the women had aspirations for working at the checkout counter and felt they had the basic computer skills. However, many of them were told that they would have to learn better English to work at the counters. A minority of the Seelampur women found work at lower-level call centers that involved long hours and dealing with difficult customers. Shahnaz's comment signified the contradictions in her situation after completing the GRC program, "We are willing to work day and night. I have no fear of hard work. I have had jobs before and really need to support my parents. I am working hard now. But I often feel that we are here to learn computers without a plan."

Contrary to the training narrative at the center that emphasized speed in the form of "efficiency" and "discipline," the days of the Seelampur women passed slowly at the center waiting for their instructors, classes, electricity, and computer and internet access. In their lives outside the center, the women experienced endless waiting to get jobs. The pink-collar positions that the Seelampur women occupied at the edges of information economy meant that they often performed gendered and vulnerable work involving waiting for promised incentives, better pay, and being treated with dignity. Thus, the "leapfrogging" into modernity for the ICT students translated into being at the fringes of the information economy that actually reinforced deep structural inequalities and created new ones.

"New governance" and waiting in the technologically mediated state

In 2008, Mission Convergence was introduced by the Delhi government to focus on "empowerment of vulnerable populations" especially women through the "IT enabled system" (Government of NCT of Delhi 2015). It aimed at making entitlements reach the poor through a single window system in a "hassle free manner" and to "rationalize administration" (Government of NCT of Delhi 2015). Convergence was based on a "hybrid" public-private partnership (PPP) model that included nine state departments and several civil society organizations. It claimed to establish fairness and inclusion by breaking the municipal and elected representatives who were seen as authorizing entitlements only to loyal blocks of voters. The initiative worked on two levels. It aimed to integrate 40 different social service programs of the state for marginalized communities through a single window platform. Second, it established skills training programs under its umbrella. In this section I demonstrate that the program produced more waiting for Seelampur residents and created misinformation that contradicted its claims of breaking down structural inequalities. Further, Convergence functioned through enlisting the ICT students as the face of a caring state, a position that came without power, recognition, and compensation.

The Seelampur GRC was brought under Mission Convergence in 2008. At the "community" or "field" level, the GRCs served as the first point of contact between the state and the community. The *Economist* described Convergence as follows:

> Launched in 2008, "Mission Convergence" is an ICT-driven, high-priority and award winning initiative of the government of Delhi to bring welfare benefits to the city's poorest residents. It converges Delhi's nine social welfare departments and 46 welfare schemes into a single, enabled delivery channel. Rashmi Singh, director of the mission, explains, "We are taking welfare entitlements to the poorest doorstep, not as a favor but as a duty."

Convergence won several international awards such as the United Nations Public Award and the Commonwealth Association for Public Administration and Management. The Founding Director of Convergence, Rashmi Singh, a bureaucrat belonging to the civil services, was recognized by her alma mater Humphrey School of Public Affairs with a Distinguished Leadership Award for her contributions to "inter-sectoral convergence" and "cross sector collaboration on a scale never before imagined." The seamlessness of Convergence was highlighted in policy discourse – the ICT-driven single window access would do away with "corruption," bureaucratic delays, and messiness involved in managing and administering a large number of claims. Convergence performed justice through apparently seamless state apparatuses that claimed to remove "bottlenecks" on part of marginalized citizens who no longer had to wait for social services. For Seelampur residents, Convergence was meant to ensure the end of waiting for their benefits and rights.

While Convergence was represented as speed and deftness, it actually reinforced and produced more waiting among citizens. Technology was promoted as a neutral instrument that would usher in a leveling of disparities. However, this discourse concealed the messy politics of technocratic management. Mazzarella (2006) argues that the instant "media" effect of new technologies hides the process of "mediation," which is a complex terrain of politics and negotiation between the Indian state and its multiple publics. In the case of Seelampur, the celebratory discourse concealed the complexity of the power struggles and negotiations behind the technologically-enabled, new governance program.

As a program that relied on "community participation" Convergence reached out to Seelampur residents, especially women, to participate in the new governance program. This move to elicit community participation in data collection and implementation at "field offices" was another way in which the smart city program sought to replace the bureaucratic model with the managerial one and conceptualize the citizen as the consumer-worker. This meant that Convergence drew not only on GRCs at the community level but actively sought participation of women at GRCs in the community who would be a humane interface for the program. If subaltern women were marked as significant stakeholders in Convergence, it is worth asking if they gained power and inclusion through the program.

Each week, the GRC held a free clinic for the community. The lines for the clinics would start in the small lobby of the GRC building, snake down the stairs, and often spill toward the end of the lane. Women, children, and elderly men dominated among the patients. A doctor, employed by the government, was the physician at these clinics. The computer girls, who were considered to be smarter than their peers, were elicited to help at these clinics. Most of these positions were based on voluntary labor. For example, the computer girls helped the GRC manager to order and stock supplies in addition to maintaining inventory. Additionally, they voluntarily worked as patient service representatives, doing the emotional labor of chatting with the patients to make them feel comfortable, giving out free medicines, and directing them to community and other resources. The computer girls were asked by the state to be volunteers for this program because they possessed a superior social standing both inside the ICT center and in the greater community because of their familiarity with computers and because they often had more formal schooling than the rest of the women enrolled in other skilling classes. The state and the residents perceived them to be more competent. In my other writing on the Seelampur ICT center, I have demonstrated that although the computer girls faced daily struggles for a livelihood, they were still considered to have a superior economic and social status within and outside the space of the ICT center (Sarkar 2016). The state selection of them as community leaders and volunteers placed burdens on them without due recognition or compensation. Several computer students felt that they had more privilege in relation to other residents and saw their labor as "social work." This preference for the computer girls as volunteers the state and by their administrative unit in the form of the GRC, however, excluded other Seelampur residents and women at the center from consideration for these roles because of their perceived lack of competence.

The voluntary labor that the computer girls performed was regarded by GRC staff members as "helping" and "voluntary work" instead of "skill." This is despite the fact women such as Shahnaz and Rabeena had some medical training and they checked blood pressure, dispensed medicines, and engaged in community follow-ups. Rabeena had worked as a doctor's assistant in Seelampur and Shahnaz had worked as a nurse at a nursing home in the locality. However, both of them lacked formal training that resulted in certification. While Seelampur residents were appreciative of their expertise, their lack of certification led to the devaluation of their labor.

The computer students performed a vital role as survey supervisors whose job was to correctly count residents who would be officially eligible for different welfare programs and acquire a biometric card to access these services under Convergence. Convergence aimed to include people who were excluded from the official BPL (Below Poverty Line) classification as those who earned less than 24,000 INR (about USD 350) in a year. The computer girls were selected as survey supervisors for being high school graduates, for possessing some technical skills, and their familiarity with the community. They were instructed to observe where individuals lived, ask them questions about their access to public services, how steadily they were employed, and if they were from "Scheduled Caste and Scheduled Tribe" groups that have historically been considered at the bottom of India's caste hierarchy. As I have argued elsewhere (Sarkar 2019), accurate counting placed a heavy burden on the Seelampur women. It was based on individuals and discrete family units that negated the complexity of social relationships and housing in Seelampur. For example, extended families lived in one unit to save money and migrants would often reside with families from their villages who they considered as kin. Individuals also moved between units, dividing their time among relatives and friends. This "excess" pointed to a history of poverty, migration, kinship, and community structures that could not be neatly captured in surveys and data (Sarkar 2019). The young women were also subject to the frustrations of the residents who had missing identification documents, incorrect addresses, or whose claims had not been processed – in their inadvertent role as representatives of the state.

The computer girls actively volunteered at the front desk of the GRC helping residents fill paperwork for different social service schemes under Convergence. They felt responsible for helping the residents because they were younger and better educated than most residents who came to the center. However, they lacked actual power to negotiate with the state and were not subject to much information about the programs that they were meant to represent. They often faced the frustrations of the residents when their enrollment in the welfare schemes was rejected or delayed due to missing paperwork or bureaucratic procedures. Shaira, an ICT student and survey supervisor and volunteer, reflected on her role:

> I volunteer many hours here at the help desk helping people so that they can be included under the Mission Convergence schemes. I help with their questions and filling the forms. It is like social work for me. I am better educated than many of them so I help. But then they think I am working for the government. I say to them that I don't know many other things they ask for but I can try to help them fill their forms.

The Indian state is increasingly partnering with civil society organizations that include NGOs and corporate foundations. The state takes on "hybrid" and "flexible" forms in its partnership with civil society. This "horizontal" collaboration between the state and various civil society actors is supposed to facilitate more efficiency in public administration based on private sector models (Przeybilovicz et al. 2016). The state delegates its functions to private actors and there is an outsourcing of state functions from the center to the lowest or outermost unit (Osborne & Gaebler 1993; Sarkar 2019). Significantly, the bureaucratic model is replaced with the managerial one that leads to a rethinking about citizens as "clients" (Sarkar 2019). John Harriss (2001) understands this process as "depoliticizing development" (Harriss 2001). "Development" is perceived as a neutral emphasis removed from political realities and inequalities related to structural power. Under e-governance programs, the state's role is not as much reduced as it is transformed to coordinating networks between public and private organizations (Przeybilovicz et al. 2016). In their ethnographic study of Mission Convergence in different sites in Delhi, Dhanju (2011) makes a similar observation that the hybrid state depended on subaltern women to present its humane face and enable marginalized residents to form empathetic understandings of the program. However, as Dhanju argues that while this creates "a mirage of a caring state" (275), the emotional labor performed by the women is not accompanied by actual power to make a change in the community. This "social work" also was regarded as akin to other forms of low paying, gendered labor that the computer students performed after graduating from the skills program (Sarkar 2019).

In the next section, I focus on the Ladli program under Convergence. The familiarity of the computer girls with computer skills gave them a higher status at the center and they emerged as important translators of the program. This led to misinformation and subverted the aims of the program. "Development interventions" can depoliticize political realities and questions of power often by diverting attention from more engaged and radical forms of citizenship (Ferguson 1994; Murray Li 2007; Sharma 2008). However, I argue that the engagement of the computer girls with Convergence simultaneously led them to sometimes inadvertently emerge as critics of the new governance and skilling programs of the state.

Ladli

Under Mission Convergence, the Ladli scheme of the Delhi government originated in 2008. It constituted an important social service scheme to be "converged" under the smart city program allied to the goal of "empowerment of women." The introduction of the Ladli scheme under the ICT-integrated Mission Convergence was meant to ensure easy access to the program. "Ladli" translated means the beloved girl child. This image was meant to counteract the declining sex ratio in India and in Delhi. Under Ladli, the Government of NCT of Delhi would regularly deposit cash in the bank account of eligible, poor families for a girl child from her birth to grade 12 or the end of high school. The objectives of the scheme were to bring down the rate of sex selective abortion, improve school employment and ameliorate "insecurities" of parents having only daughters (Nanda 2010).

In Seelampur, GTech Foundation had been active in awareness drives on female infanticide and selective sex abortion. The *Antarashtriya Patrika*, translated as the International Newspaper, was a community-based newspaper published by GTech Foundation. The instructor of the ICT class usually worked as the Editor of the newspaper and the articles were written by staff and students of the Gender Resource Center in Seelampur. The circulation of this newspaper was limited to about 200 to 300 copies that are mainly disseminated in the Seelampur area. In 2008–2009, the newspaper included one article on selective sex abortion and female infanticide. In January 2009, *Antarashtriya Patrika* featured an article discussing the reasons why people preferred to have male children that included feeling under pressure to save money for a girl's wedding and dowry.

During the first four months since the launch of the Ladli Scheme in 2008, the Delhi government opened 6,000 fixed deposit accounts and another 23,000 claims were being processed (Sharma & Haub 2010). The convergence of different social service schemes facilitated by ICT under Mission

Convergence allowed for the state to effectively register and process claims to programs such as Ladli. It was considered as easier for poor urban residents to access such programs through a centralized system of registering claims. At the Seelampur Gender Resource Center, the Ladli Scheme gained popularity because of the single window access to the program.

The Delhi government pointed to the success of Ladli by demonstrating a higher number of female registered births that indicated a decline in the rates of female infanticide and foeticide (Sharma & Haub 2010). However, critics have argued that this rise in the registered numbers of girl children could have factors other than the success of the Ladli scheme – including migrants from other states registering births in Delhi to avail of the scheme and more registration of non-institutional births (Sharma & Haub 2010). Further, some better-off families registered as BPL ones with the help of elected representatives and local leaders (Bansal, Bharadwaj & Chugani 2014).

Though Mission Converge sought to eliminate the role of "middle-men" between the state and the "beneficiaries" through an ICT-driven interface, the computer girls emerged as important intermediaries between the two parties. Other students Seelampur residents relied on them for information about the program. Talk of Ladli at the Seelampur GRC however produced an understanding of the program that ran contrary to the vision of the state.

The computer girls praised Ladli because they felt that the government was helping young women gain access to funds to pay for their weddings. They compared the Ladli scheme to another program run by a local organization that explicitly stated its aims as loans with low interest rates to help poor families toward their daughters' weddings and off-set the cost of expected dowries that met the demands of the groom's family. Several young women felt that the practice of asking for dowry was harmful for the status of women but felt that the money from Ladli could be a benefit for women from poor families who would have otherwise remained unmarried. This corresponds to Nanda's findings (2010) that parents and young women who participated in the Ladli scheme stated their highest priority as spending the money on their marriage. Nanda (2010) reported that beneficiaries of the Ladli program considered spending the money on their daughters' education to be ideal but that the chances of spending it for marriage are significantly higher.

While the role of the computer girls as mediators produced more complex and messy messaging about Ladli that ran contrary to the aims of "efficiency" by the PPP, the involvement of the women also led them to question the skilling programs. Amira, an ICT student, said:

> I can get my younger sister enrolled in the Ladli (Girl Child) program but what use is that money for her if she cannot live?

Amira's poignant question pointed to responsibility from the state not just as a client of a cash-transfer, interfaced, governance program but of a citizen who faced deep structural inequalities in her everyday life. In the case of the Ladli scheme, reciprocal obligations on part of the state or educational institutions regarding attendance, quality of education, access to basic health care, and transportation were not linked to this program (Nanda 2010). The Seelampur women spoke to their immediate needs that were embedded in the challenges of urban poverty, persecution, and violence. These needs pointed to the shortcomings of the state and civil society in bringing deeper, structural transformations.

Shahnaz saw the skilling programs as an inadequate gesture by the state:

> What has the government done? Just because it has opened a GRC does not mean that the government has done everything. If the government cannot go in and see whether a stove has been lit in a home or if a quarrel is brewing in the streets? Our learning computers does not mean our problems have ended.

Shahnaz pointed to the limitations of the skills programs that did not bring about the promised mobility and structural transformations. For other students like those enrolled in the Dress Design program, it was hard to start small businesses or sell clothes because of the surfeit of dress making businesses in the locality and in surrounding neighborhoods (Sarkar 2019). The Beauty Culture students felt that the GRC program only taught them basic skills and that they would need to enroll in privately run programs to get jobs in the better paying salons in the city. Most women could not afford the fees for these courses. Several students had attempted to start beauty salons in their homes but these had not succeeded.

The ICT students became unwitting mediators and the humane faces of the Convergence program. However, their involvement with the residents and their participation in the skills program also led them to see the contradictions in the policy discourse that focused on skills training as a means to level structural inequalities. It also led them to voice their concerns for more accountability from the government in providing basic public goods and services that remained elusive for many Seelampur residents despite the technology-led, new governance program that promised an end to the waiting for inclusion for marginalized residents.

Conclusion

Although Mission Convergence won international awards, it was embroiled in chaos and controversies. In 2010, the Delhi government decided that NGOs would work more toward supporting elected MLAs by conducting surveys and focusing on awareness about both social services and training programs for women. This was primarily done to conciliate the MLAs who had strongly complained about their loss of authority. In 2016, matters came to a head when the state alleged that the NGOs had misused funds though civil society governments blamed the government for mismanagement and unpaid salaries. The AAP (Aam Aadmi Party) worked on transitioning Convergence into privatized centers. The ICT skills training program moved from the GRC building to another space in Seelampur that was further away from public transportation. The controversies that Convergence was embedded in revealed the power struggles and contestations behind its apparently smooth interface.

In this chapter, I have focused on the Seelampur ICT skills training program, which has a long history of being hailed as an exemplar for technology-led modernization programs for urban, poor communities. Policy and program literature promised an end to waiting for marginalized residents who would be both included in social service programs and receive skills training for economic and social mobility. The residents were framed as "traditional" and as outside "modern" occupations and economy. However, a preliminary mapping of Seelampur reveals that the area already had a surfeit of computer training programs. The locality formed an important node of the global, modern economy with its denim industries and cloth market directed toward export. The understanding of Seelampur as "lumpen" and "backward" negated the rich ecology of skills in the area including technological capabilities.

The skills program represented "learning computers" as the "leapfrogging" means to achieve mobility. The ICT students did enjoy a higher status as the computer girls within the space of the center. However, they were still caught in the waiting room, where their aspirations for a better life were in a state of permanent deferral. Inside the center, the women spent a lot of time waiting to learn. This waiting was mirrored in their everyday lives outside the center – in endlessly searching for jobs or in working in precarious and low-paid occupations at the edge of the information economy.

Due to their higher status associated with familiarity with technology, the computer girls emerged as crucial representatives for the state's new e-governance program, Mission Convergence. While Convergence promised more inclusion for marginalized residents through a single window access of social service programs, it led to more delays and waiting for Seelampur residents. Subaltern women such as the ICT students assumed the work of emotional labor for the state and emerged as its humane face. However, this role did not bring power to actually impact state policy and actions and was largely uncompensated. Thus, the association of expertise with technology skills placed more burden of invisible work on the shoulders of the computer girls similar to their work in the denim industry or in pink-collar occupations. The example of how the computer girls were influential mediators of Ladli demonstrated that they could unknowingly advocate messages against the vision of the state. At the same time, the involvement of the girls with the urban governance program also led them to point out the limitations of the state and its skilling programs in transforming structural inequalities.

The CAA/NRC protests by the women in East Delhi including Seelampur remind us about their political struggles related to structural inequalities of religion, class, caste, and gender. The women's claims amplified in the context of their relationship with the state that has been based in historical trajectories of violence. The protests make women, who have been otherwise rendered largely faceless and voiceless in media and policy discourse, more visible in public spaces and highlight their everyday lives. Finally, they remind us that development interventions such as the computer skilling programs, despite their powerful promise of mobility, can be divorced from political claims for structural inequalities and can in fact end up amplifying and reproducing these inequities. The women's participation in the face of police violence is a call for recognizing political struggles that development interventions can serve to diffuse or tame.

Critical and feminist scholars have further called attention to multiple publics who engage with policy shifts as consumers and citizens (Chakravartty & Sarikakis 2006; Sarkar 2016; Sharma 2008). Policy has usually been studied from "above" such as the perspectives of states, civil society organizations or think tanks (Chakravartty & Sarikakis 2006; Schiller 1996). Ethnographic research enables us to more fully comprehend "policy from below," through the lives of marginalized individuals in the community, at home, at training centers, at work and on the streets. The lives of the Seelampur computer girls demonstrated the deep limitations of the promise of skilling programs for inclusion in the "new" India.

Note

1 The Shaheen Bagh protests were peaceful, sit-in protests led by women, in the north-eastern, largely Muslim locality of Delhi to protest the CAA and the NRC. Women of all ages, including the elderly and young girls, protested each day in thousands with allies, including students. The protest captured global attention and was embedded in tensions between the protestors and the state. It started on December 15, 2019, and ended with the police removing the remaining protestors following the outbreak of the COVID-19-pandemic-related lockdown in March 2020 (Venugopal 2020).

References

Abu-Lughod, L. 2005. *Dramas of Nationhood: The Politics of Television in Egypt*. Chicago: University of Chicago Press.

Afshar, H., & Maynard, M. (ed.). 1994. *The Dynamics of Race and Gender: Some Feminist Interventions (Feminist Perspectives on the Past and Present)*. London: Taylor & Francis.

Ahmed, L. 1993. *Women and Gender in Islam: Historical Roots of a Modern Debate.* New Haven, CT: Yale University Press.
Alhassan, A., & Chakravartty, P. 2011. 'Postcolonial Media Policy under the Long Shadow of Empire'. In R. Mansell, & M. Raboy (eds.), *The Handbook of Global Media and Communication Policy*, pp. 366–382. Oxford: Blackwell Publishing.
ANI. 2020. *Women Stage Dharna in Delhi's Seelampur against CAA/NRC.* Available online at https://www.aninews.in/news/national/general-news/women-stage-dharna-in-delhis-seelampur-against-caa-nrc20200117191048/ (downloaded on 04/04/2023).
Bansal, P., Bharadwaj, U., & Chugani, M. 2014. 'Delhi Ladli Scheme 2008: A Parental Perspective'. *Journal of Nursing Science & Practice*, 4(3): 43–48.
Baviskar, A. 2003. 'Between Violence and Desire: Space, Power, and Identity in the Making of Metropolitan Delhi'. *International Social Science Journal*, 55(175): 89–98.
The Caravan Magazine. 2020. *Spilling onto the Streets: The Women of Seelampur Stand against the NRC.* Available online at https://www.facebook.com/watch/?v=196350901737107 (downloaded on 08/04/2024).
Chakravartty, P., & Sarikakis, K. 2006. *Globalization and Media Policy: History, Culture and Politics.* Edinburgh: Edinburgh University Press.
Daniyal, S. 2020. *Driven by Delhi Violence, Anxious Muslims First Flock to Jaffarabad Road Blockade – Then Clear It.* Available online at https://scroll.in/article/954319/driven-by-delhi-violence-anxious-muslims-first-flock-to-jafrabad-road-blockade-then-clear-it (downloaded on 08/04/2022).
Dhanju, R. 2011. *Reaching the Unreached: (Un)making an Inclusive and World-Class Delhi.* PhD Thesis, College Station, Texas A&M University.
Douglas, M., Heap, S. H., & Ross, A. 1992. *Understanding the Enterprise Culture: Themes in the work of Mary Douglas.* Edinburgh: Edinburgh University Press.
Ferguson, J. 1994. *The Anti-Politics Machine: Development, Depoliticization, and Bureaucratic Power in Lesotho.* Minneapolis: University of Minnesota Press.
Gooptu, N. 2009. 'Neoliberal Subjectivity, Enterprise Culture and New Workplaces: Organized Retail and Shopping Malls in India'. *Economic and Political Weekly*, 44(22): 45–54.
Government of NCT of Delhi. 2015. *Mission Convergence.* Available online at http://web.delhi.gov.in/wps/wcm/connect/doit_dcwest/DCWest/Home/Mission+Convergence (downloaded on 08/04/2023).
Harriss, J. 2001. *Depoliticizing Development: The World Bank and Social Capital.* New Delhi, India: LeftWord Books.
Hasan, Z., & Menon, R. 2004. *Unequal Citizens: A Study of Muslim Women in India.* Delhi: Oxford University Press.
Hindu. 2006. *Over 150 Held for Riots in Delhi.* Available online at https://www.thehindu.com/todays-paper/over-150-held-for-riots-in-delhi/article3079520.ece (downloaded on 04/01/2023).
Irani, L. 2019. *Chasing Innovation: Making Entrepreneurial Citizens.* Princeton, NJ: Princeton University Press.
Jeffrey, C. 2010. 'Timepass: Youth, Class, and Time among Unemployed Young Men in India'. *American Ethnologist*, 37(3): 465–481.
Kumar, R. 2013, November 9. 'N-E-Delhi – City's Social Underbelly'. *The Daily Pioneer*, New Delhi.
Kumar, U. 2020. *Jamna-Par Has Provided Delhi with an Unforgettable Reality Check.* Available online at https://www.thecitizen.in/index.php/en/newsdetail/index/9/18395/jamna-paar-has-provided-delhi-with-an-unforgettable-reality-check (downloaded 01/04/2023).
Mankekar, P. 1999. *Screening Culture, Viewing Politics: An Ethnography of Television, Womanhood, and Nation in Postcolonial India.* Durham: Duke University Press.

Mazzarella, W. 2003. *Shoveling Smoke: Advertising and Globalization in Contemporary India*. Durham: Duke University Press.
Mazzarella, W. 2006. 'Internet X-Ray: E-Governance, Transparency and the Politics of E-Governance in India'. *Public Culture*, 18(3): 473–505.
Mohanty, C. T. 2003. *Feminism without Borders: Decolonizing Theory, Practicing Solidarity*. Durham, NC: Duke University Press.
Murray Li, T. 2007. *The Will to Improve: Governmentality, Development, and the Practice of Politics*. Durham, NC: Duke University Press.
Nanda, B. 2010. *The Ladli Scheme in India:* Leading *to a Lehenga or a Law Degree?* paper presented at the Academic Forum Indo Brazil South Africa (IBSA) Summit, Brasilia, Brazil, April 12-13.
Neff, G. 2014. *Venture Labor: Work and the Burden of Risk in Innovative Industries*. Cambridge, MA: MIT Press.
OpIndia. 2019. *Anti-CAA Seelampur Riots*. Available online at https://www.opindia.com/2019/12/seelampur-riot-caa-raees-arrested-petrol-bomb-injured/ (downloaded on 01/03/2023).
Osborne, D., & Gaebler, T. 1993. *Reinventing Government: How the Entrepreneurial Spirit Is Transforming the Public Sector*. New York: Plume.
Pathak, R., & Katiyar, A. 1993. *Thugs Stomp Grey Area between Respectability and Rejection*. Available online at https://www.indiatoday.in/magazine/cover-story/story/19930115-thugs-stomp-grey-area-between-respectability-and-rejection-810586-1993-01-14 (downloaded 08/04/2023).
Peters, M. 2001. 'Education, Enterprise Culture and Entrepreneurial Self: A Foucauldian Perspective'. *Journal of Educational Enquiry*, 2(2): 58–71.
Przeybilovicz, E., Macaya, J., Cunha, M., & Albuquerque, J. 2016, September 11–12. 'Investigating the Echoes of New Public Management and Electronic Governance in Smart City Projects in Brazil'. *Working Paper 10.13140/RG.2.2.35125.06888*, Dublin: Pre-ICIS Workshop on E-Government.
Rajagopal, A. 2001. *Politics after Television: Hindu Nationalism and the Reshaping of the Public in India*. Cambridge: Cambridge University Press.
Rediff. 2006. *Lumpen Elements Triggered Violence: Delhi Police*. Available online at https://www.rediff.com/news/2006/sep/21delhi6.htm?print=true (downloaded on 31/01/2025).
Rose, N. 1992. 'Governing the Enterprising Self'. In P. Heelas, & P. Morris (eds.), *The Values of the Enterprise Culture*, pp. 141–164. London: Routledge.
Sarkar, S. 2010. 'Women at Home and Work: New Technologies and Labor among Minority Women in Seelampur'. *Journal of Community Informatics*, 5(3–4). Available online at https://openjournals.uwaterloo.ca/index.php/JoCI/article/view/2443/3020 (downloaded on 01/04/2024).
Sarkar, S. 2016. 'Beyond the Digital Divide: The Computer Girls of Seelampur'. *Feminist Media Studies*, 16(6): 968–983.
Sarkar, S. 2019. 'A Mission to Converge for Inclusion? The Smart City and the Women of Seelampur'. *Media, Culture & Society*, 41(3): 278–293.
Saxenian, A. 2002. 'The Silicon Valley Connection: Transnational Networks and Regional Development in Taiwan, China and India'. *Science Technology & Society*, 7(1): 117–149.
Schiller, H. 1996. *Information Inequality: The Deepening Social Crisis in America*. New York: Routledge.
Sharma, A. 2008. *Logics of Empowerment: Development, Gender and Governance in Neoliberal India*. Minneapolis: University of Minnesota Press.
Sharma, O.P. & Haub, C. 2010. 'Delhi scheme comes to the rescue of daughters.' *The Tribune*, Chandigarh, 9 March.
Singh, P. 2009. *Delhi Ladli Scheme: An Appraisal*. New Delhi: CCS India.

Statista. 2021. *India: Youth Unemployment Rate from 1999 to 2021*. Available online at https://www.statista.com/statistics/812106/youth-unemployment-rate-in-india/ (downloaded on 08/04/2024).

Steinmueller, W. E. 2001. 'ICTs and the Possibilities for Leapfrogging by Developing Countries'. *International Labor Review*, 40(2): 193–210.

Tarlo, E. 2003. *Unsettling Memories: Narratives of the Emergency in Delhi*. London: Hurst & Company.

Venugopal, V. 2020. *Delhi Lockdown: Anti-CAA Protesters Removed from Shaheen Bagh, Other Places*. Available online at https://economictimes.indiatimes.com/news/politics-and-nation/coronavirus-lockdown-delhi-police-vacate-protesters-at-shaheen-bagh/articleshow/74785253.cms (downloaded on 08/04/2024).

PART IV

Sociology of vocational training

11

TOWARDS A GENDER TRANSFORMATIVE VISION OF TVET IN INDIA

Student experiences and labour market trajectories in India's contemporary TVET

Saikat Maitra and Sadaf Sethwala

Introduction

The global pandemic of 2020–21 brought on major disruptions to the learning landscape. This was particularly significant for low-skilled youth and adults in India whose struggles to secure decent work opportunities were amplified by the loss in learning. While advanced economies demonstrated greater resilience to the pandemic by adapting to alternative modes of working and providing support for upskilling workers, India's Technical and Vocational Education and Training (TVET) system suffered from much deeper effects. In this chapter, we attempt to situate the impact of the pandemic on students enrolled under the newly introduced dual system of training (DST) programme within the context of the growing support and advocacy for TVET in the country, and to highlight how the pandemic made transparent the weaknesses, and reinforced the poor reputation associated with TVET in India.

With expanding urban job markets and economic growth, TVET has progressively been gaining salience and has assumed a pivotal role in India's policy discourse and framework over the past decade and half (Agrawal, 2012). It was estimated that over 70% of India's population will be of working age by 2025 (Hajela, 2012), and, given deepening globalization and rapid changes in occupational patterns, a skilled workforce has been heralded as a pathway towards economic prosperity. Consequently, the government prioritised skill development efforts, resulting in a rapid expansion of TVET activities since the mid-2000s.

This commitment is exemplified by the establishment of the Ministry of Skill Development and Entrepreneurship (MSDE) (2014), which provided an

DOI: 10.4324/9781003604846-15

institutional framework for scaling up efforts to enhance skill development in India (Maitra et al., 2022). Subsequently, in 2015, the 'Skill India Mission' was launched with the goal of providing institutional capacity to skill over 400 million individuals by 2022 (Government of India). With a total budget allocation of over 27,850 million rupees for skilling in 2020, the state's vision for youth development is accompanied by discourses of increased employment and socioeconomic mobility. However, in a context of growing job precarity resulting from informalization, the state's aim of capitalising on the 'demographic dividend' has in fact pushed people towards an expanding sector of precarious and low-paying jobs, in contrast to their aspirations for professional employment. While India experiences a demographic dividend, many young people struggle to acquire skill sets that are demanded by employers (Comyn, 2014). Despite various reforms and efforts at capacity development, links between training institutes and employers continue to remain weak and fractured (Comyn, 2014). Currently, there exist approximately 15,000 Industrial Training Institutes (ITIs) in India offering a total of 136 specialised courses related to manufacturing and services. The government's vocational training programmes are primarily implemented through these ITIs, which cater to about 36% of the seven million individuals receiving training (Government of India). While 85% of these are run by the private sector, 15% are publicly funded and have a combined capacity to train nearly 2.5 million students annually.

With 12 million people predicted to enter the work force each year (Tandon et al., 2022), India faces significant challenges in attempting to enhance the skills of its population. A 2017 report from the Federation of Indian Chambers of Commerce and Industry (FICCI) predicted that by 2022, there will be a 37% increase in jobs that require significantly new skill sets (Shukla et al., 2017, p. 11). Perceived as facilitating access to labour markets for historically marginalised groups, the government has shown interest in skill development programmes as a means to engage and utilise the potential of India's growing youth population (Pilz and Ramasamy, 2022). However, this expansion has been unplanned and lacking in vision, and without clear goals of ensuring employability (Mehrotra, 2021).

Given this context and the common criticisms of TVET in India, the Indian government introduced the German-inspired DST model in 2016 as a pilot in a limited number of ITIs. Positioned as an aspirational model of skill development, the DST model has been accompanied by a rhetoric of productivity for companies and better employment outcomes for young trainees with smoother transitions to the labour market. It also hopes to transform the commonly held low-status perceptions often associated with TVET in India by making it aspirational for students. Drawing on the success of dual TVET systems globally and the model's association with smoother school-to-work transitions, many governments in developing countries, including India's, have adopted this model with the aim of improving young people's employability and boosting economy growth (Valiente and Scandurra, 2017). Hoping to bridge the currently existing disconnect between ITI trainees' learning outcomes and industry requirements, the DST offers an opportunity to ITIs to partner with industries which provide on-the-job training to students at industry sites for a fixed duration of their course (one or two years).

Combining classroom theoretical learning with basic practical training, DST allows students to simultaneously learn on the job within industry settings, departing from the traditional apprenticeship model where students first complete their course and then work in the industry. Additionally, the DST emphasises instilling students with not just theoretical and practical knowledge but also crucial professional skills essential for diverse job roles.

This model aims to address a common criticism of India's TVET ecosystem; the limited involvement of industries or employers (Mehrotra, 2021) and the associated low perceptions linked with TVET. By cultivating partnerships and integrating vocational education with industry prospects, the DST model endeavours to elevate the prestige of vocational training. Its goal is to establish vocational education as a respected and viable career path, departing from its current perception as a secondary or less desirable choice. While DST has been positioned as an aspirational model that hopes to shift perceptions of vocational education from a fallback option to one that equips individuals with practical skills and immediate career opportunities, the pandemic also revealed the vulnerabilities of the model and made transparent the continuing low status of vocational education in the country. In the following section we look at literature on how the pandemic impacted students in low- and middle-income countries, including India. While the impact varied over regions, overall, the pandemic revealed the vulnerabilities in the TVET sector.

Challenges to TVET during the COVID-19 pandemic

The global literature on the impact of COVID-19 on TVET students in low- and middle-income countries shows how the pandemic exacerbated pre-existing problems in accessing TVET, including limited access to mobile and internet technologies. In the context of South Africa, Allais and Marock (2020) highlight the plight of TVET students who were already disadvantaged under a system that was struggling to live up to its aims and objectives even before the pandemic struck. South African TVET students hail from some of the poorest socioeconomic backgrounds and do not possess the 'facilities for online learning or the prior educational background' (Allais and Marock, 2020, p. 65) that can equip them to deal with a suddenly transformed TVET system. In Ghana and Kenya too, students who opt for TVET instead of a general education track usually come from families with lower socioeconomic status (Allais and Marock, 2020). The lack of social support from schools and governments only added to students' struggles as they tried to cope with the effects of the pandemic. In South Africa, TVET colleges closed and examinations were postponed, resulting in students missing out on almost four months of instruction in certain programmes. Although the government adopted several measures, such as disseminating tutorials through radio, YouTube, Facebook, and WhatsApp, most students could not access the content as they did not have suitable devices and internet access (Allais and Marock, 2020). Even when devices were provided to some students, they often faced further challenges such as the absence of a quiet space at home in which to study. A lack of free learning resources was yet another challenge encountered by students.

Even in regions such as Gujarat, India, which is industrially and economically developed and offers better employment prospects than many other parts of India, the pandemic had significant consequences for student trainees. For women in particular, while the DST provided them with the capability to negotiate very strong patriarchal expectations related to marriage and family, the pandemic prompted many to retreat to the domestic sphere instead of entering the labour market. While there have been multivariate attempts by several international organizations and donor agencies to document the efforts of countries in navigating this crisis, there is little academic and empirical evidence on the lived experiences of trainees, especially in India. Moreover, while most existing scholarship analyses issues of access to education, there exists a scarcity of research that attempts to understand how the pandemic altered the career and life trajectories of young trainees contending with the already precarious transitions offered by vocational education. As such, this chapter attempts to examine and contrast the initial expectations accompanying the DST policy with how the pandemic impacted students enrolled under the programme. Drawing on interviews with policymakers, ITI principals, employers and student trainees provides valuable insights into the attitudes and perceptions amongst various DST stakeholders. It also reveals whether the promises accompanying TVET reforms, like the introduction of the DST model, have actually been successful in enhancing the reputation of TVET in India.

Despite human capital theorists acknowledging the crucial role of TVET in a country's economic growth and development (Mouzakitis, 2010), it remains largely undervalued in most countries (Billett, 2013). In India, TVET is often perceived to be associated with low-paying manual labour jobs and is viewed as a sub-sector primarily suitable for lower-caste youth or those with low educational attainment. As a consequence, TVET programmes are perceived as lower in status than general education programmes (Agrawal, 2012). Studies (e.g. Maitra and Maitra, 2018) have shown how state level vocational education programmes in India often prepare students for low level service jobs; in contrast to their aspirations for professional employment. The Organisation for Economic Cooperation and Development (OECD, 2010) highlights how vocational education is often overshadowed by an increasing emphasis on general academic and university education. Such low status can have significant implications, not only for those directly participating and working in vocational education, but also for how it is supported, funded, and administered (Billett, 2013). Poor perception of TVET can discourage people from considering this educational option and can lead to reduced industry sponsorship and support. Additionally, as Billet (2013) points out, negative perceptions of TVET can push young people to increasingly pursue higher education over TVET, including university programmes that offer no direct employment outcomes and possibly limit employment prospects upon graduation. This trend can potentially inhibit a country's ability to achieve its social and economic goals in the long run. The chapter proceeds by outlining the methodology adopted for the study. Thereafter, it elaborates the findings that help deconstruct the challenges of the DST model. The concluding section juxtaposes the rhetoric surrounding the potential of the DST model in India against the systemic challenges that came to fore during the pandemic preventing models like DST from being successful.

Methodology

The findings of this chapter are based on a total of 31 semi-structured qualitative interviews conducted with policymakers and senior officials part of the TVET ecosystem in India (4), ITI principals (2), industry partners (5), and students (20) enrolled under the DST programme in the state of Gujarat, India. Interviews with students (10 male and 10 female) were conducted in two waves between 2019 and 2021. The first wave was conducted with students either at the start, or during the second half of their course but before the onset of the COVID-19 pandemic, while the second wave of interviews was conducted after the pandemic started and students had completed the programme. The interview guide for the second wave was modified to help us understand the changes experienced by students during the pandemic and to capture their perceptions of how the pandemic had impacted their transition to labour markets.

The interviews were designed to understand students' motivations for participating in the programme, their perceptions of learning quality at the ITI and in the company, experiences with peers and trainers, their aspirations, their perceptions of the labour market value of their training and degree, and overall experiences with transitioning to the labour market. Interviews with principals were aimed to gain insights into the implementation of the DST programme at the ITI level and the challenges encountered. Interviews with industry personnel were conducted to understand their reasons for participating in the policy, how they interpreted goals of the DST, their perception of students enrolled in the programme, and the challenges they faced. These interviews helped us analyse the implementation gaps between the text in the policy document and the practices and experiences of the actors directly involved with the DST programme. The choice of field was guided by the locational advantages that the state of Gujarat offers. The urban industrial landscape of Gujarat provides a rich ethnographic field in terms of the aspirational trajectories and employment opportunities available to students after their training. A growing number of industrial enterprises in the region are accompanied by a significant demand for labour, and, as such, the region is home to a large number of migrants from all over the country. The selected ITI was also the first in the country to introduce the DST.

Research findings

Interviews with principals and employers

Discussions with principals underscored the top-down approach adopted in implementing the DST policy. Principal 1 recounted being informed about the DST model through a notification sent by the office of the Directorate General Training (DGT), the apex organisation responsible for the overall development and coordination of vocational training in India, and which oversees the vast network of ITIs across the country. Although the choice to adopt the DST model is left to the discretion of the states and ITIs, the implementation process, as also observed by Maitra and Maitra (2018), remains entrenched in a bureaucratically driven hierarchical framework.

Both principals interviewed spoke of the challenges they faced in persuading industries to partner and collaborate with the ITI to actualise the DST model. Principal 1 said:

> The main concerns that the industries have is that they do not want to come under the obligations of the labour laws in the event of an accident. Despite trying to tell them that the government provides insurance to students at the time of admission, it still takes a lot of convincing to have the industries on board.

Additionally, Principal 1 noted that while larger industries were able to absorb students trained under DST, the smaller and medium-sized industries lacked the capacity to absorb all the trained students. Consequently, many students remain unemployed or have to seek job opportunities elsewhere. On the other hand, Principal 2 spoke of some of the advantages of collaborating with smaller scale industries. According to him, students received more personal attention and were trained better as compared to the larger industries that were unable to provide the student trainees with adequate time and training.

Despite these challenges, both principals emphasised the need of a programme like DST, which provided the opportunity for ITI trainers and students to stay abreast with evolving industry technology, given that many ITI trainers lacked exposure to latest industry practices. Principal 2 highlighted:

> DST is very much needed, especially in a country like India where bringing about infrastructural change in ITIs cannot keep up with the changes in technology being adopted in the industry. Unless we collaborate with the industry, this latest technology will not be available for students. So, partnership with the industry is key.

From a policy perspective, the appeal of the DST model, also emphasised by the Principals, lies in the effective cooperation between industry and ITIs. Yet, our interviews with 5 industry personnel reveal little evidence of employee involvement in the overall DST partnership. Three of the 5 industry trainers we spoke to were unaware of the DST programme specifically, viewing both DST and non-DST students as regular ITI students. For example, Mr. Abhijit, the line in charge at one of the industries said that he would receive instructions from his manager to train a certain group of ITI students, and that was it. Mr. Das, a quality check manager at Jaba industries, reiterated this saying:

> I'm not sure who is from DST. They have interviews with HR. For me, DST and non-DST students all receive the same training.

Mr. Kamal, a training manager at Zen automobiles, additionally expressed concerns over the outdated ITI curriculum and its inability to prepare students for real industry practices. He said:

> I was also a student of ITI. There have been no changes in the syllabus since. Many carbonator systems and engines are outdated but students continue to study the same old thing. There is an urgent need to update the syllabus.

Mr. Menon highlighted the difficulties in aligning ITI curriculum with their operational needs. He pointed that their industry operations were tailored to production needs, not curriculum requirements. He said students often expressed confusion when tasks beyond their syllabus were assigned in the company. Moreover, the industry struggled with the limitation of training students due to the vastness of their production stations and emphasised that their primary role was manufacturing, not student training. He also spoke of the challenges under the DST partnership. He said that as partners they were forced to engage every DST student on the shop floor irrespective of organisational criteria like fitness of a student or colour blind. Even if students were irregular and undisciplined, it was mandatory that they train all DST students since they had signed the MoU with the government.

Interviews with policymakers

Our interviews with four policymakers make evident the primary policy objective of the DST initiative; the need to bring India's vocational education ecosystem closer to the world of work. Mr Chandan, a senior personnel of a leading think tank in India, mentions that while the model has been adopted from the German Dual TVET system, the DST has been customised to the Indian ecosystem. The success of the German model lies in its large-scale industries and strong public-private partnerships that are absent in the Indian context. In fact, one of the main challenges highlighted by Mr. Aromar, a senior policy officer in the Ministry of Skill Development and Entrepreneurship, was partnering with industry. He spoke of how the world of work in India is mired in small industries that on an average employ anywhere between 1 and 15 people but occupy nearly 80% of the industry ecosystem. As a result, there is a need to cajole, request, and push industries to come forward and participate in this programme to unlock the full potential of the DST. As mentioned in our earlier interviews, the burden of forging these partnerships falls on the ITI principals who often times struggle to convince industries to join the initiative. Although the DST policy is moving in the direction of creating work opportunities for students, the movement is slow.

While there seems to be a unanimous consensus on the potential benefits and needs of the DST model amongst our interviewees, a common characteristic of the Indian TVET ecosystem that was highlighted was the poor quality of learning that has little connect to the world of work. They mentioned that industries were being restructured and the pace of change in technologies used in industry was very fast, and that Indian ITIs lacked the infrastructure and capacity to keep up with this change. In this context, the DST model thus offers the opportunity to unlock the capacity of ITIs by closely partnering with the industry. As Mr Aromar told us:

> The government of India invested heavily in setting up TVET institutions to produce skilled workforce. However, lately they realised that upgrading the equipment, upgrading the infrastructure, upgrading the curricula, every time to keep pace with all these technological changes, was not possible. We are not able to match the speed of what it is going to change every time.

Mr. Das, Director of a prominent skill development programme run by an international organisation, highlighted how skill acquisition in India is not aspirational due to the wage structure that exists in Indian labour markets. However, degrees as a social perception are aspirational with parents aspiring for their children attain a graduate degree or diploma certificate. In this context, a programme like the DST becomes aspirational as it addresses students' desire for a degree certificate while enhancing their employability. Another senior policy officer, Mr. Nanda, reiterated that the DST programme will carry significant brand value as students will be better trained and have more practical work experience through this initiative.

Interviews with students

Interviews with 20 DST students, 10 male and 10 female, were conducted to learn about their experiences under the programme. The students, aged between 17 and 25 years, came from disadvantaged socioeconomic backgrounds. Many were second-generation migrants, whose families had moved from rural villages in pursuit of better education and job opportunities. Most students belonged to disadvantaged caste backgrounds, with family education levels limited to secondary schooling. Parents often worked service jobs as a driver or security guard or ran small scale businesses as tailors, carpenters, or bangle makers.

At the time of the interviews, a noticeable gender divide was observed within the ITI. Only the Computer Operator and Programming Assistant (COPA) programme had female students enrolled, while other DST courses like electrician, fitter, and motor mechanic were completely male dominated, with no female participants. Talking to students about their aspirations and motivations, many of them expressed a strong desire for government jobs, viewing ITI certification as crucial for these exams. They viewed the DST programme as a path towards competitive exams, often selecting their trades accordingly. For instance, Mr. Ranjit (machinist trade), who chose his programme based on his professor advice.

> My professor told me that my chances of getting a government job would be higher if I took up the machinist trade. Therefore, I chose it.

Likewise, Mr. Abid (Mechanical Draughtsman), highlighted the benefits of acquiring a technical certificate:

> Last year, I got a job in the Railways, and they informed me that a technical certificate was necessary for eligibility. Having a technical certificate enhances the chances of selection [for a government job]. So, I enrolled for the DST course under the sports quota.

For many students who had discontinued school or viewed their options for pursuing a general degree programme as limited due to high entry requirements and related expenses, enrolling at the ITI represented a viable safety net. This has also led to the widespread perception that ITIs are for students who are academic and socioeconomically disadvantaged. As articulated by one student trainee, Mr. Shourjo (Electrician):

> DST wasn't helpful in finding a job. It's for candidates like me who don't know what to do next. I failed 12th [grade] and since I wasn't interested in continuing with my studies, my brother suggested that I enroll in an ITI for practical hands-on learning.

Counter to policy expectations, Mr. Shourjo's remarks indicate that DST was not viewed as a useful route to employment by some students. On the other hand, some students opted for DST to enter the workforce quicker than a standard three-year general degree course. This was echoed by Ms. Bina (COPA):

> I was never keen on studying. I feel that DST certification will help me secure a good job and build my career in lesser years compared to a degree college.

Students mentioned that they were initially unaware of the programme due to its recent introduction, and that their decision to enrol in dual training was primarily influenced by the counselling provided at the institute. Principals and teachers advertised the DST as offering more employability than other programmes, and students perceived better employment prospects in a programme that offered practical training.

Experiences under DST

A few students mentioned being denied admission to the DST programme due to the limited number of seats. Admission was granted based on school leaving grades or performance in a regular ITI course. For instance, Ms. Anwesha (COPA), was initially denied admission to the DST programme but was later transferred after improving her performance in a regular ITI course. She said:

> When I first came here, I was refused admission to the DST programme as my grades were not good enough. But after performing well in my regular ITI course, and a vacancy under DST, I was allowed to join it.

When students were asked about their learning experiences, while some mentioned that the knowledge they gained was useful and supported them in their job search, a majority of them echoed that the theoretical component was not particularly useful as the curriculum was outdated. Students mentioned that teachers and faculty were helpful and supportive, creating WhatsApp groups for students to ask for help. However, students felt that there was little connection between what was taught at the ITI and the training they received at the company. For example, Mr. Aman (fitter) commented:

> The first 15 days at the company were spent studying, followed by 3–4 months of training, which was very different from what we had learnt at the ITI. This made it confusing for me. It felt like the theoretical lessons at the ITI were pointless.

The disconnect between ITI curriculum and industry practice was repeated by industry partners as well. In fact, one of the most frequent concerns raised by students regarding their experience at the ITI was the outdated equipment and poor infrastructure. Additionally, the ITI lacked library facilities and career centres. While students were appreciative of the faculty and their overall support, a few students did mention that lectures were often irregular. One student mentioned that certain faculty members would take attendance and then leave the class for other work. Moreover, with the onset of the pandemic, the ITI struggled to transition to a remote learning environment. Issues pertaining to poor connectivity, lack of devices, and online learning resources were reported. The impact was particularly significant for students in vocations such as motor mechanic and electrician, where a large component of learning occurs through hands-on practical experience. Students reported that while online lectures did resume, many students discontinued their studies for the remainder of the semester. As Mr. Bharat (Motor-mechanic Vehicle) noted:

> The [online] lectures ran for only a month. The professor was managing 3 batches simultaneously, so it was tough to handle them together. Eventually, our lectures were stopped due to time constraints.

The ITI tried to adapt and move to a distant mode of learning using low-tech solutions, yet students struggled to cope with the transition. Students found it hard to grasp online material without its corresponding practical training. Ms. Pushpa (COPA) mentioned how without practical lessons, understanding the course became difficult. Similarly, Ms. Simran (COPA) highlighted how the absence of in-person interactions meant missing out on valuable learning experiences.

> The way we ask questions in front of our teachers and understand what solutions they provide is quite different from what we do in online classes. There is a lack of communication, and studying in a virtual classroom on the mobile is not the same as studying.

While the ITI faculty tried to help students' prepare by sharing online study videos and mock tests, many students reported feeling overwhelmed with information and struggling to maintain motivation levels. One student, Ms. Salma (COPA), reported that no online classes were conducted for their cohort:

> Online classes were discontinued by the institute for 8–10 months. We had to educate ourselves by sourcing syllabus topics from different materials. For a subject like computers, practical lessons are more important than the theory. Applying theory to practice helps in our understanding of the topic. And not every student has a PC or a laptop. So everything felt stagnant and aimless.

Additionally, several students lacked access to devices such as laptops and smartphones which hindered their online learning. Internet connectivity was another issue that students reported. Mr. Jacob (Fitter), who resides in the city, also mentioned being burdened with additional internet costs. Furthermore, the indefinite postponement of ITI exams had an adverse effect on students' interest in education. They reported having forgotten much of the syllabus that had been taught due to repeated delays in exams. As Ms. Ankita (COPA) described:

> There was a substantial loss of learning this year. All the topics that were useful, interesting, and exciting were skipped due to the Covid lockdown, dampening our enthusiasm for studies in the process.

Our interviews highlighted the disconnect between the vision of skilling contained in the DST policy document and students' expectations and experiences – an issue only compounded by the significant impact of the pandemic. The above responses underscore how the DST lacked the capacity and resilience to respond to sudden shocks like the pandemic. The ITI struggled to shift to a remote learning environment as teachers were untrained in online pedagogical techniques. Additionally, teachers were overburdened with multiple classes leading to irregular online lectures for students. Most importantly, as a result of the pandemic, students were unable to complete their company-based training. In interviews, most students cited the expectation of gaining practical hands-on experience of the latest technologies, thus enhancing their employment prospects, as a primary motivation for joining the DST programme. However, in a pandemic landscape and without any practical training or certification, students encountered difficulty in applying for jobs. Ms. Archana (COPA) who shared her job hunting struggles said:

> Employers are not hiring freshers in the market. They often demand some sort of work experience to hire us. Completing the practical training would

> have provided us with valuable experience and the certificate would have made it easier to secure a job.

After completing her Higher Secondary Certificate, Ms. Archana enrolled in the DST with the hope that the three months of practical training under DST would help her secure a job with decent pay. However, post lockdown, she changed her job three times for reasons such as low pay, lengthy commute times, and health concerns. At the time of wave two interviews, she was actively searching for a job and felt disappointed that her post-DST expectations of finding employment and earning a decent salary had not been met.

Students were initially optimistic about securing jobs in the companies where they would receive their training. Unfortunately, many students lost out on this opportunity as companies ceased hiring during the lockdown and vacancies fell drastically. As a result, some students stopped actively searching for work and either joined family businesses or continued to passively search for employment. Mr. Rajesh (Fitter) said:

> I had inquired with my DST company, but they hadn't called back the existing employees to work so there was no chance that they would recruit new hires. Eventually, I stopped searching for a job.

Without social security to fall back on, students were forced to take up jobs in the informal or gig economy to secure some form of livelihood, often in roles unrelated to their DST trade. For instance, Ms. Simran (COPA) faced severe financial difficulties during the pandemic when both her father and brother lost their jobs. She switched jobs twice during the pandemic as the work was stressful, did not offer her a fixed salary, and was located very far from her home. To make ends meet, she and her mother started a small imitation jewellery business at home, which provided them with some source of income. When asked about how the pandemic had impacted her family's finances, she said:

> Our household income fell to 50% of what it used to be. And we had no income at all during the three months of lockdown. But then we found some work making imitation jewellery from home. My mother and I continue doing it. We earn Rs 2,000 to Rs 3,000 monthly from that.

A majority of students migrated back to their villages due to the lack of job opportunities in the cities. Mr. Adil (Electrician) found employment in a local firm after his training; however, at the time of his second interview with us, he mentioned that he had resigned as he saw no prospect of growth in the company. When asked if he thought his DST training could offer him a brighter future, he said:

> No, in fact I am planning to change my field of work. There is a lot of hard work and we are not getting paid a commensurate salary. I have been trying for 2 years to get a job where I can see growth along with a decent pay scale.

The shortfall between the promised employment benefits of DST programmes and students' actual employment outcomes led many to believe that the dual training was not relevant for their career aspirations. This sentiment was particularly pronounced since the pandemic had forced companies to freeze recruitment and the number of vacancies in companies fell drastically.

Conclusion

The success of any reform depends greatly on how policy designs interact with the social and economic contexts in which they are implemented, and how the various stakeholders involved react to these interventions (Valiente and Scandurra, 2017). We have drawn insights from interviews conducted with policymakers, principals, company trainers, and students to understand the experiences and perceptions of various stakeholders involved with the DST programme. Particularly important is the experiences of students enrolled under DST. The public's perceptions of vocational education systems play a crucial role in influencing how young people select occupations and how teachers and parents advise young people about career pathways. (Billett, 2013). Perceptions surrounding TVET are often undermined by poor learning and employment outcomes, as we have seen in the case of India, and these discourses ultimately influence who accesses TVET programmes and to what end.

One of the most frequently cited deficiencies of India's current TVET ecosystem is the gap between theory and practice (Mehrotra et al., 2014). According to Wheelahan (2015a), in market-driven economies, students with TVET qualifications often do not secure jobs that are related to their qualifications due to weak links between labour markets and TVET systems. As a result, despite government policies that offer rhetorical respect to TVET, students are often trained for low-paid and low-skilled jobs. This is exacerbated by the fact that the TVET curriculum is often narrowly focused on workplace-based tasks and not occupations, thereby limiting students' chances of progression in the labour market, something we see in the case of Gujarat. Furthermore, these students are often more vulnerable to precarity as they are easily replaced in the absence of any specialised skills (Wheelahan, 2015b).

The need to integrate a practical component into India's current TVET system led to the introduction of the DST model in 2016. Drawing on the success of the German dual apprenticeship model, the Indian government has been promoting DST as an aspirational model which attracts meritorious students through the promise of bridging the gap between work and studies, thereby facilitating better employment outcomes.

One of the most desirable aspects of the DST is the strong linkage between ITI and industry which would help ITIs align their curriculum and training courses to the skills demand of the industry. This was an attempt to move towards a more demand driven model where employers could play a more active role in shaping the skills of young people, and thereby create a pool of qualified workers who could be absorbed in the industry. While in theory, this model seems like a win-win solution for both the ITIs and the industry, our interviews revealed that the DST model is yet to reach its full potential. Firstly, very few employers seemed to be aware of the model and its prerequisites, often viewing both DST and bon DST students as the same. Secondly, the top-down approach to the implementation of the model meant that the administrative burden of partnering with industry fell on the ITI principals without much support and oftentimes without the required linkages with industries. Moreover, lack in clarity of policy guidelines regarding ITI-industry partnerships meant that employers were often hesitant to partner up. Our interviews with industry trainers revealed that there was a lack of understanding of industry needs on part of the policymakers. Industry partners complained that there were no clear guidelines with regard to training students, and that they were forced to train all DST students irrespective of company policies regarding who is considered fit to work on the shop-floor. Moreover, trainers mentioned that it was not possible to provide training to students based on the curriculum followed at ITI due to the disconnect between the curriculum and varied industry practices. In fact, one of the industry partners mentioned that there were no concrete gains for them under the DST but signed the MoU to support the government. According to him, the industries work fast paced and competitive and constantly change, and they would prefer hiring workers who possess some experience and knowledge rather than training someone whom they are not sure would even work with them post the training.

While the promises of post-training employment benefits produced a preference among students for the DST programme, when the pandemic struck ITIs struggled to transition to a remote learning environment and learning quality suffered. Additionally, job opportunities reduced noticeably, in part due to the economic contraction caused by the lockdown and in part due to students' inability to gain and certify practical, in-company training. As a result, most students perceived their training in the DST programme as being of little value. In addition, pandemic conditions produced a rise in casual employment, and many students took up informal and unrelated employment in order to sustain their families, despite their aspirations for more professional employment outcomes.

While the pandemic highlighted the need for a robust skills formation system, it also reveals how programmes like the DST do not transform relations of exploitation brought on by the neoliberal market. Instead, the vulnerabilities of students in a precarious job market are exacerbated, further contributing to the continuing low status of vocational education in the country.

In order to ensure that the DST can reach its potential, there is a need to think about its workings in a more integrated way which includes better coordination, involvement of its various stakeholders, and being responsive to the needs of these stakeholders. Effort needs to be made to blend the theoretical component of the curriculum with practical training through active industry participation in developing the curriculum, and developing capacity of its faculty. It seems like the DST has fallen prey to the very same gaps that it hoped to bridge, and the pandemic only made transparent the weaknesses of India's TVET ecosystem reinforcing its poor reputation.

References

Agrawal, T. (2012). 'Vocational Education and Training in India: Challenges, Status and Labour Market Outcomes', *Journal of Vocational Education & Training*, 64(4): 453–474.

Allais, S., and Marock, C. (2020). 'Educating for Work in the Time of Covid-19: Moving beyond Simplistic Ideas of Supply and Demand', *Southern African Review of Education*, 26(1): 62–79.

Billett, S. (2013). 'The Standing of Vocational Education: Sources of Its Societal Esteem and Implications for Its Enactment', *Journal of Vocational Education & Training*, 66(1): 1–21.

Comyn, P. (2014). 'Linking Employment Services, Skill Development and Labour Market Needs: Issues for India', *The Indian Journal of Industrial Relations*, 49(3): 378–388.

Government of India. (2017). 'Grading of Industrial Training Institutes (ITIs): Framework and Methodology', Directorate General of Training, Ministry of Skill Development and Entrepreneurship, New Delhi. Available at: https://ncvtmis.gov.in/Material/GradingFramework.pdf (Accessed: 19 October 2023).

Government of India. (2014) 'National Skill Development Mission: A Framework for Implementation', Ministry of Skill Development and Entrepreneurship. Available at: https://msde.gov.in/sites/default/files/2019-09/National%20Skill%20Development%20Mission.pdf (Accessed: 19 October 2023).

Hajela, R. (2012). 'Shortage of Skilled Workers: A Paradox of the Indian Economy'. Available at: https://ora.ox.ac.uk/objects/uuid:de3a3de1-3ad3-4978-9d48-a34bd46837e5 (Accessed: 19 October 2023).

Maitra, S., and Maitra, S. (2018). 'Producing the Aesthetic Self: An Analysis of Aesthetic Skill and Labour in the Organized Retail Industries in India', *Journal of South Asian Development*, 13(3): 337–357.

Maitra, S., Maitra, S., and Thakur, M. (2022). 'Uncertain Itineraries: Dual System of Training and Contemporary TVET Reforms in India', *Journal of Vocational Education & Training*: 1–20.
Mehrotra, S. (2021). 'Technical and Vocational Education and Training in India', in *Routledge eBooks*, pp. 203–216, Azim Premji University.
Mehrotra, S. et al. (2014). 'Vocational Education and Training Reform in India Business Needs in India and Lessons to Be Learned from Germany'. Available at: https://www.bertelsmannstiftung.de/fileadmin/files/BSt/Publikationen/GrauePublikationen/GP_Vocational_Education_and_Training_Reform_in_India.pdf (Accessed: 11 December 2023).
Mouzakitis, G. S. (2010). 'The Role of Vocational Education and Training Curricula in Economic Development', *Procedia – Social and Behavioral Sciences*, 2(2): 3914–3920.
Organisation for Economic Co-Operation and Development [OECD]. (2010). *Learning for Jobs: Synthesis Report of the OECD Reviews of Vocational Education and Training*. OCED Publishing, Paris.
Pilz, M., and Ramasamy, M. (2022). 'Attractiveness of Vocational Education and Training in India: Perspectives of Different Actors with a Special Focus on Employers', in S. Billett, B. E. Stalder, V. Aarkrog, S. Choy, S. Hodge, and A. Hai Le (eds.), *The Standing of Vocational Education and the Occupations It Serves*, pp. 177–199. Cham: Springer.
Shukla, S. et al. (2017). 'Future of Jobs in India-A 2022 Perspective', *Report Submitted to FICCI*. Ernst and Young, Kolkata. Available at: https://eoivienna.gov.in/?pdf8808.
Tandon, N., Basu, P., Krishnan, O., and Bhavani, R.V. (2022). *Emerging Work Trends in Urban India: COVID-19 and beyond*. London: Routledge.
Valiente, O., and Scandurra, R. (2017). 'Challenges to the Implementation of Dual Apprenticeships in OECD Countries: A Literature Review', in M. Pilz (ed.), *Vocational Education and Training in Times of Economic Crisis*, pp. 41–57. Cham: Springer.
Wheelahan, L. (2015a). 'The Future of Australian Vocational Education Qualifications Depends on a New Social Settlement', *Journal of Education and Work*, 28(2): 126–146.
Wheelahan, L. (2015b). 'Not Just Skills: What a Focus on Knowledge Means for Vocational Education', *Journal of Curriculum Studies*, 47(6): 750–762.

12

PERCEPTIONS OF TEACHERS IN INDIAN POLYTECHNICS

An exploratory study of the attractiveness in India in the higher vocational sector

Sebastian Schneider, Natalie Grote, Usha Ajithkumar, and Matthias Pilz

Introduction

Although India has a large workforce available due to its young population and the demographic dividend, the so-called skill gap remains a major problem in the Indian employment market. The skill gap hinders India's growth, which is why political actors have recognized the need to solve this problem in order to catch up with other international economies (Badrinath 2016; Pilz & Regel 2021). In order to tackle the so-called skills gap, the Ministry of Skill Development and Entrepreneurship (MSDE) aims to reinforce VET in India. Education and economic performance show a dependence in terms of new economic opportunities as well as improved performance (Tara & Kumar 2016). Consequently, the training of skilled workers is a high priority for the Indian government to integrate young adults into the labour market (Maitra et al. 2022; Wessels & Pilz 2018). Despite the great shortage of skilled workers and the resultant opportunities for demanders, India is often said to have a low attractiveness of vocational education and training. This contradiction draws attention to the attractiveness of the VET and its institutions and the reasons for the assessments from the perspective of the people involved. The present study therefore explores the attractiveness of polytechnics (PTs). The investigation is to be conducted from the teachers' point of view, as they play a decisive role in the system and can therefore provide a deep insight into the subject matter. In addition, the teachers' self-concept is investigated and how they perceive their own role in the system.

Thus, the chapter is structured as follows. The first section introduces this topic, while the second section presents the research focus and provides an

DOI: 10.4324/9781003604846-16

overview about the relevant objects of the study like PTs, Higher VET and teacher education. The construct 'attractiveness' as well as the stakeholders of VET are introduced and defined in more detail in the third section. As special attention is drawn to teachers' perceptions, the conclusion has been made to proceed with a qualitative research method, which is introduced in the fourth section. The fifth section then covers the findings of the qualitative interviews, in which the central research results are presented regarding the perception of teachers concerning the attractiveness of PTs, while those results are discussed in the sixth section. Lastly, an outlook is given on the results of this study in a broader context of VET in India.

Research focus

Jambo and Pilz (2018) have examined the perceptions of teachers regarding the attractiveness of VET at Industrial Training Institutes (ITIs) in India. Their research concludes that the perception of teachers differs mainly from a broader perception in India's society, which highlights the different influences and awareness of VET by different stakeholders. As mentioned before, next to ITIs, PTs are also part of India's VET. Whereas a lot of research has been done on ITIs, the research on PTs is scarce. As part of VET in India and as a potential provider for India's workforce, light has to be shed on the attractiveness of PTs. In this chapter, the consideration of skills refers to the intermediate level. These include, for example, application-oriented knowledge and problem-solving skills that are taught to PTs. These intermediate-level skills are necessary in companies with supervisor positions, which are often held by PT graduates.

Due to the limited scope of this study, not all the stakeholders (like companies or society) can be brought into the centre of attention. As important actors of school systems such as VET, teachers can provide first-hand information from the schools. Consequently, this chapter chooses to further elaborate the perception of teachers in this regard. Thus, the following research question will be examined within the scope of this chapter.

How do teachers perceive the attractiveness of polytechnics in India's education system?

Since, as described here, there are already findings on the attractiveness of ITIs by teachers, these findings need to be compared in order to investigate whether there are differences between the two types of schools in VET and whether the assignment of PTs to the Higher VET has an impact on the differences. Particular attention should be paid here to whether PTs are subject to a different assessment than ITIs due to their assignment to the Higher VET. This leads to the following research question:

Are polytechnics more attractive than ITIs?

For a theoretical understanding, this chapter deals with the concept of the attractiveness of VET and how it is perceived by teachers. In order to be able to evaluate a complex issue such as the assessment of attractiveness, it makes sense to interview experts from the system (Hargreaves et al. 2006). Therefore, teachers as mediators between different stakeholders (e.g. between individuals and government) are a good way to approach the question of attractiveness. Teachers play an essential role within an education system such as VET. Several studies show this; for example, Dawson and McLendon (2000) examined the involvement of secondary vocational school teachers in the school-industry link between activities and their changing role in Australia by interviewing 32 vocational school teachers about their perceptions. Harris et al. (2005), also in Australia, conducted 64 interviews, which helped them to analyse how the changing environment affects the work of practitioners in the VET system.

The influence of teachers on the institution of school and their position as mediators of interests are of great advantage for the investigation of the research question, which is why teachers were chosen as the unit of analysis for this research. In addition to the teachers' general assessment of the attractiveness of VET, the surveys can also provide insights into how they see themselves and how they perceive their role as part of the system, which leads to the following research question:

What is their self-concept concerning their role as a teacher?

The answers to these research questions help us gain an overview of the attractiveness of PTs. In order to make the type of school PTs and the background of teacher training clearer, some selected information about the Indian education system should be given here.

Education has a great status and is perceived as a privilege in India (Y. K. Singh 2007). But next to the vast ethnic diversity, a differentiation can be made between the informal and the formal sectors of education as well as different types of schools, which consist of state, semi-state, and private schools. One part of the education system is the VET-system, in which PTs play an important role alongside ITIs.

Historically, PTs focused on supervised technician training programmes. However, over time they have begun to offer VET courses and programmes that lead to degrees (Norric (Nordic Recognition Information Centres) 2006). Especially the implementation of the National Vocational Education Qualifications Framework (NVEQF) has reinforced access to vocational courses and diploma programmes at a higher level for vocational students at the +2 level.[1] These diplomas can be obtained at PTs, which enables a pathway up to the higher education such as colleges (MHRD (Ministry of Human Resource Development) 2019b). One of the aims, for instance, is the provision of a closer integration of learning and work as well as the encouragement to continue an up-gradation of knowledge and skills (MHRD (Ministry of Human Resource Development) 2019b). There are currently 3,440 PTs with over 1.5 million students nationwide (MHRD 2019a), providing technology and services not only for people from urban areas but also for people from rural areas. Generally, PTs are approved by the AICTE (All India Council for Technical Education), if they are well equipped with, for instance, lecture halls, laboratories as well as qualified staff. Moreover, these institutions render vital help in developmental work in communities (MHRD 2019c). After grade 10, students can attend a PT and undergo a three-year diploma programme in disciplines like Civil Engineering, Mechanical Engineering, Electrical Engineering, Computer Science, or Medical Lab Technology. Next to the mentioned disciplines some institutions offer non-engineering disciplines such as Leather Technology, Printing Technology, and Sugar Technology. Moreover, PTs exist that exclusively address women. These women's PTs include areas such as Garment Technology, Beauty Culture, and Textile Design (Khare 2016). As mentioned, the goal of PTs is to create a pool of skill-based manpower to support shop floor and field operation (Khare 2016). Medium-sized industries prefer these diploma holders for their skills in reading and interpreting drawings, costing and billing and supervision, for instance (Khare 2016). Next to the generalized two-year courses, students can additionally obtain a post-diploma. This description of the PTs makes it clear that there is a difference in content to the orientation of the ITIs. While ITIs cover basic training at a lower level, for example, in the craft sector with six-month to maximum two-year training courses and are classified at ISCED (International Standard of Classification of Education) level 3, PTs move to a higher level within the VET system. In addition to practical parts, education is provided at pre-academic level, including theoretical concepts with considerable depth in some areas, which is why ISCED level 4 is applied. Thus PTs, unlike ITIs, can be described as Higher VET. Higher VET programmes offer the opportunity to acquire skills and competences and work related qualifications at a higher level. A degree in the Higher VET offers the possibility to find a more advanced position in a company, for example, in the intermediate and supervisor area. However, there is not yet a generally valid definition of Higher VET. The classification of PTs as Higher VET and thus the difference to ITIs is of interest because it creates different conditions that can significantly influence the assessment of attractiveness (MHRD 2014).

In PTs teachers play a fundamental role, as they have to provide the education to the demanders and must meet the needs and requirements of the education system. In this regard, the Second International Congress on Technical and Vocational Education and Training (TVET) states that the bridge from economic growth to human development needs to be built by qualified teachers (UNESCO 1999). Ajithkumar (2016) states that the quality of training relies on the quality of the trainer. Consequently, the quality of training impacts the attractiveness of VET. Therefore, teachers are an essential agent in an education system. As the exploration of the role within the whole education system would exceed the topic of this chapter, the analysis focuses on the training of VET teachers with regard to PTs. Wessels and Pilz (2018) differentiate between two areas of teacher education which constitutes of general and vocational education. Teaching staff in general education as well as in pre-vocational education needs a Bachelor of Education (B.Ed.) or a Bachelor of Teaching (B.T.). Teachers at the upper secondary level obtain a master's degree in the teaching area they have specialized in. Teachers at colleges must hold a Master of Education or a doctorate (PhD). For PTs, in particular, the government suggests that teachers participate in short-term training of ten days (Govt. Polytechnic 2012). The participants may complete the courses in two to three slots. One block has to concentrate on the teacher's field of expertise, and the other slots have to be interdisciplinary, such as management areas (Govt. Polytechnic 2012). Newly hired staff at PTs are in possession of a master's degree in Humanities or Applied Science or a bachelor's degree in Engineering Technology. Generally, they have not received training in teaching. In this case, the government suggests training for the faculty in fields such as pedagogy, classroom management, or lesson planning (Govt. Polytechnic 2012). Nevertheless, some of the teachers at vocational schools have obtained training in Central Training Institutes (CTIs). Graduating with an Instructor Training Certificate, teachers have undergone one-year courses providing training in skills development and principles of teaching (Norric 2006). Furthermore, faculty members have to participate in annual seminars, conferences, or workshops, which are supposed to be organized by every affiliated institution once a year. If seminars or short-term courses are not funded through AICTE, the schools mostly cover the costs (Govt. Polytechnic 2012). Moreover, it is relevant that teachers have not only an academic education but also knowledge of the working systems and processes within their field of expertise (Ajithkumar 2016). In the case of India, this would suggest that India's VET teachers need to be aware of the labour market situation in their domain. Furthermore, they need to train students accordingly to the needs of the labour market in India. Despite the required level of qualification that the government foresees for teachers, empirical findings show that not all the teachers are as qualified as required. Only 40% of 55,000 instructors at VET schools have undergone professional training (Ajithkumar 2016).

Theoretical approaches and existing studies on perception of attractiveness

Since a brief overview of the relevant objects in the Indian VET system has now been given, the attractiveness as a central aspect of the study will be defined now; it will also be explained as to why the investigation of the attractiveness of PTs has a high relevance and why stakeholders and the self-concept of the teachers are important for the consideration. The concept of attractiveness is a complex and multidimensional construct and therefore, challenging to define. There is no integrated model for the VET sector, although the issue of attractiveness is highly relevant and recurrent (CEDEFOP (European Centre for the Development of Vocational Training) 2014). However, several scholars have dealt with partial aspects of attractiveness research.

First of all, it becomes clear that the consideration of attractiveness must be multidimensional, that is via different stakeholders, since different groups perceive attractiveness differently. Consequently, it can be summarized that the attractiveness of VET lies in the eyes of the beholder and is, therefore, subjective. Berger and Pilz (2009), Winch (2013) as well as Leney and Green (2005) focus on various stakeholders of VET who perceive and influence the attractiveness of VET differently. Whereas Leney and Green (2005) focus on the way how VET is designed to meet the stakeholders' needs, the benefits of VET regarding different stakeholders is elaborated in the research of Berger and Pilz (2009). Within their study they presented (1) benefits of companies, (2) social and public benefits, (3) economic benefits, and (4) individual benefits for participants of VET (Berger & Pilz 2009). The model explicitly portrays the benefits of a range of target groups specifically in the context of vocational training. It has no specific country focus but can be adapted to local conditions. This stakeholder model makes it possible to assign respondents' statements to stakeholders and facilitates the evaluation of the collected data and that is why it was used in this study. The teachers as internal actors of the school or PT have an overall view of the various stakeholders and can therefore give a realistic assessment of their perception.

A countries' government mostly finds VET attractive at an economic level as it is the case for the Indian government. VET could reinforce positive outcomes on wages and employment opportunities and, as a result, reduce unemployment (CEDEFOP 2011b). However, a government needs to analyse and weigh the benefits and costs in an economic and social sense as well as in a political context (Winch 2013). A government can influence VET through various instruments that give them the possibility to positively influence the supply such as suitable investments in buildings and equipment, curricula, and comprehensive governance. Furthermore, trusted qualification structures as well as qualified teachers can be provided in this regard (Winch 2013). The actions of the government can then influence the stance of employers, whose lack of request for VET graduates is one of the barriers of the attractiveness of VET according to Winch (2013). Even though there is a demand of skilled workers in countries like India, mostly the inadequate return of investments is one of the barriers that hinders companies from employing VET graduates. Consequently, it is more likely for employers and organizations to invest in their own employees if a positive outcome is guaranteed (Winch 2013). Even though different stakeholders exist, they cannot be perceived separately from one another. Thus, companies' perceptions on VET influence potential VET candidates and vice versa. Winch (2013) states that there is a natural relationship between the employer demand for VET qualification and the individual demand for VET courses.

Nevertheless, the attractiveness from an individual point of view mostly relies on the desired qualification and the chance whether one can find a well-paid job and prospects for the future (CEDEFOP 2011a). This, on the other hand, is simultaneously influenced by the perception of families and society itself (Winch 2013). Parental influences have a significant impact on children's career choices (Tuli 2012). Parents, for instance, who participated in a VET programme are more likely to influence their children towards VET compared to parents who were not involved with VET (CEDEFOP 2011b). It can be stated that general education has a better status in society than VET, which is underlined by empirical findings. An explanation could be drawn onto India's historical development, in which only the higher castes had greater access to general education than others (Bayly 1999). The way VET is perceived depends on the individual's environment, which is influenced by religious affiliations, historical as well as cultural influences such as India's caste system (Y. K. Singh 2007).

The way VET is perceived by an individual depends on the individual's environment, which is influenced by religious affiliations and historical as well as cultural influences such as India's caste system. Furthermore, institutions such as schools and their teachers are categorized as stakeholders. According to Winch (2013) the attitudes of schools play a major role in terms of the attractiveness of VET. Especially, the schools' knowledge and awareness of the labour market can be linked to the attractiveness of VET. Schools in countries like Germany, for instance, have secure connections to the labour market and therefore an implemented vocational orientation in secondary education.

Little research exists concerning the attractiveness of PTs and VET in general. In India, most of the research focuses on quantitative data, such as drop-out rates or enrolment rates. Jambo and Pilz (2018) explored teachers' perception of the attractiveness of ITIs in India, which offer a more fundamental kind of VET compared to PTs. Their findings conclude that VET in India does not have a good reputation in broader society (Jambo & Pilz 2018). However, most of the interviewees perceived it as a convenient alternative to general education for students, especially in terms of starting their own business. Moreover, some teachers also stated that the job opportunities for ITI students are better than for University graduates (Jambo & Pilz 2018). In this case, the main problem is the employment of temporary teachers, who are less qualified (Jambo & Pilz 2018). Okada (2012) additionally states that general education is perceived higher in society and that VET is perceived as the second choice. This perception is also underlined by T. Agrawal and A. Agrawal (2017), who state that poor labour market outcomes are associated with VET within the Indian society. Their research examined VET from a labour market perspective, which poses that even employers think that they would be better off by recruiting young individuals from a non-vocational stream (Agrawal & Agrawal 2017). Schneider and Pilz (2019), on the other hand, state that the broad range of specializations at PTs benefits companies as they do not have to invest a significant amount of time on newly recruited diploma holders regarding their on-the-job training. Their research on the embeddedness of PTs in the Indian education system shows that jobs such as supervisor positions are typical for diploma holders and in demand in the labour market (Schneider & Pilz 2019). Furthermore, their findings show that PTs offer the possibility to pursue a higher degree or become an entrepreneur (Schneider & Pilz 2019). Most of the results of previous studies on the attractiveness of vocational education and training relate exclusively to the perception in relation to ITIs. Since PTs, as explained here, are part of the Higher VET, it is important to check whether the findings on attractiveness found for ITIs also apply to PTs. Therefore, this study focuses on the perception of PTs itself and explores its attractiveness in the Indian education system.

Besides the attractiveness of the school form, the self-concept of the respondents, that is the teachers, also plays a role in the assessment. Just like attractiveness, self-concept is a complex construct that has approaches from various sciences such as sociology, philosophy, and psychology. Self-concept is about how individuals describe, evaluate, and understand themselves. However, self-concept is also related to the social environment, because this is constituted by interactions with the environment since early childhood. Moreover, the idea of self-concept is contextualized by various social and historical dimensions such as caste or class (Dyer et al. 2004; Joy & Kolb 2009; Nissilä et al. 2015; Pilz et al. 2022). Furthermore, the expectations of society with regard to self-concept are important, as well as how the teacher sees himself or herself as part of the school organization (Baumeister 1987; Mead 1934). As is the case for other stakeholders, teachers' assessments are strongly influenced by their personal backgrounds, their own educational histories, their family relationships, their origins, and their religion or caste. These personal backgrounds can strongly influence their assessments and self-perceptions.

Methodology

A qualitative research approach has been chosen for this study as it aims to reveal detailed descriptions of the attractiveness of VET regarding the stakeholders, teachers' experiences, and their perception of PTs and their self-concept. The teachers in India were recruited through local partners in Delhi. In the course of the research, 17 interviews were held at 4 different PTs in Delhi. Three government institutions and one private PT were visited in two weeks in January 2020. Since this work is an explorative analysis of perceptions of PTs from the perspective of teachers at Indian PTs, no nationwide total survey was intended. Accordingly, the field of inquiry is limited to Delhi. Delhi, as the capital, represents an industrially developed and metropolitan region of India. However, it must be noted that India is a heterogeneous country due to its size in terms of territory and population. English language was used for the medium of communication. Semi-structured interviews suit this study as the interviewer gains insight into individual perceptions. The semi-structured interview questions were included in an interview guideline. The guideline included 28 questions with categories like the general perception of VET, the reasons to become a teacher or the perceptions with regard to different stakeholders. The categories related to the stakeholders were deductively derived from the model of Berger and Pilz (2009) and constructed in such a way that teachers can adopt the different perspectives of the stakeholders like society, companies or individuals (see the third section). In order to examine teachers' understanding of the attractiveness of VET in relation to their own situation as teaching staff, the categories were structured in such a way that the individuals' point of view, self-concepts, and attitudes could be worked out. The data was transcribed and analysed by using qualitative content analyses according to Mayring (2014). Since the interviews dealt with attitudes and personal insights to the attractiveness of PTs, particular care had to be taken not to question or evaluate the professionalism critically and the opinion of the teachers interviewed. Furthermore, additional methodological and ethical considerations were used by conducting interviews for a cross-cultural environment (Peters & Giacumo 2020). For example, the questionnaires were pre-screened by local researchers for cultural sensitivity and special consideration and respect was given to cultural beliefs; the researchers' own cultural experiences and expectations were reflected upon in advance, and culturally sensitive interview techniques were used.

Findings

In this section, the results are examined by interpreting the interviews according to the research questions mentioned earlier. The findings are divided into two parts. The first part refers to the attractiveness of VET in India and is structured by the four analytical categories that are derived from Berger and Pilz's model (2009), namely companies, role of government, individuals and families, and finally society. The second part then refers to the teachers' self-concept and their individual status.

Companies

Teachers think that the way and quality of their teaching, as well as the reputation of PTs, contribute to the perception of companies and society.

> *It depends on the name also. Some institutions have been in demand. It also depends on the placement if they have a good placement (rate and connections), if they have a good name in society; otherwise, society does not generally consider their child to get (an) education at a Polytechnic.*
> *(Interviewee A2)*

Companies are interested in PTs as they require qualified workers which PTs provide. The findings suggest that the job opportunities for diploma holders are perceived as positive. The reasons for this are, on the one hand, the practical knowledge that PT students have acquired through their training at PTs. On the other hand, companies find the lower wages of diploma holders attractive compared to those of degree graduates.

> *Because they are in between worker and higher level, they are intermediate level. They can work as (a) supervisor and junior engineers. So, they are (a) lot of vacancies. Industries also like the diploma students, because industries can pay them less compared to graduates or M.Tech. students.*
> *(Interviewee P3)*

The interviewed teachers, however, stay in close connection with companies and former students and receive positive feedback from both sides.

> *For the diploma courses, companies are satisfied because they need (a) technician. And for being a technician, the basic requirement is (a) diploma. . . . They are well equipped. They gain a lot of knowledge and precision.*
> *(Interviewee A3)*

Nevertheless, some companies invest in newly recruited students as they train them for their own needs. Some of them even established their training institutions which could be an indicator that they are not as satisfied as some teachers believe them to be.

It can thus be assumed that a connection exists between the quality of PTs and the companies' satisfaction.

Role of the government

Although theoretical research shows that the government is interested in VET in order to meet the country's needs in qualified workers, the results pose the opposite. Besides the fact that the government tries to reinforce students to attend PTs, which can be assumed by the high number of students in a class, the lack of teaching staff and the need of more space suggests that the government could spend more monetary resources on the development of PTs in terms of buildings and qualified faculty.

> *Because our government is focusing too much on structural aspects. Now we are floating too many courses. . . . We are running three sections. The market demand (of skilled workers) is higher. So, the government pushes (our institution) to take more students on. We are running two shifts in the morning, one shift in the evening, and one shift in part-time also. . . . So, we are providing courses from 6 am to 9 pm in the evening. So, they are also older persons 40 years or 50 years. Because we have an incapacity (of space and teachers).*
>
> *(Interviewee P4)*

Numerous political initiatives also illustrate that the focus of government agencies is increasingly directed towards the VET system and its institutions, which shows the growing appreciation for VET within the government (MSDE 2019).

Individuals and families

According to the teachers the families and students were perceived as happy and satisfied with the education in the PTs, which has several reasons. PTs seem to enjoy a high reputation due to the existing job opportunities for students in the PT field in India. Also, the skill training that is part of the PT education is valued by the individuals as it makes them stand out in the labour market. However, the perception of students and their families stands in a discrepancy with the general perception of PTs. The general societal perception of PTs will be pointed out later in the chapter.

The length of the diploma courses, as well as the cost, seems to be suitable factors for students and their families. According to the responses, the students mostly come from lower-strata and middle-class families, who cannot afford to send their children to colleges in order to pursue a degree. Additionally, a PT is preferred as the students get a diploma at a young age and can, consequently, start working at a young age to support their families. Most of the teachers do not interact with the students' families. Nevertheless, some of them mentioned that families feel satisfied with the education and jobs that their children attend. Other teachers, on the other hand, mentioned that aspects such as poor infrastructure and the lack of equipment lead to dissatisfaction among students and their families. Additionally, some teachers pose that self-employment is an additional reason why students perceive PTs as attractive. Nevertheless, some students want to improve their knowledge and want to pursue a degree. However, some teachers pose that diploma holders find a job quicker as they are cheaper for the companies. One teacher even referred to her situation as she explained:

> *I had also struggle to get a job and I have seen it. I am a degree holder and those who were diploma holders were getting jobs earlier.*
>
> *(Interviewee A2)*

This shows that teachers believe that there are more job opportunities for diploma holders than for degree holders, which has a positive influence on the attractiveness of PTs.

Society

Within the Indian society, VET and their institutions like PTs do not enjoy a high reputation according to the results as well as previously explored studies. It should be noted, however, that the view of society presented here is a very condensed and generalized view due to the narrow focus of this study. Indian society is very heterogeneous in terms of religion, caste, education level, levels of wealth, and so on (M. Singh 2001). An explanation could be given by examining the people who visit PTs. The target population at PTs refers to students from rather poor socioeconomic backgrounds, who might set their surroundings as a benchmark when assessing their career opportunities. Furthermore, India's profoundly rooted history might still influence the perception of VET, which is still perceived as a second-best choice. According to the responses of this work VET enjoys a low reputation in society.

> *Society has a very basic opinion, not a very good opinion on Polytechnic. They think [a] Polytechnics degree is not enough for student's career.*
>
> *(Interviewee A4)*

Consequently, it can be concluded that general education has a better status in society than VET, which is underlined by empirical findings.

Teacher's self-concept and individual status

In addition to the teachers' assessment of the various stakeholders, light will now be shed on their own assessment of the PTs, their background, and their role in the system.

Concerning the teachers' personal education the degrees of the interviewees range from a bachelor's degree to a Ph.D. Some of the teachers also visited a PT to obtain a diploma and used the pathway to higher education. It can be concluded that some of the interviewees had worked in different jobs before they became a teacher at a PT. Most of them worked within their field of interest, in which they also obtained a degree. The jobs mentioned range from technician or chemist to an office worker or science assistant. As a result, some of them gained work experience in relation to their subjects. Regarding the preparation as a teacher, different perceptions can be observed. Some teachers claim that they receive mandatory short-term courses each year, which address their subject as well as teaching methods. Others, on the other hand, say that no training is provided. At this point, it needs to be highlighted that those who mentioned that no training was provided belonged to the private institution that was visited, which underlines a difference between private and governmental PTs. Nevertheless, most of the teachers said that no specialized training was provided at the beginning of their teaching career except one. One of the teachers studied a Bachelor of Education, which included one month of practical training at a school in general education.

As reasons for the choice of school the teachers feel that they are addressing the country's needs by training the workforce that the market requires. Some of the teachers mentioned that the interaction improves the knowledge of the students and vice versa. Moreover, the working hours and the time for leisure activities are additional aspects that teachers described as attractive.

Next to all the mentioned benefits there are also some challenges according to the interviewees. Some teachers mentioned that due to the high number of students and the lack of teaching staff, the quality of teaching suffers. The number of regular teachers is a problem that most of the institutes face. Some teachers complain about substitute teachers who do not take their work seriously. Therefore, teachers wish to have a higher number of regular faculty. Next to the low number of teachers stands the high number of students. The overcrowded classrooms were mentioned as challenging by most of the teachers. Furthermore, the equipment was another aspect of improvement. The latter can be underlined by the empirical findings which note that the lack of equipment and the lack of qualified teachers are commonly found at vocational institutions (Okada 2012: 189). For some of the interviewees, it was the first job so it could be possible that they could not compare it to other institutions that are well-equipped.

The teacher's status is generally perceived as positive and valuable. They feel that they are respected in the Indian society. Nevertheless, this does not only depend on PTs, specifically. Most teachers believe that a teacher is highly valued in Indian society regardless of general or vocational education.

> *When my mother in law tells [other people at a gathering] that her daughter in law is a lecturer at Polytechnic, they are happy with it. I get positive*

responses. And most of the times they do know about Polytechnics, that there are Polytechnic courses.

(Aidtya: Interviewee 2)

In general, a teacher is perceived as pure and honest according to the responses. Nevertheless, some teachers are convinced that a technical teacher is more respected while others believe that a teacher in general education is more respected.

However, the methodological approach has to be borne in mind as solely teachers at PTs were questioned within the scope of this research. Some of the interviewees became teachers due to different conditions other than the pure conviction to become a teacher. Nevertheless, some teachers came from teaching backgrounds and have also obtained a diploma and have actively chosen to become a teacher at a PT. Thus, it can be assumed that the attractiveness of PTs influences this. Furthermore, being in a government job secures safety and benefits as the unemployment rate in India remains high.

Regarding their situation, teachers perceived PTs as attractive. Furthermore, they perceived VET as an essential system for the society and the labour market. Nevertheless, only a few actively chose the path as a teacher at PT. For others, it was at first solely the decision to be employed as no other option was in sight. However, all the interviewees enjoy their job as a teacher, which is a promising outlook for the future development of VET.

Discussion

The study on the perceptions of the attractiveness of PTs among PT teachers in Delhi aimed to shed light on the perceived differences between different stakeholders as well as on the self-concept of the teachers. Furthermore, the available results can be compared with already existing studies on ITIs.

One of the most important findings concerns the general perception of PTs from society. Based on their personal experiences, teachers believed that VET, including PTs, is not highly valued in broader Indian society. General education still perceives a higher reputation within Indian society as vocational education is mostly perceived as craft and physical work, which does not enjoy a high reputation. This perception is still deeply rooted in the Indian society. This assessment of low attractiveness expressed by teachers is remarkable as it is contrary to the opinion of other stakeholders. Furthermore, no differentiation between VET and Higher VET can be identified, although this could have been expected, since education at Higher VET institutions offers more chances and opportunities for graduates. In particular, participants in PT courses and their parents consider PT education to be attractive and conducive for finding an adequate job. Notably, the good placement opportunities and the chance of adequate self-employment are a decisive factor for the attractiveness for parents and students. According to the respondents, companies also share this positive assessment, as they value the employability of graduates and their practical knowledge. Nonetheless, the assessment would depend substantially on the quality of the educational institution. In relation to the government, aspects such as the provision of guidelines and equipment were mentioned. These aspects, however, do not yield information on the government's perception regarding the attractiveness of PT. As the government aims to meet the mismatch situation through VET, it can be presumed, on the one hand, that VET is regarded as attractive by the government. On the other hand, the overcrowded classrooms and the lack of a certain amount of qualified faculty propose that the government could invest more effort regarding PTs. Here, the Indian government in particular must proceed with caution, as many approaches introduced in the past were not sustainable and the will to invest in TVET was not strong enough (Schneider & Pilz 2019). In particular, care must be taken to ensure that the government's focus is not only on quantitative benchmarks, but also specifically on advancing the qualitative component of skill training to increase the attractiveness of PT education (Ramasamy et al. 2021).

Moreover, the perception of each stakeholder influences the other, and therefore they cannot be looked at separately but must instead be set into context (Berger & Pilz 2009). As stated in the literature review, the concept of attractiveness is perceived and influenced differently, which can be underlined by the results of this chapter.

A comparison of the teachers' self-perception as opposed to the stakeholders' external perceptions is also of interest. As described in the results section, the teachers are largely satisfied with their work in the PTs and feel acknowledged; this also applies to the satisfaction of the students. What is most significant is that both actors are in direct contact with the PT; that is they experience the advantages and disadvantages of the institution directly and personally. The critical assessments of the attractiveness of the PTs come mainly from society, which to a large extent has no direct contact with the PTs and only reflects traditional opinions without knowing the possibilities of the PTs in detail. This shows that only marginal distinctions can be made between VET and Higher VET in this regard, as these facts also apply to ITIs.

Another key finding refers to the institution. Although the teachers were highly qualified, the overcrowded classrooms, the maintenance of equipment, and as the outdated curriculum prove to be quite challenging in their everyday life. Nevertheless, due to close contact to former students and companies, teachers perceived their students' career opportunities positively especially in comparison to students from general education, which depends on the reputation of the institution as well. The conditions and programmes offered were perceived as useful and attractive for young people. This view stands in discrepancy to the literature (e.g. Ajithkumar 2016; Majumdar

2016; Okada 2012; Pilz et al. 2022; Pilz & Gengaiah 2019), which states that VET in India suffers from outdated equipment and insufficient teaching quality. Furthermore, the shortage of instructors is a significant influence on the quality of teaching.

Of particular interest are the available results on estimates of the attractiveness of PTs against the background of existing surveys on the attractiveness of ITIs. As mentioned, both institutions are part of the VET system, although PTs can be added to the Higher VET (see earlier). Compared to the findings of Jambo and Pilz (2018), similarities can be analysed towards both school forms regarding the interviewees' perceptions, skills-development, and job opportunities. Both studies pose that the institutions in question are perceived as attractive by the interviewees (Jambo & Pilz 2018). We can also note some differences between vocational training in ITIs and higher vocational training in PTs in terms of the programmes and certificates awarded by the institutions. Whereas with the ITI degree a certificate is obtained, which entitles the holder to move directly to the labour market or to register at the PT, with the Certificate Polytechnic, which is widely known as a diploma, it is also possible to enter the job market, but in a higher position (e.g. supervisor level) or even to transfer to the engineering college.

It is evident from the results of this research project that some students visited an ITI before pursuing a diploma, which indicates a close connection between both institutions. Based on the findings provided, it cannot be stated whether a PT is perceived as more attractive than an ITI. This seems remarkable, as PTs generally provide higher educational qualifications and should therefore be more attractive. There can be various reasons for this. For example, studies have shown that informants rate their own institution, either ITIs or PTs, and their individual position in such research more positively (Joshi et al. 2014: 95). The situation is similar when respondents are not familiar with research approaches. They tend to give more positive answers, assuming that this is what field researcher from abroad would like to hear (Ritchie & Lewis 2003).

Conclusion

An analysis of all mentioned stakeholders' perception on the attractiveness of VET would exceed the scope of this work, but a closer look at any educational system reveals that teachers are important actors within school systems. Therefore, they play a significant role in terms of the attractiveness of VET as well. The present study provides a clear statement from teachers about the attractiveness of PTs. VET is a strategically significant factor in India's further social and economic development.

Results show that skill training is still not seen as a desirable solution by society and various stakeholders in India and is therefore not considered very attractive. Theoretical and academic education is still considered the gold standard (Wessels & Pilz 2018). Skill training, which is possibly still related to manual activities, is mainly attributed to lower social classes (M. Singh 2001). This assessment is made especially from the point of view of society, in which vocational education or skills training enjoys a bad reputation, although skills training offers young people more and more opportunities for the future. As a result, skill formation has long led a backseat, as it has not received much attention from government authorities. Accordingly, the quality of skill formation institutions was also negatively impacted. This shadowy existence is slowly changing, which is reflected in the assessments of the business community and families of students.

As mentioned, PTs are part of the Higher VET sector. This sector in particular can play an important role in India's future development. This is shown by the international trend, according to which Higher VET is becoming increasingly important in many countries, including the United Kingdom. There are several reasons for this, for example, to ensure connectivity to academic education. PTs as links between VET and academic education are of great importance from a systemic point of view and have numerous international role models, such as the Berufsakademien in Germany or the Higher Diplomas in the UK (Deißinger et al. 2013; Young & Raffe 1998). Good permeability and well-linked connectivity to education programmes enables the targeted training of skilled workers and the efficient use of opportunities for those who need education. Moreover, it is clear that economic progress in India is leading to a slow but steady transformation of the national economy. Therefore, from an organizational and technical point of view, an upgrading of the skills of the workforce is necessary, as more complex and versatile work is required. Here the PTs provide many opportunities for upgrading skills and act as a link between VET and academic education (Raffe & Howieson 2013).

In this respect, recommendations for future studies could be conducted regarding different perspectives. A focus could lie on more stakeholders like companies for instance, after which a comparison could be drawn onto existing studies to see if and how the perceptions of the different stakeholders vary. In a further step, former PT students could be interviewed to reveal their experiences in terms of job opportunities as well as on-the-job training when in employment. In addition, the attractiveness of PTs could be examined in pilot studies to see if it can help to make the education system in India more inclusive in terms of gender, class, and castes (Bagde et al. 2016).

At this point, it has to be noted that the results have to be carefully interpreted. The study solely focused on a small sample of teachers at PTs in Delhi. Due to the small sample focusing on teachers only and just in one region in India, the interviews offer a very restricted insight into the perception of attractiveness. For future data collection, which will extend the exploratory character of this study, further regions (urban vs. rural, industrially developed vs. less developed) in India have to be included in order to get a broader picture of the perceptions of the teaching personnel in Indian PTs. In the scope of stakeholders, it is evident from the results that families, companies, the society, and the government perceive the attractiveness of PTs differently. Moreover, it can be concluded that they influence the attractiveness in different ways, which stands in alliance with the concept of stakeholders of VET.

Note

1 Vocational students at +2 level refer to students who have passed the 11th grade (MHRD 2019c).

References

Agrawal, T., and Agrawal, A. 2017. 'Vocational education and training in India: A labour market perspective', *Journal of Vocational Education & Training*, 69(2): 246–265.

Ajithkumar, U. M. 2016. 'Training of teachers: Institutionalising training and development of academic faculty of TVET institutions for realising excellence', in M. Pilz (ed.), *India: Preparation for the world of work: Education system and school to work transition*, pp. 183–210. Wiesbaden: Springer VS.

Badrinath, V. 2016. 'Further education and training, retraining: Skilful India – a dream or reality', in M. Pilz (ed.), *India: Preparation for the world of work: Education system and school to work transition*, pp. 231–259. Wiesbaden: Springer VS.

Bagde, S., Epple, D., and Taylor, L. 2016. 'Does affirmative action work? Caste, gender, college quality, and academic success in India', *The American Economic Review*, 106(6): 1495–1521.

Baumeister, R. F. 1987. 'How the self became a problem: A psychological review of historical research', *Journal of Personality and Social Psychology*, 52(1): 163–167.

Bayly, S. 1999. *Caste, society and politics in India from the eighteenth century to the modern age*. Cambridge: Cambridge University Press.

Berger, S., and Pilz, M. 2009. 'Benefits of VET', in U. Hippach-Schneider, and B. Toth (eds.), *ReferNet Research-Report Deutschland/Germany 2009*, pp. 6–49. Bonn: Bundesinstitut für Berufsbildung.

CEDEFOP. 2011a. *The benefits of vocational education and training*. Luxembourg: Publications Office of the European Union.

CEDEFOP. 2011b. *Vocational education and training is good for you: The social benefits of VET for individuals*. Luxembourg: Publications Office of the European Union.

CEDEFOP. 2014. *Attractiveness of initial vocational education and training: Identifying what matters*. Luxembourg: Publications Office of the European Union.

Dawson, M., and McLendon, E. 2000. 'School-industry links and the secondary VET teacher perceptions and involvement', in National Centre for Vocational Education Research (ed.), *Proceedings of the 9th annual vocational education and training research conference*, p. 10. Brisbane: North Coast Institute of TAFE.

Deißinger, T., Wern, R., Heine, R., and Ott, M. 2013. 'Progression from VET into higher education via hybrid qualifications in Germany: Context – policy – problem issues', in T. Deißinger, J. Aff, A. Fuller, and C. H. Jorgensen (eds.), *Hybrid qualifications: Structures and problems in the context of European VET policy*, pp. 111–145. Bern: Peter Lang.

Dyer, C., Choksi, A., Awasty, V., Iyer, U., Moyade, R., Nigam, N., Purohit, N., Shah, S., and Sheth, S. 2004. 'Knowledge for teacher development in India: The importance of "local knowledge" for in-service education', *International Journal of Educational Development*, 24(1): 39–52.

Govt. Polytechnic. 2012. *Training policy for polytechnic faculty/staff*. Retrieved from: http://www.gpadampur.ac.in/training-policy-for-polytechnic-facultystaff.html (Accessed Feb 12th 2020).

Hargreaves, L., Cunningham, M., Everton, T., Hansen, A., Hopper, B., McIntyre, D., and Turner, P. 2006. *The status of teachers and the teaching profession: Views from inside and outside the profession – interim findings from the teacher status project*. Cambridge: University of Cambridge.

Harris, R., Simons, M., and Clayton, B. 2005. *Shifting mindsets: The changing work roles of VET practitioners*. Adelaide: National Centre for Vocational Education Research.

Jambo, S., and Pilz, M. 2018. 'Perceptions of teachers in industrial training institutes: An exploratory study of the attractiveness of vocational education', *India International Journal of Training Research*, 16(1): 4–18.

Joshi, S., Pandey, G., and Sahoo, B. K. 2014. 'Comparing public and private vocational training providers', in S. Mehrotra (ed.), *India's skills challenge: Reforming vocational education and training to harness the demographic dividend*, pp. 86–128. Delhi: Oxford University Press.

Joy, S., and Kolb, D. A. 2009. 'Are there cultural differences in learning style?', *International Journal of Intercultural Relations*, 33(1): 69–85.

Khare, M. 2016. 'Higher education/university: Taking the skills march forward India – transitioning to the world of work', in M. Pilz (ed.), *India: Preparation for the world of work: Education system and school to work transition*, pp. 103–139. Wiesbaden: Springer VS.

Leney, T., and Green, A. 2005. 'Achieving the Lisbon goal: The contribution of vocational education and training', *European Journal of Education*, 40(3): 261–278.

Maitra, S., Maitra, S., and Manish, T. 2024. 'Uncertain itineraries: Dual system of training and contemporary TVET reforms in India', *Journal of Vocational Education & Training*, 76(3): 556-575

Majumdar, S. 2016. 'Foreword: Reflections on opportunities and challenges of skills development in India', in M. Pilz (ed.), *India: Preparation for the world of work: Education system and school to work transition*, pp. 7–13. Wiesbaden: Springer VS.

Mayring, P. 2014. *Qualitative content analysis: Theoretical foundation, basic procedures and software solution*. Klagenfurt: Beltz.

Mead, G. H. 1934. *Mind, self & society*. Chicago: University of Chicago Press.

MHRD. 2014. *Indian standard classification of education*. New Delhi: Government of India, MHRD.

MHRD. 2019a. *All India survey on higher education 2018–19*. New Delhi: Government of India, MHRD.

MHRD. 2019b. *Revised centrally sponsored scheme of "vocationalisation of higher secondary education"*. New Delhi: Government of India, MHRD.

MHRD. 2019c. *Vocationalisation of secondary education*. Retrieved from: https://mhrd.gov.in/vocationalisation (Accessed Dec 26th 2019).

MSDE. 2019. *Annual report 2018–2019*. New Delhi: Government of India, MSDE.

Nissilä, S.-P., Karjalainen, A., Koukkari, M., and Kepanen, P. 2015. 'Towards competence-based practices in vocational education – what will the process require from teacher education and teacher identities?', *Center for Educational Policy Studies Journal*, 5(2): 13–34.

Norric. 2006. *Report on the system of education in India*. Retrieved from: http://norric.org/files/education-systems/India-2006.pdf (Accessed Dec 23rd 2019).

Okada, A. 2012. 'Skills development for youth in India: Challenges and opportunities', *Journal of International Cooperation in Education*, 15(2): 169–193.

Peters, D. T., and Giacumo, L. A. 2020. 'Ethical and responsible cross-cultural interviewing: Theory to practice guidance for human performance and workplace learning professionals', *Performance Improvement-International Society for Performance Improvement*, 59(1): 26–34.
Pilz, M., and Gengaiah, U. 2019. 'Teacher training education for VET teachers in India', in S. McGrath, M. Mulder, J. Papier, and R. Stuart (eds.), *Handbook of vocational education and training: Developments in the changing world of work*, pp. 1733–1746. Cham: Springer.
Pilz, M., and Regel, J. 2021. 'Vocational education and training in India: Prospects and challenges from an outside perspective', *Margin – the Journal of Applied Economic Research*, 15(1): 101–121.
Pilz, M., Schlögelmann, A., and Gengaiah, U. 2022. 'VET teachers and teacher trainers in India', in S. Loo (ed.), *Teacher educators in vocational and further education*, pp. 13–27. Cham: Springer.
Raffe, D., and Howieson, C. 2013. 'Hybrid qualifications in a credit-based system: Scottish higher national certificates and diplomas', in T. Deissinger, J. Aff, A. Fuller, and C. H. Jørgensen (eds.), *Hybrid qualifications: Structural and political issues in the context of European VET policy, studies in vocational and continuing education* (Vol. 10), pp. 149–164. Bern: Peter Lang.
Ramasamy, M., Regel, J., Sharma, H., Rajagopalan, A., and Pilz, M. 2021. 'Measuring quality in Indian VET institutions: Development steps towards a framework adapted to the national context', *International Journal for Research in Vocational Education and Training*, 8(4): 44–66.
Ritchie, J., and Lewis, J. (eds.). 2003. *Qualitative research practice: A guide for social science students and researchers*. London: Sage.
Schneider, S., and Pilz, M. 2019. 'The function and institutional embeddedness of polytechnics in the Indian education system', *International Journal for Research in Vocational Education and Training*, 6(3): 284–308.
Singh, M. 2001. 'Reflections on colonial legacy and dependency in Indian vocational education and training (VET): A societal and cultural perspective', *Journal of Education and Work*, 14(2): 209–225.
Singh, Y. K. 2007. *History of Indian education system*. New Delhi: APH Publishing Corporation.
Tara, S. N., and Kumar, S. N. S. 2016. 'Primary and upper primary (1–8) education: Initiative for the world of work at the primary and upper primary education in India', in M. Pilz (ed.), *India: Preparation for the world of work: Education system and school to work transition*, pp. 25–40. Wiesbaden: Springer VS.
Tuli, M. 2012. 'Beliefs on parenting and childhood in India', *Journal of Comparative Family Studies*, 43(1): 81–91.
UNESCO. 1999. *ICT competency standards for teachers*. Paris: Harper Collins Publisher.
Wessels, A., and Pilz, M. 2018. *International handbook of vocational education and training: India*. Bonn: Bundesinstitut für Berufsbildung.
Winch, C. 2013. 'The attractiveness of TVET', in UNESCO-UNEVOC (ed.), *Training, revisiting global trends in TVET: Reflections on theory and practice*, pp. 86–122. Bonn: UNESCO-UNEVOC.
Young, M., and Raffe, D. 1998. 'The four strategies for promoting parity of esteem', in J. Lasonen, and M. Young (eds.), *Strategies for achieving parity of esteem in European upper secondary education: Post 16 strategies*, pp. 35–46. Jyvaskyla: University of Jyvaskyla.

13

EMPLOYMENT CHALLENGES OF THE INDIAN YOUTH

An overview of the Indian VET sector

Muthuveeran Ramasamy

Introduction

The Indian labour market has the potential to have a higher proportion of youth; half of its population is under the age of 25, and the country has a core labour force of 433 million; also, on average, another 6 million to 8 million youths will be entering the labour force every year for the next decade and a half (Ghose 2016; ILO 2024). Studies have highlighted that investment in youth human capital enhances the economic growth of developing economies (Sianesi & Van Reenen 2002). Also, it is highly valuable that such a workforce should possess the needed skills leading to gainful employment by allocating adequate resources and imparting skills to the labour force. This agenda has been a critical mandate within the country's development strategy for several decades (Meky 2015). While India is one of the world's fastest-growing economies, unemployment remains a challenge in its development process, primarily attributed to the present education and training system (Bhalla & Meher 2019). The challenge of youth employment, however, is highly dependent on how to correspond to a complex interaction of demographic, social and economic factors (Assaad & Levison 2017). On the one hand, the young population in India represents one of the potential human capitals to serve the skilled workforce both nationally and globally; on the other hand, the country is facing a challenge in absorbing skilled human power into the labour market (Mehrotra 2014b; Mitra & Verick 2013; Pilz 2016b).

The VET system is one of the formal institutional frameworks established in India and has also been perceived as a vital component of skill development in the country. The correspondence between VET and the labour

DOI: 10.4324/9781003604846-17

market considered rests largely on knowledge and skill the VET transfer to the students and in-turn into the labour market. However, there are several challenges and barriers that are yet to be addressed to facilitate that transition. Notably, issues such as skill mismatch, quality of VET (Aggarwal & Gasskov 2013; Ramasamy et al. 2021) and inadequate support for the school-to-work process (Bisht & Pattanaik 2021; Pilz 2016a; Smith et al. 2014) make it difficult for many young people to acquire the right skills demanded by employers. Against this backdrop, this chapter aims to explore the challenges related to the transition from education to the workforce, the factors influencing the framework of school-to-work transition and the challenges faced by VET graduates in India.

This chapter is structured into seven sections. The first section sets the aim and context of the chapter. Structural changes in the economy, labour market trends and youth employment challenges are briefly presented in the second section. The third section outlines the demographic transition and youth unemployment issues, focusing on VET. The following (fourth) section discusses the challenges in the demand and supply-demand and quality-quantity issues in VET. The fifth section describes the pathways of VET in the school-to-work process and issues at each level. The sixth section discusses the possible measures and the seventh includes limitations and policy implications

Structural change in the labour market

The term 'structural change' here refers to changes in the relative importance of the main sectors of an economy (agriculture, industry, services and so on) during economic growth and its link between structural change and employment (Majid 2019). The Indian labour market structure is complex and highly segmented (Mundle 2017), broadly categorized into two sectors: formal and informal.[1] The informal sector consists of all unincorporated private enterprises owned by individuals or households engaged in the sale and production of goods and services operated on a proprietary or partnership basis and with less than ten total workers (Mehrotra 2019). The informal sector is dominated by own-account workers, workers and apprentices in micro-enterprises; unpaid family workers, casual labourers, home-based workers and migrant labourers; out-of-school youth and adults in need of skills; and farmers and artisans in rural areas. The formal sector has a majority of its working force on a contractual basis or as casual workers with very little or no security benefits. The informal worker is defined as a worker with no written contract, paid leave, health benefits or social security. More than 90% of people in India work in the informal sector, which involves employment in both the organized and unorganized sectors (Ramasamy 2016).

As Mehrotra (2019) states, employment growth elasticity is based on major economic sectors and is dependent on the progressive change in

TABLE 13.1 Employment trends in India (15–29 years of age)

	2004–05	*2011–12*	*2017–18*
		Share of works in percentage	
Agriculture	55.6	44	36.1
Manufacturing	14.5	16.1	16
Non-manufacturing	7.5	14	15.4
Service	22.4	25.9	32.5

Source: (Mehrotra 2019).

employment associated with structural changes in output between the primary, secondary and tertiary sectors (Mehrotra 2019). Nevertheless, more than 70% of the Indian population live in rural areas. The country remains predominantly an agrarian-based society and a large proportion (48.9%) of the workforce still depends on the agricultural sector (ILO 2018). In this context, while the agricultural sector has seen moderate growth since independence, despite a substantial increase in agricultural production, there has been a shift by which employment in agriculture fell by 27 million during 2011–12 and 2017–18 (see Mehrotra & Parida 2019) and continued to move to non-agriculture activities. Only limited jobs were created in the non-agriculture sector compared to the last ten years due to slow growth in the Indian economy's GDP since 2012–13 (Mehrotra & Parida 2019). Therefore, economic growth in this period did not generate sufficient jobs in non-agriculture to absorb those entering the labour force and those wishing to leave agriculture for non-agricultural jobs (Mehrotra 2019: 8). This scenario is reflected in Table 13.1, which shows that a broad shift in the occupational structure of the Indian economy has created a demand for new skill requirements among the emerging workforce in the non-agricultural sectors such as industry, construction, and services, to keep pace with the growth of potential job seekers (Tara & Kumar 2016; Thomas 2020).

The industry, which consists of both the manufacturing and construction sectors, has declined sharply in recent years. Further, a large proportion (85%) of the non-agricultural workforce is in the informal sector, which is vast and contributes about 60% of the GDP (Mehrotra 2019). Most employees acquire their skills and knowledge in an area of the economy that is informal (Wessels & Pilz 2018).

Some analysts like Verick (2018) argue that the traditional economic development process in a developing economy is primarily characterized by the movement of resources and workers moving from agriculture to manufacturing. In the Indian case, it has not happened and they failed to be employed in the manufacturing sector; rather, the country witnessed service-led economic growth and employment perspective (Verick 2018). Employment in the age group of 15–29 years, the share of workers in agriculture, has declined from 55.6% in 2004–05 to 36.1% in 2017–18. Also, the gradual rise in the service sector increased from 22.4% to 32.5% in 2004–05 and 2017–18, respectively.

Consequently, the low-skilled workers in rural areas tend to move out of agriculture, absorbed in traditional services, construction or unorganized manufacturing and none of these areas does employment come with social insurance (Mehrotra 2019). India's service sector represents a key driver of economic growth, accounting for more than half of economic output but a relatively low share of employment (Verick 2018). In this context of labour market transition, the increasing youth population who enter the labour market and the challenges of youth employability, skill demand and supply are discussed in the subsequent section.

Demographic transition, educational attainment and youth employability

According to the National Policy for Skill Development and Entrepreneurship, more than 54% of India's population is part of the working age group of 15 to 59 years and 29.1% of the total workforce in the country comprises young[2] people (NSDC 2020). Such a demographic transition greatly influences the demand on the labour market to create jobs and absorption of labour when a large cohort of youth enter the workforce apart from the existing workforce (Assaad & Levison 2017). Leveraging necessary measures would harness its benefits to the young people not only to provide employment opportunities within the country but also globally. According to an ILO (2021) report, 83.3% of the total unemployed in the country in 2019 were in the 15–29 cohort. When such young people remain unemployed for a period, it is likely to affect the economic prospects of the unemployed as their skills and motivation deteriorate and employers may disfavour them as potential recruits (Ryan 2001). Table 13.2 depicts that the incidence of

TABLE 13.2 Unemployment rates in percent for persons aged 15 years and above with different educational attainments

General educational level	*Year*			
	2004–05	*2009–10*	*2011–12*	*2023–24*
Not literate	0.45	1.1	0.45	0.25
Literate and up to Primary	1.7	0.9	1.25	0.50
Middle	4.3	2.6	2.37	1.35
Secondary and above	10	7.7	6.9	8.25

Source: Authors' calculation based on NSS 61st (2004–05), 66th (2009–10), 68th (2011–12) and PLFS 2023–24 (NSSO 2024).

unemployment is higher among those who completed secondary level of education and above, about 8.35%, compared to illiterate persons at 0.15%.

Young people who attain a degree, including technical and other professional education, suffer from the highest proportion of unemployment. Significant reasons for unemployment among better-educated graduates of technical, vocational and professional education include lack in skill levels, disconnect between the theoretical learning and practical knowledge being imparted at the institutions and suffering from employability and skill mismatch in the labour force (Mamgain & Tiwari 2016). As Majumdar (2016) points out, the lack of general education and employability skills pushes young unemployed VET graduates towards relying on low-productivity labour and low earnings (Majumdar 2016). The illiterate and the less-educated end up with underemployment in the informal sector and low-productivity jobs. As mentioned at the beginning of this section, as more young people enter the labour force, unemployment among young people increases. It mirrors the factors that high demand for the semi-skilled and skilled labour force, the quality issues are of more significant concern that need attention to address challenges, hence matching employment opportunities by skilling the large section of the young population to accelerate the availability of a skilled workforce to meet regional and global demand. In the next section, we discuss the issues of demand-supply aspects and issues of the VET-trained workforce.

Demand and supply of vocational skills – quality and quantity

Ghose (2016) estimates that of the 16 million persons who will join the labour force annually over the next 15 years, 4 million will be low skilled (with up to primary education), 7 million will be medium skilled (up to above primary and higher secondary education) and 5 million will be highly skilled (with tertiary education). It is essential to address the employment challenges, not only to create 16 million jobs every year but also to create jobs for the low to medium skilled, which account for 11 million people (Ghose 2016).

The PLSF (2023–24) data on receiving VET in the age group of 15–29 denotes that only a small proportion (4.9%) of young people had received formal vocational or technical training (see Table 13.3). Most of the skilled population in India acquires skills through non-formal training, including hereditary passing of skills, on-the-job, self-learning and informal apprenticeship (Pilz & Wilmshöfer 2015; Ramasamy & Pilz 2019).

Indeed, policy-makers often consider VET, both formal and non-formal, as a significant means for equipping young people with the necessary skills for sustainable employment. The acquisition of knowledge and skills by VET graduates is one of the most crucial determinant factors for employability (Neroorkar & Gopinath 2020). However, research (see Mehrotra 2014c;

TABLE 13.3 Percentage distribution of persons aged 15 to 29 years by the status of vocational/technical training in India

	Male	*Female*	*Persons*
Received/received formal vocational/technical training	4.8	5.0	4.9
Received vocational/technical training other than formal vocational/technical training	28.2	13.9	21.2
Did not receive vocational/technical training	67.0	81.1	73.9
Total	100	100	100

Source: PLSF 2023–24.

Pilz & Ramasamy 2022; Tara & Kumar 2016) demonstrates that the quality of VET graduates who enter the labour market does not possess the skills that the industry expects, causing higher unemployment of youth trained in VET. Scholars (Ramasamy et al. 2021; Tara et al. 2016) have identified several challenges confronting VET institutions in India, such as no quality standards, heavy theory-centred rather than practical components, poor infrastructure/resources, inadequate equipment and outdated curricula. In addition, the availability of qualified instructors/teachers in VET institutions deteriorated the quality. Many instructors at the VET institutions had not received pedagogy training and were not sufficiently prepared for teaching (see Pilz et al. 2022). These issues affect VET graduates' ability to acquire skills needed by employers, which impacts their employability. In addition, when the school-to-work process is less effective and efficient, young people tend to face the problem of increasing their level of education and gaining adequate general work experience rather than the job-specific skills and competencies demanded by the industry. Therefore, facilitating youth transition from school-to-work is a significant task in the education systems.

To ensure a better transition of young people into the labour market, it is essential to reinforce vocational education within school-based education and minimize the skill gap between the VET system and the labour market (Zimmermann et al. 2013). In addition, inadequate educational attainments, high unemployment, increasing job turnover and weak links between schooling and employment are crucial factors that cause poor school-to-work transition (Ryan 2001). The school-to-work transition framework facilitates young people in preparing them for the world of work (see Pilz 2016a) The following section will delve into the various challenges associated with each stage of this transition in the following section.

School-to-work transition

Education and training are considered core factors in determining the chance of a successful transition into work (Zimmermann et al. 2013). The transition from school to work is structured differently across countries and regions. The education system in India has multiple challenges in realising the school-to-work transition process and equipping young people for the labour market (Pilz 2016a). As discussed in the introduction, despite India experiencing a 'demographic dividend', many young people find it difficult to acquire the appropriate skills demanded by employers for a successful school-to-work transition (Comyn 2014). Aside from country-specific dynamics in demographic and economic development, the patterns of youth employment are heavily influenced by regulatory policies on the one hand and the education system, which is illustrated in Figure 13.1, on the other (Zimmermann et al. 2013). Subsequently, taking account of the work's length and scope, the author discussed only the VET component within the border education system here.

Overview of VET in the Indian education system

The schooling system[3] in India comprises 12 years, known as the 10+2 system. The Right to Education (RTE) Act, 2009, in the Constitution of India, entitled every child between the ages of 6 and 14 to the right to free and compulsory education. Elementary education is divided into primary school (classes 1 to 5) and upper primary (classes 6 to 8). When students attain the mandatory completion of schooling (Class 8), that is at the age of 14, children can make their transition to the two-year lower secondary (class 9 and 10) and senior secondary education consists of two years (class 11 and 12). Students can pursue higher education after passing the higher secondary or class 12. Graduation education can take three to five years, and postgraduate education can take two to three years, depending on the stream.

VET at the school education level

The pre-vocational education at the secondary education level is offered to impart training in simple and marketable skills to students in classes 9 and 10, develop vocational interests, and allow for self-exploration of vocational preferences. It also facilitates students' choice of vocational courses at the higher secondary level (classes 11 and 12) and prepares students for participation in work experiences (Tara & Kumar 2016). At the school level, VET starts only at the upper secondary level (classes 11 and 12) in schools, providing general education and lasts for two years.

Vocationalization of secondary education was launched in the year 1988 by the Ministry of Human Resource Development (MHRD)[4] as a centrally sponsored scheme. This scheme provides vocational education instruction in secondary schools and is considered an alternative to the general stream of education in schools (MHRD 2017). This scheme offers 150 vocational

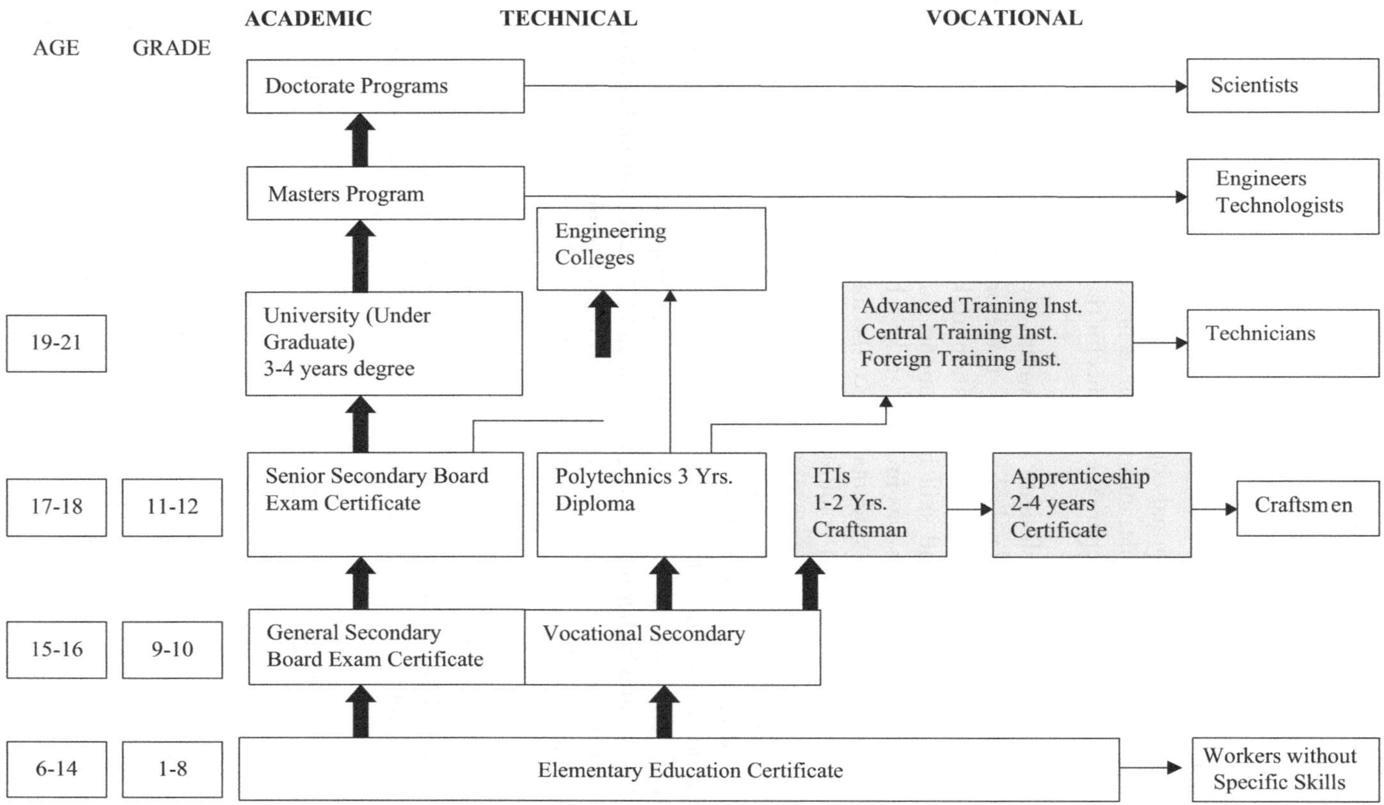

FIGURE 13.1 VET in the Indian education system

Source: Adapted from Skill Development in India: The Vocational Education and Training System (World Bank 2008).

courses of two-year duration at the higher secondary level (class 11 and 12). The Secondary and Higher Secondary educations are essential stages in the school education system of general education since only at this point do the young people decide his/her pathway on whether to pursue higher education or vocational education (Planning Commission 2009). Also, it integrates vocational education with general education and provides horizontal and vertical mobility to the students (MHRD 2017). In total, 7,448 schools across the country offer 150 vocational courses covering 17 sectors, including agriculture, apparel, automobile, information technology, logistics, insurance, hospitality and media, to prepare the students for the world of work (MHRD 2017).

The key focus of India's Eleventh and Twelfth Five-Year Plans was on imparting technical and vocational education. Therefore, the government is emphasising shifting focus from general education to skill education to improve the quality of education and skill base among students (Bhalla & Meher 2019). Vocational education was initiated at the school level to enhance the employability of individual students, reduce the mismatch between the demand and supply of human resources, and provide an alternative to those seeking to pursue higher education.

Since vocational education is offered only at the higher secondary level, class 11 and 12, students are limited or do not have an opportunity to acquire any vocational skills until they complete their secondary schooling (Mehrotra 2014a). However, this scenario is due to higher dropout at the secondary level (20.7%) and higher secondary (10%) in 2014. Further, the higher dropout rate at the secondary level (see Table 13.4) makes young people take up unskilled, low-productivity jobs in the informal economy.

VET system at the higher level

The formal technical education in India comprises a three-tier system, namely Industrial Training Institutes (ITI) at the first level, Polytechnics at the middle

TABLE 13.4 Percentage of dropout/discontinued persons between 5 and 29 years

Education level	*2007–08*	*2014*
Primary	12	10.1
Upper primary	26.5	16.2
Secondary	30.2	20.7
Higher secondary	19.2	10.8
Diploma	2.3	4.4
Graduate	8.4	4.7
Postgraduate and above	4	4.7

Source: NSS 71st round NSS Report No. 575, Education in India.

level and professional courses, which offer engineering degrees in colleges/universities at a higher level (British Council 2016; Pilz & Regel 2021). In India, Vocational Training programmes are offered through two principal schemes called the Craftsmen Training Scheme (CTS) and the Apprenticeship Training Scheme (ATS). The CTS and the ATS are offered by the Directorate General of Training (DGT) under the Ministry of Skill Development & Entrepreneurship (MSDE 2020).

Craftsmen Training Scheme

The CTS is the most important in the field of Vocational Training to meet the existing as well as future manpower needs through the vast network of ITI, which is the oldest and most trusted method of the VET system (Mehrotra 2014c) and is expected to play a crucial role in enabling youth to enter the world of work (Kumar 2016).

Students who completed class 8 of school education can join vocational training courses in ITIs, some courses requiring entry-level class 10. The first ITI was opened in India in 1950 and until 2007, there were around 7,000 ITIs in India. There are more than 15,000 ITIs, where private ITIs increased from 4,119 in 2007–08 to 15,024 in 2023 and a total seating capacity of about 2.6 million (MSDE 2024). Government ITIs have also grown, but their growth rate is significantly lower than that of private ITIs (MSDE 2021).

The country is expected to create a pool of skilled manpower through various measures to strengthen vocational training, including expanding its network and establishing more Centers of Excellence with the active participation of the Public-Private Partnership (PPP) (Kumar 2016; MSDE 2018b). The data from MSDE reports illustrate that there is a surge in seating capacity, which was close to 1.1 million in 2016–17 compared to 2015–16; the recent years have seen a decrease to 7% between 2017–18 and 2018–19

TABLE 13.5 Number of ITIs and seating capacity

Year	*Government ITIs*	*Private ITIs*	*Total ITIs*	*Seating capacity (million)*
2015–16	2,293	10,812	13,105	1.865
2016–17	2,150	11,200	13,350	2.84[5]
2017–18	2,161	11,751	13,912	2.96
2018–19	2,738	12,304	15,042	2.28
2020–21	3,262	11,892	15,154	2.66
2023–24	3,291	11,733	15,024	2.62

Source: MSDE annual reports of 2015–2021 and 2023–24.

(Table 13.5). The poor utilization of seating capacity can be attributed to several factors. Key among these are low placements and underqualified instructors with low salaries and high dropout rates (see Maitra et al. 2022; Pilz & Ramasamy 2022), which significantly dampen student interest in enrolling in ITIs.

Apprenticeship Training Scheme

The Apprenticeship Act 1962 in India comprises four types: (a) Trade Apprenticeship, (b) Technician (Vocational), (c) Technician and (d) Graduate. The DGT is responsible for the first type and the MHRD is responsible for the remaining three types of apprenticeships. The first and second types of apprenticeships are primarily to create a cadre of shop floor skilled and semi-skilled work. In contrast, the third and fourth are to train youths as potential managers for manufacturing in the organized sector (Mehrotra 2014a). The Trade Apprenticeship and Technician (Vocational) scheme is aimed at youth aged 15–18 and intended to provide practical on-the-job training to those who graduated from ITI after a two- to four-year course and those who have received no training in any ITI, respectively. The Technician and Graduate types of training are for people 18–22 years of age, with a higher level of skill training ITI graduates and a diploma in polytechnics and degree in technical engineering institutions. There are 266 designated trades under the ATS, in which 30,165 establishments conduct training of 0.23 million trade apprentices (MSDE 2024). Kumar et al. (2019) argue that India's apprenticeship system is ineffective, as the country only has 0.27 million apprentices, whereas a million persons are in the working-age cohort. The private sector is reluctant to show interest in offering apprenticeships as they do not get any incentives to incur the cost (Kumar et al. 2019). Mehrotra (2014b) pointed out that only 20% of Indian firms offer any form of training and it is lower when compared to developed economies. According to MSDE (2019), the current scenario of apprenticeship training is mainly (80%) associated with students from ITIs and most of the apprenticeships are associated primarily with the manufacturing industry. While more than 89% of the overall apprentices engaged are from the engineering sector, the potential of the services sector, which is the primary driver of the economy, has remained untapped (MSDE 2019). Apprenticeship provides contextualized learning to practical problems at the workplace and offers better understanding and improved motivation, especially among low achievers (Ryan 2001). Unfortunately, the apprenticeship system also faces issues due to factors such as poor coordination and delivery/monitoring mechanisms, ineffectively designed apprenticeship programmes, lack of trainers and inability to attract practitioners from industries as guest faculty (GoI 2015).

Post-secondary education: technical education

While vocational education refers to a lower level of education and training for young people to produce skilled or semi-skilled workers, technical education after post-secondary school leavers technicians at the supervisory level. Technical education offers various courses in engineering, technology, management, architecture, pharmacy and hotel management (Venkatram 2016). There has been a mushrooming growth of technical education intuitions in the country during the last two decades, which has affected the quality of vocational and technical education in the country (Mamgain & Tiwari 2016). Mamgain and Tiwari (2016) noted that the demand for degree-level technical education in private institutions has declined sharply, and the seating capacity is under-utilized. On the other hand, the need for diploma-level qualified technician graduates has increased in the labour market, and they are paid comparatively less than the former (Pilz & Ramasamy 2022).

Polytechnics

Polytechnic education offers three-year generalized diploma courses after class 10 with a duration of between one and three years. It primarily offers courses in conventional engineering disciplines such as civil, electrical and mechanical engineering. However, since early 1990, polytechnics also started offering courses such as electronics, computer science and medical Lab technology to increase employment opportunities for students in the diversified labour market (Khare 2016). In India, there were 43 Polytechnic colleges with an intake capacity of 3,400 in 1947 and by 2018, there were around 3,440 polytechnics in India with an intake capacity of 1.5 million (MHRD 2019).

Although the aim of polytechnic education is to create a pool of skill-based workforce to support shop floor and field operations as a middle-level link between technicians and engineers (Khare 2016), these types of institutions are also often suffering in quality and relevance in terms of lack of demand-oriented courses, lack of upgraded machines, inadequate funds, poor infrastructure, lack of training of trainers, outdated curriculum and lack of industrial exposure (Maitra et al. 2022; Schneider & Pilz 2019), resulting in only 15% of polytechnic students being employable (Shrotriya et al. 2018). The India Skills Report 2016 (Wheebox 2016) highlights that technical engineering institutes across the country are supplying close to 1.5 million engineers each year and one-fifth to one-third of students out of this group may have to face unemployment (Shrotriya et al. 2018). By contrast, Bhalla and Meher (2019) claim that technical education proved to be a vital factor in eradicating unemployment. Bhalla and Meher (2019) highlighted that a 1% increase in enrolment in diploma courses correlates with a 0.5% reduction in the unemployment rate. This finding underscores the positive relationship between technical and vocational education and unemployment, suggesting that enhanced investment in technical education is crucial at this juncture.

The supply of a well-educated and trained labour force is highly important for a country's development; however, enrolment into educational institutions does not adequately translate into human capital with the required skills and knowledge (Thomas 2020). The above-discussed issues are not only at the VET level but also at the graduate level, which is consistently increasing (Shrotriya et al. 2018). Although the youth unemployment rate has risen sharply across all education categories, the increase is the highest for those with graduate plus degrees (see Table 13.2) and the technical and vocational education categories. Many highly educated graduates are forced to take up jobs much below their educational qualifications or enter unsuccessful entrepreneurial pursuits (Khare 2016). It is implicit that the increased youth enrolment in higher education does not transform into the successful school-to-work transition of the younger generation in the Indian labour market (Bisht & Pattanaik 2021). A growing proportion of diploma and engineering graduates are undertaking forms of employment that are not commensurate to their level of education and skills. This raises the issue of the balance of supply and demand of graduates in the labour market. This situation prevails due to the poor supply of graduates from the VET institutions and the employability of diploma and engineering graduates. This context raises concern about the greater potential for displacement between levels of education and occupational position. Consequently, the diploma and engineering graduates may also perceive a potential mismatch between their qualifications and their returns in the job market (Schneider & Pilz 2019). The following sections will explore the intricacies of these challenges and possible interventions.

Discussion

Skill education and youth employment

This chapter has explored the factors affecting youth employment in India, mainly through the lens of school-to-work transition and VET. One of the key findings is that there is a higher dropout rate at the secondary level (see Table 13.4) compared to higher secondary and to join the workforce (GoI 2020). Consequently, this phenomenon forced young people to find possible opportunities in the informal sector in low productivity activities. This reinforces the need for skill education for early school leavers to enter work and find decent employment (Vincent & Rajasekhar 2021). Another constraining factor is that, as Mundle (2017) puts it, India's school education policy has not been effective as it focuses more on inputs rather than learning outcomes, often favours higher education than primary or secondary education and has a higher incentive structure for government school teachers regardless of performance. Thus, integration of VET with general education starting from the upper primary level is highly important and pre-counselling on various VET courses during various stages of schooling will also be helpful (Vincent & Rajasekhar 2021). Furthermore, the result of the school-to-work transition in the market-led economy associated with a lack of focus on aspects concerning quality and quantity of training provisions further complicates access to the labour market (Rubery & Grimshaw 2003).

Labour market inequalities and industry participation in VET

Moreover, the scale and scope of demand for labour would, in the long run, be influenced by structural changes in the economy or other factors like globalization and technological advancement or de-industrialization (Islam 2016). As mentioned in the earlier section, the VET system in India is facing a multitude of problems. It cannot meet the demands of the industry unless it addresses the issues of quantity, quality and relevance (Kumar et al. 2019). While the country needs a more significant number of semi- and medium-skilled workers in the coming years, only about 4% of the total Indian workforce has acquired VET skills formally compared to more than 70% in developed countries like UK or Germany and about 80% to 90% in East Asian countries like Japan and Korea (Ghose 2016; Mundle 2017). Furthermore, from a labour market perspective, many job-seekers are unemployable, as they do not have adequate exposure to practical aspects of education and training (Mamgain & Tiwari 2016). This is in line with the recent study findings of Pilz and Ramasamy (2022) on employers' perspectives on VET graduates: the vocational training provided at ITIs is deficient in terms of providing practical skills to perform in the workplace. These factors emphasize the need to embed hands-on practical components to be integrated into VET provision and an effective apprenticeship system (Pilz & Ramasamy 2022). Also, industry associations, sector councils and companies could play a more significant role (Majumdar 2016). The recent reforms, such as adopting the Dual System of Training (DST) in 2016, are one initiative in this direction. The primary purpose of DST is to ensure that students in formal VET institutions, particularly in the state-owned ITIs, devote equivalent time to classroom theoretical learning and on-site industrial training during their period of education (Maitra et al. 2022). In India, around 60% of government ITIs have been adopted by corporate companies under the public-private partnerships scheme (Neroorkar & Gopinath 2020). The companies often upgrade the infrastructure and provide training in the latest technology and other assistance to the VET institutions. Such measures may help VET institutions up-to-date industry needs, technological advancement, and new methods and knowledge that can be imparted to VET graduates.

However, the private sector is unwilling to bear the financial burden of creating in-house training infrastructure and recruiting employees due to the poaching problem (Mehrotra 2014b). Another essential factor is that training for new VET graduates is expensive (Pilz & Pierenkemper 2014). For example, in the case of manufacturing sectors often concerned about the duration of (apprenticeship) training which the ITI graduates receive in the form of on-the-job training, the companies can get the return on investment only after they productively contribute and return to the company. If the training period of ITI graduates exceeds the stipulated period, then the scrap rate will be higher, and the production rate will be lower (Pilz & Ramasamy 2022). Indian companies focus more on reducing costs, and training must be undertaken as economically as possible. These are the reasons why companies are reluctant to collaborate with VET institutions despite the government providing incentives to the companies.

Also, most VET institutions are running only engineering courses. According to the MSDE report, more than 80% of all the apprentices come from the ITIs and apprenticeships are dominantly provided in engineering trades. In contrast, the service sector, though an essential driver of the economy, does not provide training in substantial numbers (MSDE 2015). The structural changes in the economic growth and labour market changes, the growing non-agriculture sector has increased and the expansion of service sectors has created the demand for skilled labours. Nevertheless, ITIs have been the mainstay of skilled manpower for the manufacturing sector and have served their purpose well in the last two decades and a half. The ITIs, therefore, must also transform to meet the emerging demand from the services sector, which contributes 60% of the GDP and will have to start running more trades that provide skilled manpower to the service sector. Currently, 37 Sector Skill Councils are approved, covering all the priority and high-growth sectors, including Retail, Healthcare, Food Processing, and Beauty & Wellness (MSDE 2024).

Regional disparities and inclusivity in VET

The challenges of regional disparities in industrial development and economic growth in the country affect the VET graduates' ability to enter the labour market. For example, rural areas often have no access to companies unless they are located near an industrial hub. Industrial visits and other kinds of industry exposure to ITI trainees are also unavailable. This affects ITI graduates' employability, especially when competing with graduates from urban institutes (Neroorkar & Gopinath 2020) and severely affects the integration of young people into the labour market. Vocational qualifications are the best suitable options and of high value for low-ability individuals and those who work in low and medium-skill jobs (Kumar et al. 2019). Thus, students with less academic performance ability and hail from lower socioeconomic backgrounds mostly take up vocational education and often, their parents were less educationally qualified (Kumar et al. 2019). Nevertheless, it is implicit that VET is perceived as a poor public perception, low-standing manual work and low-paying employment in India (Ajithkumar & Pilz 2019; Pilz & Ramasamy 2022). These conditions can be attributed to several socio-cultural, historical and economic factors (Singh 2012). Furthermore, factors like access to VET, attitude towards women's education and economic participation remain crucial issues in developing countries like India.

The inclusive growth strategy of India has aimed at ensuring that individuals across society have equal opportunities in access to education and VET, irrespective of gender, age, race, caste, ethnicity and religion, and to acquire skills and facilitating young people to find employment in the labour market (Mehrotra 2017; Ramasamy 2016). These considerations are also reflected, and measures are taken through national policy agendas. For example, these issues are essential, and the recent National Policy on Education (MHRD 2020) document outlined the actions aimed at addressing disparities in access to education and vocational training based on gender or for any underrepresented groups (MHRD 2020: 24–25) for better integration of young people, predominantly female graduates into the labour market across sectors.

While the efforts are laudable, there is still a critical need for effective employment measures and improvements in quality and standards. Although there are significant efforts and reforms in VET in India, it remains a challenge, which impedes better jobs for young people. These arguments show that despite reasonable economic growth, issues of declining employment and increasing unemployment persist as a significant challenge to a successful school-to-work transition for the country's younger population.

Outlook

In a country like India, where only a limited section of the population has access to quality higher education, a larger section of the population finds difficulties in being employed in productive activities. In this context, the VET can be viewed as an instrument that influences the enhancement of labour productivity and efficiency and makes a meaningful contribution towards various sectors of the economy (Shrotriya et al. 2018). In addition, VET increases the productivity of individuals/workers and yields good returns when jobs for learners are ensured and when training is closely linked to existing employment demand (Middleton et al. 1993; Wallenborn 2010). Therefore, India requires an efficient and quality-driven vocational skill development system to transform the high youth population of India into productive human capital (Saini 2015). As VET institutions primarily prepare trainees for vocational purposes, programs must match the requirements of both learners and employers concerning skills and competencies to enhance their employment opportunities for VET graduates. As discussed in the earlier section, skill mismatch and quality of VET are some of India's most significant challenges; many industries lack skilled workers, leading to employment challenges for the young population (Sanghi & Srija 2014). Another important factor is that a general lack of connection between the VET institutes and industry leads to a lack of exposure to modern technologies among trainers and instructors. This arises due to the absence of comprehensive planning based on a spectrum of studies of the skill requirements, providing information on the current and future trained workforce needs of all categories of skilled personnel required by different sectors of the economy, along with weak links with industry. Therefore, the link between VET institutions and industry should be strengthened to enhance the employability of VET graduates. Thus, industry-institute cooperation is recommended so that every VET institution is connected to small-, medium- and large-scale enterprises at the regional level. The Institute Management Committee (IMC), institute management and staff members will have to take the lead. Furthermore, demand-driven curriculum (Ramasamy 2016) development in consultation with industry representatives, experts and academia by the competent bodies would also be an option to provide quality training and gainful employment in line with the latest market trends for a better transition of youth from education into the labour market. Further to demand-driven provisions, more emphasis shall be placed on good governance of the VET system and delivering the VET agenda that responds to individual and integration of young people into labour market.

There are significant limitations to this work. The vocational skill formation process in the Indian system is predominantly by informal structures and processes, where more than 92% of India's workforce is in the informal sector where the rate of job growth in the informal sector is estimated to be twice that of the formal sector (Ramasamy & Pilz 2020; Wessels & Pilz 2018). Thus, one of the biggest challenges in Indian VET is to meet the skill demand of the informal sector worker in the skilling landscape.

The labour market policies and institutions have high effects on youth employment and earnings. As discussed in the preceding section, there has been a rapid increase in VET institutions, especially ITIs, during the past decade (see Table 13.5). Some developed countries witnessed policy success in effective vocational education, apprenticeship and labour market programmes, which increased employment prospects for young people (Ryan 2001). Focusing only on supply-side factors and working on quantifiable achieving targets can lead to overcrowding and bumping out of low-skilled workers, leaving the Indian economy with a large pool of unemployed skilled and unskilled workers. Therefore, addressing these issues, such as input factors affecting the learners who graduate from VET institutions and get into the labour market, is a more significant challenge. It requires stringent regulation and nationally integrated quality assurance is crucial at this stage. The Ministry of Skill Development and Entrepreneurship launched the National Quality Assurance Framework (NQAF) in 2017, aimed to improve the quality of all education and training/skills programmes in India. Furthermore, the recent National Education Policy (NEP) launched in August 2020 by MHRD proposed various changes in the educational system and hoped for better employment prospects for youth and school-to-work transition in the coming years.

Notes

1 The terms 'unorganized sector' and 'informal sector' are used interchangeably in the Indian context.
2 The terms 'young people', 'youth' and 'younger generation' are used interchangeably, which in the Indian context, represents individuals aged 15–29 years.
3 A new education policy was launched by the Government of India in August 2020, which pushed for a 10+2 structure of school education; the new NEP pitches for a '5+3+3+4' design corresponding to the age groups 3–8 years (foundational stage), 8–11 (preparatory), 11–14 (middle) and 14–18 (secondary).
4 The name of the Ministry of Human Resource Development (MHRD) was changed to Ministry of Education in August 2020 (Source: https://www.timesnownews.com/india/article/president-gives-assent-for-changing-name-of-hrd-ministry-to-ministry-of-education/638584). However, the authors have used MHRD in this chapter.
5 Number of seats including supernumeraries (see MSDE 2017: 57).

References

Aggarwal, A., and Gasskov, V. 2013. *Comparative analysis of national skills development policies: A guide for policymakers*. Geneva: International Labour Organization (ILO).

Ajithkumar, U., and Pilz, M. 2019. 'Attractiveness of Industrial Training Institutes (ITI) in India: A study on ITI students and their parents', *Education and Training*, 61(2): 153–168.

Assaad, R., and Levison, D. 2017. 'Facing the global challenge of youth employment', in H. Besada, L. M. Polonenko, and M. Agarwal (eds.), *Did the MDGs work? Meeting future challenges with past lessons* (pp. 151–189). Bristol: Policy Press.

Bhalla, R., and Meher, S. 2019. 'Education, employment and economic growth with special reference to females in Kerala', *The Indian Journal of Labour Economics*, 62(4): 639–658.

Bisht, N., and Pattanaik, F. 2021. 'Revisiting the shift in youth labour market vis-à-vis the economic development in India', *Millennial Asia*: 1–22.

British Council. 2016. *Overview of India's Evolving Skill Development Landscape*. Available online at https://www.britishcouncil.org/sites/default/files/18.10.16_overview_of_skill_landscape.pdf (downloaded on 10.03.2023).

Comyn, P. 2014. 'Linking employment services, skills development & labor market needs: Issues for India', *Indian Journal of Industrial Relations*, 49(3): 378–388.

Ghose, A. K. 2016. *India employment report 2016: Challenges and the imperative of manufacturing-led growth* (1st ed.). New Delhi: Oxford University Press.

GoI (Government of India). 2015. *National Policy on Skill Development and Entrepreneurship 2015*, New Delhi. Available online at http://www.skilldevelopment.gov.in/assets/images/Skill% (downloaded on 15.02.2023).

GoI (Government of India). 2020. *National Education Policy 2020*. Available online at https://www.education.gov.in/sites/upload_files/mhrd/files/NEP_Final_English_0.pdf (downloaded on 19.06.2021).

ILO (International Labour Organization). 2018. *Emerging Technologies and the Future of Work in India, ILO Asia-Pacific Working Paper Series*, ILO DWT for South Asia and Country Office, India.

ILO (International Labour Organization). 2021. *Young Persons Not in Employment and Education (NEET) in India: 2000–2019*, ILO Brief, New Delhi: ILO DWT for South Asia and Country Office for India. Available online at https://www.ilo.org/newdelhi/whatwedo/publications/WCMS_789243/lang--en/index.htm (downloaded on 14.09.2025).

ILO (International Labour Organization). 2024. *India Employment Report 2024: Youth Employment, Education and Skills*, India: ILO DWT for South Asia and Country Office. Available online at https://www.ilo.org/sites/default/files/2024-08/India%20Employment%20-%20web_8%20April.pdf (downloaded on 17.02.2025).

Islam, R. 2016. 'Pursuing the employment goal: Need for re-thinking development strategies', *The Indian Journal of Labour Economics*, 58(2): 195–216.

Khare, M. 2016. 'Higher education/university: Taking the skills march forward in India – transitioning to the world of work', in M. Pilz (ed.), *India: Preparation for the world of work-education system and school to work transition* (pp. 103–139). Wiesbaden: Springer VS.

Kumar, K. 2016. 'ITIs/ITCs: Industrial training institutes/industrial training centres', in M. Pilz (ed.), *India: Preparation for the world of work-education system and school to work transition* (pp. 65–80). Wiesbaden: Springer VS.

Kumar, R., Mandava, S., and Gopanapalli, V. S. 2019. 'Vocational training in India: Determinants of participation and effect on wages', *Empirical Research in Vocational Education and Training*, 11(3): 1–17.

Maitra, S., Maitra, S., & Thakur, M. 2022. 'Uncertain itineraries: Dual system of training and contemporary TVET reforms in India', *Journal of Vocational Education & Training*, 76(3): 556–575. https://doi.org/10.1080/13636820.2022.2042724.

Majid, N. 2019. 'Structural change and employment in India', *ILO/Sida Partnership on Employment Working Paper No. 1*, ILO, Geneva.

Majumdar, S. 2016. 'Foreword: Reflections on opportunities and challenges of skills development in India', in M. Pilz (ed.), *India: Preparation for the world of work-education system and school to work transition* (pp. 7–10). Wiesbaden: Springer VS.

Mamgain, R. P., and Tiwari, S. 2016. 'Youth in India: Challenges of employment and inclusion', *Journal of Social and Economic Development*, 18(1–2): 85–100.

Mehrotra, S. 2014a. *India's skills challenge: Reforming vocational education and training to harness the demographic dividend*. New Delhi: Oxford University Press.

Mehrotra, S. 2014b. 'Quantity and quality: Policies to meet the twin challenges of employability in Indian labour market', *Indian Journal of Industrial Relations: Economics & Social Dev*, 49: 367–377.

Mehrotra, S. 2014c. 'From 5 million to 20 million a year: The challenge of scale, quality and relevance in India's TVET', *Prospects*, 44(2): 267–277.

Mehrotra, S. 2017. 'Vocational education and training in India: Challenges and critical issues', *IASSI-Quarterly*, 36(2–3): 290–303.

Mehrotra, S. 2019. 'Informal employment trends in the Indian economy: Persistent informality, but growing positive development', *Employment Policy Department*

Employment Working Paper, No. 254, Employment Policy Department, ILO, Geneva.
Mehrotra, S., and Parida, J. 2019. 'India's employment crisis: Rising education levels and falling non-agricultural job growth', *CSE Working Paper #23*, Azim Premji University, India.
Meky, M. S. 2015. 'Labor market impacts and effectiveness of skills development programs in 5 states in India: Assam, Andhra Pradesh, Madhya Pradesh, Odisha, and Rajasthan (English)', *World Bank Working Paper*, World Bank Group, Washington, DC.
MHRD (Ministry of Human Resource Development). 2017. *Annual Report 2016–17*, New Delhi: Government of India, and New Delhi. Available online at: https://aishe.gov.in/aishe/viewDocument.action;jsessionid=3176A0D12A8A3A94F7458C690743CC4E?documentId=239 (downloaded on 16.04.2024).
MHRD (Ministry of Human Resource Development). 2019. *All India Survey on Higher Education 2018–19*, New Delhi: Government of India, MHRD, and Department of Higher Education. Available online at: https://aishe.gov.in/aishe/viewDocument.action;jsessionid=3176A0D12A8A3A94F7458C690743CC4E?documentId=262 (downloaded on 16.04.2024).
MHRD (Ministry of Human Resource Development). 2020. *National Education Policy 2020*, New Delhi: Government of India. Available online at: https://www.education.gov.in/sites/upload_files/mhrd/files/NEP_Final_English_0.pdf (downloaded on 16.04.2024).
Middleton, J., Ziderman, A., and Adams, A. V. 1993. *Skills for productivity: Vocational education and training in developing countries*. New York: Oxford University Press.
Mitra, A., and Verick, S. 2013. 'Youth employment and unemployment: An Indian perspective', *ILO Asia-Pacific Working Paper Series*, ILO, New Delhi.
MSDE (Ministry of Skill Development and Entrepreneurship). 2015. *National Policy for Skill Development and Entrepreneurship 2015*, Government of India, New Delhi.
MSDE (Ministry of Skill Development and Entrepreneurship). 2016. *Annual Report 2015–16*, New Delhi: Government of India. Available online at: https://www.msde.gov.in/sites/default/files/2019-09/Annual%20Report%202015-16%20eng.pdf (downloaded on 28.05.2023).
MSDE (Ministry of Skill Development and Entrepreneurship). 2017. *Annual Report 2016–17*, New Delhi: Government of India. Available online at: https://www.msde.gov.in/sites/default/files/2019-09/Annual%20Report%202016-2017%20-%20English.pdf (downloaded on 28.05.2023).
MSDE (Ministry of Skill Development and Entrepreneurship). 2018a. *Standing Committee on Labour, Industrial Training Institutes (ITIs) and Skill Development Initiative Scheme* (Thirty-Third Report), New Delhi. Available online at: https://eparlib.nic.in/bitstream/123456789/762503/1/16_Labour_33.pdf (downloaded on 17.05.2023).
MSDE (Ministry of Skill Development and Entrepreneurship). 2018b. *Annual Report 2017–18*, New Delhi: Government of India. Available online at: https://www.msde.gov.in/sites/default/files/2019-09/Annual%20Report%202017-2018%20%28English%29.pdf (downloaded on 28.05.2023).
MSDE (Ministry of Skill Development and Entrepreneurship). 2019. *Annual Report 2018–19*, New Delhi: Government of India. Available online at: https://www.msde.gov.in/sites/default/files/2020-09/Annual%20Report%202018-2019%20%28English%29.pdf (downloaded on 07.06.2023).
MSDE (Ministry of Skill Development and Entrepreneurship). 2020. *Annual Report 2019–20*, New Delhi: Government of India. Available online at: https://www.msde.

gov.in/sites/default/files/2020-12/Annual%20Report%202019-20%20English.pdf (downloaded on 28.05.2023).

MSDE (Ministry of Skill Development and Entrepreneurship). 2021. *Annual Report 2020–21*, New Delhi: Government of India. Available online at: https://www.msde.gov.in/sites/default/files/2021-08/English-%20Anual%20Report%20of%20MSDE%20for%202020-21.pdf (downloaded on 29.05.2023).

MSDE (Ministry of Skill Development and Entrepreneurship). 2024. *Annual Report 2023–24*, New Delhi: Government of India. Available online at: https://www.msde.gov.in/static/uploads/2024/02/a58c37c42f8511ec0cadde5f64b4cce0.pdf (downloaded on 16.05.2023).

Mundle, S. 2017. 'Employment, education and the state', *The Indian Journal of Labour Economics*, 60(1): 17–31.

Neroorkar, S., and Gopinath, P. 2020. 'An employability framework for vocational education and training graduates in India: Insights from government VET institutes in Mumbai', *TVET@Asia*, 15: 1–18.

NSDC (National Skill Development Corporation). 2020. *An Overview of Technical Vocational Education and Training Ecosystem in India*, New Delhi: NSDC. Available online at: https://skillsip.nsdcindia.org/sites/default/files/kps-document/TVET%20Landscape%20and%20Stakeholders_February2020_0.pdf.

NSSO. (2024). *Periodic Labour Force Survey (PLFS), July 2023-June 2024*, Ministry of Statistics and Programme Implementation, Government of India.

Pilz, M. 2016a. *India: Preparation for the world of work.* Wiesbaden: Springer Fachmedien.

Pilz, M. 2016b. 'A view from the outside: India's school to work transition challenge – strengths and weakness', in M. Pilz (ed.), *India: Preparation for the world of work-education system and school to work transition* (pp. 345–357). Wiesbaden: Springer VS.

Pilz, M., and Pierenkemper, S. 2014. 'Apprenticeship programs – lessons from Germany & German companies in India', *The Indian Journal of Industrial Relations: A Review of Economic & Social Development (IJIR)*, 49(3): 389–400.

Pilz, M., and Ramasamy, M. 2022. 'Attractiveness of vocational education and training in India: Perspectives of different actors with a special focus on employers', in S. Billett, B. E. Stalder, V. Aarkrog, S. Choy, S. Hodge, and A. H. Le (eds.), *The standing of vocational education and the occupations it serves: Current concerns and strategies for enhancing that standing* (pp. 177–191). Cham: Springer Nature.

Pilz, M., Schlöglmann, A., and Gengaiah, U. 2022. 'VET teachers and teacher trainers in India', in S. Loo (ed.), *Teacher educators in vocational and further education* (pp. 13–27). Cham: Springer.

Pilz, M., and Wilmshöfer, S. 2015. 'Formal, nonformal, and informal learning in rural India: The case of fishing families on the Chilika Lagoon', *Prospects*, 45(2): 231–243.

Pilz. M., and Regel, J. 2021. 'Vocational education and training in India: Prospects and challenges from an outside perspective', *Margin: The Journal of Applied Economic Research*, 15(1): 101–121.

Planning Commission. 2009. *Sub-Committee on Remodelling India's Apprenticeship Regime Report and Recommendations*, Government of India, New Delhi.

Ramasamy, M. 2016. 'Demand-driven approaches in vocational education and training: A case study of rural population in South India' (Doctoral Dissertation, Wiesbaden: Springer).

Ramasamy, M., and Pilz, M. 2019. 'Competency-based curriculum development in the informal sector: The case of sewing skills training in rural South India', *International Review of Education*, 65: 905–928.

Ramasamy, M., and Pilz, M. 2020. 'Vocational training for rural populations: A demand-driven approach and its implications in India', *International Journal for Research in Vocational Education and Training*, 7(3): 256–277.

Ramasamy, M., Regel, J., Sharma, H., Rajagopalan, A., and Pilz, M. 2021. 'Measuring quality in Indian VET institutions: Development steps towards a framework adapted to the national context', *International Journal for Research in Vocational Education and Training*, 8(4): 44–65.

Rubery, J., and Grimshaw, D. 2003. *The organisation of employment: An international perspective*. London: Palgrave Macmillan.

Ryan, P. 2001. 'The School-to-work transition: A cross-national perspective', *Journal of Economic Literature*, 39(1): 34–92.

Saini, V. 2015. 'Skill development in India: Need, challenges and way forward', *Abhinav National Monthly Refereed Journal of Research in Arts & Education*, 4(4): 1–9.

Sanghi, S., and Srija, A. 2014. *Youth Unemployment in India*, Confederation of Indian Industry. Available online at: https://www.ies.gov.in/pdfs/sunita-sanghi-and-a-srija.pdf (downloaded on 05.01.2025).

Schneider, S., and Pilz, M. 2019. 'The function and institutional embeddedness of Polytechnics in the Indian education system', *International Journal for Research in Vocational Education and Training*, 6(3): 284–308.

Shrotriya, S., Dhir, S., and Sushil. 2018. 'Innovation driven ecosystem for quality skill development in India', *Benchmarking: An International Journal*, 25(8): 2997–3020.

Sianesi, B., and Van Reenen, J. 2002. 'The returns to education: A review of the empirical macro-economic literature', *IFS Working Papers, No. 02/05*, Institute for Fiscal Studies, London.

Singh, M. 2012. 'India's national skills development policy and implications for TVET and lifelong learning', in M. Pilz (ed.), *The future of vocational education and training in a changing world* (pp. 179–211). Wiesbaden: Springer.

Smith, E., Kemmis, B. R., and Comyn, P. 2014. 'How can the expansion of the apprenticeship system in India create conditions for greater equity and social justice?', *Australian Journal of Adult Learning*, 54(3): 368–388.

Tara, N., and Kumar, S. 2016. 'Initiatives in skill upgrading: The case of industrial training institutes (ITI) in Karnataka, India', in M. Pilz (ed.), *Vocational education and training in times of economic crisis* (pp. 151–170). Cham: Springer.

Tara, N., Kumar, S., and Pilz, M. 2016. 'Quality of VET in India: The case of industrial training institutes', *TVET @Asia*, 7: 1–17. Available online at http://www.tvet-online.asia/issue7/tara_etal_tvet7.pdf.

Thomas, J. J. 2020. 'Missing the demographic window of opportunity? Labour market changes in India, 2005–18', *Economic & Political Weekly*, 55(34): 57–63.

Venkatram, R. 2016. '(Technical) colleges: Technical education in India – the strengths and challenges', in M. Pilz (ed.), *India: Preparation for the world of work-education system and school to work transition* (pp. 81–102). Wiesbaden: Springer VS.

Verick, S. 2018. 'The puzzles and contradictions of the Indian labour market: What will the future of work look like?', *IZA Discussion Paper, No. 11376*, IZA, Bonn.

Vincent, A., & Rajasekhar, D. 2021. 'Who participates in vocational education and training in India? An analysis of socio-economic determinants', *Journal of Vocational Education & Training*, 75(5), 890–909.

Wallenborn, M. 2010. 'Vocational education and training and human capital development and future options', *European Journal of Education*, 45(2): 182–198.

Wessels, A., and Pilz, M. 2018. *India: International handbook of vocational education and training* (BIBB ed.). Leverkusen: Barbara Budrich.

Wheebox. 2016. *The India Skills Report*, Gurgaon: Wheebox, People Strong, CII, Linkedin, and Association of Indian Universities. Available online at https://wheebox.com/logo/ISR-2016-small.pdf (downloaded on 14.01.2023).

World Bank. 2008. 'Skill development in India – the vocational education and training system', *World Bank Working Paper Series*, World Bank, Washington, DC.

Zimmermann, K. F., Biavaschi, C., Eichhorst, W., Giulietti, C., Kendzia, M. J., Muravyev, A., Pieters, J., Rodríguez-Planas, N., and Schmidl, R. 2013. 'Youth unemployment and vocational training', *Foundations and Trends® in Microeconomics*, 9(1–2): 1–157.

INDEX

For Product Safety Concerns and Information please contact our EU representative GPSR@taylorandfrancis.com Taylor & Francis Verlag GmbH, Kaufingerstraße 24, 80331 München, Germany